SHOOTING IN Sh*tty LIGHT

THE TOP TEN WORST PHOTOGRAPHY LIGHTING SITUATIONS AND HOW TO CONQUER THEM

Lindsay Adler
Erik Valind

Shooting in Sh*tty Light

The Top Ten Worst Photography Lighting Situations and How to Conquer Them

Lindsay Adler and Erik Valind

Peachpit Press
www.peachpit.com

To report errors, please send a note to errata@peachpit.com
Peachpit Press is a division of Pearson Education.

Acquisitions Editor: Ted Waitt
Project Editor: Valerie Witte
Production Editor: Lisa Brazieal
Developmental Editor: Linda Laflamme
Copyeditor: Linda Laflamme
Proofreader: Erin Heath
Composition: WolfsonDesign
Indexer: Rebecca Plunkett
Cover Photo: Lindsay Adler
Cover Design: Charlene Charles-Will
Interior Design: WolfsonDesign

ISBN-13: 978-0-321-86269-3
ISBN–10: 0-321-86269-4

9 8 7 6 5 4 3 2 1

Printed and bound in the United States of America

*To everyone who knows it's not the camera that makes the photo.
It's the photographer.*

To everyone who wants to be a master of their craft.

*To all those people who know it's the camera that makes a photo great.
Just kidding!*

Acknowledgements

Thank you to all my friends and family who stick by my side through life's ups and downs. Having great people like you in my life provides the stability to know that I can take on anything that comes my way. People like Mom, Dad, Alicia, Lila, Brooke, and more give me the foundation I need to continue to grow and succeed!

A big thank you to the Peachpit team for pushing through this first project together! You embraced my outlandish title and allowed me to be me. I wasn't always easy to work with, but I'm excited for this book and to work together on future projects. Thank you to Ted, Linda, and Valerie for helping to bring this book to fruition!

Also, I continue to be blessed with so many people who support and follow my career. Thank you to the thousands of you who keep in touch through social media, at conferences, and in person. Your support allows me to write books like this and travel the world doing what I love. Thank you for allowing me to share and for sharing with me! I sincerely hope this book helps you as you embrace your passion and perfect your craft.

Finally, a huge thank you to Erik Valind. It was fate that we met, and I'm glad we have been able to build a personal and professional relationship. I've enjoyed the late-night book nights filled with ice cream, mac and cheese, and bonding. I love our "book baby," and I look forward to seeing our continued success!

—Lindsay

A huge thank you to my friends and family for your support over the years as I pursued a career in the creative arts rather than the cubicle. Most of you have stood in front of my camera countless times, helping me hone my craft. You all made it possible, and I'm happy to be able to share in this book some of what I've learned along the way.

To my grandfather, whose career began in WWII while hanging out of an aircraft's bomb bay doors to get "the shot," then transitioned into a successful commercial photography career, which enabled him to raise a family. Thank you for showing me that it can be done, and the amount of passion that is required to do so, no matter what genre.

To my mom, for encouraging creativity in the home, and for always sharing yours with the world. Without your love of sharing photography and letting me "borrow" your old cameras, who knows where I'd be today?

To my dad, a voracious reader. Seeing you with a book in hand every evening must have left an impression. There was never a shortage of reading material in the house or want for a recommendation on what to pick up next.

To Alicia, my biggest fan. We've been friends forever, but I'm most thankful for your love and tireless support over the last three years. You've pushed me to be better in life and photography. Your sunshine and positive influence can be seen in both.

To Lindsay Adler, a great friend and incredible photographer! It has been a blast working together with you on this book-building adventure. Here's to many more years of being photo friends, other new and exciting projects, weathering creative challenges together, and the fun photos that they will all produce!

Finally, thank you to everyone who helped in creating the countless images for this book, the entire crew at Peachpit Press, and our editors: Ted, Linda, and Valerie. You embraced a unique title, and it has been a pleasure working together to bring it to fruition. I'm excited for our first completed project together, and to empower photographers in their battle in overcoming sh*tty light.

—Erik

CONTENTS

Introduction

As photographers, we all fantasize about capturing that perfect shoot under the ideal lighting conditions. Nothing feels better than clicking the shutter knowing that you have captured that beautiful scene. Perhaps you show up to a portrait session with the sun low in the sky, creating a heavenly glow of light around your subject. She is tall, slender, and in a flowing dress on the beach as waves crash behind her. Sometimes you really do have those striking visuals in front of you, just waiting to be recorded.

Other times, reality is not so pleasant, even bordering on brutal. You show up to the midday shoot to find harsh sunlight with no shade in sight and a concrete building for a background. Or perhaps the event you're photographing is indoors lit by sickly green, overhead fluorescent lights.

The reality can sometimes be miserable, but your images don't have to be. You can't always control everything on your shoot, but as portrait, wedding, and fashion photographers, lighting is an essential ingredient we must master.

Think of *Shooting in Sh*tty Light* as your survival guide for terrible lighting situations. No longer will you feel overwhelmed or confused when approaching challenging or unpleasant lighting. We, Lindsay and Erik, are here to demystify the light and give you practical, effective solutions to common lighting challenges. Whether you're a beginning photographer or experienced professional, this book will help you feel confident in creating quality images no matter how undesirable the light you encounter. You will know how to assess the scene and use your photographic toolbox to take control if it.

In this book we will teach you how to handle the ten most common scenarios of bad lighting. Some crappy lighting situations are actually a blessing in disguise—if you know how to work them! Other crappy light situations are just...well...crappy and leave you with very few options. This book will not provide every solution or every elaborate lighting formula possible. Instead, it focuses on educating you on efficient and proven techniques for overcoming the lighting challenges you face. Our goal is to share with you the most common, most efficient, and most effective solutions. You don't need to know every single trick in the book, just the solutions that fit your style!

First, let's start with five foundation tips. If you take this advice to heart, though, you may be able to stop reading right now.

Tip 1: Don't Shoot in Sh*tty Light

Light is so important to a good image that you must consider it as a major element of the shoot. Without it, you don't have a shot. Don't schedule your shoots in the middle of the day or in a room lit solely by fluorescent light. It's your image, and the light will make or break it. The best way to deal with sh*tty lighting is to avoid it at all costs.

In photography it's okay to be a control freak. Your job is to control every element of the photo that you can. While in other parts of your life people may torment you for being anal, detail oriented, or OCD, photography is one of those fields that embrace these traits!

So be a control freak. Take control of your light. Don't shoot in sh*tty lighting.

Tip 2: Educate Your Clients

Most of your clients aren't photographers (even if some think they are), and most are not visual artists. Chances are they don't understand light—but you do. You are the expert! Too often we are so eager to please our clients, we let them select every element of the shoot: the location, the clothing, and the time of day. This is a guaranteed recipe for sh*tty light. *You* are the expert and know what it takes to make a great shoot, so you need to share this knowledge from the start.

Understanding light is both an art and a science, and it's also your job as a photographer. A lot of clients will schedule their portrait sessions or wedding ceremonies in the middle of the day or in direct sunlight because they don't know any better. It's your responsibility to educate them. Let them know what time of day, location, or clothing will help make the best photograph. Show them your expertise, and help make the shoot the most successful it can be!

If a wedding client approaches you for advice, recommend that they not hold the ceremony at high noon, or perhaps recommend that they situate the alter beneath the shade of a tree. Chances are they never even thought about light when planning their big day.

Speak up! Let them know. A bride will certainly pay attention to you if you let her know that light can be the difference between her looking like Snookie and Kim Kardashian. Feel free to exaggerate. Recommend good locations. Recommend lighting conditions. Show your clients you care about how they look. We promise your images will improve markedly.

Consider showing clients comparative samples of portraits or weddings. Show them the difference between images shot at different times of day or at different locations. Most times, showing is a lot better than telling. Another approach is to have your clients look at your work to determine which images they are most attracted to. Be sure to emphasize the importance of light to the success of these shots, and let them know what they can do to help be part of that success.

Educating your clients will enagage them as active partners in helping you create successful images.

Tip 3: Read This Book

When all else fails, read this book. You will face times when you have no choice but to shoot in sh*tty lighting. Maybe the venue cannot be changed, or the time of day is set in stone, or you simply cannot sway your client. Sometimes the light is going to be a massive challenge. This book was written for such times.

You don't have to dread terrible light. Instead, approach it confidently and knowing you can bend it to your will. It's not magic! We will discuss light, techniques, and other tips and tricks. Everything from shooting in direct sunlight, to shooting in mixed light, to shooting in low light with no flash—we cover it all! By understanding how to conquer sh*tty lighting, you're on your way to becoming the miracle worker your clients expect you to be. The good part is, it's no miracle. It's just about understanding the light.

We've added a few features that we hope you find useful in understanding how to conquer light. As a quick reference, a red ✗ next to a photo means the shot failed to conquer the light and needs a bit of improvement. By studying these, you'll learn to quickly identify some of the pitfalls of unflattering light. We've also added green check marks (✔) next to the lighting results we prefer. By comparing the two, you'll be able to quickly reference problems and solutions.

Next, if you need help understanding some of the more technical terminology we use, watch for words that are color coded. You'll find these words and their definitions in Appendix A's glossary.

Tip 4: Equipment Doesn't Make the Shot, but It Can Help

We photographers do like our "toys" (huge telephoto lenses, fancy flash modifiers, light meters, the list goes on), but we sometimes tend to forget these toys are really just tools. You don't need a ton of equipment to solve many of the most challenging lighting situations. You just need the *right* equipment.

When you read this book, we hope you will realize that buying more equipment is usually not the solution. Typically, you need just a few simple tools (a reflector and a flash) to conquer nearly every situation. In fact, even more important than equipment is seeing the light. You must see and analyze the light to help you determine which tools and solutions are best.

We wrote this book so that you can achieve almost all of the techniques with any digital camera that allows you to adjust your basic settings: aperture, shutter speed, and ISO. Furthermore, you don't even need an expensive lens. While we recommend a faster lens (see Appendix B, "Equipment"), most images can be achieved with the basic kit lens included with your DLSR.

The most important thing in any photographer's toolbox is an understanding of light and how to interact with it. So before you stress out about filling up your kit with expensive equipment, fill it with knowledge. Your credit cards will thank you later.

Tip 5: Practice Makes Imperfect Light Perfect

We will provide you with various suggested tools and options, but remember that it's all about which option works for *you.* Don't just take our word for it. Try out these techniques. We mean it: Try them out, see what fits best with your photographic style, your budget, and the challenges ahead of you. *Practice* before you need to perform on a big job, like photographing someone's wedding day. Practice makes perfect, and this book will help you perfect that imperfect light!

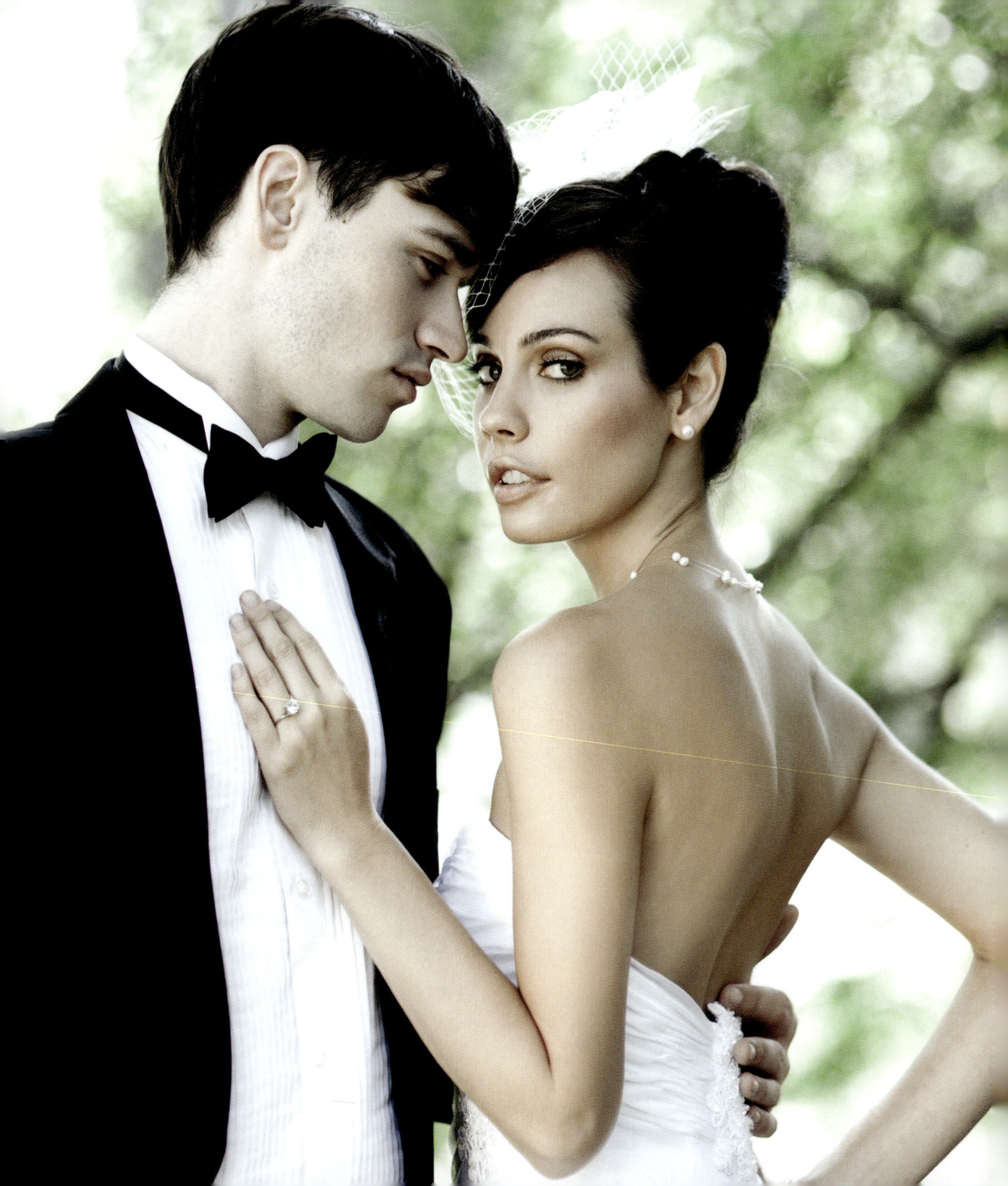

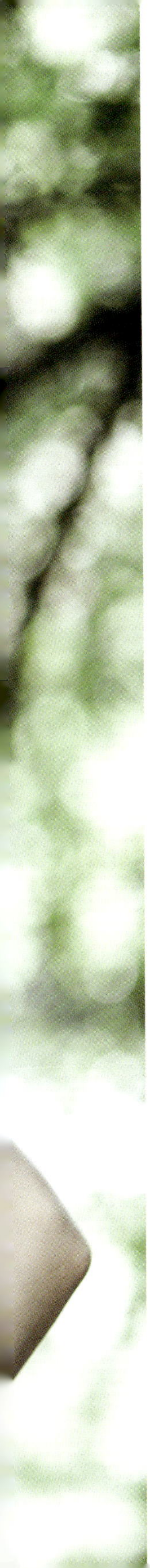

CHAPTER ONE
Direct Sunlight

A bright and sunny day can be a blessing for a photographer, but it can also be a curse. What do you do when you must shoot at high noon with the sun blaring down? Natural light can be beautiful and sweet, but at times it can also be brutal and harsh. Luckily, if you pay close attention to your surroundings, you can rise to the challenge. You can turn high noon and direct sunlight into the ideal type of light. You can make your subjects glow and bend the natural light to your will. It's not magic, and it's no secret.

In this chapter, we'll explain some of your options when your portrait session, wedding, or other event takes place in direct sunlight. Specifically, we'll spend the middle of the day in Central Park to illustrate how to handle the challenging light of the midday sun.

Take Cover!

On a bright and sunny day, the first thing you should do is get out of the sun and take cover. Search your surroundings for cover, such as large trees providing shade, porches, or the shadowed side of a building. Try to find an area that is in the shade but still gives you a pleasing background.

WATCH IT! Pay attention to your backgrounds.

Pay attention to your backgrounds. If you put your subjects in the shade, they will be darker than their surroundings. Compose your shot to place an equally dark environment behind your subjects. If you don't, you may create a very distracting, brightly lit background that detracts from your photograph. On the other hand, if the background is lighter, consider using a shallower depth of field so that the highlights are not rendered crisp, but seen as more subtle blurs of light instead.

Putting your subjects in the shade will:

- Help them to avoid squinting
- Get rid of bright highlights on the face, thus creating a more pleasing illumination
- Save you a ton of headaches

Even if you have no reflectors, no diffuser, and no flash, just moving your subjects out of the direct sunlight is going to make a huge difference, as you can see in **Figures 1.1** and **1.2**. If you are an event photographer, do whatever you can to make the action happen in the shade. Educate your clients and encourage them to have the competition, ceremony, or other part of the event out of direct sunlight.

TAKEAWAY ACTION

Get your subjects out of direct sunlight.

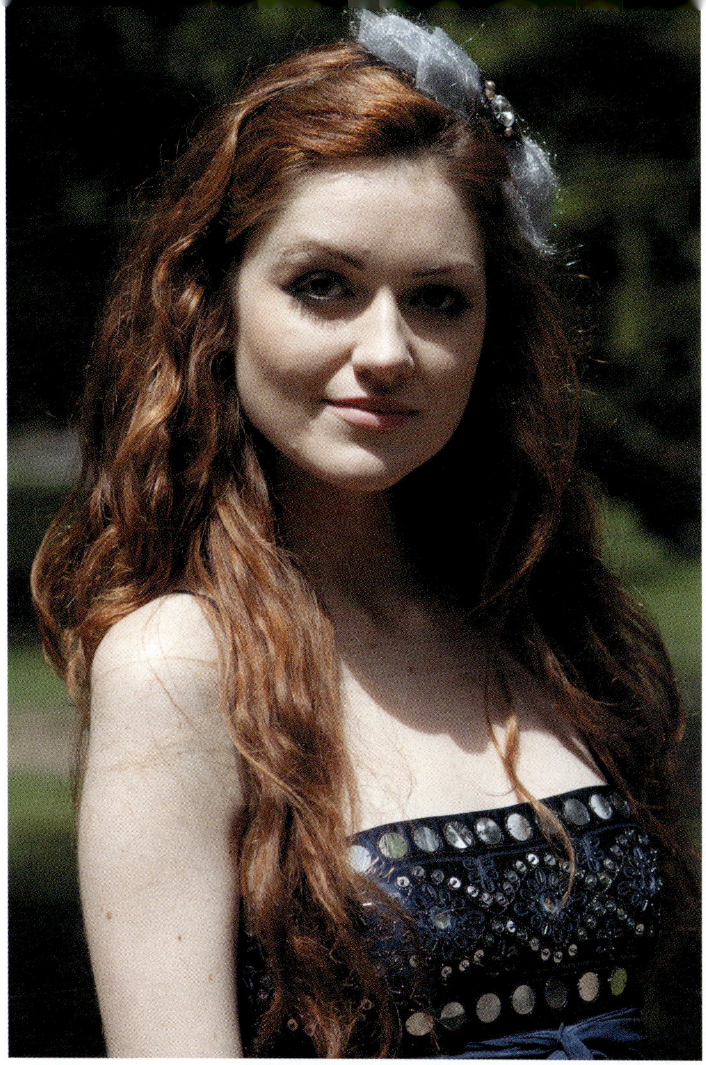

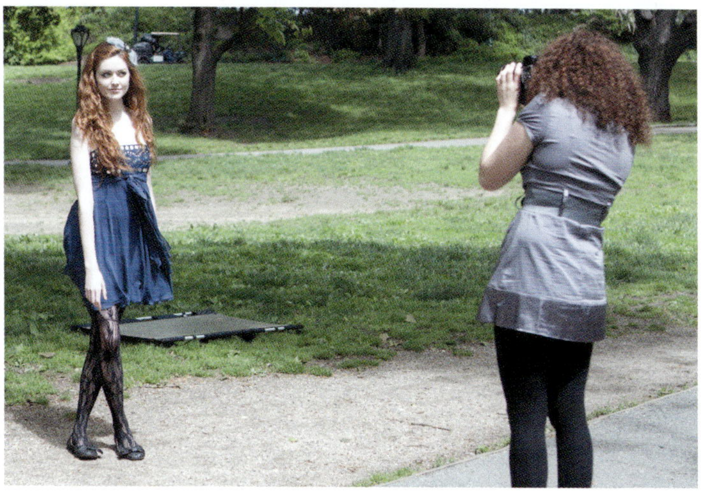

FIGURE 1.1
Our subject is in direct sunlight. The contrast, highlights, and shadows on her face are unflattering.

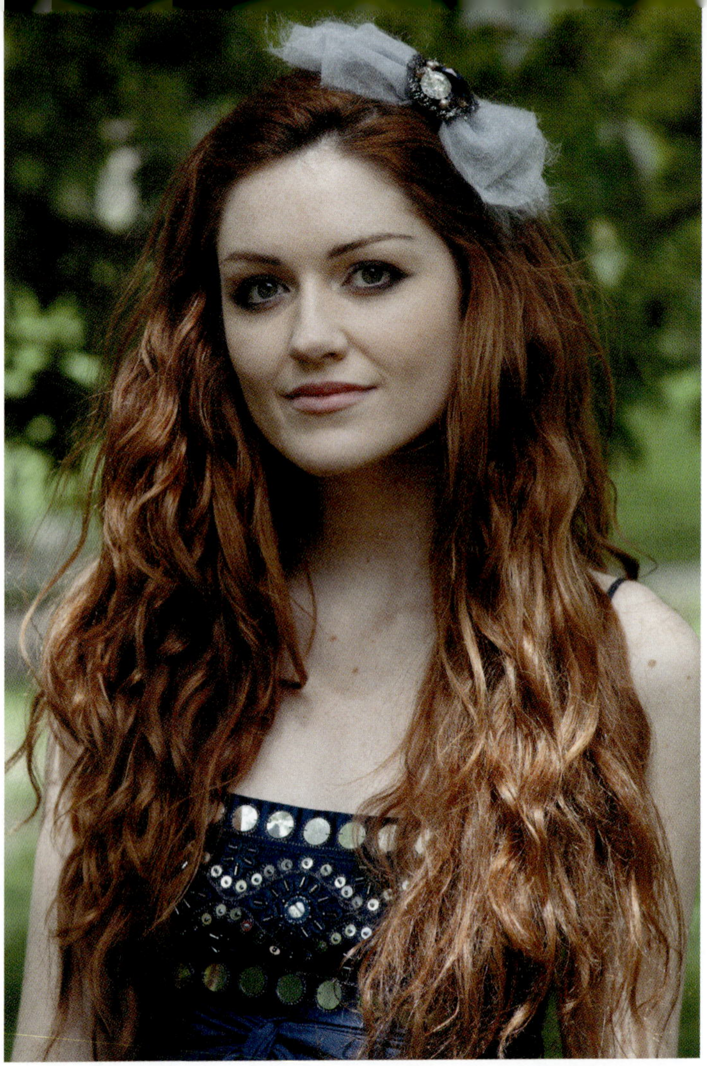

✔ FIGURE 1.2
The first solution for handling direct sunlight is to put your subject in the shade. In this instance, the subject is in the shade of a tree. The light of the open sky above her illuminates her face, as you can see by the **catchlights** in her eyes.

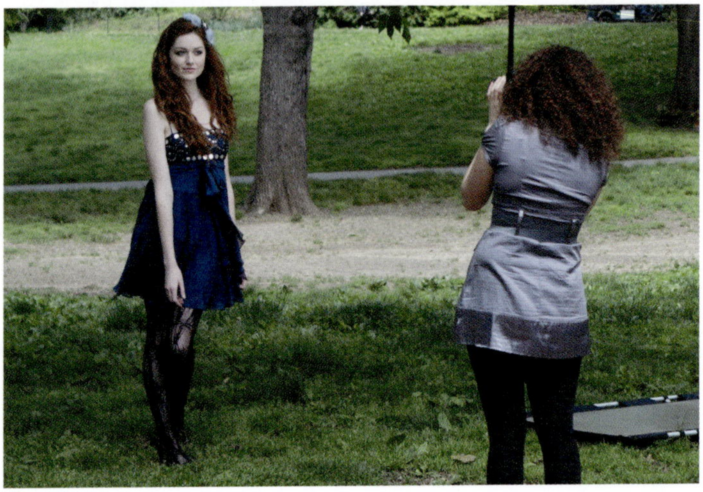

WATCH IT! Analyze the light on the face.

When shooting a portrait session, pay close attention to the light on the subject's face. Even though someone is in the shade, that doesn't mean your lighting job is done. Nor does it mean the light is flattering. Even shade has a direction of light to it. *Study* the face, and ask yourself these questions:

- Where is the overall illumination coming from?
- Where are the highlights on the face?
- Where are the shadows?
- Is this where I want the highlights and shadows to be?

Sometimes simply turning your subject a different direction in the shade is enough to fix the light. Rotate the subject, and wait for the light to be more even or flattering. As you will see throughout the book, all shade is not created equal!

Beware of Overhead Light

When shooting in natural light, watch out for overhead light. Overhead light rarely contributes to a better photograph—very rarely. Instead, it usually gives you those nasty highlights on the nose and forehead as well as ugly shadows in the eyes. When you hear your client later complain, "Oh my God, my nose looks so big," overhead lighting and an oversized nose shadow are often the cause.

To remedy this situation, be selective about the *type* of shade you take cover under. Often you don't want simple open shade, but instead need to seek out covered shade. **Open shade** involves no direct, overhead covering and is the kind of shade you find in the shadowed side of a building. **Covered shade** is the kind created by an overhang, such as a porch or a doorway.

Look for a setting with some sort of overhang above the subject—a roof, a roof's eaves, the ceiling of a doorway, or leaves from branches hanging close above the subject's head. Putting something almost directly over the subject's head helps eliminate overhead light. The illumination becomes frontal and, therefore, much more flattering. To see just how much a shady overhang can improve a shot, compare **Figures 1.3** and **1.4**.

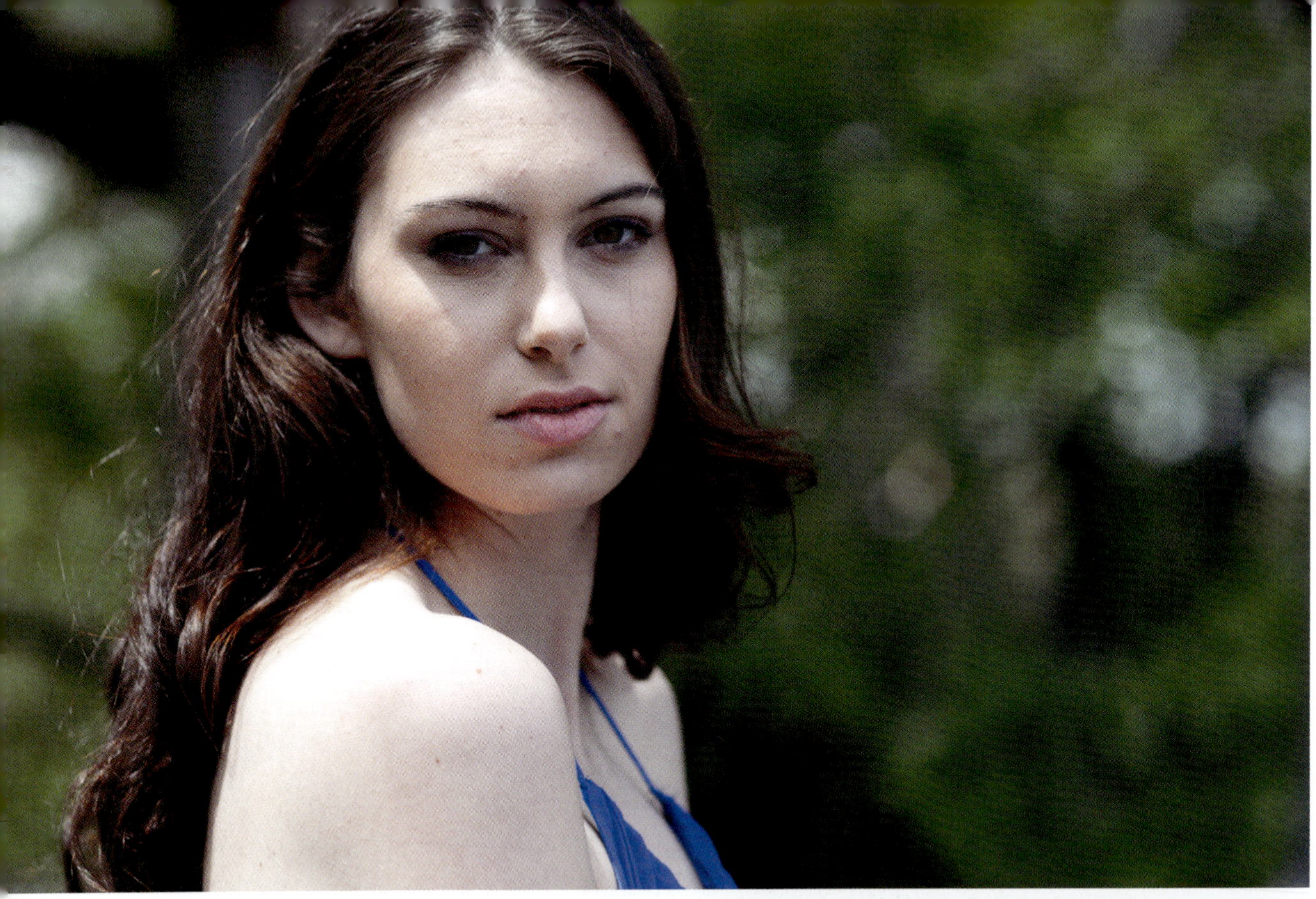

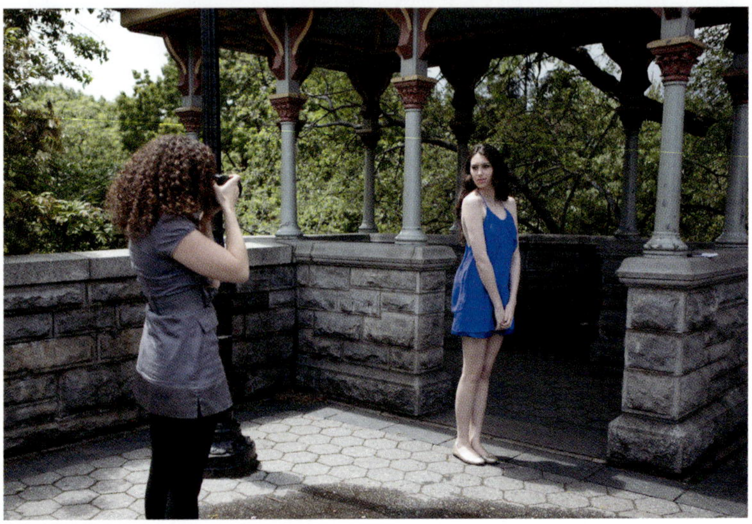

FIGURE 1.3
Here the subject is in mixed sunlight and shade. The sunlight hits half of her face (creating undesirable highlights), while the open shade illuminating the right side of the face still leaves some shadows in the eyes. The best solution is to eliminate the sun and open shade.

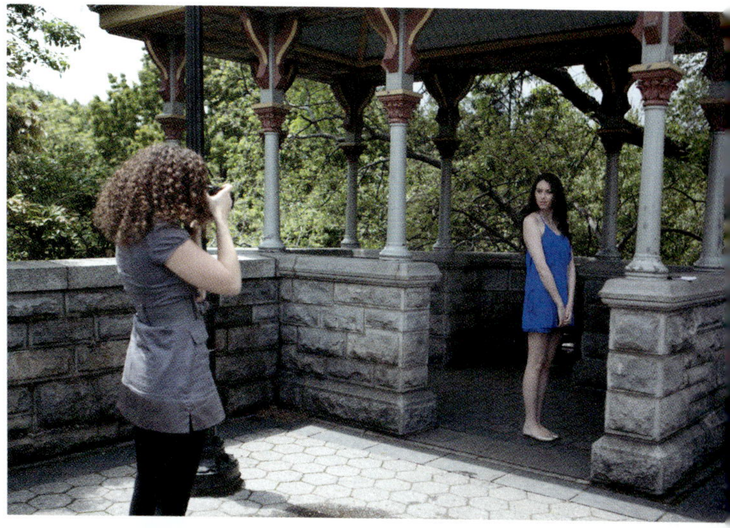

✔ FIGURE 1.4

To handle the challenging light, we moved the subject back a few feet so she was standing beneath an overhang in the park. The roof blocks off the overhead light, removing the unwanted highlights, as well as changing the direction of the light. The result is frontal, even lighting without having to use a reflector or diffuser.

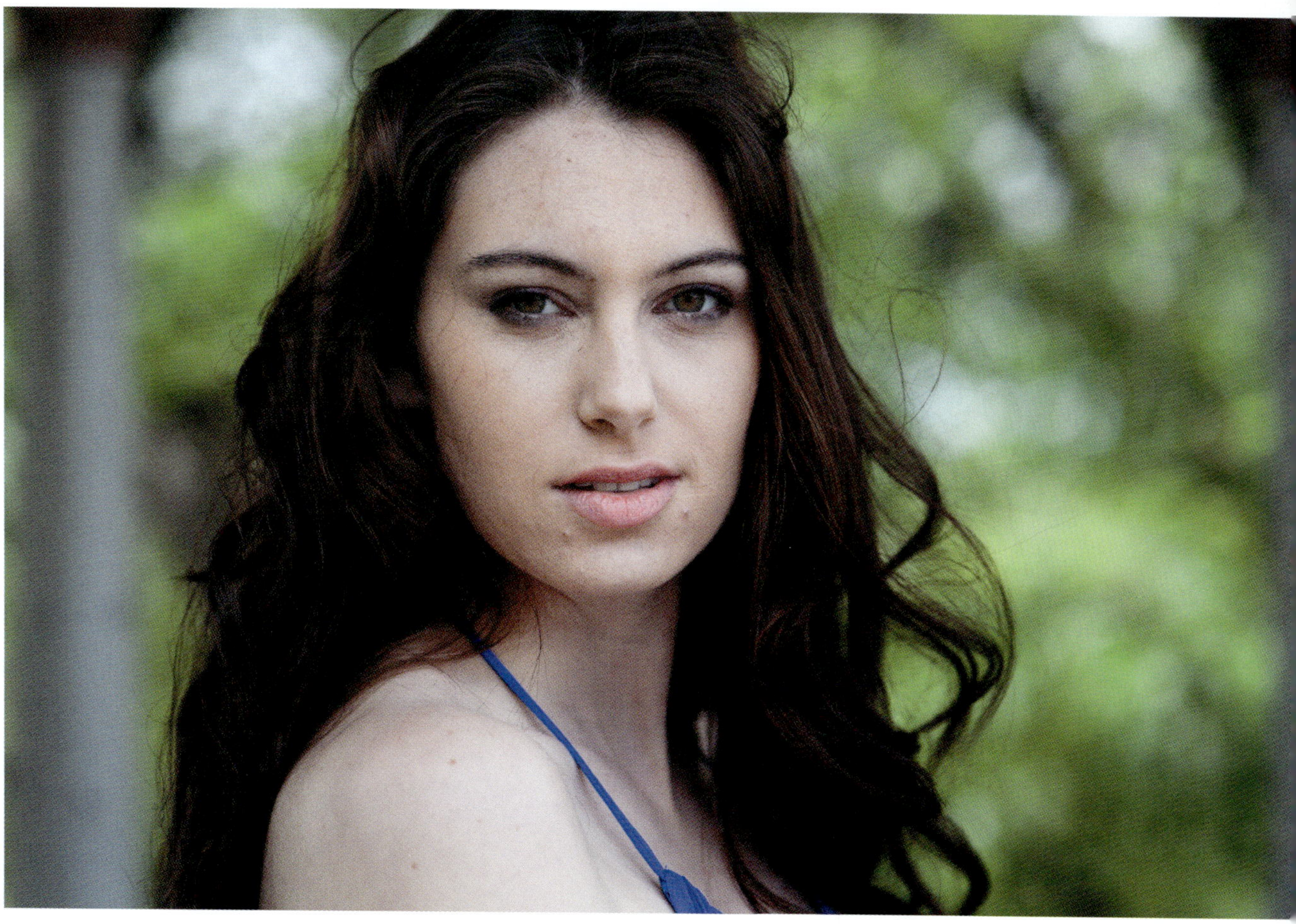

Consider a second example: During a bright sunny day, we found an area of shade on the side of an old cabin. Although the shade significantly helped this shot, in **Figure 1.5** you can still see the highlights on the model's nose and forehead, as well as the shadows in her eyes. When we stepped the subject back underneath the overhang of the porch just four feet behind her, notice how the light changed drastically. The light is all frontal and even in **Figure 1.6**.

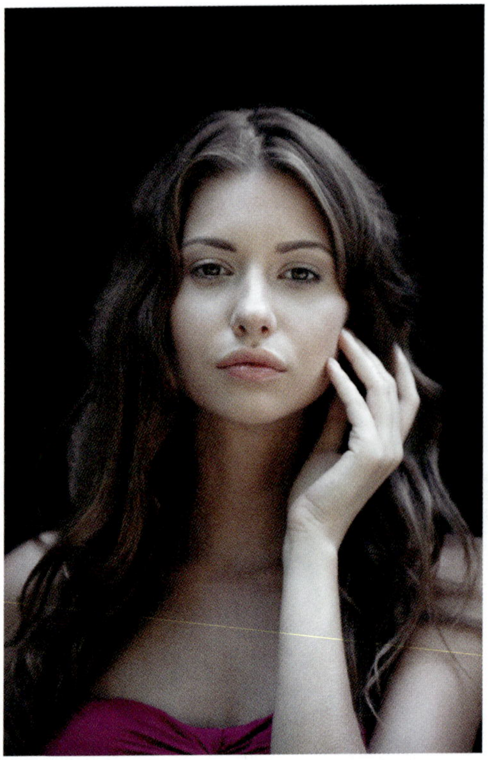

FIGURE 1.5
The subject is in open shade—shade on the side of a building with no overhang above her. Notice the shadows and highlights on the face.

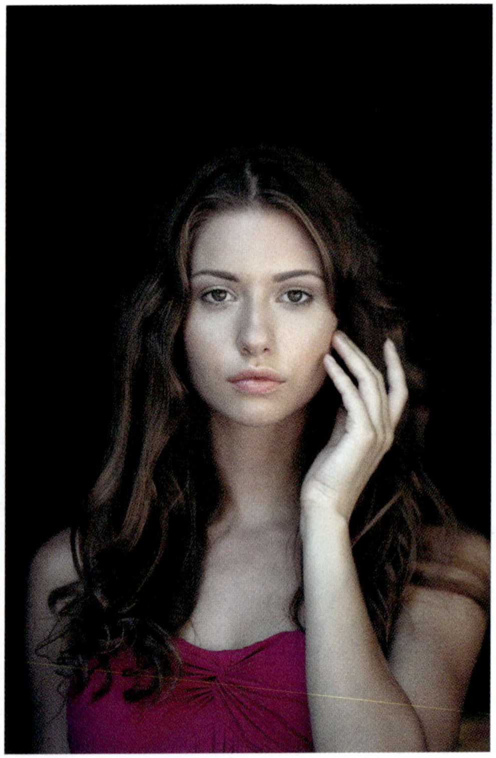

FIGURE 1.6
When the subject steps back just four feet to an overhang of a porch, the light changes completely. It is now even and much more flattering.

Create Your Own Shade

What if you don't have an overhang on hand to block off the light? Create your own shade! Chapter 2, "Direct Sunlight, No Shade in Sight," will address this problem in detail, but for now compare **Figures 1.7** through **1.9**. All three images were taken in the same setting, just minutes apart. The subject stands in direct sunlight in Figure 1.7, and all elements of the light are unflattering. When a cloud passes over (Figure 1.8), the light becomes softer, but the direction of light is still unflattering. Notice the highlights on her forehead and nose. For Figure 1.9, an assistant held a piece of white foam core (available at most office supply and craft stores) over the subject's head. Notice how the direction of light changes; it is now more flattering. If you want to kick even more light into the eyes, you can add a reflector under her chin, as you'll learn in the next section.

Whether in sunlight or on an overcast day, putting that foam core overhead eliminates overhead light and does wonders for making the light more even.

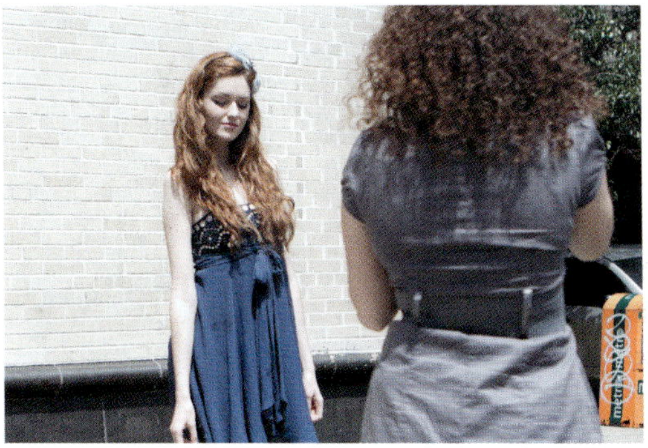

✗ FIGURE 1.7
The subject is standing in front of a light-colored brick wall in direct sunlight. The light is miserable and completely unflattering.

TAKEAWAY ACTION

Be aware of overhead light.

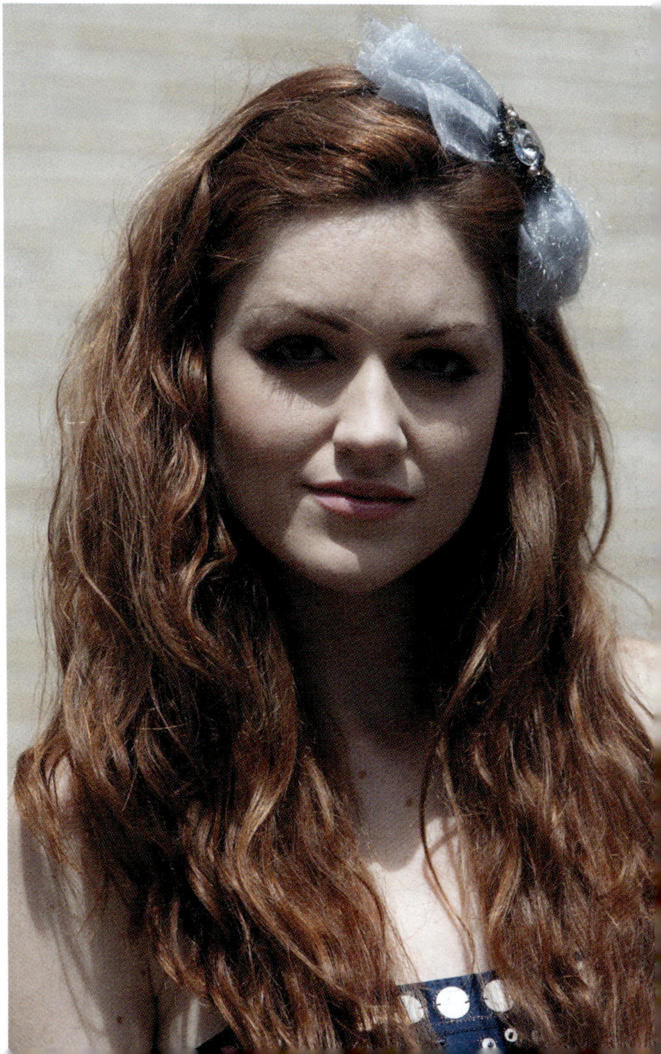

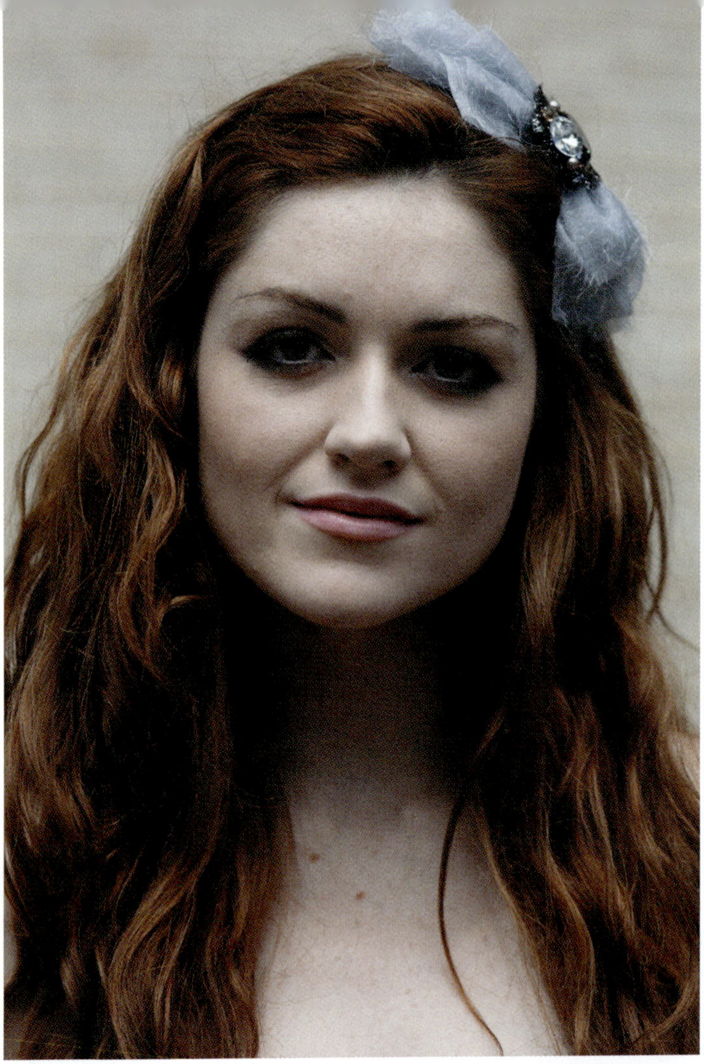

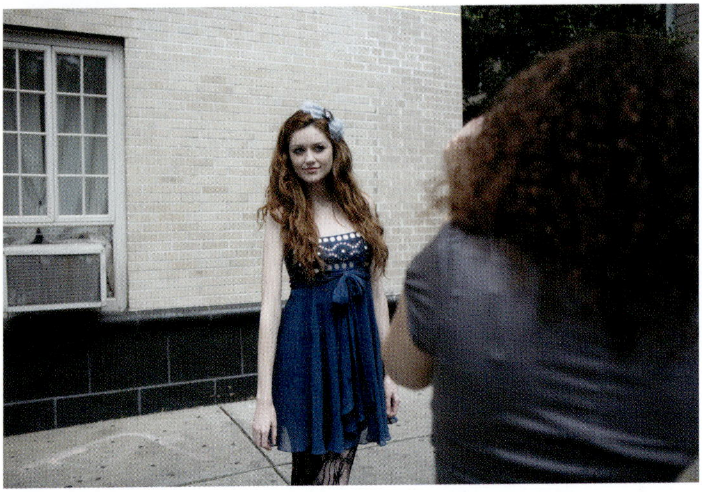

FIGURE 1.8
When a cloud passes over the scene, the light becomes much softer, but notice that the light is still coming from overhead. Being in this open shade does not mean the light will be good. In fact, the light is unflattering due to the combination of the shadows in the eyes and the highlights on the nose and forehead.

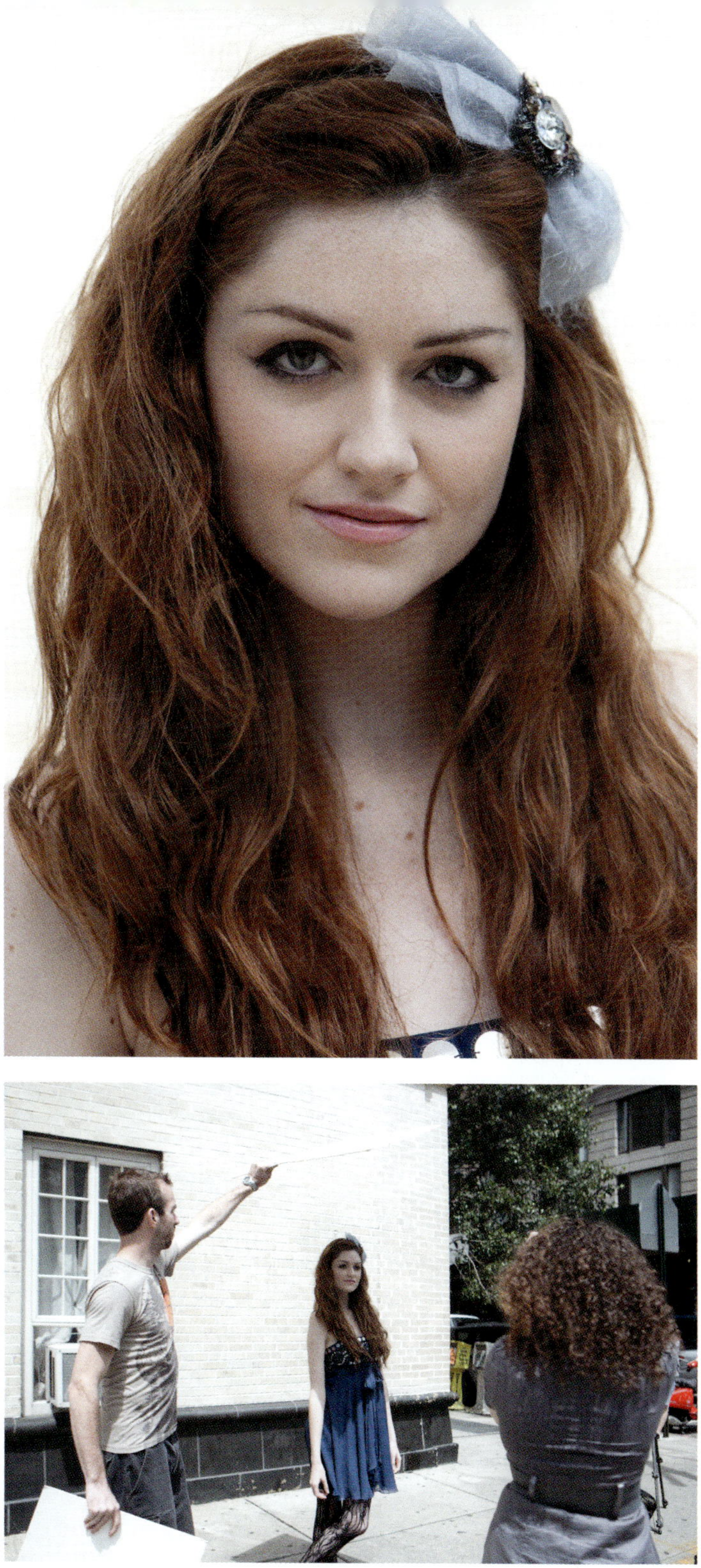

FIGURE 1.9
When there is no overhang in sight to block off overhead light, you can create your own. Here an assistant holds a piece of white foam core over the subject's head when the sun comes back out. With the overhead light eliminated, the light is now frontal and even.

For a third example, we positioned the subject in open shade on the side of a building and held a piece of foam core over her head to even out the light. The difference between **Figures 1.10** and **1.11** is a result of the apertures we used. Notice how soft and subtle the background of Figure 1.11 is compared to Figure 1.10. Figure 1.10 was shot at f/5.6 aperture (kit lens), while Figure 1.11 was shot very wide at f/2.0. You will need a specialized lens with a wide aperture to achieve this effect, but the beautiful background is often well worth the cost!

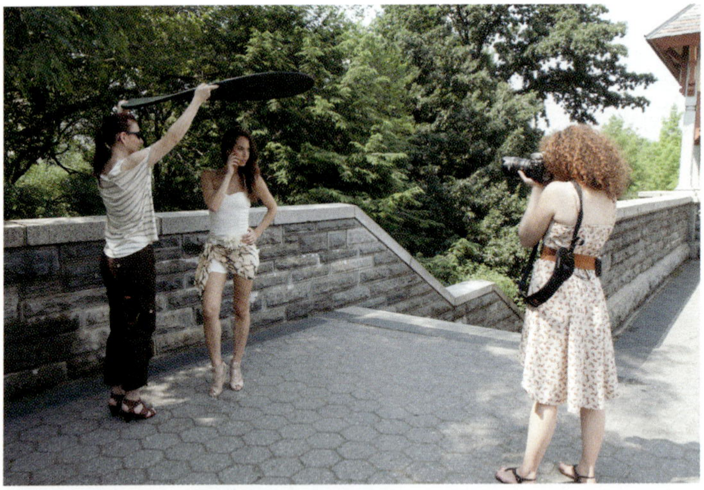

FIGURE 1.10
We blocked off overhead light to make an even illumination on the subject's face. This image is shot at f/5.6, producing a good amount of detail in the background.

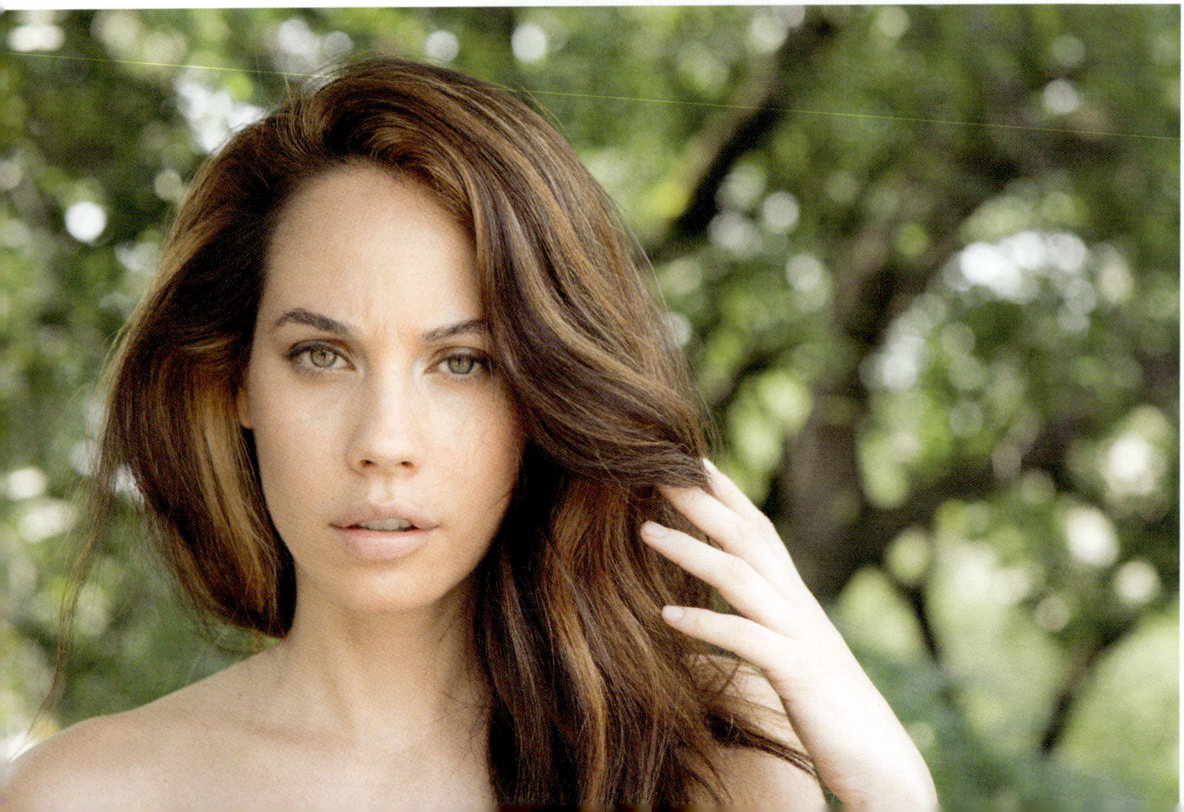

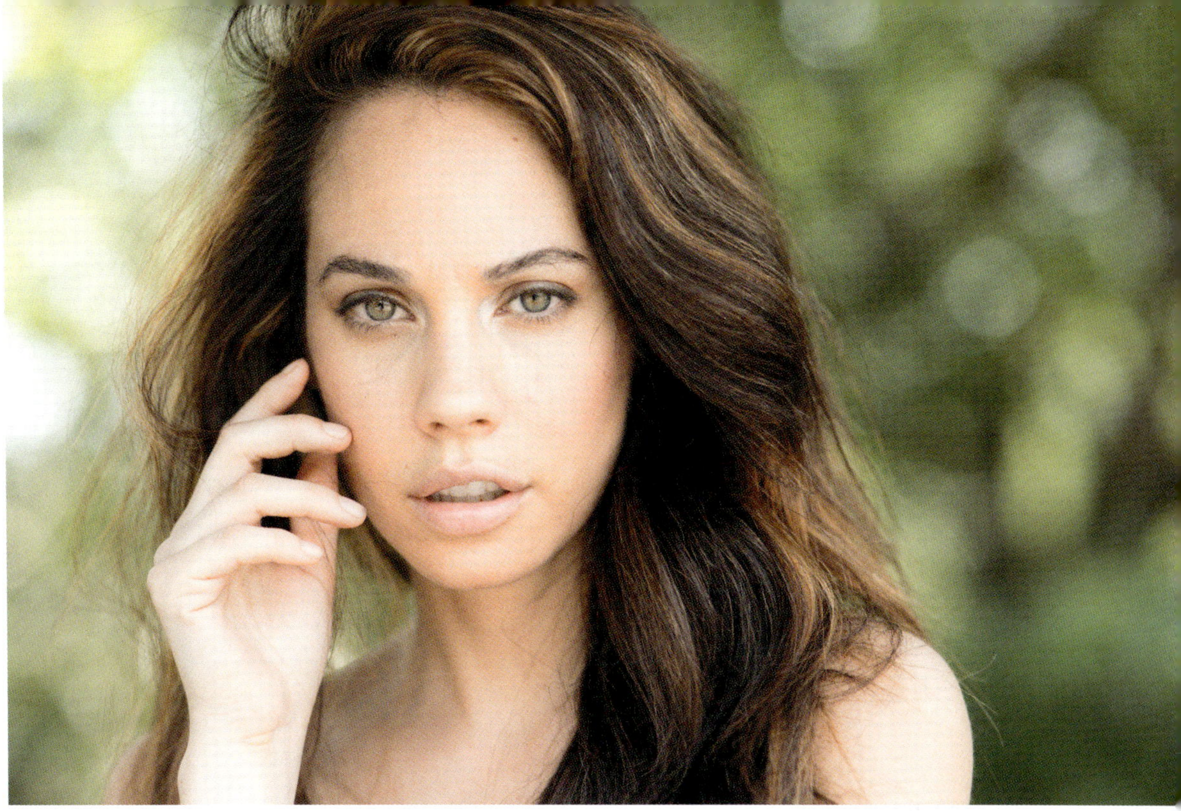

FIGURE 1.11
We blocked off overhead light to make an even illumination on the subject's face. This image is shot at f/ 2.0 using the Sigma 85mm 1.4 lens. The result is a simplified background and more attention drawn to the subject.

BEGINNER TIP Stare a lot.

Find someone to stare at. It may sound creepy at first, but we are serious! Whether you use a friend, fellow photographer, or significant other, find someone who you feel comfortable with and study the light on his or her face. Likewise, as you wander around a scene, stop and pause when you run into "good" light, then analyze the contributing elements of the scene. For example, ask yourself:

- Is there an overhang near the subject?
- Where is the light coming from—a window, reflected off the floor, a lamp?
- Is it sunny or overcast?

Pausing to study and ask questions is a great way to learn to identify good lighting conditions and what contributes to them.

Combine Shade and a Reflector

One of the most common lighting techniques on a sunny day is to combine shade and a reflector. Place your subjects in the shade, and use a reflector to bounce light to fill in the shadows in their eyes. Often this produces flattering and even light. By adding a reflector, you also can reflect a catchlight into the eyes, which adds a spark of life to your subject. **Figure 1.12** illustrates one of the most common lighting solutions for a sunny day. The subject is in the shade of a tree, and an assistant is bouncing light back into her eyes using a silver-gold-mix reflector. (In Chapter 2, we will discuss angles of reflection in depth, as well as our recommended reflecting tips.)

EQUIPMENT TIP Choose the right reflector for the task.

Reflectors come in a wide range of shapes and sizes. What's the difference, you ask? A smaller reflector will not be able to catch as much light and usually casts a harsher quality of light on the subject. More commonly used outdoors, a round reflector will give round catchlights in the eyes and also a more circular area of illumination. A larger, rectangular reflector will give more even light and a rectangular catchlight, similar to that of window light or studio softboxes.

When shooting with shade and a reflector, keep a few things in mind. First, you don't *always* need a reflector; sometimes the shade is enough. Many novice photographers discover the power of the reflector and then overuse it. If the light of the shade is crisp enough and flattering on the face, don't succumb to the urge to use a reflector or use it *too* much. The light in **Figure 1.13**, for example, is relatively flattering. The situation doesn't require a reflector, yet you still could use one to add a bit of sparkle to the eyes with catchlights if you prefer. The main problem with Figure 1.13 is that the face lacks contrast. A reflector would remedy this but might also lead photographers into a second problem.

The second mistake photographers make is to reflect too much. Many peoples' instincts are to catch as much light as possible and throw it back at the subject. This tends to add too much contrast and very harsh highlights. In **Figure 1.14**, the reflector is overpowering the photograph and creates unpleasant results, such as crisp and harsh shadows, or bright highlights. In other words: Back off! Oftentimes less is more when it comes to fill light with reflectors.

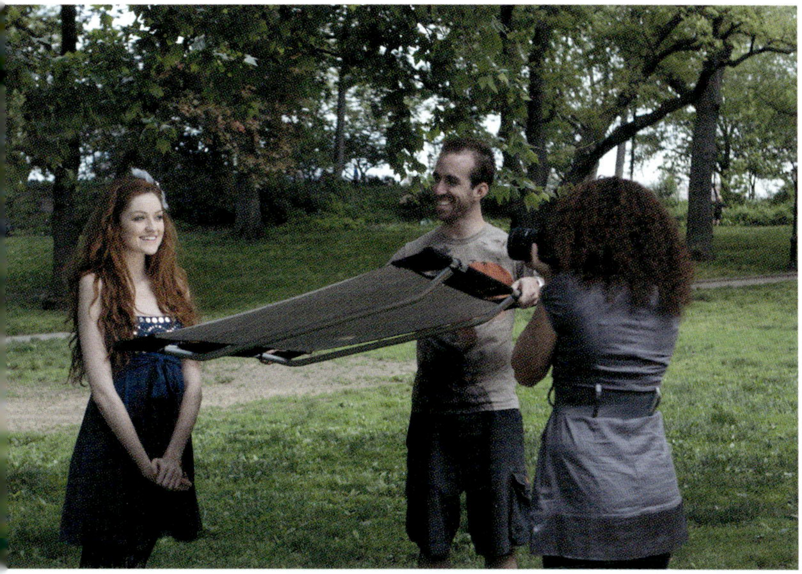

FIGURE 1.12
Our subject stands in the shade of a tree while an assistant uses a silver-gold-mix reflector to bounce light back into her eyes. In this instance, a rectangular reflector helps catch more light, which is visible in the rectangular shape of her catchlights.

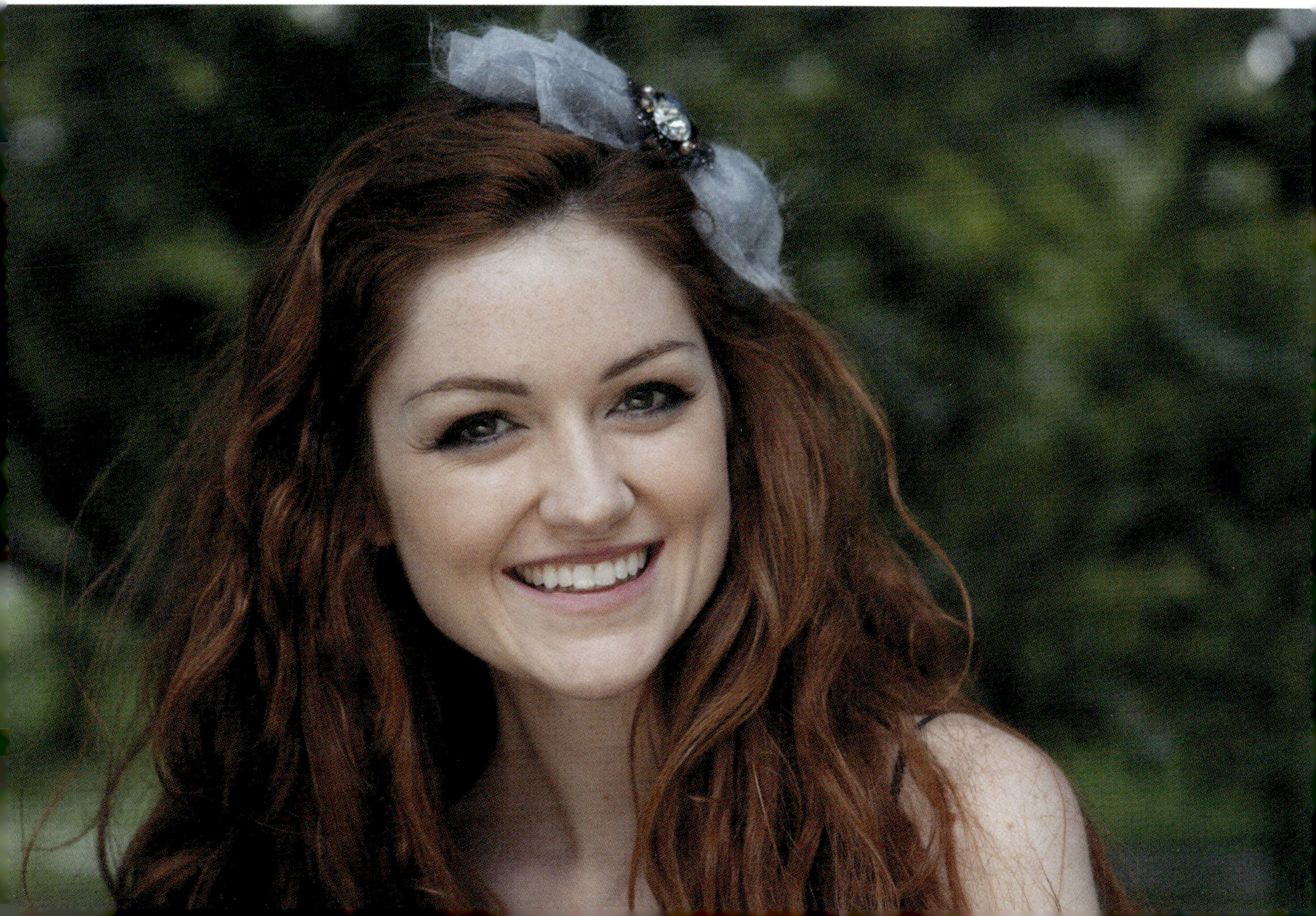

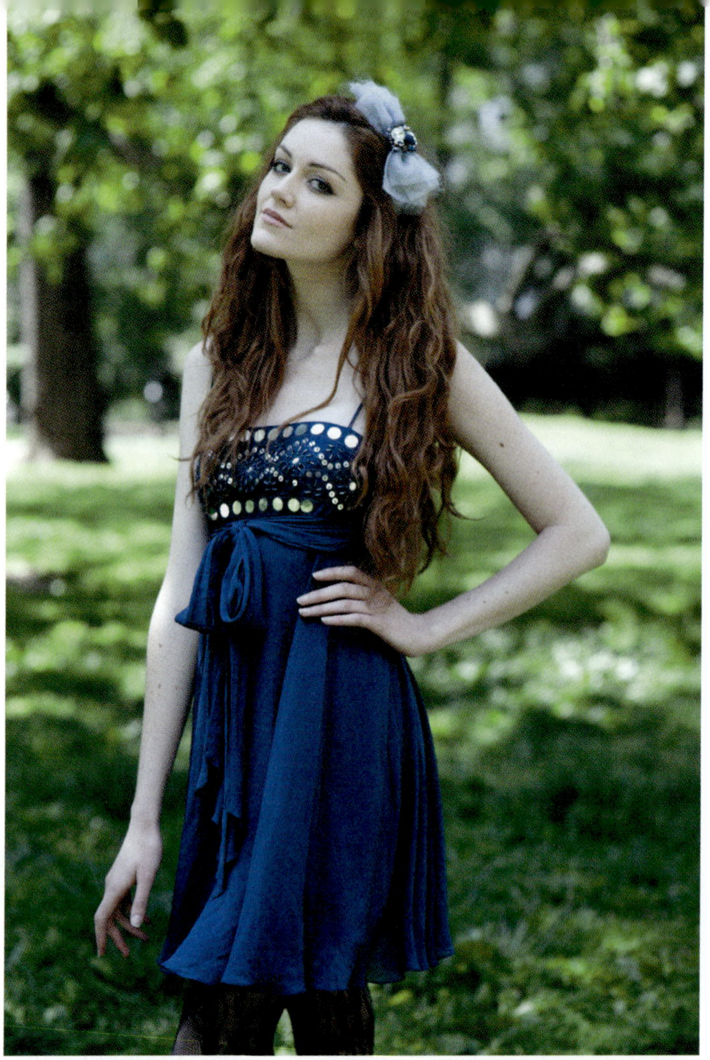

FIGURE 1.13
By placing the model in the shade, we eliminated harsh light on her face. In some instances, you do not need a reflector when the subject is in shade. This scenario is a toss up. If you like a softer, more natural look, you might shoot this image without any reflection at all.

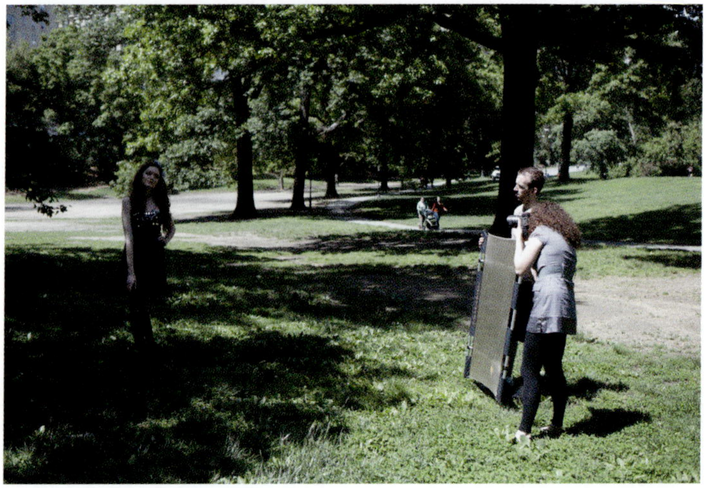

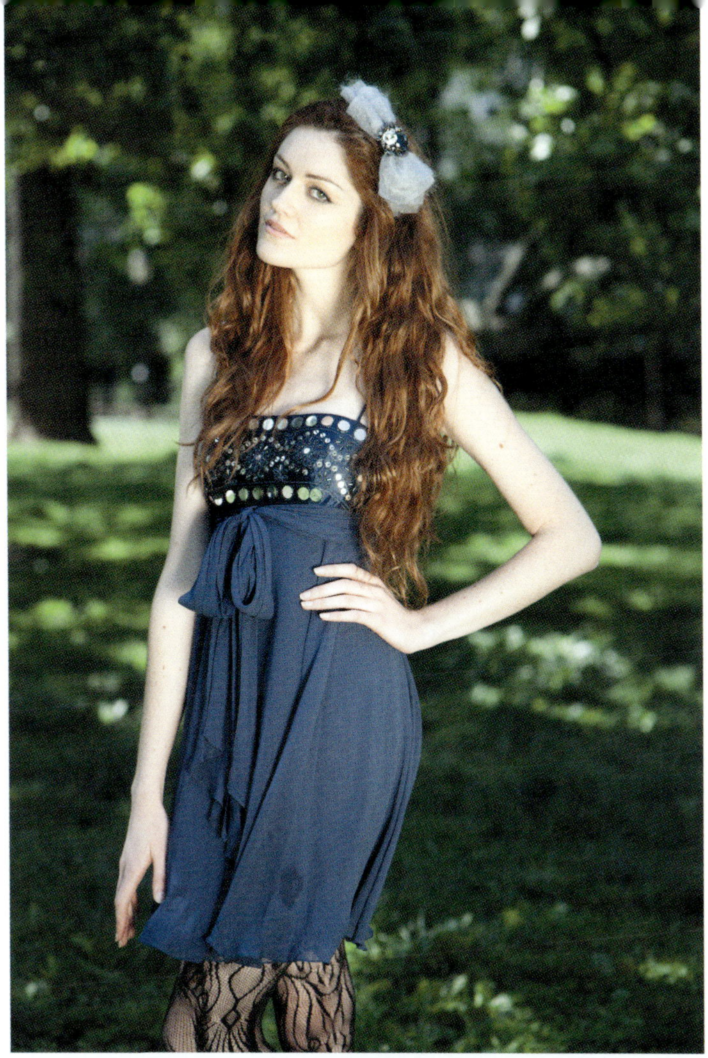

FIGURE 1.14
Many novice photographers over light their portraits. Here the three- by four-foot silver-gold-mix reflector is catching too much light and overpowering the subject.

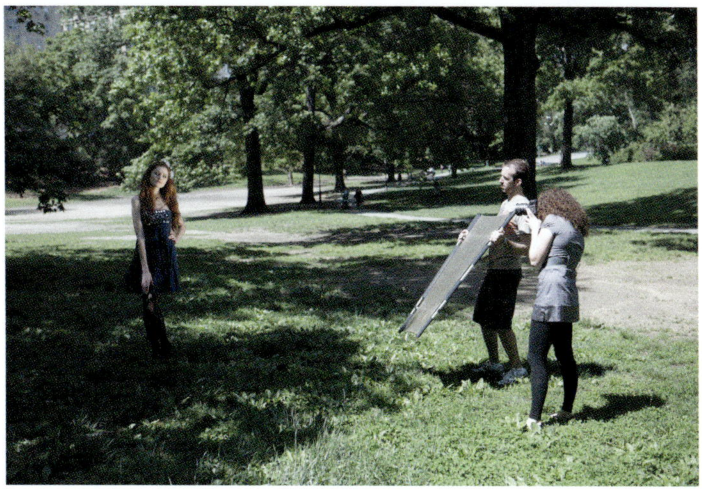

The solution to a more flattering use of reflector is to **feather** the light: Vary the angle of the reflector to just catch the edge of the light. This will bounce a tiny bit of light back into the face, just enough to increase the contrast a bit and add catchlights. I recommend trying a variety of angles. Rotate the reflector left to right, raise it up and down, and just look for a bit more flattering light in the face without overpowering the image. In **Figure 1.15**, an assistant feathered the light by holding the reflector at a high angle to control the light's direction. (Chapter 2 discusses this technique in depth.)

Finally, avoid illuminating a subject unevenly. Think of light as water and a reflector as a bucket. If you are close to your subject and throw a small bucket of water, it will hit a very concentrated area only. If you want to spread the water out, you back up and throw the water from a farther distance. This way the water begins to spread out and evenly soak your subject. What's the problem now? There isn't much concentration to the water, and it becomes weak and ineffective. Instead, if you want to soak your entire subject (or group), you need to back up *and* use a bigger bucket.

The same principle applies to light. If you want to illuminate a focused area on the subject, get close, with a smaller reflector. If you want to illuminate a greater area and more evenly, back up and use a large reflector! Keeping this water-light comparison in mind will help you figure out how to solve some of the reflector issues you may encounter.

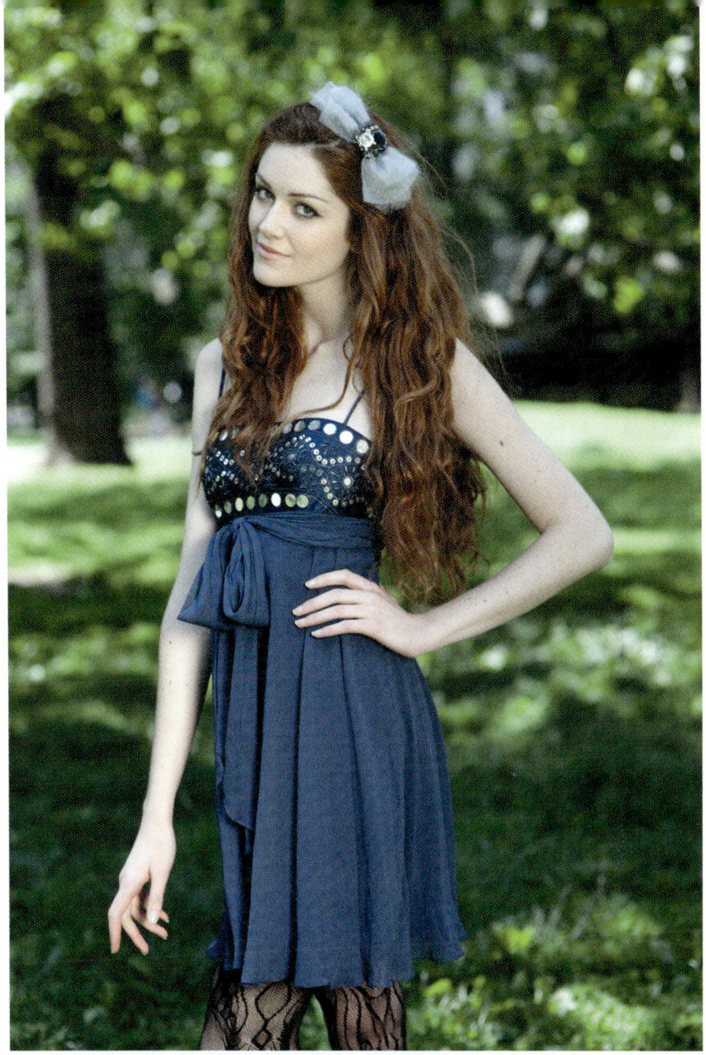

FIGURE 1.15
To get a flattering amount of reflection, you should feather your light. By changing the angle and height of the reflector, you are able to catch just enough light to add contrast to your image and a catchlight in the subject's eyes. There is no need for more reflection than this.

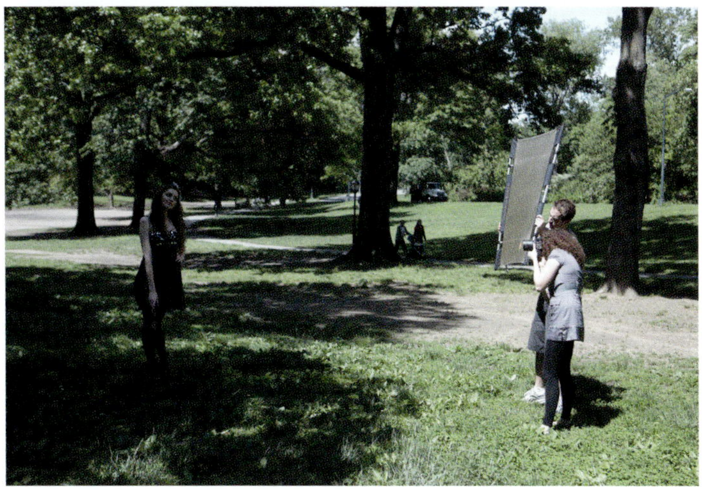

Make Use of Your Surroundings

If you pay close attention to your environment, you can actually let the environment do the heavy lifting for you! When you are out on location on a sunny day, look for a large neutral surface being lit by the sun. Preferably this surface will be light in tone. Look for large concrete walls, white sidewalks, white trucks—anything that is large, white or gray, and hit by the sun. The surface will act as a giant natural reflector to help illuminate your subject. Simply put the subject across from this illuminated surface. Consider moving the subject in the shade if the highlights from the sun on the subject are too harsh.

The example setup in **Figure 1.16** uses a large pale-colored apartment building in New York City. When the sun illuminates this wall, it becomes a giant, even light source. While in Figure 1.16 the wall is to the model's back, when I turn her around in **Figure 1.17**, the wall becomes a large, natural reflector that illuminates the subject with an even and glowing illumination on her face.

Using a large surface as a natural reflector is a great technique for achieving flattering, even light when photographing one person or large groups. Furthermore, you don't need to carry any equipment, hold reflectors, or even have an assistant. It's easy to do and provides great quality of light.

What happens if your natural reflector is not completely neutral? In **Figure 1.18**, the wall used as a reflector is actually slightly yellow. Notice the warm tones on the subject's face. The light is beautiful and glowing, but likely a bit too yellow to represent her true complexion.

TAKEAWAY ACTION

Pick a neutral surface for your natural reflector to avoid unwanted color tints. If you use a large light green wall as your natural reflector, for example, a light green tint will appear, ruining your photograph.

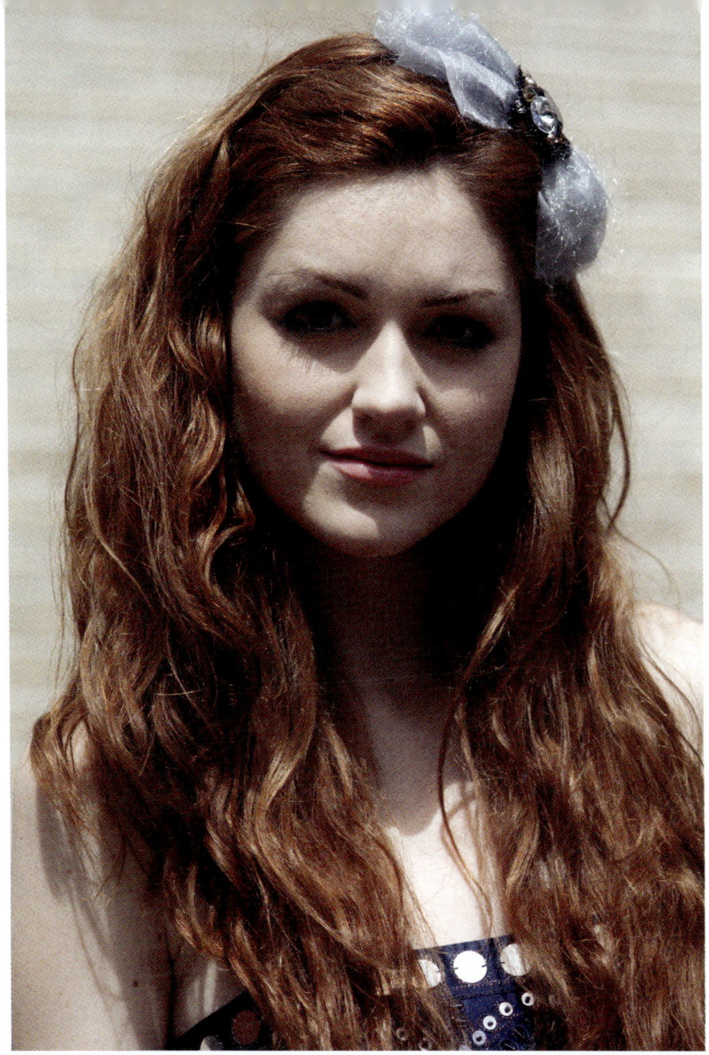

FIGURE 1.16
When the subject faces away from the wall, her face is illuminated by harsh midday sunlight. You can see the brightly illuminated wall behind her.

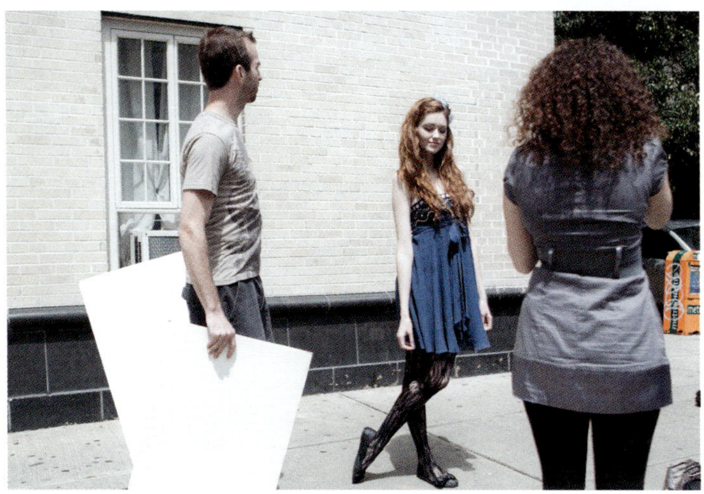

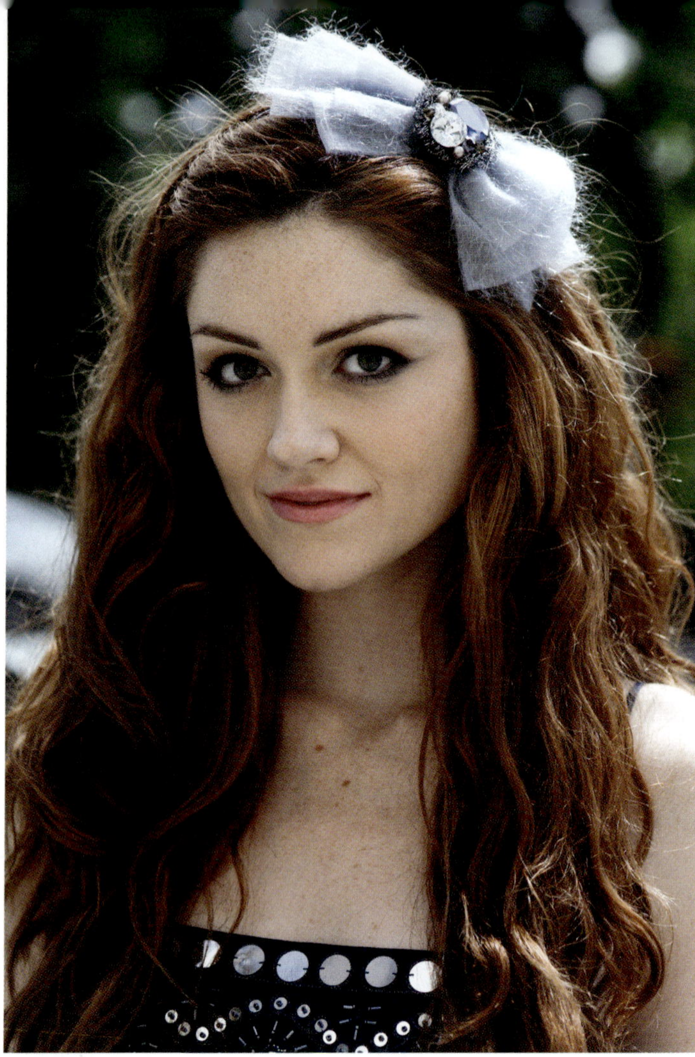

FIGURE 1.17
When the subject faces the wall, the large lit surface now evenly illuminates her face. The resulting light is a natural reflector that is glowing and soft on her face.

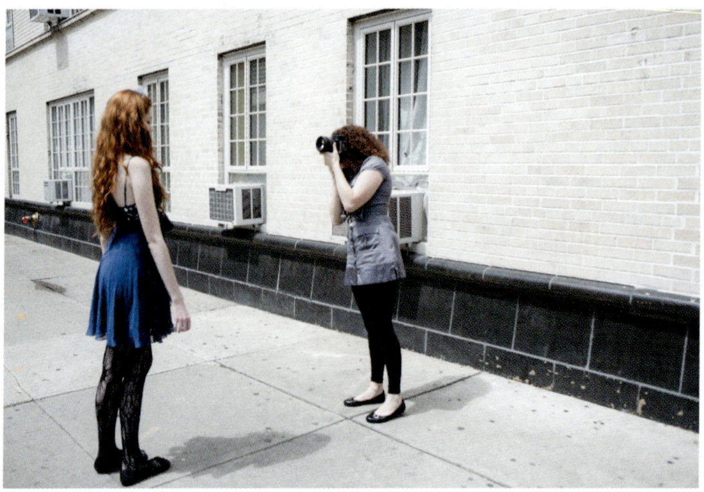

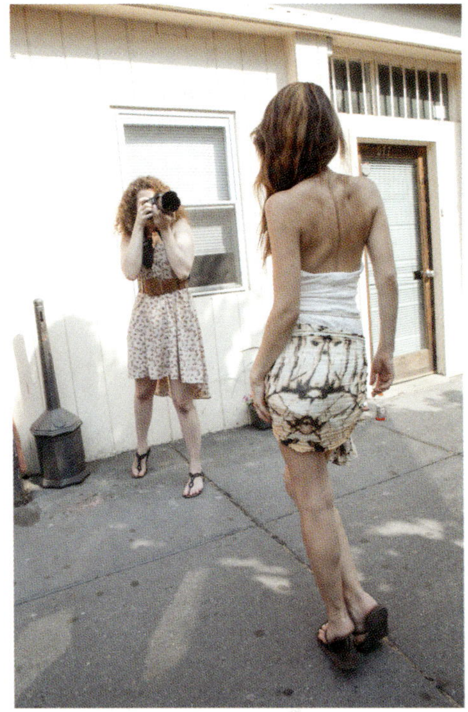

FIGURE 1.18

We found a large natural reflector, but the wall is slightly yellow. Notice the yellowish tones on the subject's face. The color of your reflector matters! Even subtle colors will affect the final image.

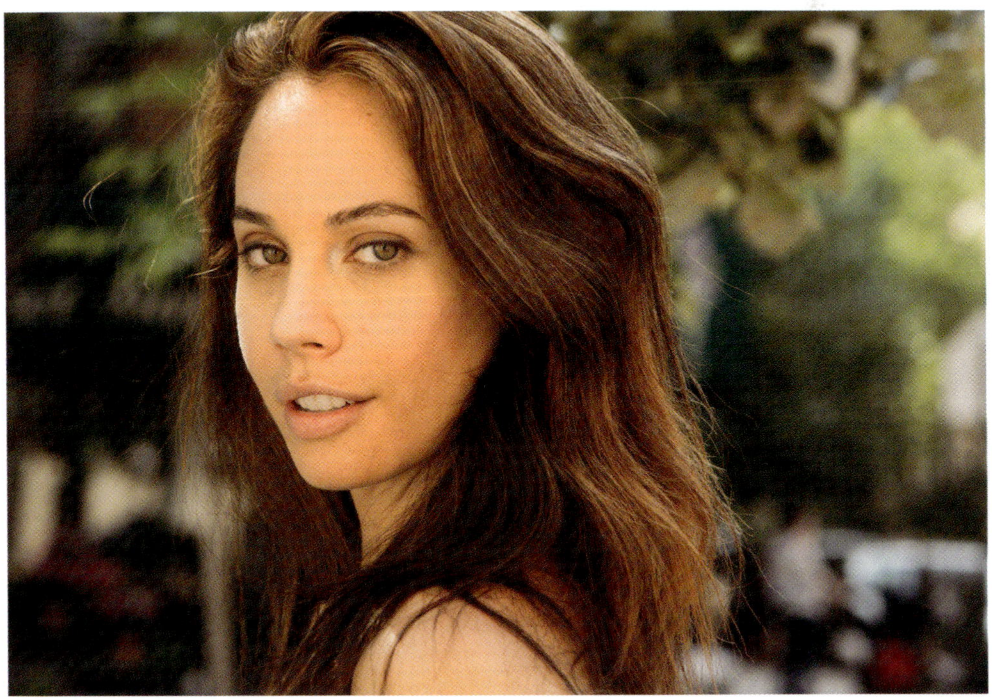

Think outside of the box! How about trying a large neutral colored stone as a reflector? In this instance, we found a gray stone in Central Park. First we photographed the subject in front of the stone (**Figure 1.19**), then we faced the subject toward the stone—success and beautiful light! (**Figure 20**)!

Another amazing solution is to combine two things we've discussed already: covered shade and natural reflectors! If you can find a porch or overhang that has a natural reflector illuminating the scene, then you've got a perfect recipe for portrait success! For **Figure 1.21**, we found an overhang of a bridge and the illuminated sidewalk. Throw in a bit more of a reflector for catchlights in the eyes, and you have a striking image!

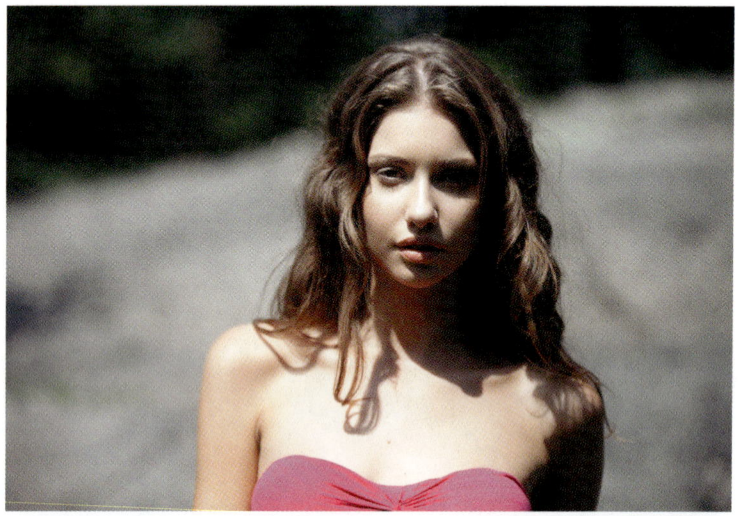

FIGURE 1.19
Think outside the box and use unusual natural reflectors. The stone behind the model shows promise.

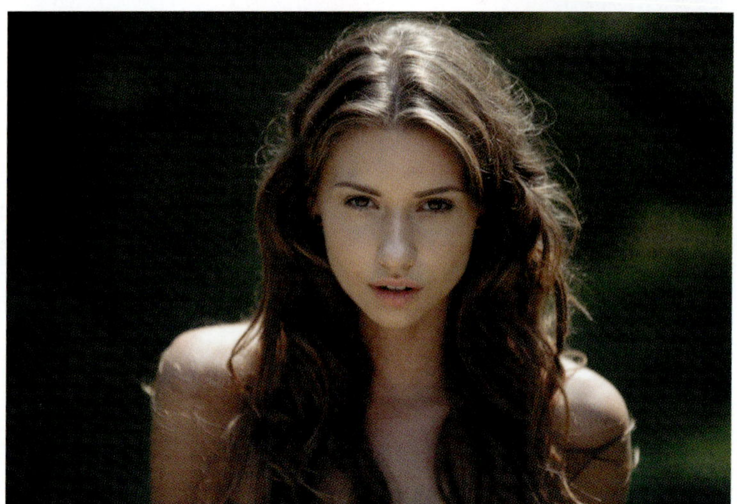

FIGURE 1.20
Here we used the extremely large sun-lit rock in Central Park as the main illumination on the subject's face by turning her towards the rock.

FIGURE 1.21
Using existing structures, we were able to create a striking image much like if we had used a combination of diffusors and reflectors out in the open. A large bridge overhead created shade for the model, while the bright sidewalk in front of her reflected enough light back onto her face for a fill.

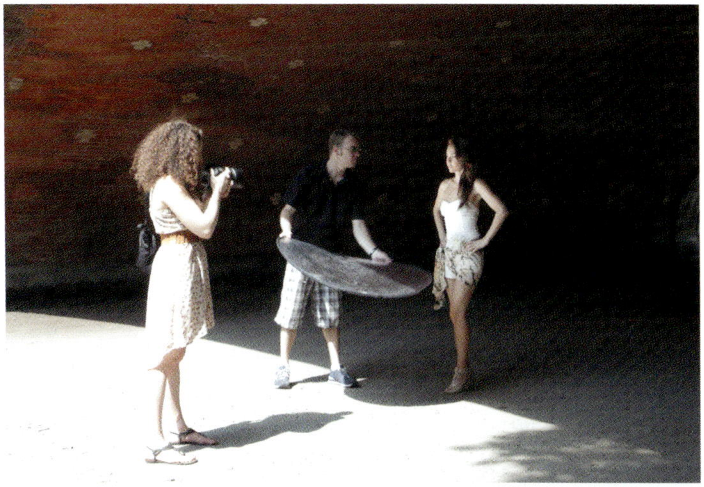

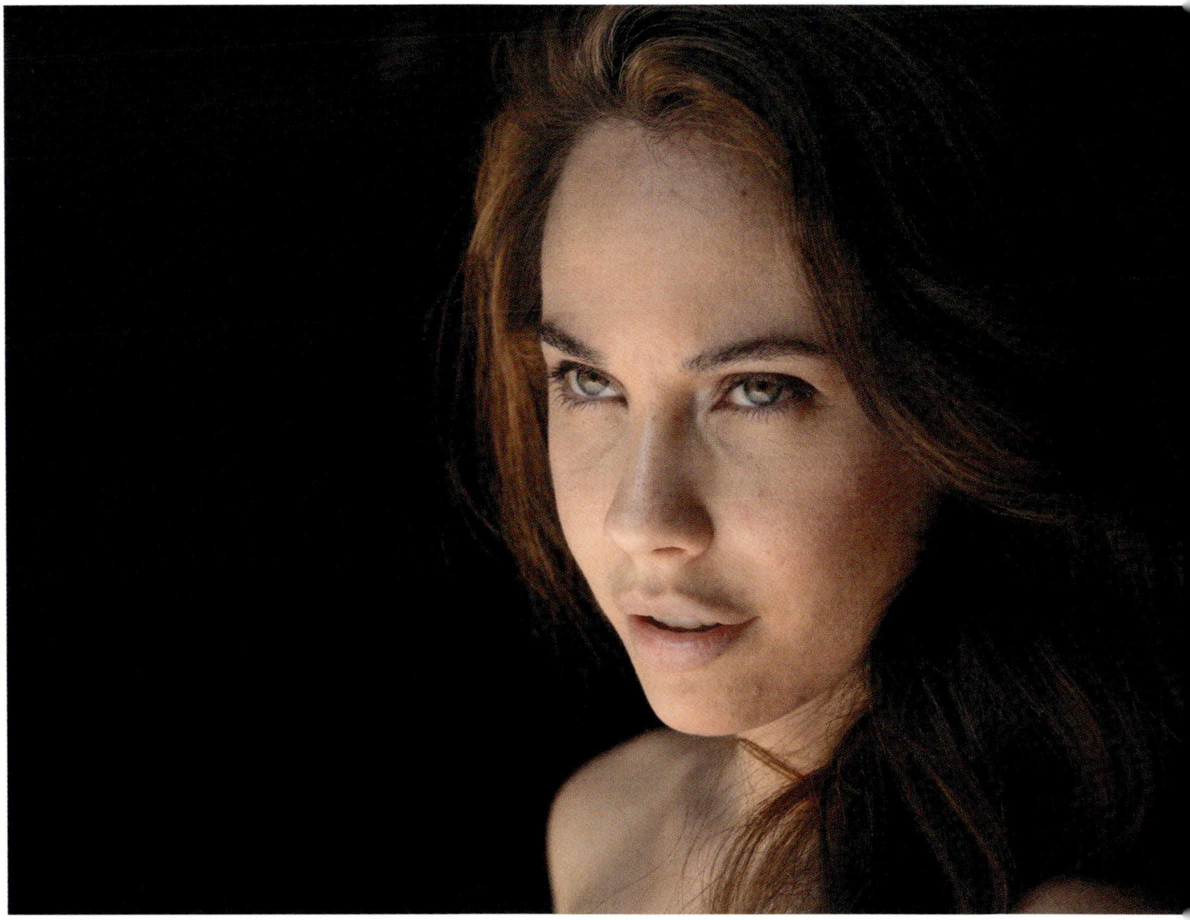

Look for Backlit Leaves on Trees

On extremely sunny days, one of our favorite lighting situations is to find backlit leaves on trees. Look at the angle of the sun to determine which leaves are then backlit, place your subject in front of these leaves. When you shoot with a wide aperture (f/1.4, f/1.8, f/2.8), these leaves will become a dreamy background of highlights and what looks like bubbles of light (the smooth quality of this out-of-focus area is referred to as **bokeh**).

Lovingly referred to as "dreamy bubbles" by Lindsay, this technique works best on a sunny day when the sun is not at its peak; earlier in the morning or later in the afternoon is preferred. This gives a little angle to the light and makes it easier to catch it coming through the leaves. On an overcast day, you can still get light coming through leaves, which will provide a similar lighting situation, with slightly less pop. Either way, by shooting the backlit leaves on trees as a background, the bokeh (blur) of the lens will create this stunning effect. In **Figure 1.22**, we took advantage of an overhang of leaves that were backlit by the sun. Because we were shooting at a wide aperture, the leaves became a soft blur and beautiful background for a portrait.

TAKEAWAY ACTION

Place your subject in front of backlit leaves on trees shoot at a wide aperture for great portraits.

If the backlit leaves are too low in the frame to show up behind your subject, get down on your knees or lie on your stomach. You can't move the tree, but you can move yourself: Position your body in whichever way necessary to put those beautiful leaves directly behind the subject.

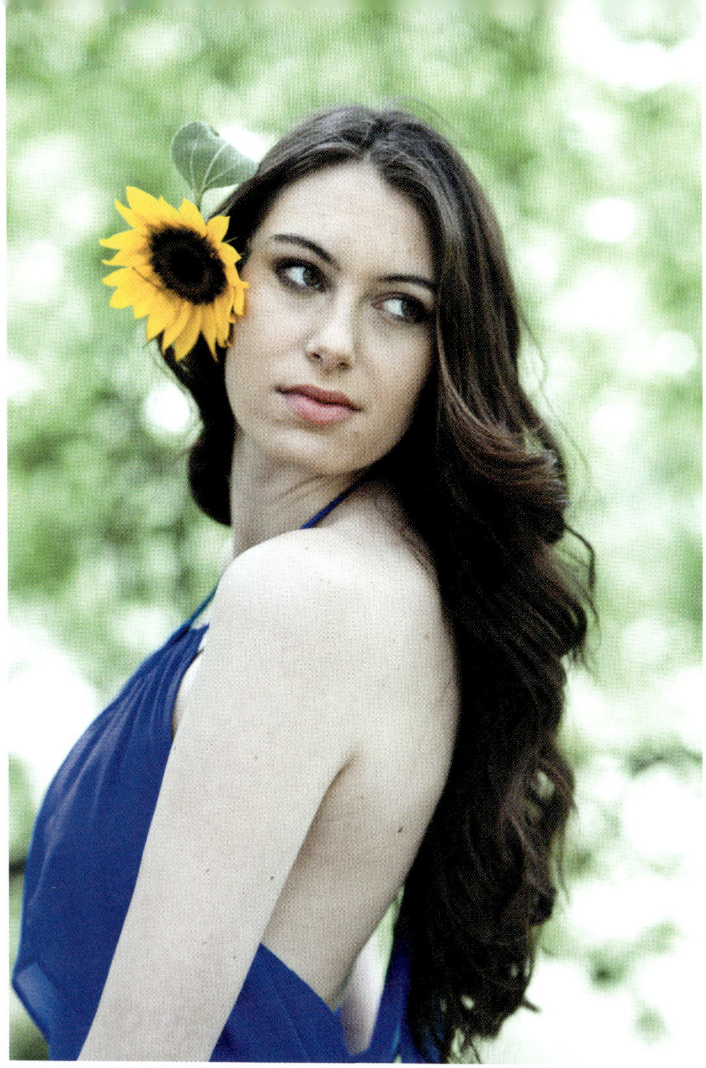

FIGURE 1.22
When shooting in a park or near trees, look for an environment with backlit leaves on trees. Placing the subject in front of backlit leaves and shooting at a wide aperture (f/2.8) created this soft and textured background.

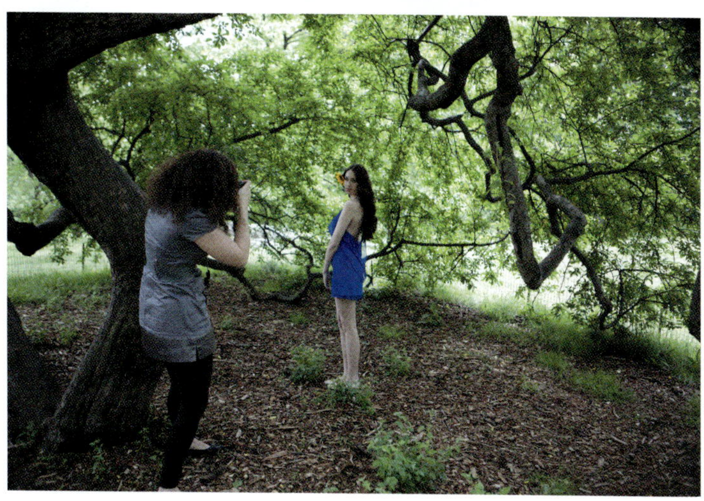

Shoot in Direct Sunlight

In 99% of situations, you shouldn't shoot in direct sunlight, but what about that last 1%?

The time of day changes the equation, for example. When the sun is lower in the sky at the beginning and end of the day, the sun's rays are softened by traveling through more of Earth's atmosphere and become more flattering. They create a beautiful glow on the face or great backlight on the hair. We all know *that* light. Such directional sunlight is called golden hour for a reason. It can be pure gold in color and for your wallet. If you choose to shoot in golden hour and use direct sunlight, be aware that the light might be too warm, applying an orange "fake tan" look to your subject's skin.

In fashion photography the rules change a bit, as well. When photographing a man with a chiseled jaw or a woman with a structural face, shooting in harsh midday light will enhance these features and contribute to the overall mood of the scene or editorial. In general, we stay away from this approach, however. It can work, but it fails more often (a lot more) than it succeeds. **Figure 1.23** shows more fashion potential for direct sun: The subject stands in direct sunlight with her face turned slightly to catch the rays. In fact, we angled her face to create a triangle of light below the right eye, called *Rembrandt light*.

WATCH IT! Avoid harsh shadows.

If you are an event photographer, shooting in direct sunlight later in the day can create some really dramatic images, especially when playing with shadows. Just be sure to watch the light on the face so that the shadows aren't harsh and unflattering.

When You Are Stuck

Sometimes none of these solutions work. There is simply no shade in sight. You are in a large open field with no trees, or you can't budge the bridal couple from the alter in the sun. The sun is baking down, and you're sweating because you can't think of a way to salvage this scene. What do you do?

Read Chapter 2.

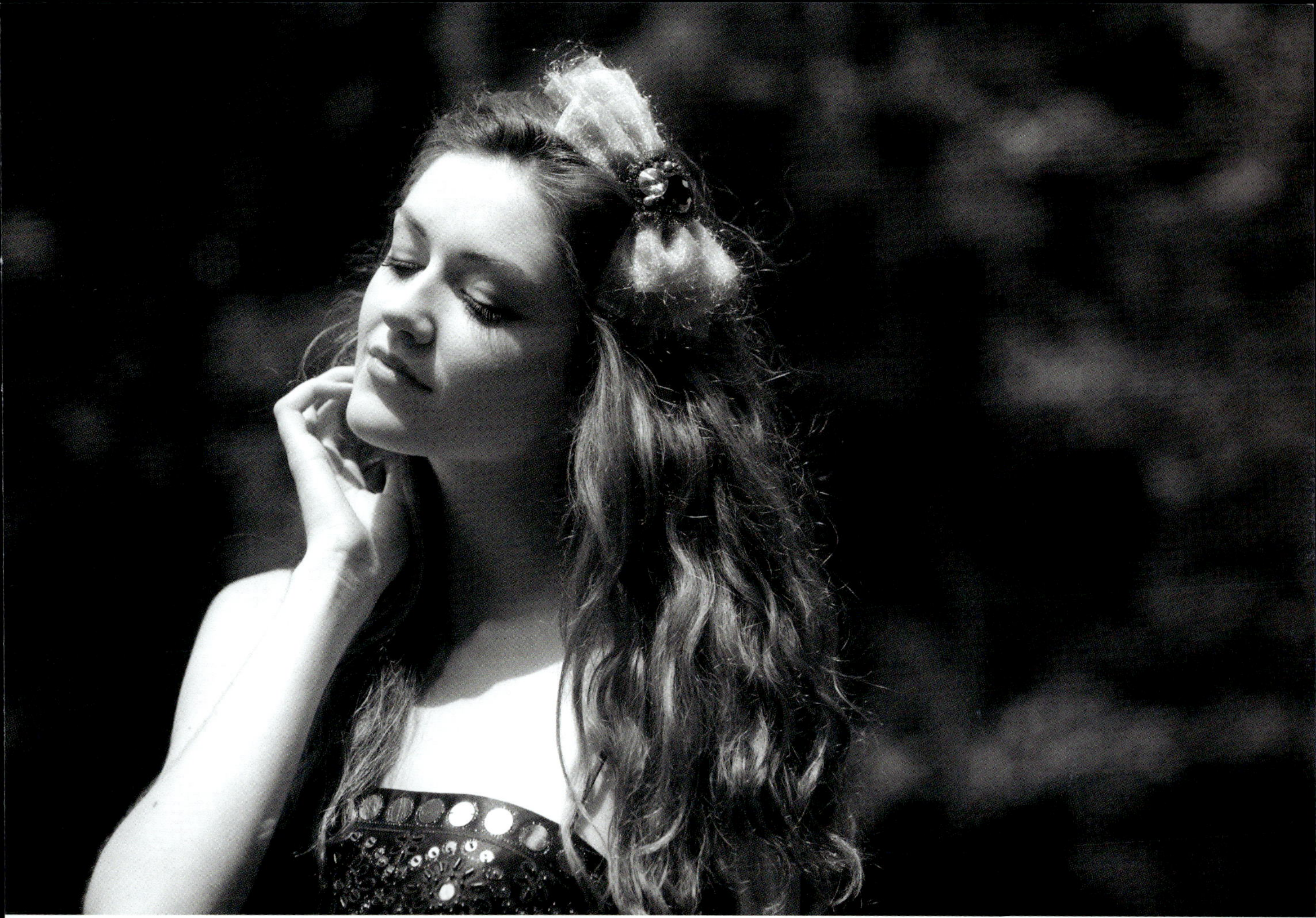

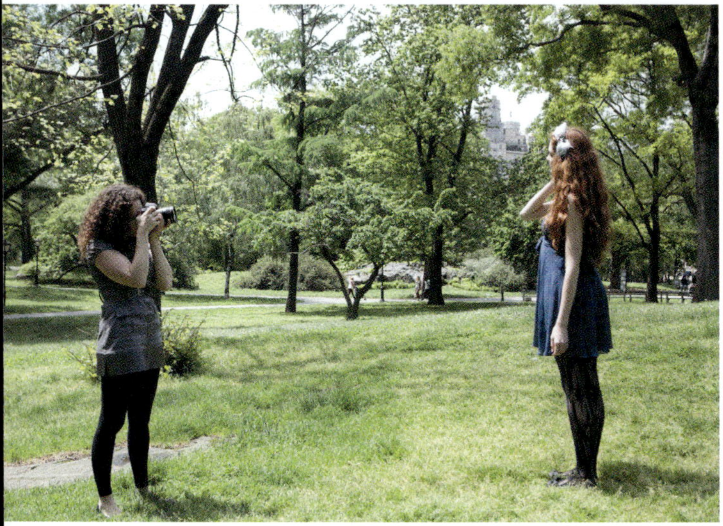

FIGURE 1.23
In some rare instances, shooting in midday's direct sunlight can create interesting light. Here we have angled the subject so that her face caught the direct sunlight, which created Rembrandt light on her cheek. Although this technique isn't typically recommended, you can use it for dramatic effect.

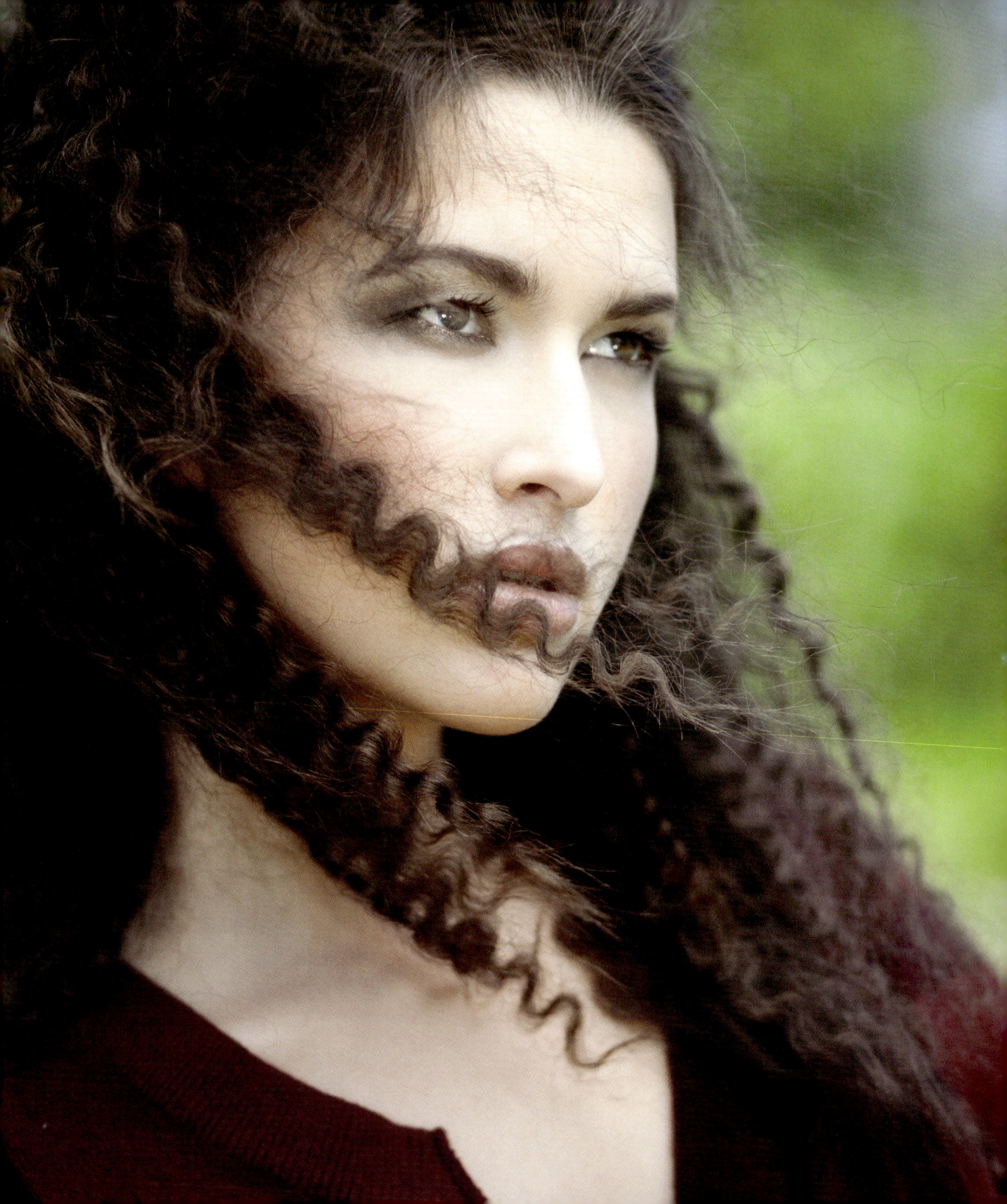

CHAPTER TWO
Direct Sunlight, No Shade in Sight

Sometimes you are asked to shoot in direct sunlight with no shade in sight—a portrait session in the middle of a field, a wedding ceremony at high noon. When the sun is blaring down and you can't take cover, what do you do?

Try to sculpt the light. When you take control of the direct sunlight, you can bend it to your will to help create a glowing radiance on your subject. Although controlling the light is easier for portrait shoots than event photography, several solutions can help you make striking images—even in direct sunlight with no shade in sight.

Create Your Own Shade

When no natural shade is available, get resourceful and create your own! This is a quick and easy solution for a single-person portrait. In **Figure 2.1**, you can see how miserable the illumination created by direct sunlight is on the face.

To block off overhead light, you can use a reflector, a piece of cardboard, or a piece of white foam core (which can be found at most office supply or art stores). Simply hold it over the subject's head.

We recommend, however, that you create a *light trap* or a *light sandwich*: Block overhead light with a board or reflector (the black side of a 5-in-1 reflector works great here), and use a reflector to fill from below or from the side. When you block off overhead light, you really don't have much light on the face. In fact, often the image will look flat and lack contrast. Instead, use a white, silver, or silver-gold reflector to bounce the natural sunlight back onto the face. The results are often very flattering and create even, glowing light, as seen in **Figure 2.2**.

This trap or sandwich technique, however, works best when you're photographing only one person at a time. For a couple or group, you'll need something extremely large to block out the light.

Because putting someone in the shade reduces the light on the subject, you must increase your exposure to compensate. The problem with this, however, is that you can easily overcompensate, making backgrounds blown-out and distracting. Be acutely aware of your background when creating your own shade. You may need to change the angle of shooting or recompose to position the subject against a darker toned (therefore less distracting) background. **Figure 2.3** was composed to put a darker background behind the subject. Compare it to Figure 2.2 where the background is lighter toned.

WATCH IT! Don't light too much from below.

When using the sandwich technique, photographers frequently fall into the trap of reflecting too much from below. Because the subject needs light on the face, novice photographers tend to throw in a reflector right underneath the subject's chin. If the reflector is catching direct sunlight, it will create terrible under-light (highlights under the nose and with shadows possibly going upwards, much like you would see when telling ghost stories around the campfire at night). Instead, use a reflector slightly off to one side or raised a bit higher. You may also consider using a white reflector (even a white piece of foam core) that will produce a much more subtle fill effect.

FIGURE 2.1
Direct sunlight is harsh and unflattering. It often makes your subject squint or puts unsightly highlights and shadows on the face.

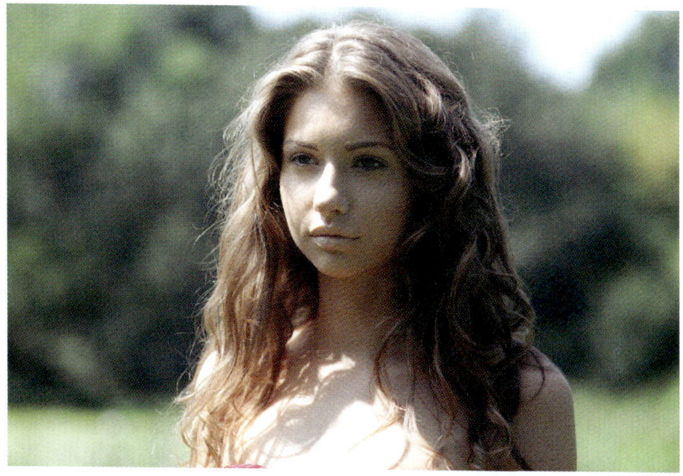

FIGURE 2.2
Try blocking off overhead light with a piece of white foam core and using a reflector to add contrast and illumination to the face.

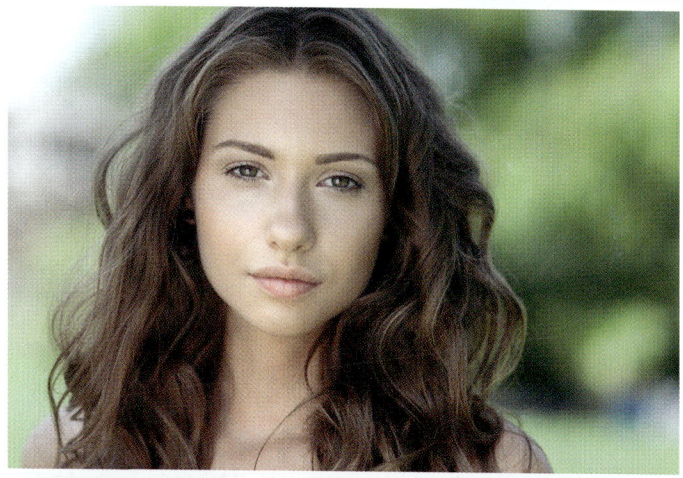

FIGURE 2.3
To make the subject stand out from the background, consider reframing your shot to put a darker background behind your subject. Backgrounds are always important, and up to personal taste. Just remember, keep them clean and simple.

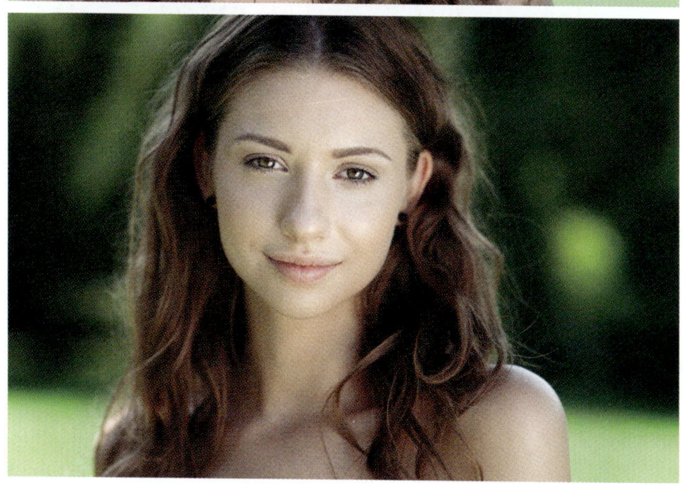

Later in the day, the sandwich technique can create very striking results, as seen in **Figure 2.4**. If you let the sun hit the back of the hair, it will create striking hair light, while the reflector and overhead block give you beautiful catchlights in the eyes and illumination on the face.

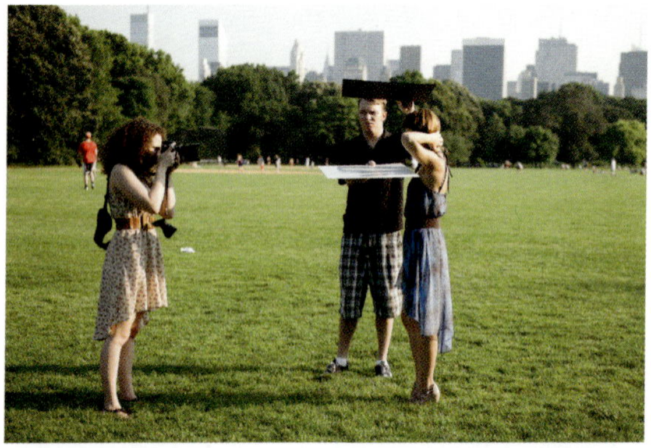

FIGURE 2.4
You can sandwich your subject between two pieces of foam core for a striking effect. You block off overhead light and fill the shadows in the eyes. The effect is quite beautiful later in the day, as seen here.

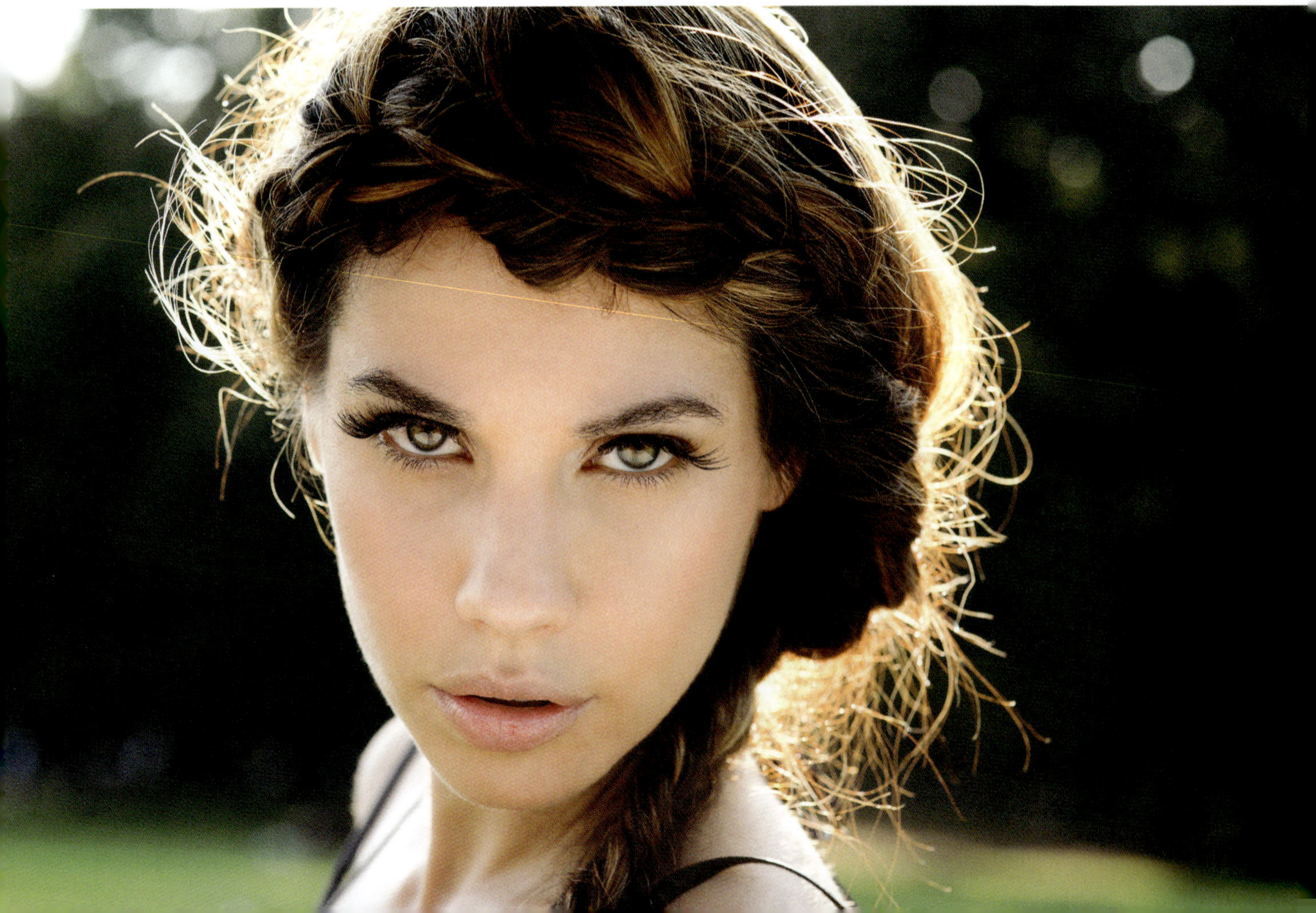

Soften the Light

Direct sunlight is usually unflattering because it is harsh and has a lot of contrast. A variety of tools on the market enable you to make this light soft and glowing. By diffusing the light, you can completely change its properties and make it great for your portrait photography. In fact, you can make that light appear *almost* like a softbox on location.

To do this, you will need something called a **scrim** or **diffuser**. A diffuser is basically a slightly translucent piece of fabric. As light passes through this fabric, it becomes soft and diffused. Diffusers come in a host of shapes and sizes. Many reflector kits have a translucent center, giving you a diffuser included in the kit. For small reflector kits, this diffuser has limited use because the area of light it diffuses is quite small. The benefit, however, is portability.

When using diffusers, you often must balance a trade-off between effectiveness and portability. For example, the bigger the diffuser, the greater area of light it diffuses, yet the more difficult it is to transport. Keep this in mind when making diffuser selections.

Using a scrim is a way to diffuse a much larger surface area. A scrim with diffusion material is like a very large frame with a bed sheet stretched over it. Diffusion material is actually available in stops; you can cut out different amounts of light depending on the translucency of the fabric.

Scrims and diffusers come in a variety of sizes and range drastically in price. If you are photographing a child, you can often just use the diffuser included in the 5-in-1 reflector/diffuser kits available at most camera stores. Simply place the diffuser between the subject and the direct sunlight, and you have pleasing, even illumination! You can get a 5-in-1 reflector/diffuser for under $50. If you are photographing adults or multiple subjects, you will need more diffused area. One great way to get more is with the of use a Scrim Jim (F.J. Westcott, westcott.com), which is shown in **Figure 2.5** and is available in several sizes. The Scrim Jim also breaks down to be relatively compact, so you're not sacrificing portability for size.

The challenge, however, is getting the diffuser to soften the area you want it to. If you have a group of people and the sun is high in the sky, you basically need the diffuser raised above them. This is not easy to do with one or even two assistants. If you need this type of elevation for your scrim, there is a solution. California Sunbounce offers the Sun-Swatter (www.sunbounce.com). Shown in **Figure 2.6**, the Sun-Swatter has a four-by-six-foot diffuser on a pole that a single person can hold out over a group. This is a fantastic tool for whenever you need to raise your diffuser and have only a single helper. On a windy day, however, beware! You may create a very amusing circus-style entertainment as your assistant goes flying through the air while holding such a large "sail."

FIGURE 2.5
A scrim (specifically Westcott's Scrim Jim here) is used to soften the light and decrease the contrast in a scene. When photographing a single person or when you don't require a full-length shot, a scrim can be very effective. In some circumstances, however, you may require multiple assistants or a bigger setup to use the scrim to its full potential.

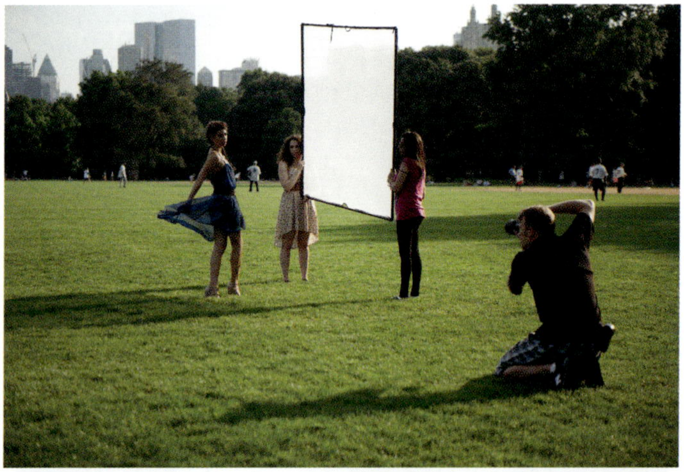

FIGURE 2.6
The Sun-Swatter from California Sunbounce enables you to elevate your scrim over a scene or subject and can be held by one person. While it is more expensive, it also offers a greater reach than basic scrims.

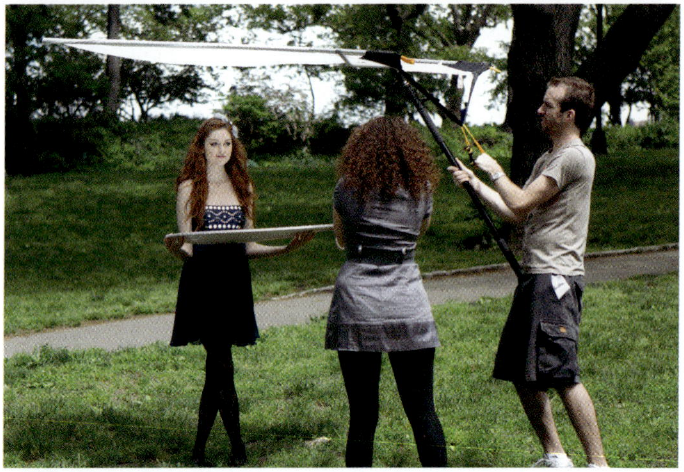

FIGURE 2.7
Try using a large, shoot-through umbrella as a make-shift, portable scrim that also provides pleasant illumination.

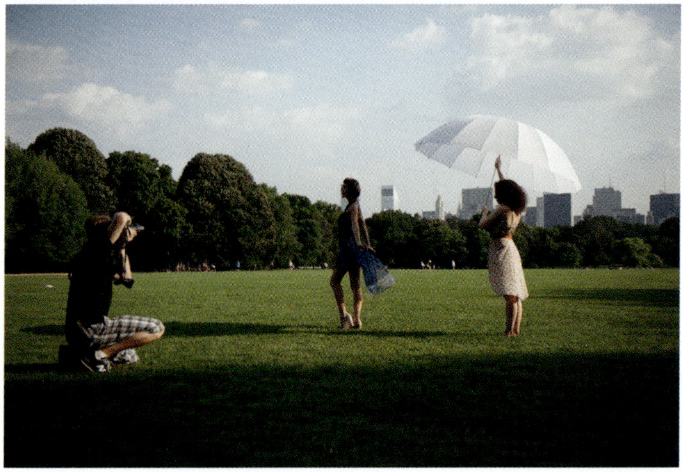

A third solution is to use a large, shoot-through umbrella to diffuse the scene (**Figure 2.7**). Westcott makes a seven-foot, shoot-through parabolic umbrella that can be a *great* tool to diffuse a scene on a bright day, even if you don't have an assistant. Your subject can hold the umbrella, and you can easily make beautiful headshots. If you have an extra hand on set, ask that assistant hold the umbrella farther from the body to create more full-body diffusion!

Use a Scrim or Diffusion Material

Scrims really are amazing tools for turning harsh overhead light into soft, glowing light. There are a few tips you need to keep in mind when using these tools.

First, scrims change the *quality* of light (soft versus hard), not the *direction* of light (left, right, up, down). In other words, if you use a scrim to diffuse the light that is high and to the left of the frame, the light will still be coming from this angle. This is something to consider when posing your subjects. There will still be a bright side of the face and frame; use this knowledge to your advantage. You will likely want to pose the subjects facing that light, or just make sure the direction of light doesn't create unflattering highlights and shadows on the face. **Figure 2.8** is the raw, direct sunlight whereas **Figure 2.9** has been diffused.

A diffuser is a great option when you want to knock down overhead light, because it still maintains a level of light on the hair while giving shape to the face. Notice in Figure 2.9 how you still see highlights on her hair and how the direction of light has defined her cheekbones. When overhead light is eliminated, the light on the face becomes very flat and does not sculpt. In Figure 2.9, however, the light is quite sculpting.

✗ **FIGURE 2.8**
Direct sunlight on the face is extremely undesirable.

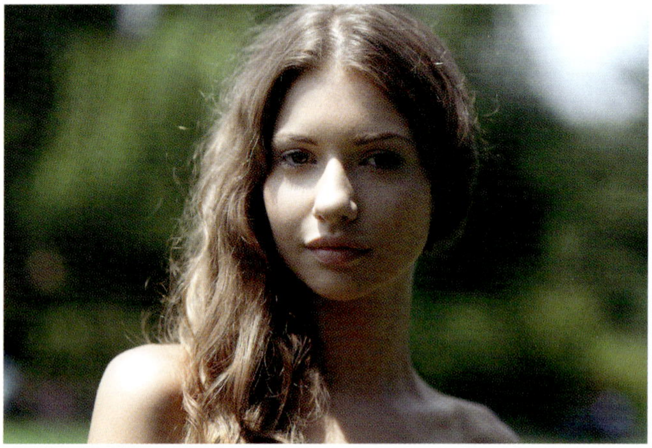

FIGURE 2.9
Here we added a diffuser above the subject. Notice how there is still a strong direction of light (from above and to the left), but the quality of light is much softer and more flattering.

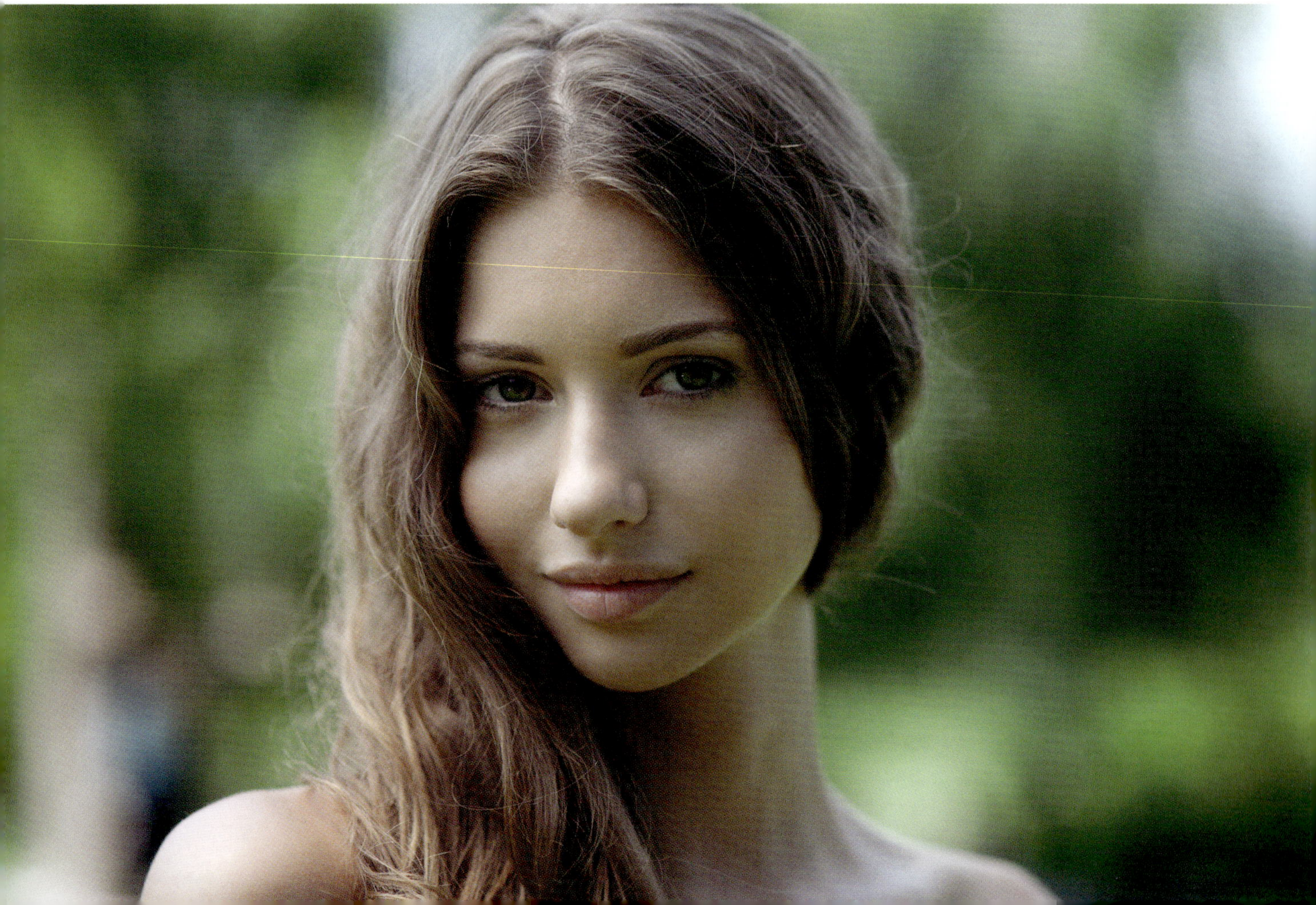

Use a Scrim and a Reflector

As we said, a scrim does not change the direction of light. If your shoot is in the middle of the day in direct sunlight, the sun is still coming from a very high angle. In fact, it can come from directly overhead and give the raccoon-eye look—highlights on the nose and forehead with shadows in the eyes. Not usually a good look, even for the most attractive of subjects. You must find a way to help even out the light and put illumination back into the subject's eyes.

You have two options. First, you might stand elevated above your subjects. This will lift their heads and chins up, and help them to catch the light in their eyes. Basically, you are lifting their eyes up to a light source. It is as if you have placed a large softbox above the model's head.

Another option is to use a reflector to bounce light back into their eyes. In this instance, you would use a scrim to soften the overhead light, then you would use a reflector (silver, silver-gold mix, or white) to catch some of that sunlight and give a sparkle to their eyes (**Figure 2.10**).

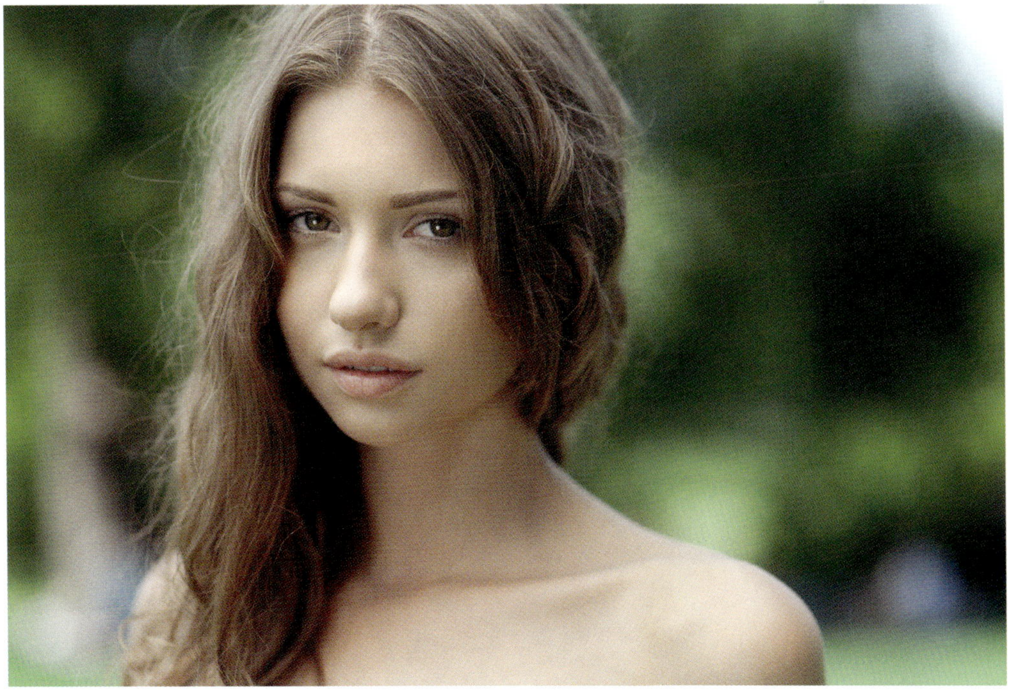

✔ FIGURE 2.10
Here we used a scrim so we can keep the direction of light on the face but have a much softer quality of light. By introducing a reflector in this image (silver), we were able to add a catchlight to the eyes and reduce the shadows.

Notice how this solution keeps the beautiful sculpted shape to the face in Figure 2.10, but also adds sparkle and illumination to the eyes. The photo has more depth than simply blocking overhead lights, but is much more gentle and flattering than direct sunlight.

The results can be quite beautiful, though perhaps a bit complicated. If you are just starting out as a photographer, always try to keep your solutions as simple as possible. You don't want equipment and excessive tools that get in the way of your interactions with the subject. That being said, the reflector solution can be striking.

Don't forget your angle of reflection and to **feather** the light; both are key to proper illumination. You could also use a flash to introduce a catchlight, but for the purposes of this book, we recommend a reflector as a great solution.

Take another look at this effect side by side: **Figure 2.11** was shot in direct sunlight, **Figure 2.12** with a diffuser, and **Figure 2.13** with a diffuser and reflector. Notice that we did not feather the reflector and used it from a lower angle; we nearly eliminated the direction of light. It's all a matter of taste, although we prefer the end result of Figure 2.10 with a bit more shape to the face. Notice, however, that even with a diffuser in Figures 2.11 through 2.13, the direct overhead light gives the subject raccoon eyes that we must remedy. By using a silver reflector, we are able overpower the shadows and fill the light in the eyes.

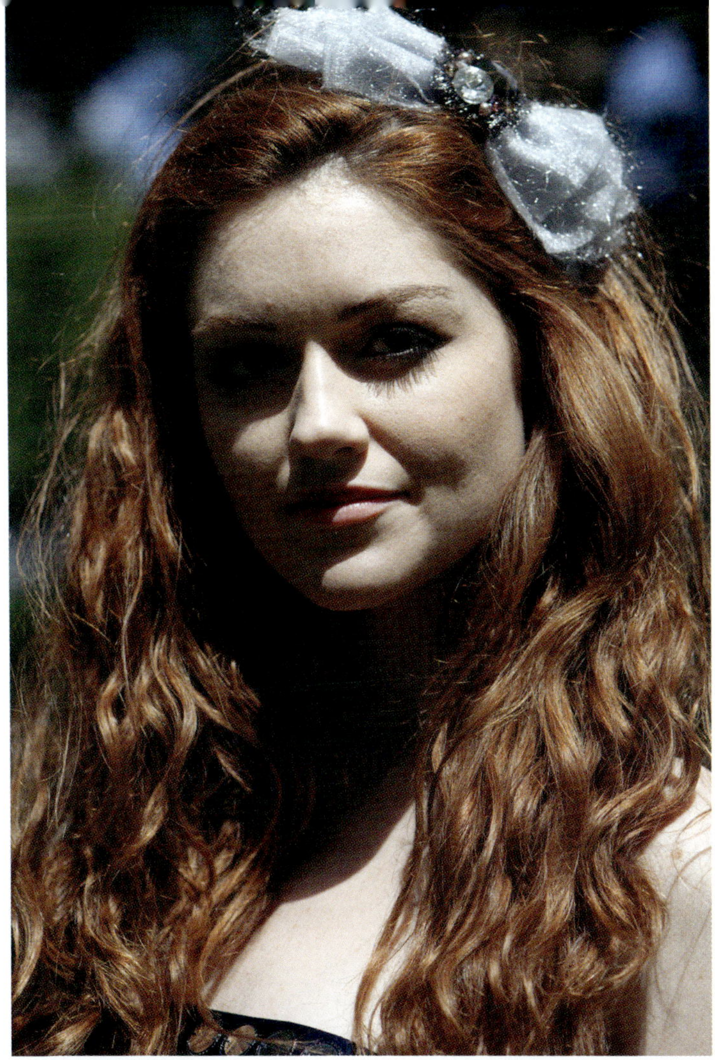

FIGURE 2.11
Here our subject is in direct overhead sunlight. The raccoon eyes are miserable and unflattering.

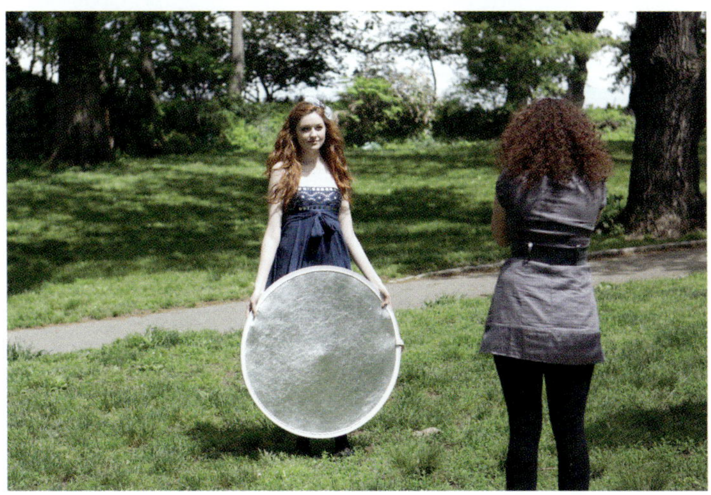

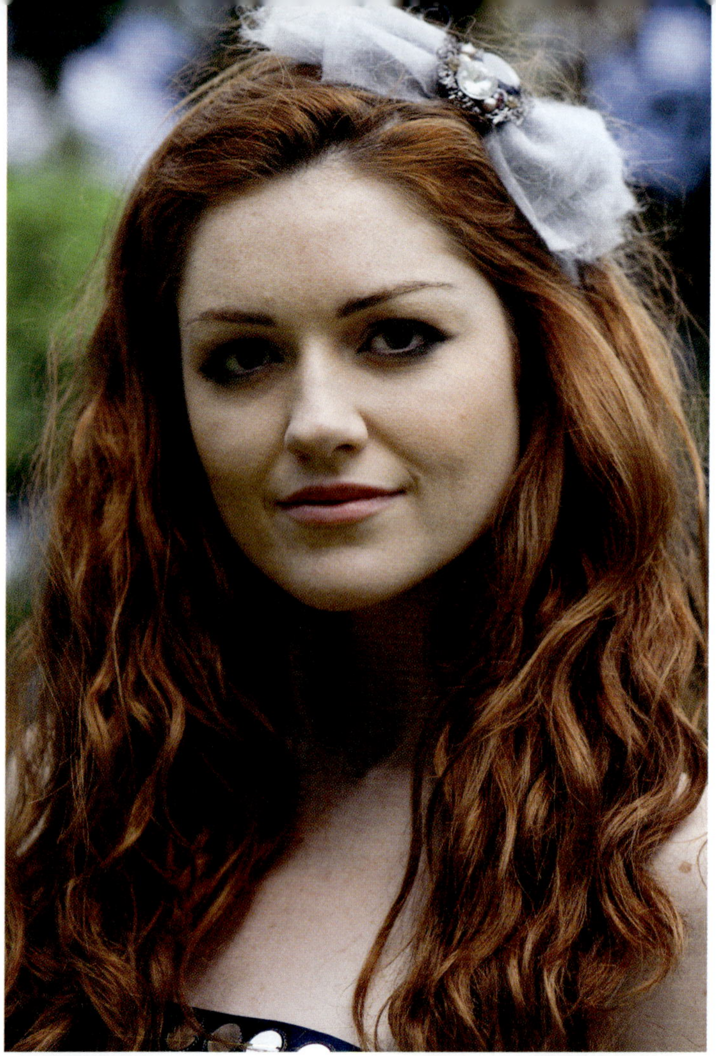

FIGURE 2.12

By adding an California Sunbounce Sun-Swatter overhead, we softened the light and reduced the harsh contrast. The light, however, is still overhead and gives unflattering shadows to the eyes.

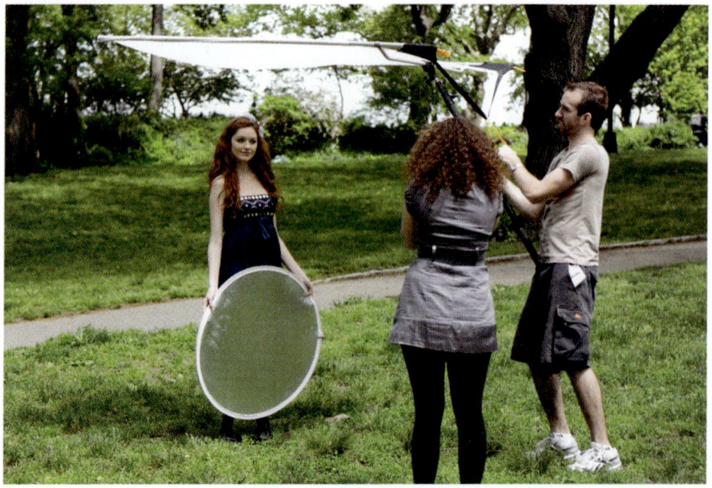

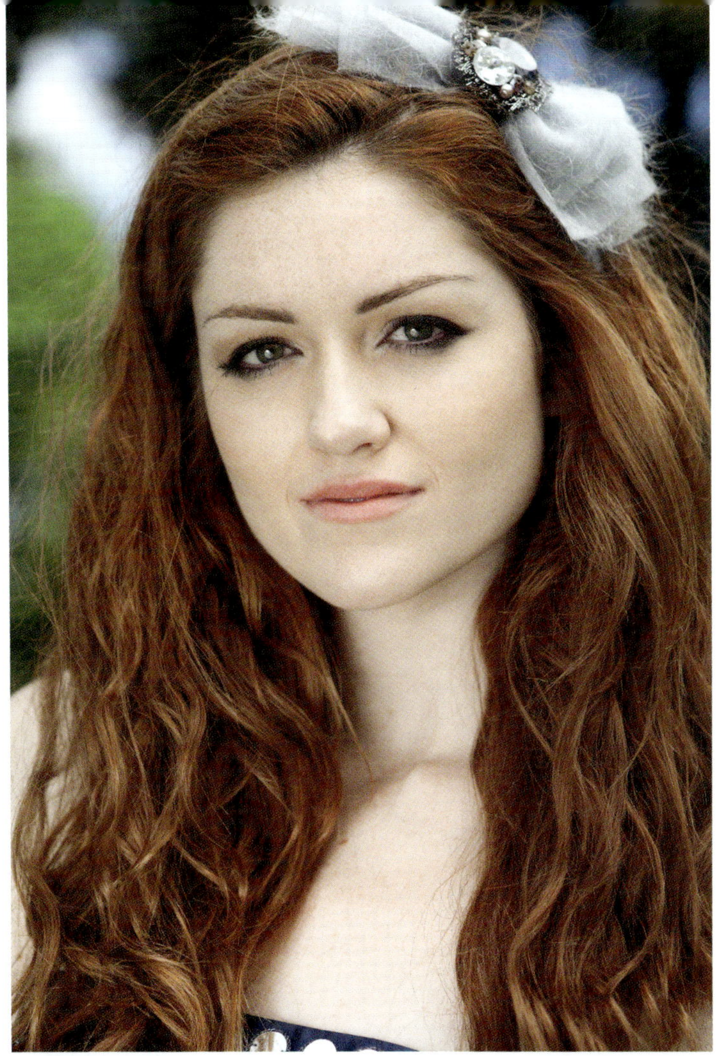

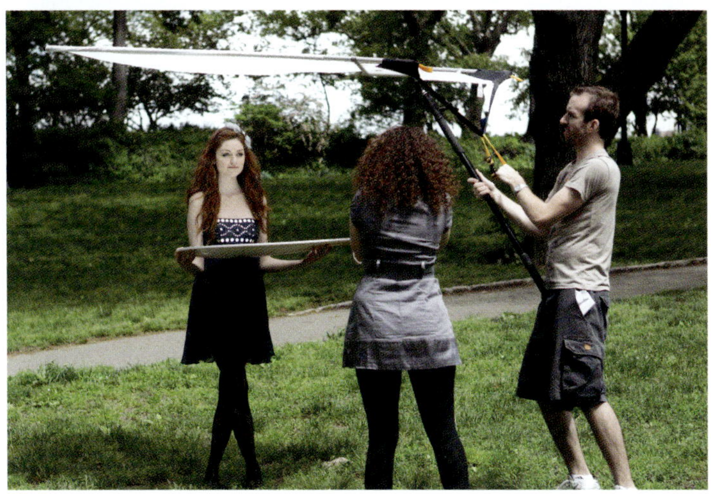

FIGURE 2.13
By introducing a silver reflector to the scene, we were able to overpower the shadows and fill the light in the eyes.

Face Subjects Away from the Sun

If you have no choice but to shoot in direct sunlight, put the subject's back to the sun. Obviously you don't want your subjects staring into the sun because the light will be just as unpleasant as are their expressions. If you have no other choice—you can't find shade and can't use a diffuser—putting the person's back to the sun is a good way to start improving your image.

Unfortunately, this technique has two pitfalls: lack of contrast on the face and overexposed highlights on the hair. You'll be happy to know, however, that our solution takes care of both problems!

When you put the light to the subject's back, you will create a hair light that acts to separate the subject from the background and often gives the person a heavenly glow (**Figure 2.14**). So far, so good. Unfortunately, when in direct sunlight, these highlights on the hair become too bright and create overexposed and distracting highlights. This problem is particularly severe on people with light blonde hair. The second problem you encounter is that the light on the subject's face is often flat and lacks contrast. There really isn't a source of light, and compared to the bright highlights in the hair, the face just looks dull. The solution is *not* to fix it in Adobe Photoshop, but instead in camera! Here is what we recommend.

To tame the exposure and improve the quality of light on the face, you must introduce a new light source. To do this, you may either use a flash or a reflector. For the purposes of this chapter, we recommend a reflector to illuminate the face. The key to this approach is not to over-illuminate the face and to be mindful of the angle of your reflector. Some photographers catch as much light as possible and reflect it back into the face. Doing so, however, can create unpleasant highlights and harsh light. Instead, feather the reflector by skimming the some of the reflected light past your subject, allowing only a controlled portion to illuminate the face.

By introducing this "second" light, you will even out exposure between the subject and the background. Because of this, the highlights on the hair will register less overexposed, and you'll get that glow on your subject's face as you intended. Furthermore, your reflector gives a pleasant direction and quality of light to the face when used correctly (correct angles and feathering). In other words, this can be a pretty potent and easy solution!

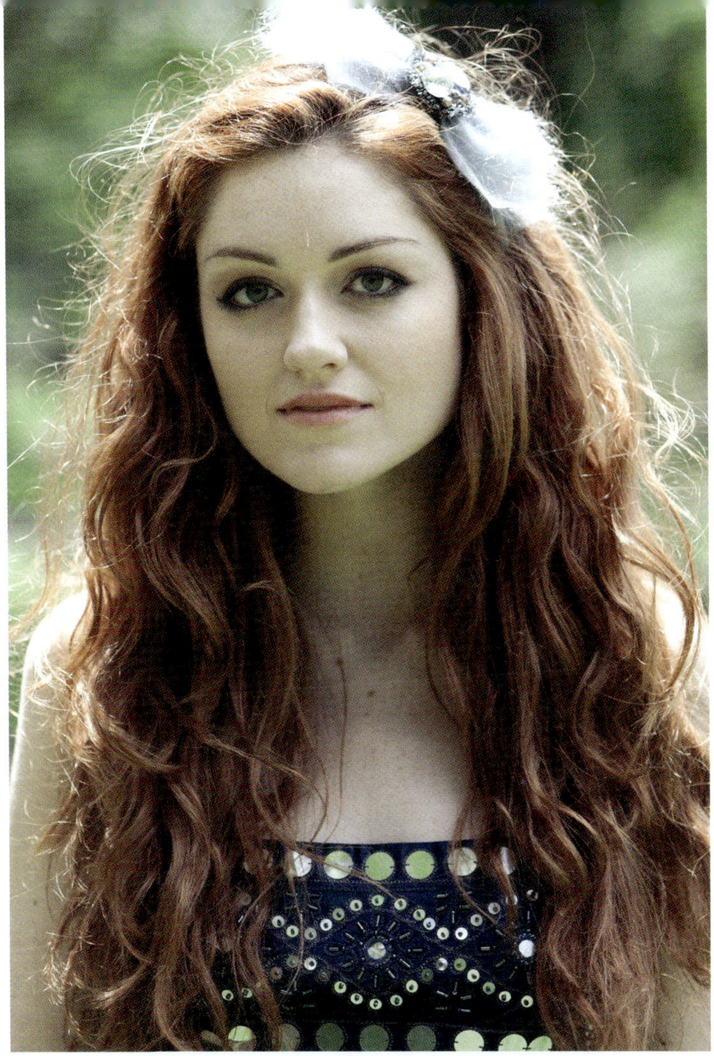

✘ **FIGURE 2.14**
We put the subject's back the sun, but the light on her face is flat and dull, plus it has a green cast from the grass. The highlights on her hair from the sun are overexposed.

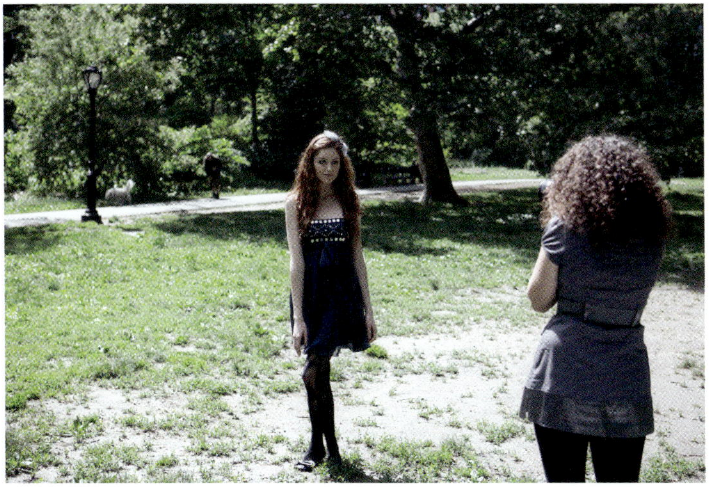

Now is a good time to talk about angles of reflection and different types of reflectors. With no reflection, the light is flat and muddy. In Figure 2.14, there is no contrast and a green color cast (from light reflecting off the green grass). To remedy this, we added a reflector. You can use white, silver, or silver-gold, but for **Figure 2.15**, we chose silver to give us more contrasty light.

When we introduced the reflector to illuminate the face in Figure 2.15, the angle of reflection was far too low. Many beginning photographers fall into this trap. Do *not* just put the reflector beneath the subject's chin. This gives unpleasant under-light which will draw attention to the subject's chin and nostrils and is generally unflattering.

When we raised the reflector to a higher angle, the quality of light improved, but as you can see in **Figure 2.16**, this resulted in too much reflection. When you are reflecting light onto the face, you don't want to reflect at full power. This creates an unflattering contrast and quality of light. Instead you want to change the angle of reflector to just catch the edge of the light.

In the **Figure 2.17**, our favorite, we elevated the reflector. By raising the reflector above the subject, we were able to cast the light downward. This is a more natural and flattering angle that helps carve out the subject's cheekbones and jawline. Notice how, by feathering, we still introduced light and contast to the face without having an overpowering amount of light.

Take a look at one more example of this effect by comparing **Figures 2.18** (before) and **2.19** (after). Instead of using a traditional silver reflector in Figure 2.19, we opted for a white reflector that produces softer, more subtle lighting. When using a white reflector, you may need to move in closer to your subject to achieve sufficient illumination on the face. Notice again that by introducing a reflector, we changed the color tones on the face, added a direction to the light, put catchlights to the eyes, and helped tone down the bright highlights in the hair.

Late in the day, this soft, subtle lighting effect takes on a dream-like and romantic quality, which is great for portraits of couples, bridal sessions, and pretty much any photo subject. (You'll learn more about this effect in Chapter 9, "Strong Backlight.")

For portraits, a reflector is generally a great solution, and you can use a larger reflector farther from the subjects if you must light a group of people. For events, however, a reflector may be quite impractical. Instead, a fill flash from a speedlight or an off-camera flash might be your best solution for portability and power.

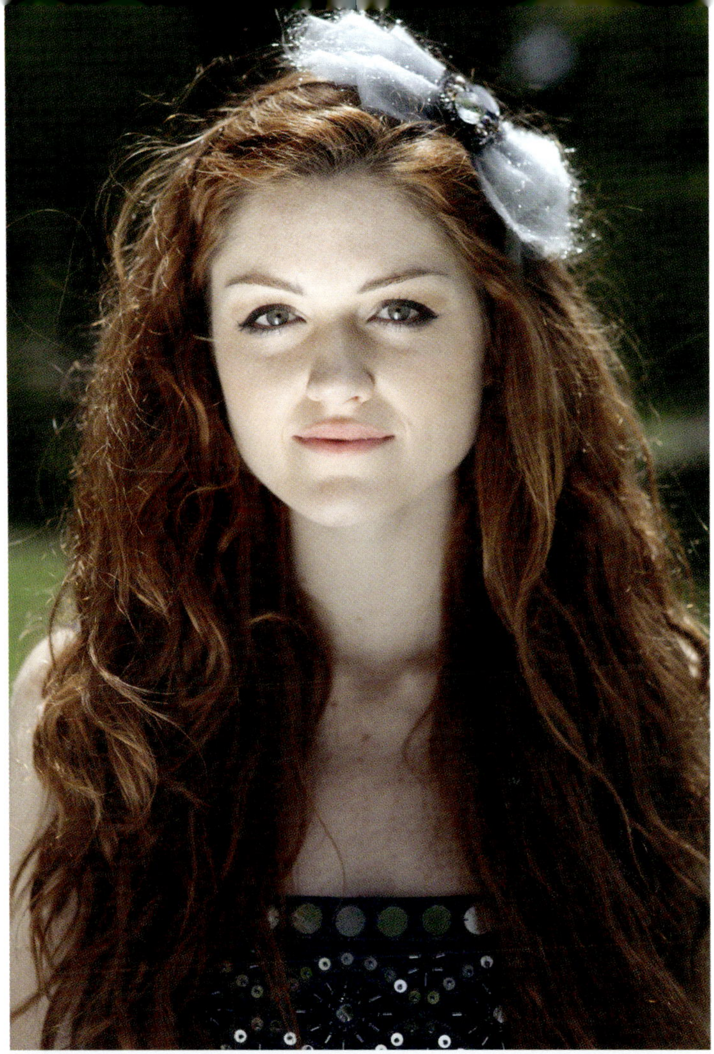

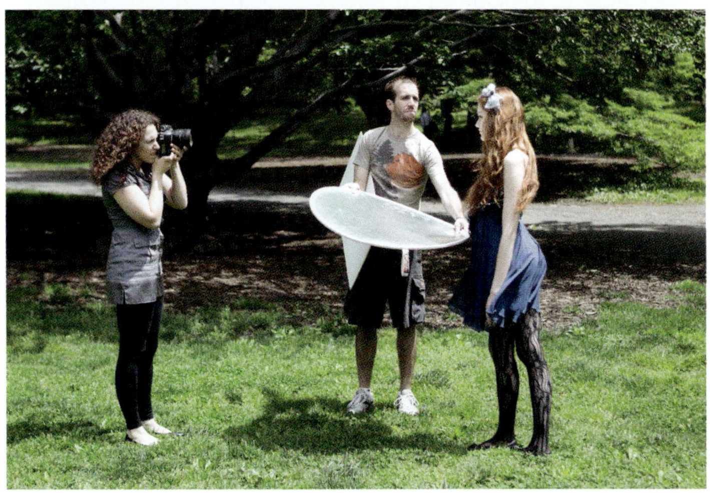

FIGURE 2.15
By introducing a reflector, we helped decrease exposure on the bow and hair by compressing the exposure range of the scene. In other words, we made the face exposure similar to the exposure on the hair. The silver reflector we used, however, is at too low of an angle. This "monster light" is unflattering.

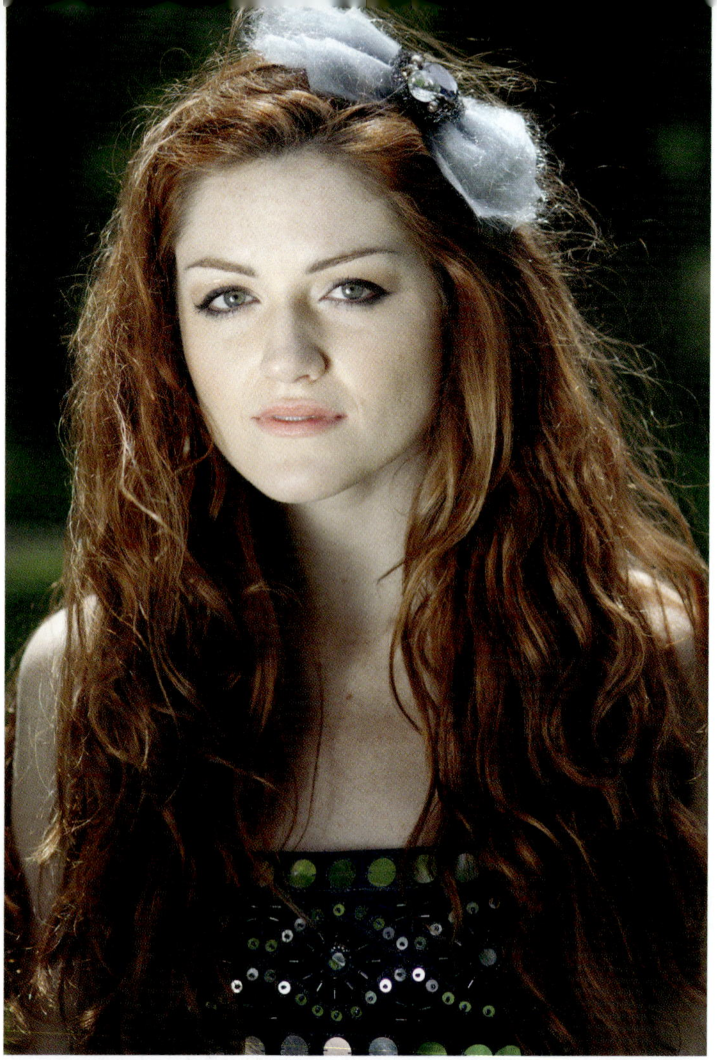

FIGURE 2.16
We chose a higher angle of reflection, but now are reflecting too much. In portraits, you want to avoid the over-reflected look with harsh contrast and highlights on the face.

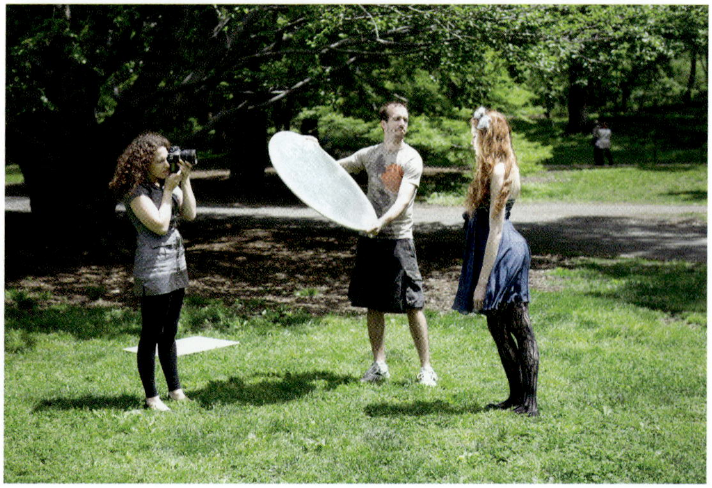

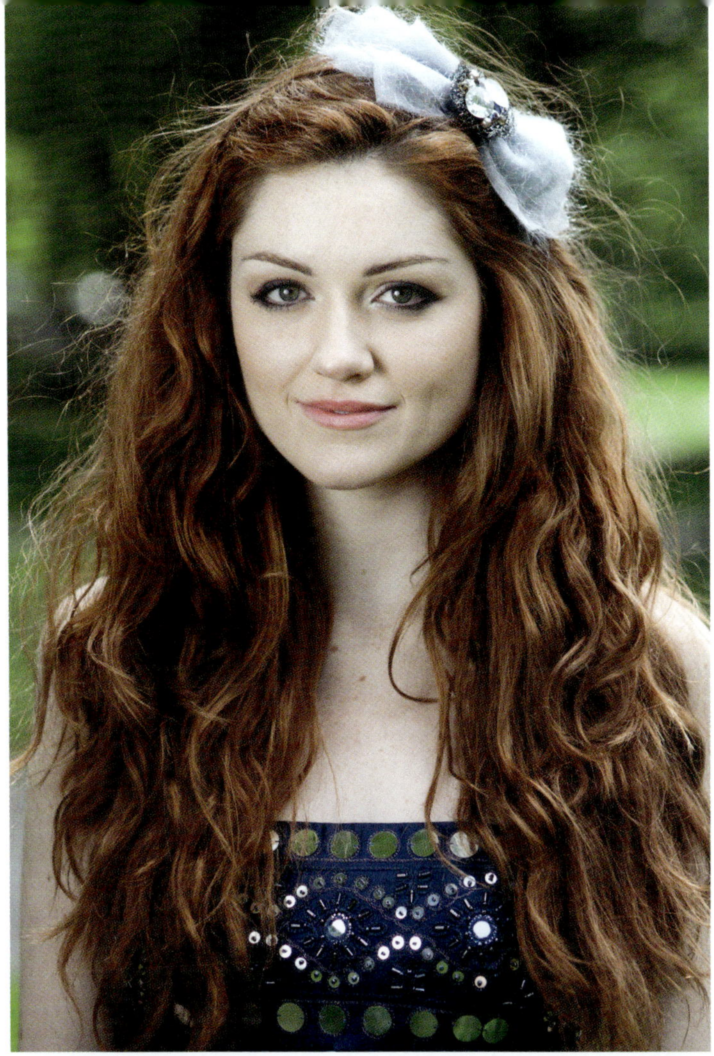

FIGURE 2.17
By increasing the angle of the reflector, we created a much more flattering shape to the face. We emphasized her cheekbones and jawline while introducing catchlights into the eyes. We also feathered the reflector (angled it away from the subject) so that the reflected light does not have so much contrast.

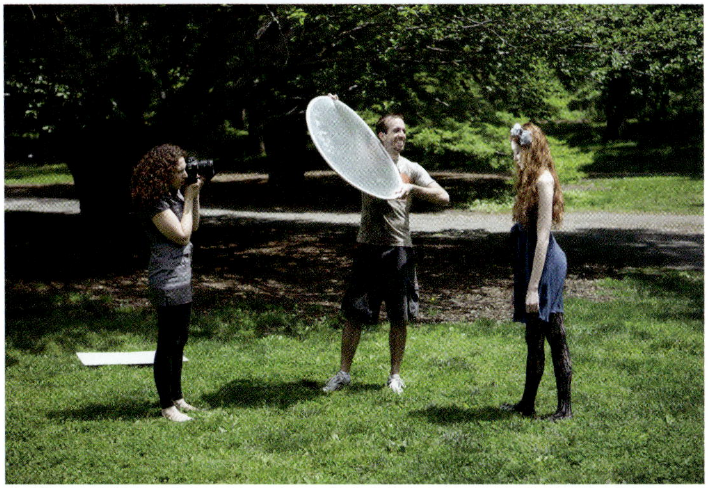

FIGURE 2.18
This angle allows us to quickly remove the immediate issue of bright highlights on the face, yet suffers from a green cast and lack of contrast. The image benefits, however, when a reflector is added into the equation as seen in Figure 2.19.

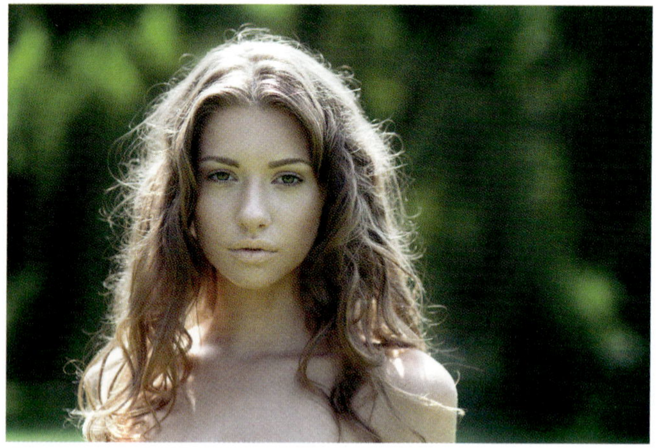

FIGURE 2.19
A white reflector held close to the subject adds a soft and flattering quality of light on the face and showcases the halo of hair created by the backlit sun. By using a high angle of reflection, we also achieved much more flattering light on the face.

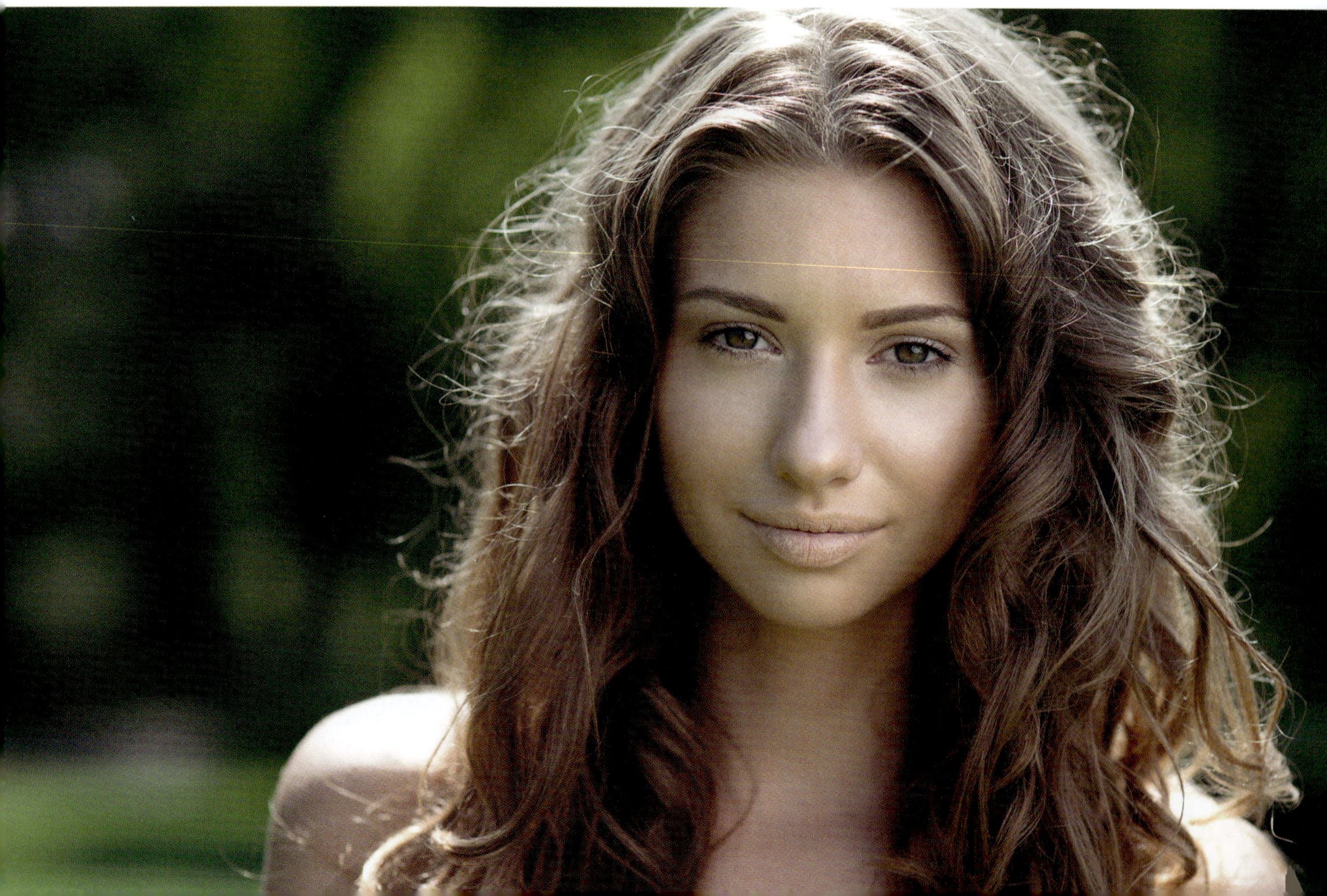

Use Flash on Location

You absolutely could use a flash on location to help overpower the sun and fill in the shadowed side of the face. Instead of a reflector, you could use your flashes to illuminate shadows or even out exposure between your subject and the background. Chapter 8, "Dappled Light, High Contrast," discusses using flash on location to help even out dappled light. Throughout this book, we will explore how flash can be used on location to build in good contrast, to improve the quality of light on your subject, and to even out exposure in a scene. Although we won't go into detail here, feel free to experiment with flash on a sunny day as one of the tools in your kit. For best results, we recommend that you first put the subject's back to the sun or use flash in conjunction with another tool such as a diffuser. Be sure to get out there and experiment with these different techniques, working from the more simple solutions, all the way on up.

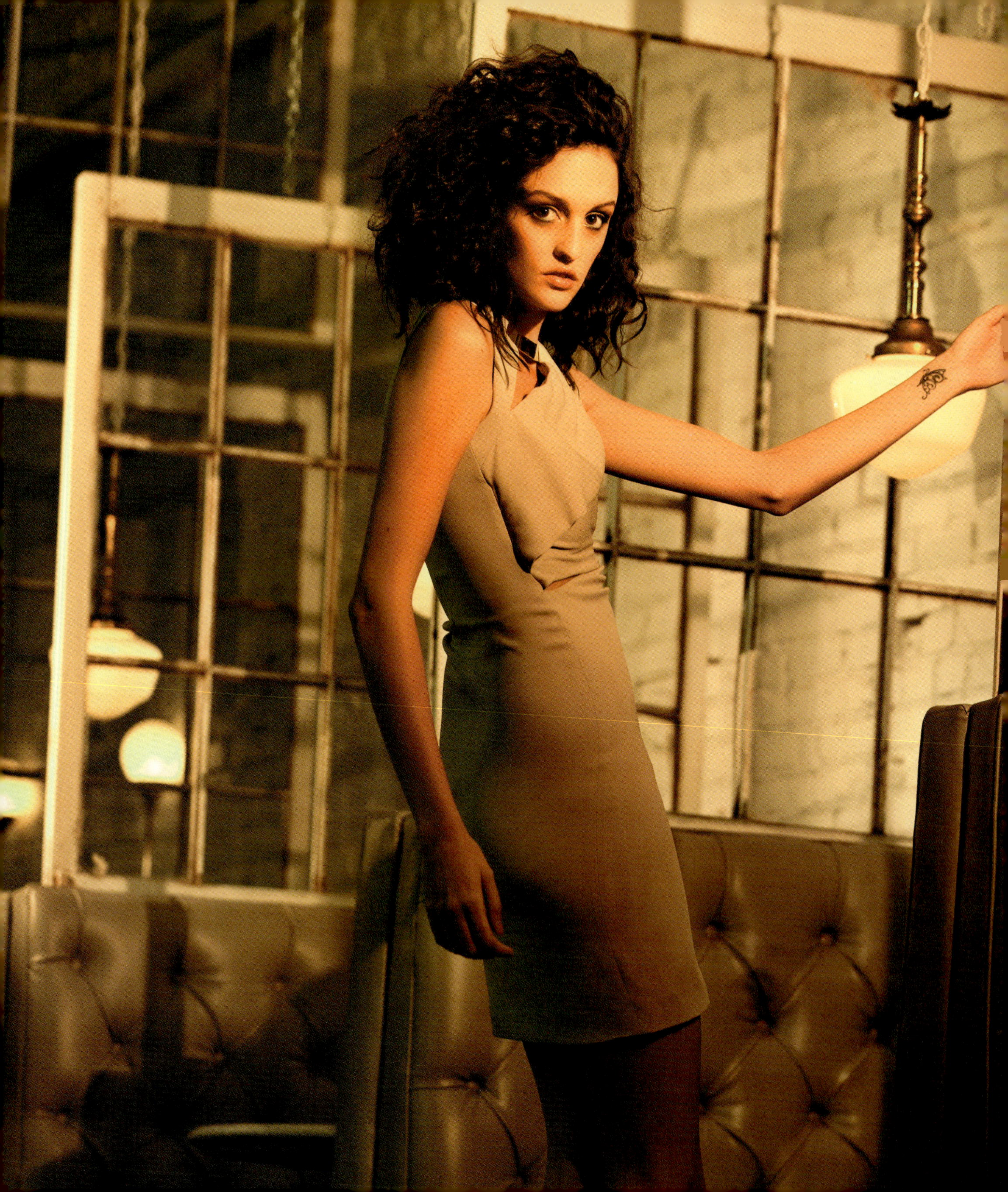

CHAPTER THREE
Fluorescent Light

Ever walk into a building or event hall, fire off a few photographs, and upon looking at the back of camera screen, wonder why everyone looks so green? Welcome to the nightmare of fluorescent overhead lighting. To the naked eye, common fluorescent light doesn't appear so sickly green, but when compared to the cool light from a flash or the midday sun, it can be downright gross. The photos you shoot don't have to be unsightly though! In fact, by following a few simple techniques you can avoid fluorescent frustration and produce pleasing results.

Set Your White Balance

Different light sources actually have different color tints to them. Fluorescent light looks green, for example. Tungsten light is orange. Midday light is blue. The human eye more or less automatically corrects for these color tints in a scene, helping to neutralize the appearance of light as white. The tint of a light source, or its **color temperature**, corresponds to a value on the Kelvin temperature scale. Tungsten light is around 3200K (degrees Kelvin), for example, whereas daylight is around 6500K. Interesting, but what does this mean to you?

Cameras aren't as good as the human eye when it comes to eliminating color cast from a scene. (Auto White Balance is your camera's weak attempt to do so.) For optimum results, you must tell your camera which light source you are using so it can adjust accordingly. You do this by manually setting your **white balance**. In other words, you need to tell your camera what a neutral white should look like in the photo under your current lighting conditions. Establishing this reference point ensures your subject's skin tones are represented correctly as well.

Because fluorescent light in particular is often discolored green, it creates unflattering skin tones when you shoot. **Figure 3.1** was taken with the camera set to Auto White Balance. You can see the green discoloration created by the fluorescent lights. You have a few options for setting your white balance and helping define the color temperature:

- Set one of your camera's white balance presets.
- Shoot a gray card to reference while editing on the computer later.
- Create a custom white balance on location.

Take a closer look at each variation.

Default White Balance Presets

Thankfully, most camera manufacturers anticipate different lighting scenarios and include some pretty decent white balance presets to help you get started, beyond the Auto White Balance option. Go to the White Balance menu on your camera, and take a look at the options, which will be similar to those in **Figure 3.2**. The Fluorescent setting tells the camera that the neutral white point under these lighting conditions is around 4000 to 5000K, compared to a daylight temperature of 5000K to 6500K. Choosing the Fluorescent setting improves the results, as you can see in **Figure 3.3**. In other words, you are telling your camera to shift the white balance reference point to adjust for the color of fluorescent light.

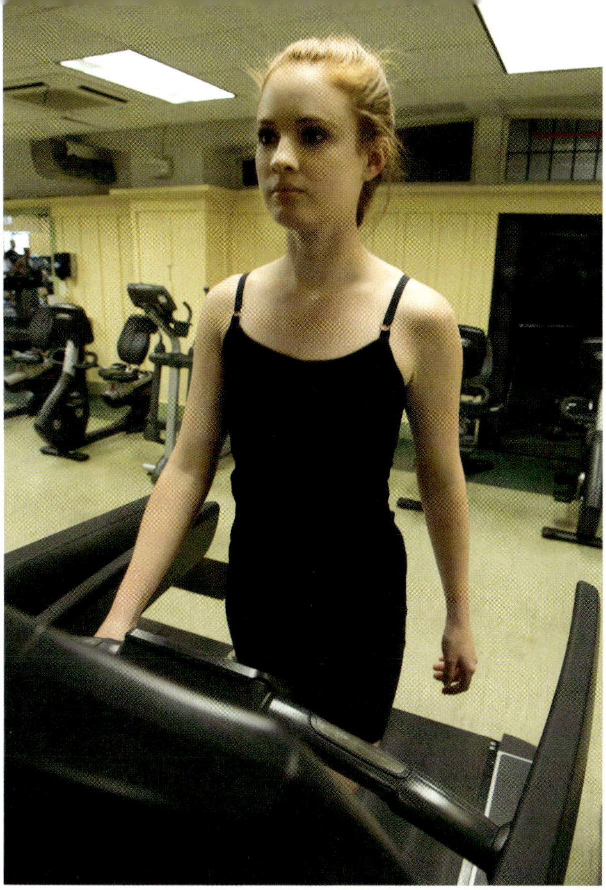

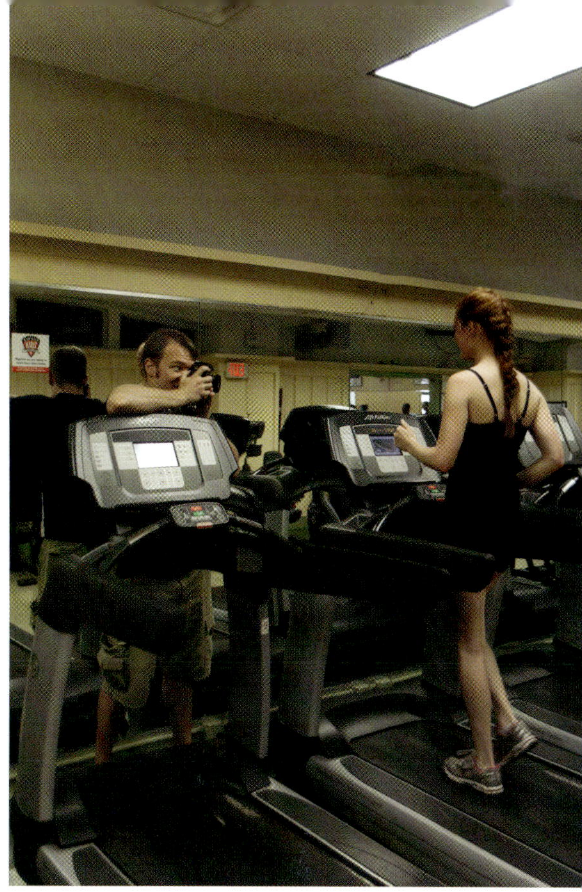

FIGURE 3.1
With your camera set to Auto White Balance, the image is sickly green from the overhead fluorescent lights.

FIGURE 3.2
Your camera has a number of white balance presets based on average color temperatures for certain light sources.

Auto
Camera sets white balance

Tungsten
Camera adds cool tones

Daylight
Camera adds warm tones

Fluorescent
Camera adds warm (red) tones

Cloudy
Camera adds warm tones

Flash
Camera adds warm tones

Shade
Camera adds warm tones

Custom
Photographer sets white balance

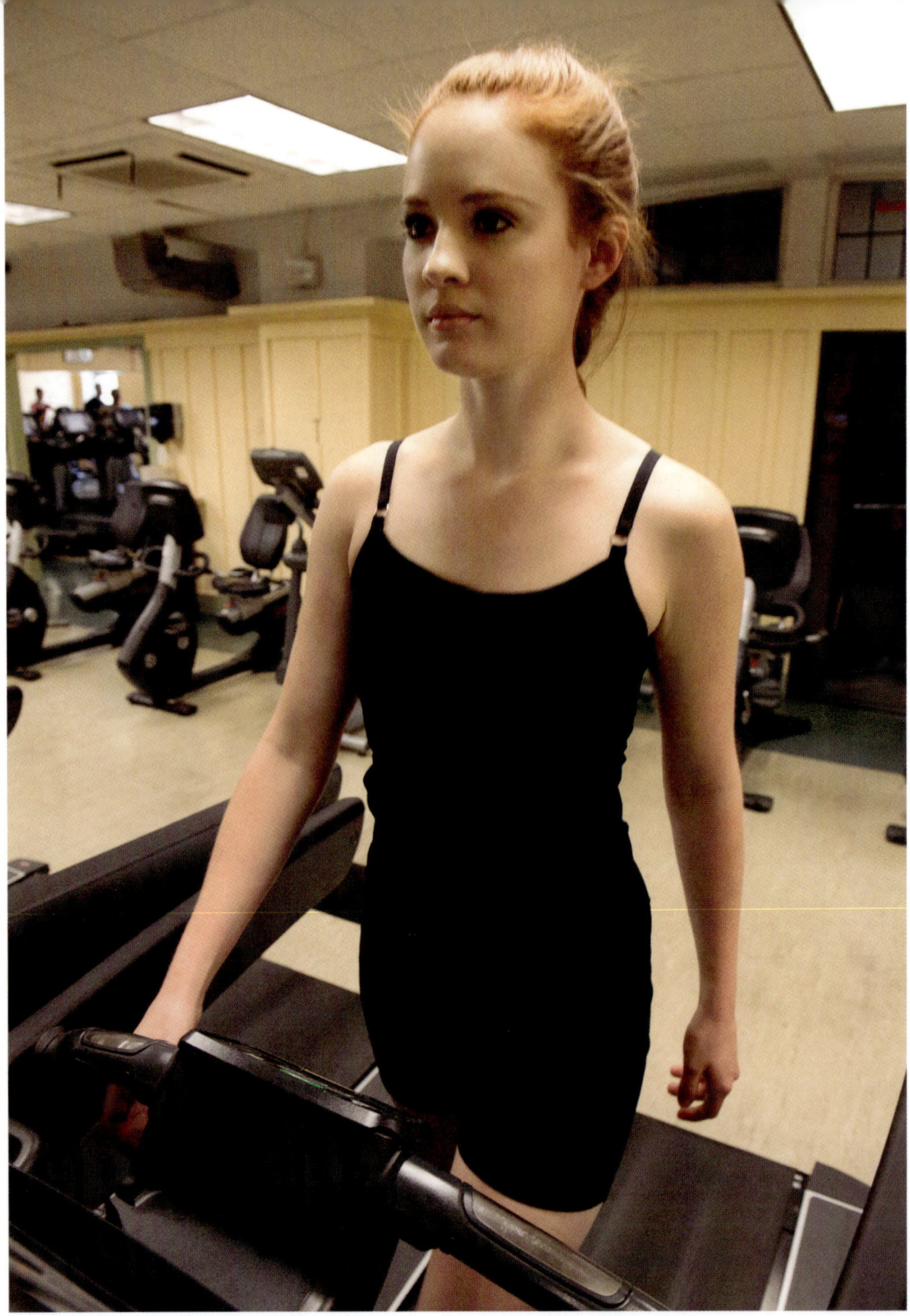

FIGURE 3.3
After setting the camera white balance to Fluorescent, we got pretty close to the correct white balance for the room.

Although the defaults are a great place to start, the manufacturers of fluorescent lights seem to have it out for us photographers. Actual color temperatures shift wildly depending on the age and model of the light, plus newer lights are designed to shift even more, some coming closer to daylight temperatures! You may even consider trying some of the other white balance presets to see if any of them get you closer to the results you want in your particular lighting scenario. Thankfully, digital cameras make this trial and error process rather quick and painless. In **Figure 3.4** we tried the Flash white balance setting, which was incorrect for this scene.

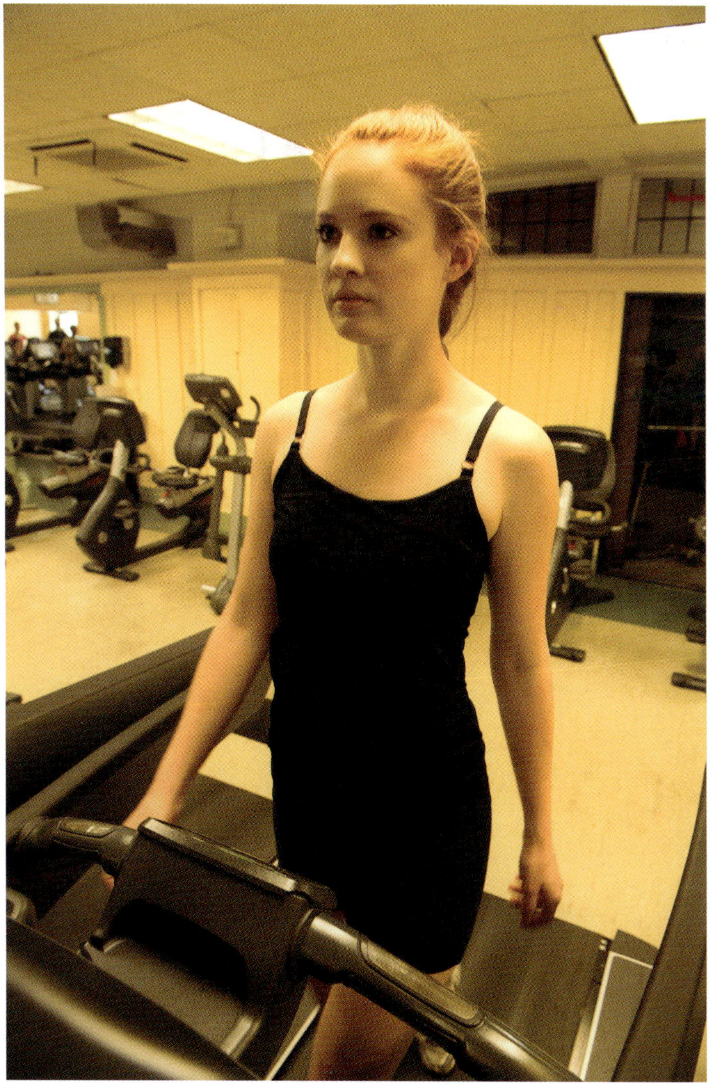

FIGURE 3.4
You can try another white balance preset, in this example, Flash, to see how it changes the color balance of the entire image. You may consider trying different presets, but Flash clearly is not correct here.

Gray Card

Because of the inconsistency in fluorescent lights, you may need to move beyond presets to get that optimal white balance. One approach is to photograph a neutral gray card in your scene to create a point of reference for correcting the white balance in post-processing (**Figure 3.5**). Basically, you load the shot into your post-processing software (Adobe Lightroom, Apple Aperture, Adobe Camera Raw, or other program), select the gray card to set the correct white balance for the image, and then synchronize all other images in the set to match. (For details on doing this in Lightroom, see the Beginner Tip, "Set white balance and sync settings," in this chapter.) Compare the original shot of the gray card with the white-balanced **Figure 3.6**; the green tone is gone and the gray is neutral again.

Using a gray card to set selective white balance in post-processing works best when you shoot RAW images. Like a digital negative, a RAW image provides every piece of information that the camera has captured, and therefore allows you to completely change the white balance of the image. You can use a gray card for a JPEG image, but if you are making extreme color shifts and color correction, you might not have the pixel information you need. It is absolutely in your best interest to shoot RAW, especially when color balance or exposure is a concern in your final image.

EQUIPMENT TIP Choose your gray.

A number of companies offer gray card solutions. These cards are sometimes called 18% gray or neutral gray, because 18% gray has been determined to be an ideal tonality to serve as a neutral point for setting white balance and exposure within an image. Not all gray cards are literally cards. Some are gray-card cubes, color checkers, and more. Check out Datacolor (www.datacolor.com) and X-Rite (www.xrite.com) for some gray card and color-correction tools.

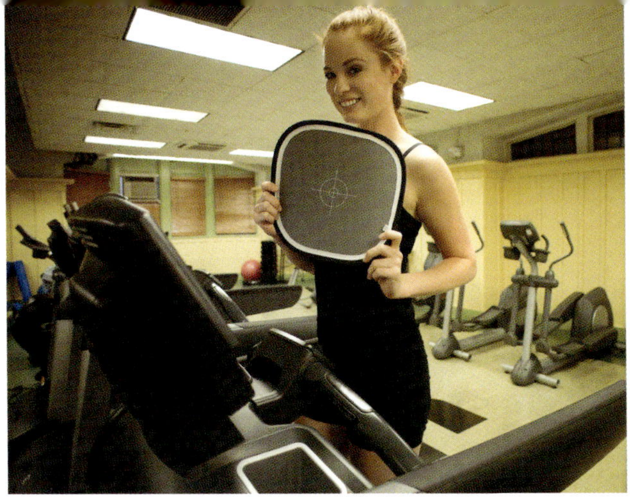

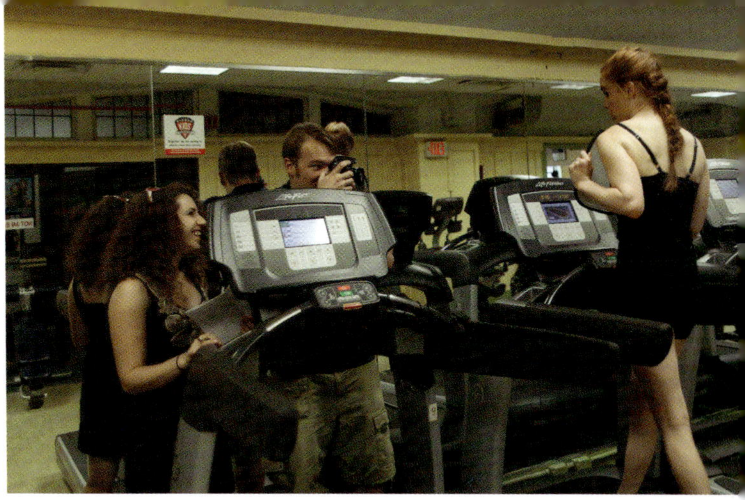

FIGURE 3.5
Have your subject hold the gray card facing the camera. Shoot in RAW, and you can use this gray card as a neutral reference point for setting white balance.

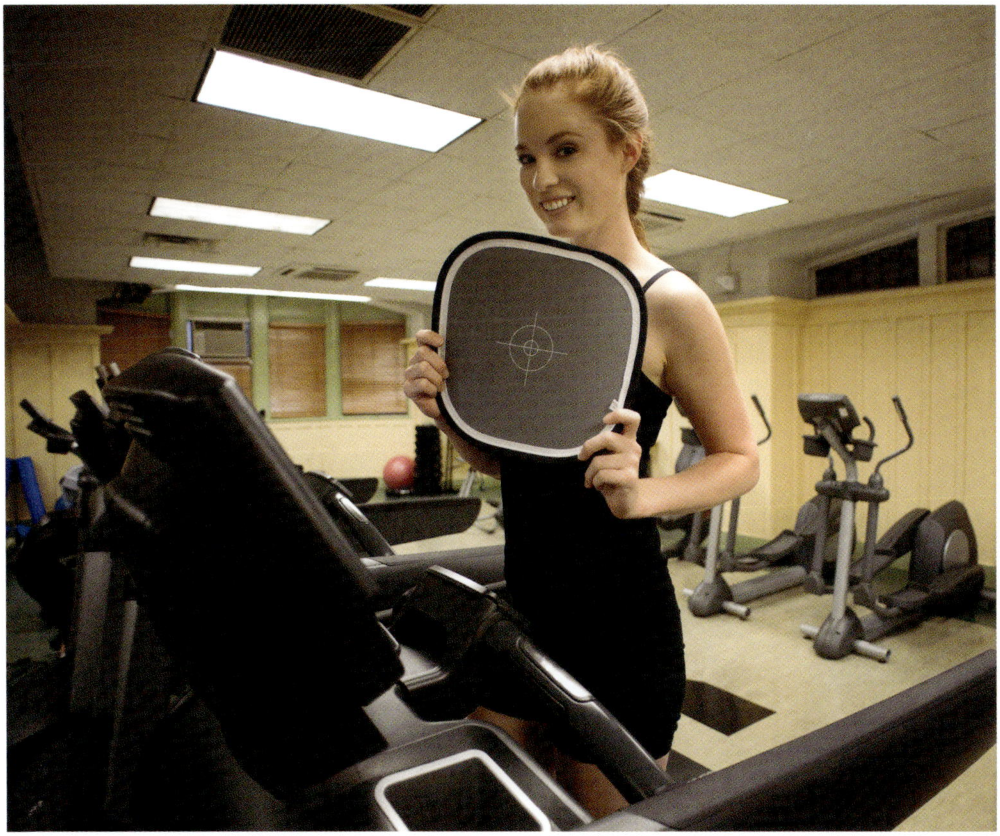

FIGURE 3.6
In post-production (Adobe Photoshop, Adobe Lightroom, Apple Aperture, or other program), you can select the gray card to set the white balance of the image.

White Balance in Lightroom

In Adobe Lightroom and most workflow management systems, you can set the white balance of a single image and then synchronize the rest of the images from the shoot to correct their white balance. Suppose you shot an indoor volleyball game in fluorescent light and have 1500 incorrectly white-balanced images. You need to correct only one image, not 1500, and then synchronize your settings. For example, we shot an athlete working out in a fluorescent-lit YMCA gymnasium, then loaded the series into Lightroom (**Figure 3.7**).

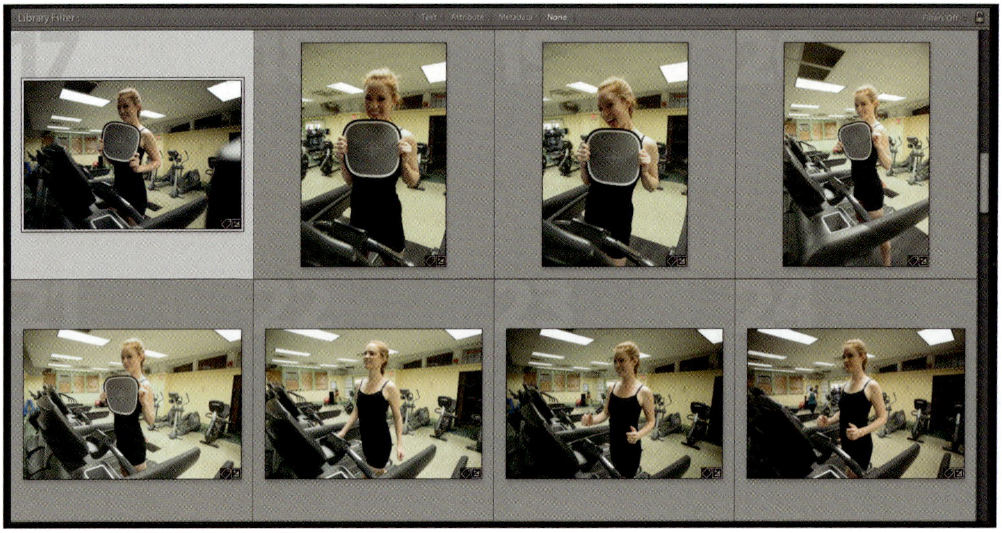

FIGURE 3.7
By managing your workflow in Adobe Lightroom, you can see that all of the images have the incorrect color balance.

In Lightroom, choose the white balance tool (click the eye-dropper or press W) in the Develop module (as seen in **Figure 3.8**) to select your gray card as the reference point. If you didn't shoot a gray card, look for a neutral color in a scene—a white jersey, dress, or shirt will often work in a pinch. **Figure 3.9** shows the correctly white-balanced image.

After Lightroom corrects the white balance, select all images that need to be adjusted (images shot under the same lighting situation). Next, in the Library module, click the Sync Settings button in the lower right. Be sure that the White Balance option is selected in the dialog box that opens, then click the Synchronize button (**Figure 3.10**). Based on your previous gray card correction, Lightroom then automatically corrects the white balance of all the selected images—saving you hours of time.

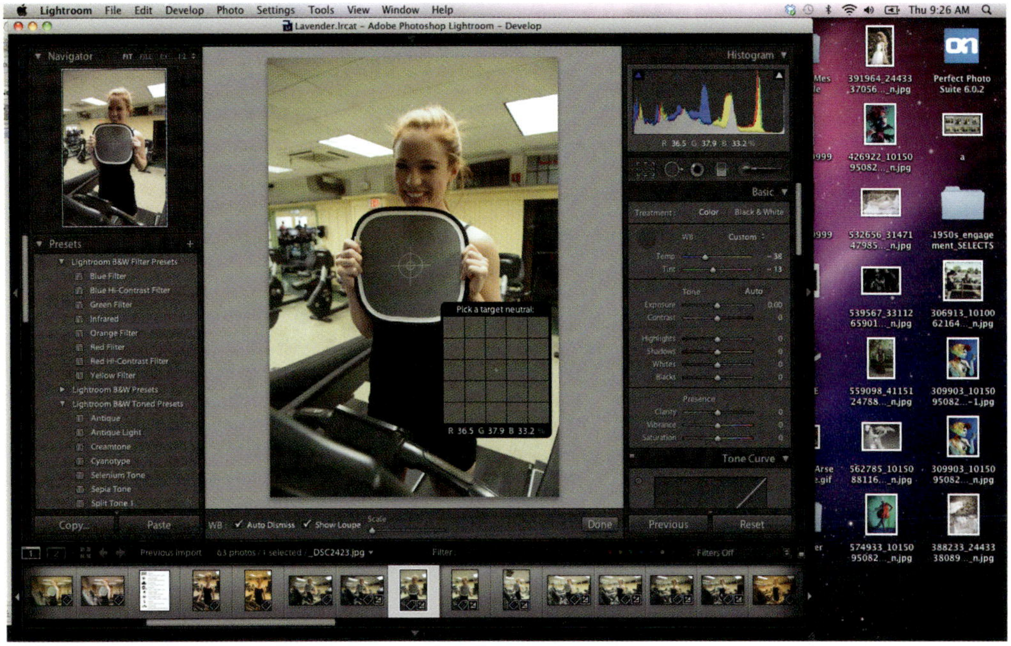

FIGURE 3.8
(above) In the Develop module, select the white balance eye-dropper. In your original image, click on the gray card to select the neutral point of reference.

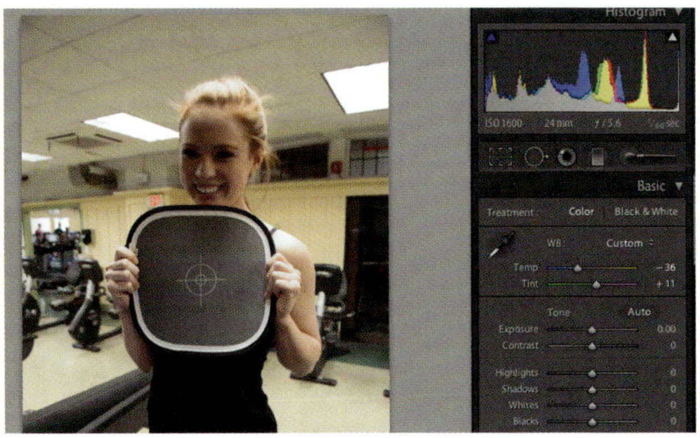

FIGURE 3.9
(left) After you select the gray card, Lightroom corrects the white balance of the image, removing the green hue in this case.

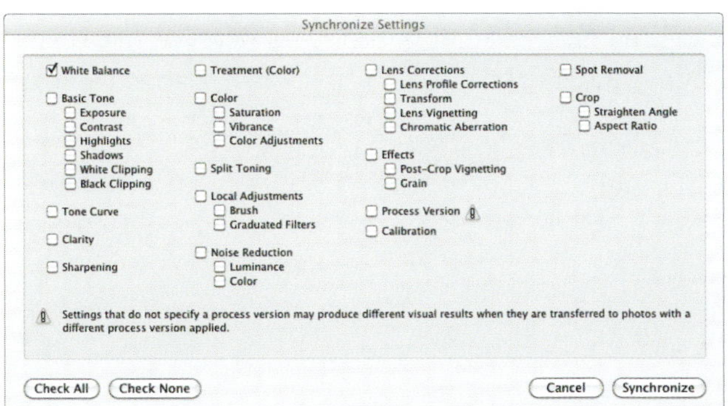

FIGURE 3.10
To adjust the white balance of a batch of shots, select the images you want to correct in the Library Module. Click Sync Settings, ensure that White Balance is selected in the dialog that opens, then click Synchronize.

WATCH IT! Adjust for shifting white balance.

Within a scene, the color balance may shift as you move around. Perhaps light reflects off a colored wall in one corner, while window light creeps into the scene elsewhere. To avoid nasty surprises in post-production, take additional shots of the gray card when your subject moves within a scene.

Custom White Balance

Your third option is to set a custom white balance for your image while shooting. When you actually set the correct white balance *before* shooting the images, this gives you a more precise white balance than the standard camera white balance presets. Custom white balance is similar to shooting a gray card and applying a custom white balance in post-production, except this time you correct the white balance in the field. Your images will be properly balanced straight out of the camera in even the most difficult lighting scenarios. As you'll see in Chapter 4, "Mixed Color Temperatures," a custom white balance can come in extremely handy when shooting in mixed lighting conditions, such as fluorescent overhead lights in a room with large sunlit windows. No preset will work here, and it may be impractical to photograph your gray card repeatedly around the room.

Because the steps for setting custom white balance vary between camera systems, you'll need to check your camera's manual or online help source for the exact procedure. In general, you photograph a neutral surface (such as a gray card) or shoot with a specialized tool, such as ExpoImaging's ExpoDisc (see the Equipment Tip "Custom white balance with ExpoDisc") and adjust your camera's settings based on the results.

EQUIPMENT TIP Custom white balance with ExpoDisc.

When you use a gray card or color-checking device, you measure reflected light. In other words, you photograph a neutral surface and the color of light reflecting off that surface. Either in post-processing or in the camera, you then adjust the white balance to align the neutral reference surface to its neutral state. The ExpoDisc from ExpoImaging (www.expoimaging.com), however, enables you to measure the light directly hitting the subject. Measuring the light from the perspective of the subject gives you a more accurate color reading. This improved accuracy is most important in situations where you have mixed light sources or drastic color shifts. For example, the white balance of **Figure 3.11** is more challenging due to slight variations in the color and age of the fluorescent bulbs.

Shooting with an ExpoDisc is simple. With the ExpoDisc held in front of your lens, place your camera at the point of view of the subject you are photographing. Next, point the camera at the main light source illuminating your subject. Take the shot, and you will see a slightly discolored white image (**Figure 3.12**). Your next step is to select this image as your custom white balance to define the color temperature influences in the room. For Nikon shooters, the process is a little different: You select and hold down the PRE setting for custom white balance. Once the text starts to blink, take the calibration photo. Your camera will indicate whether it was Good or No Good. After the confirmation, simply fire away with the proper custom white balance. In both cases, every subsequent image you take will have the same custom white balance. **Figure 3.13** shows the resulting custom white balance created specifically for the light in the scene.

Remember, as you move your subject around a room and into different light sources, the quality and temperature of light will change. If the subject moves into a different mix of light sources, you will need to repeat the process and create a new custom preset to adjust for the white balance in that scene. The ExpoDisc works best in a room with consistent lighting or if used multiple times.

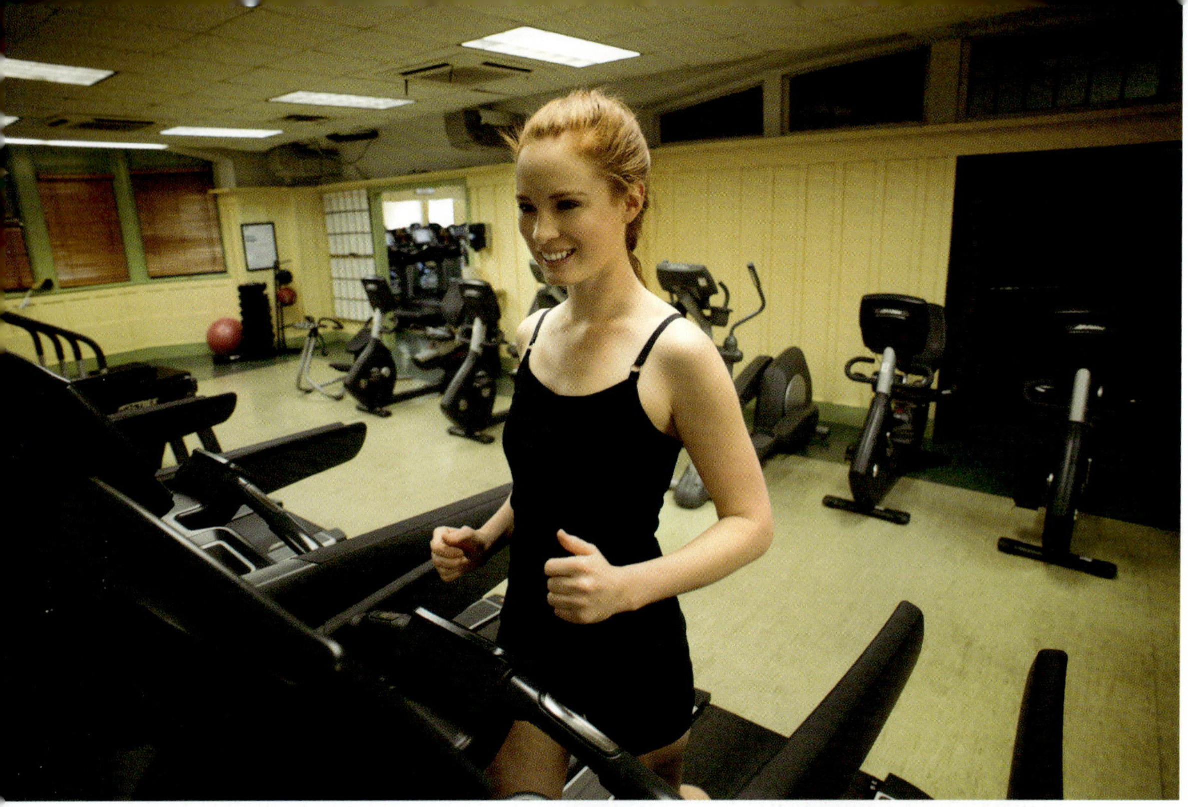

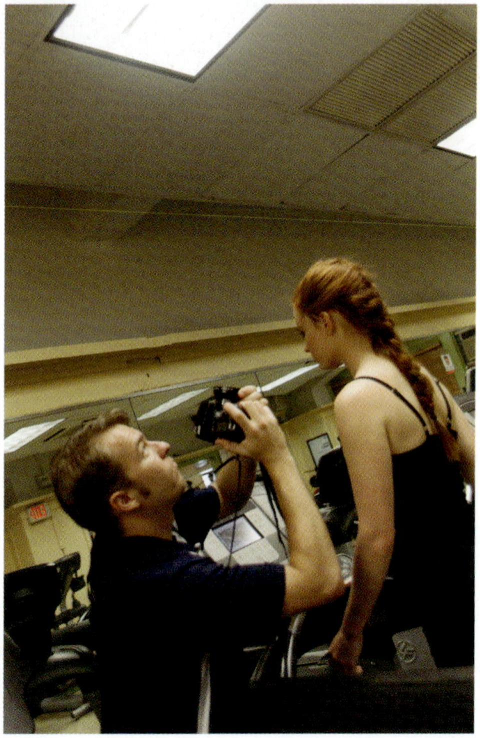

FIGURE 3.11
Here is the unmodified image before setting white balance.

FIGURE 3.12

This is an approximation of the image you will see after taking a photo with the ExpoDisc on your camera. The image will look like you photographed a slightly discolored piece of white paper. This is a representation of the mix of light sources hitting your subject.

FIGURE 3.13

If you set your camera's custom white balance to the ExpoDisc image, all subsequent images shot in the same light will be correctly white balanced.

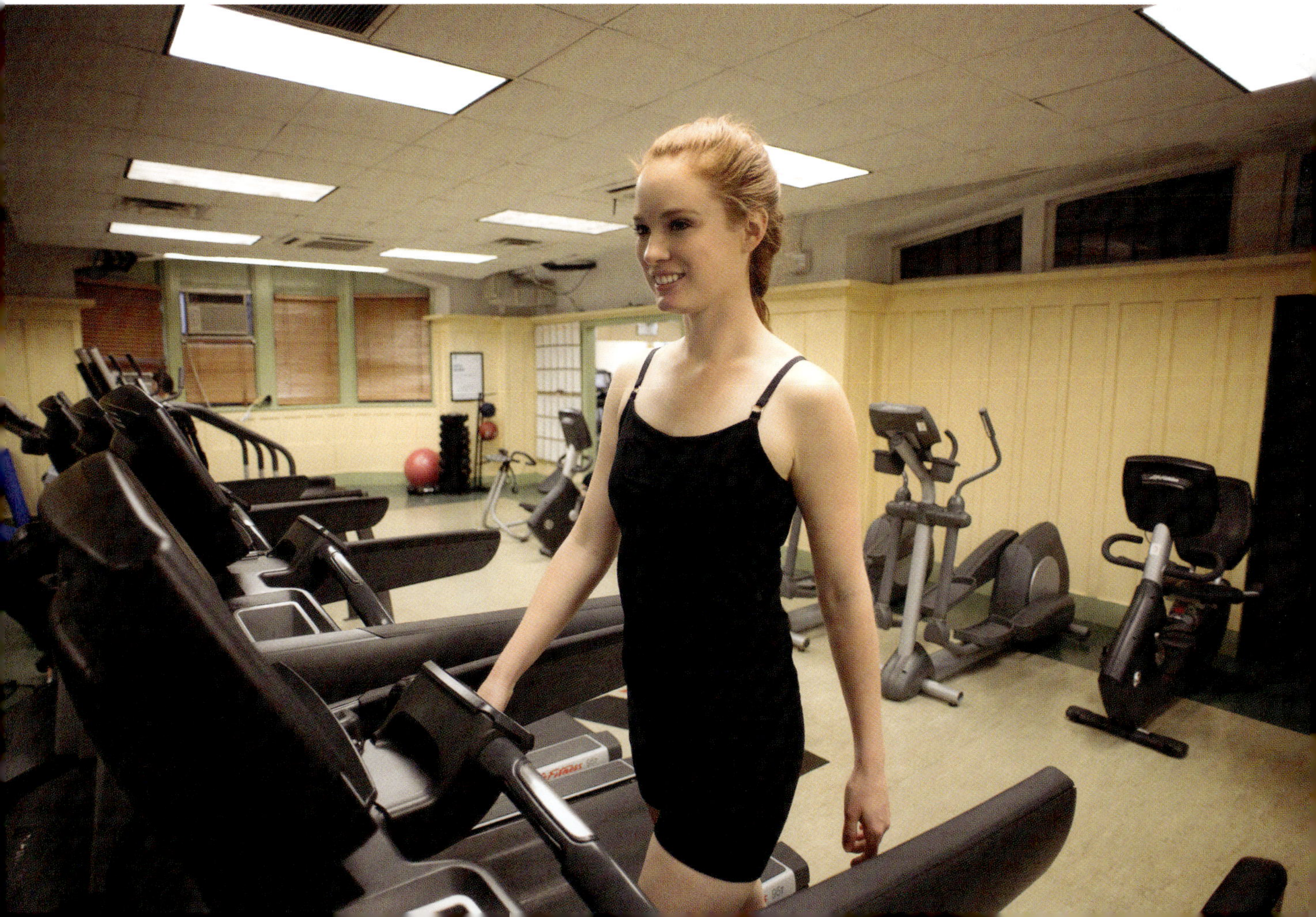

Use Flash to Augment Existing Light

If you are photographing an event, just correcting the white balance may be enough to help you achieve acceptable images. On the other hand, if you are shooting a portrait and want a better quality of light, then you'll want to add a flash into the equation to augment the ambient light. (To learn more about flash and flash exposure, see Chapter 10, "Overcast Day.")

Fluorescent lighting typically comes from overhead fluorescent panels, which is not a flattering light source, as seen in the unmodified light of **Figure 3.14**. The light may create shadows in the eyes or be diffused and without direction. Regardless, your images will benefit by introducing off-camera flash into the scene. **Figure 3.15** demonstrates this increased contrast and improved direction of light by introducing a flash.

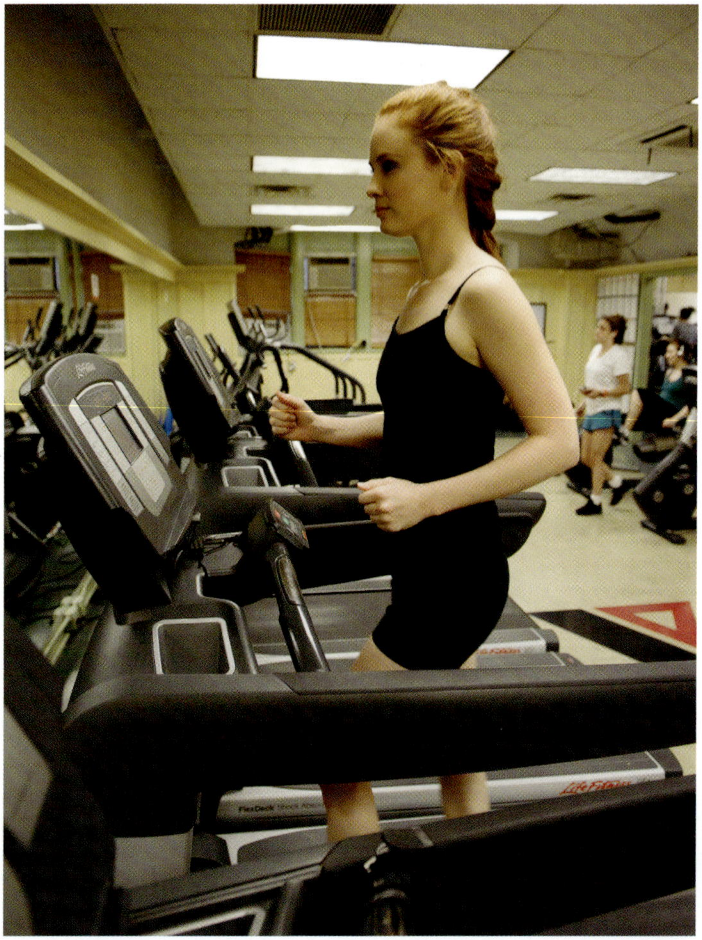

✗ FIGURE 3.14
The unmodified image in fluorescent light is discolored, flat, and unpleasant.

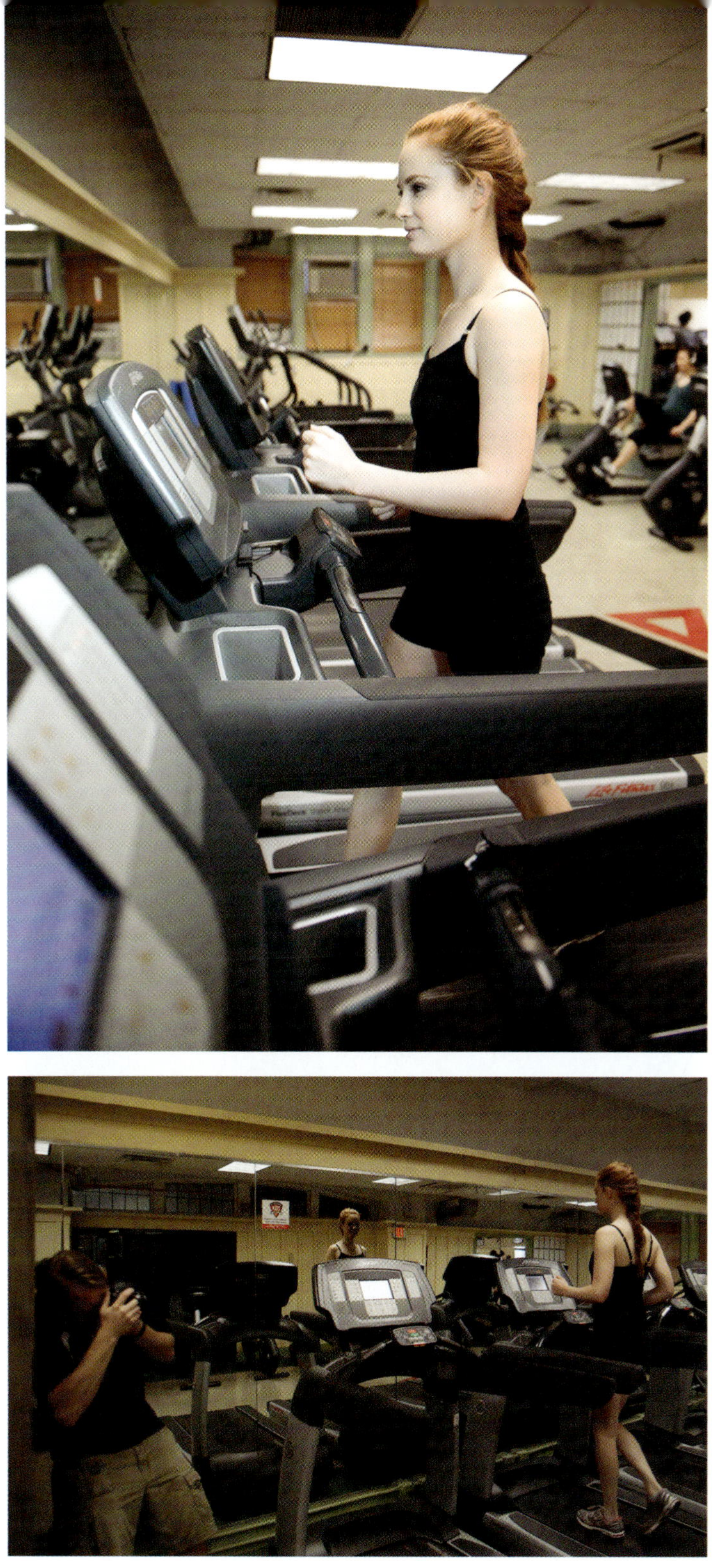

✔ FIGURE 3.15
By adding a flash to a fluorescent image, you change the direction and quality of light, creating a more pleasing photograph.

The key to mastering fluorescent light with a flash is that you must match the white balance of your flash to the white balance of the fluorescent light. To do this you must use a gel on your flash. Gels are simply translucent colored plastic. You can buy gels in *any* color of the rainbow, but what you are interested in are corrective gels. *Corrective gels* help to shift a light source from one common color temperature to another, thus "correcting" them to the desired outcome. For example, applying a green gel to your flash shifts the cool temperature of your flash to match that of the fluorescent light. If you do not gel your flash, then your ambient light will be one color temperature and the subject will be another color. The result? Extremely discolored skin!

Consider the scene in **Figure 3.16**. When a flash is introduced to the scene in **Figure 3.17**, it provides contrast but the ungelled flash's color balance is inconsistent and clashing. If you add a gel to your flash, your subject will look consistently lit, whether from the flash or ambient light. **Figure 3.18** demonstrates the improved effect when the flash is gelled to match the ambient environment.

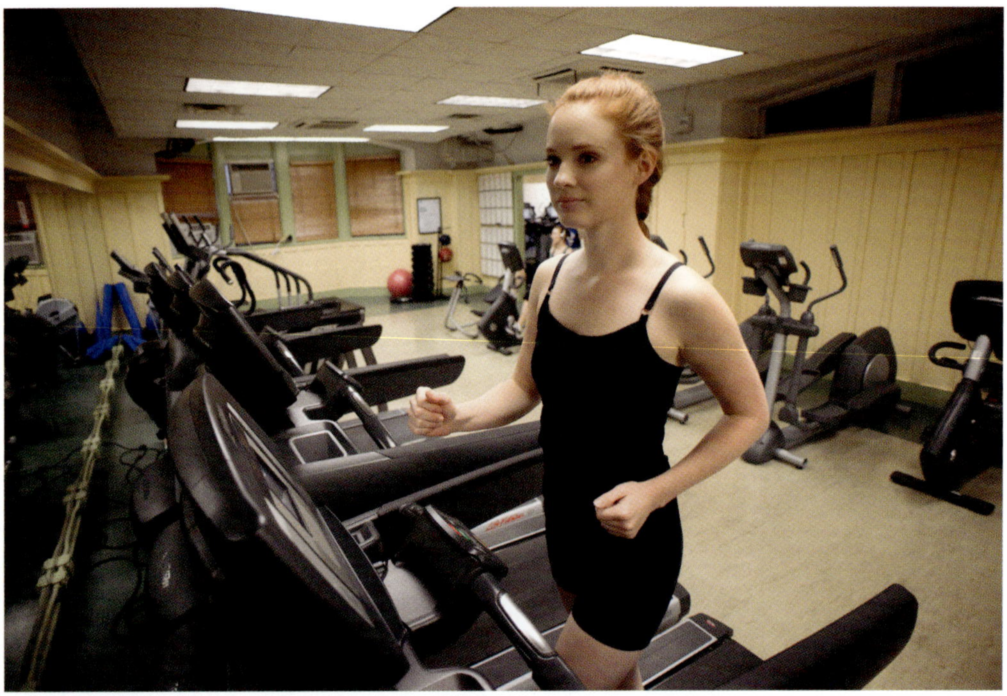

FIGURE 3.16
Using the camera's Auto White Balance setting isn't effective in this fluorescent-lit scene.

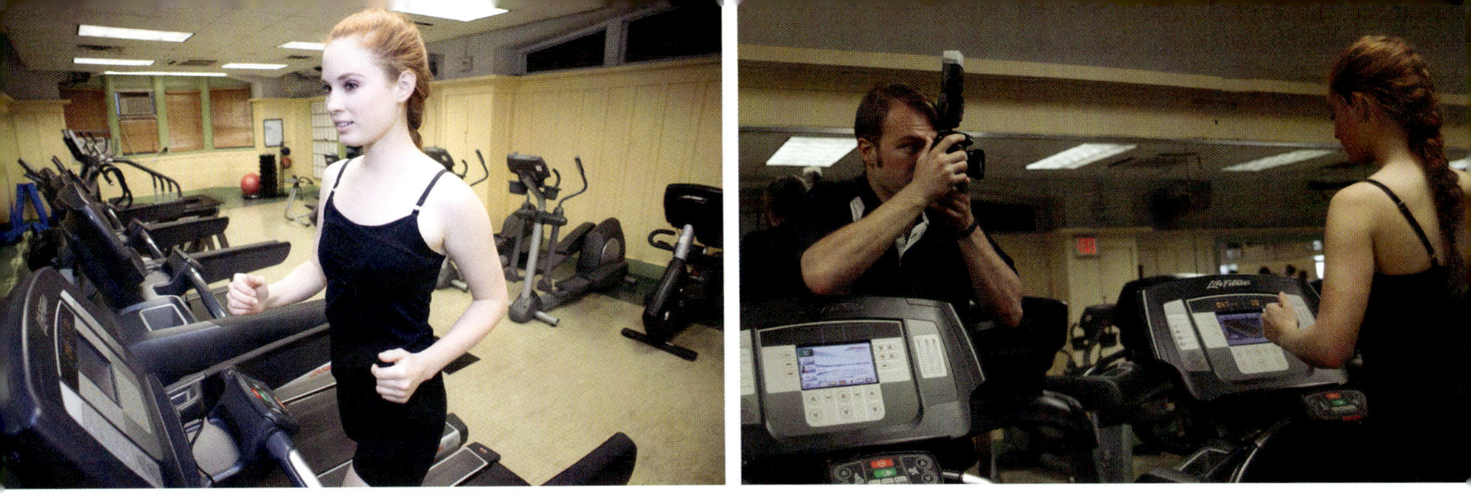

FIGURE 3.17
Adding a flash without a gel adds contrast to the model's face, but the foreground and background color tempertures clash.

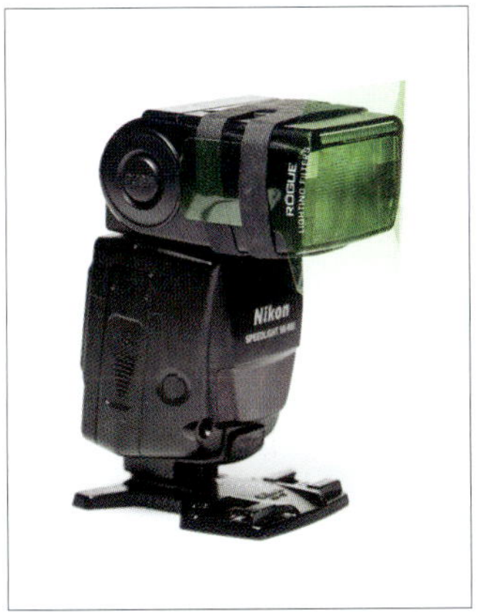

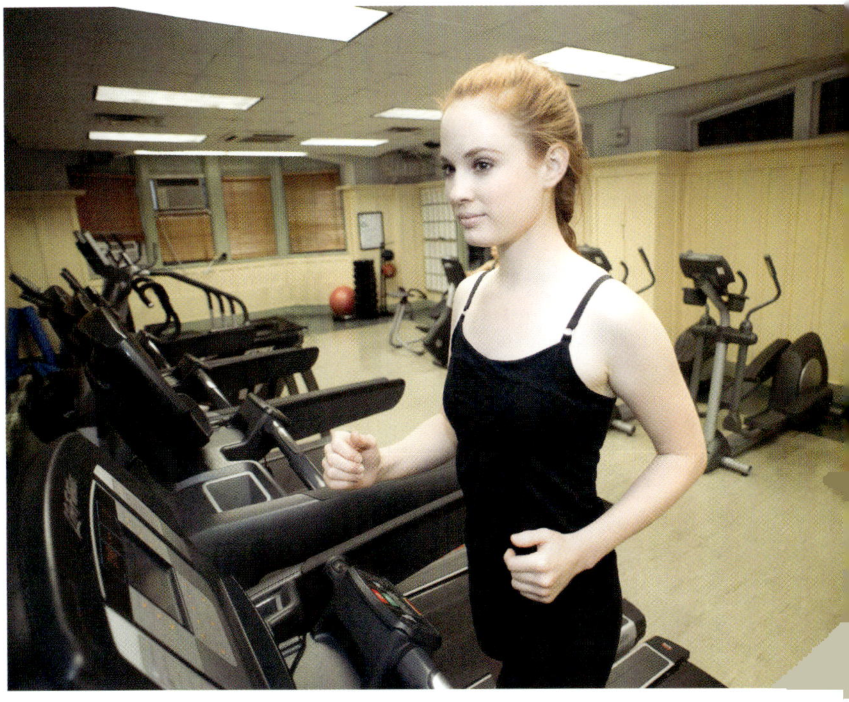

FIGURE 3.18
Gelling the flash for fluorescent light, to match the color temperture of the foreground and background, results in a more pleasing image.

EQUIPMENT TIP Know your flash gel options.

Major flash manufacturers include a set of corrective gels with most off-camera flashes. A quick look in your kit should turn up an orange and a green gel. Green will help you with fluorescent light, while orange gels will help you manage tungsten lights.

If you get a bit more advanced with your perfection of color balance, you might consider checking out Rogue Gels from ExpoImaging. The company realizes that not all fluorescent or tungsten light is the same temperature, and Rogue Gels is a kit with variations of each color to help achieve a more accurate color match. For beginners, the basic gels are a great place to start, but you can refine your image with more advanced tools.

Once you match the white balance, use your gelled flash as you would in other off-camera lighting situations, as seen in **Figure 3.19**. See Chapter 7, "Low Light with Flash," for more details on off-camera flash.

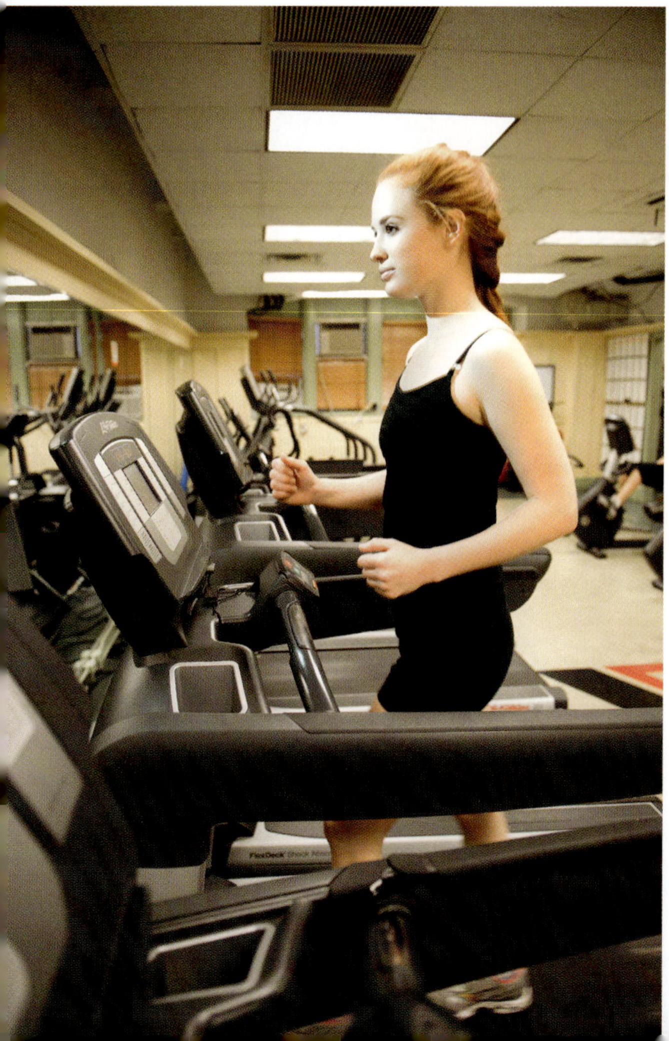

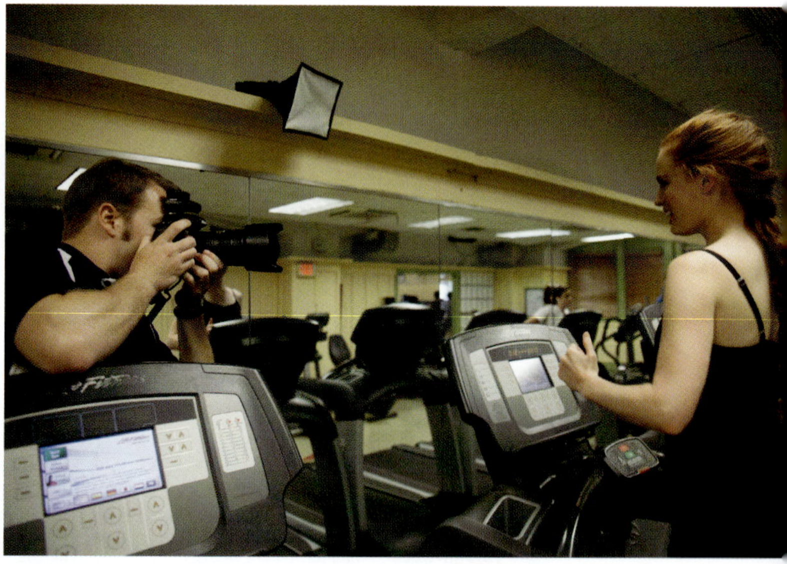

FIGURE 3.19
When you take your flash off camera or add a light modifier, you can change the direction and quality of light. This may improve your image, set a tone, or simply add visual interest.

Remember, you should still use a gray card or ExpoDisc to achieve the perfect white balance even when using flash on camera! If you match the gel of the flash to the ambient light, using a gray card is advisable. **Figure 3.20** has a green cast and unpleasant tone; once the white balance is corrected in post-production, however, the scene improves drastically (**Figure 3.21**).

FIGURE 3.20

Even when using white balance presets and a gelled flash, shoot a gray card. This image could still use a bit of additional color correction, and using a gray card can help perfect the final result.

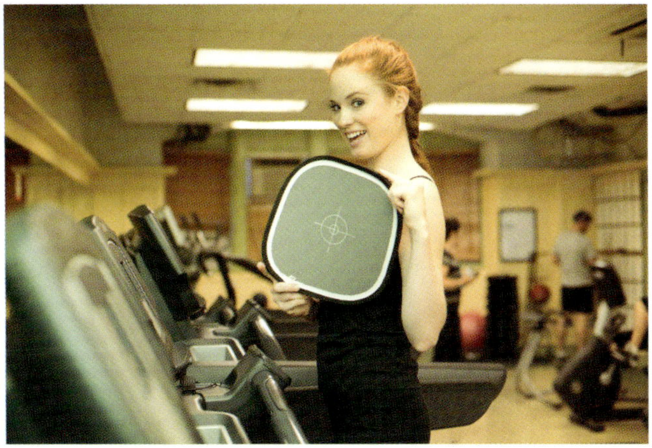

FIGURE 3.21

Even though we gelled the flash and set the white balance, using the gray card and correcting the balance in post-production had a big impact on the final image.

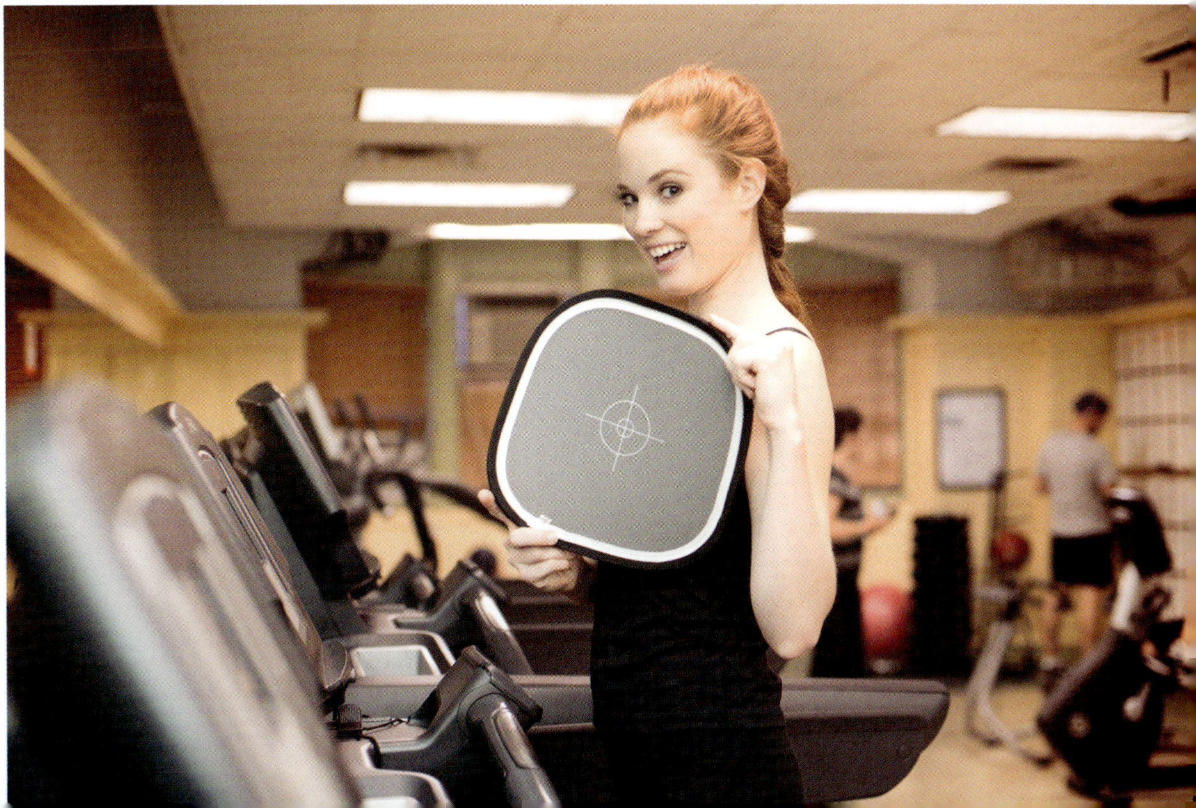

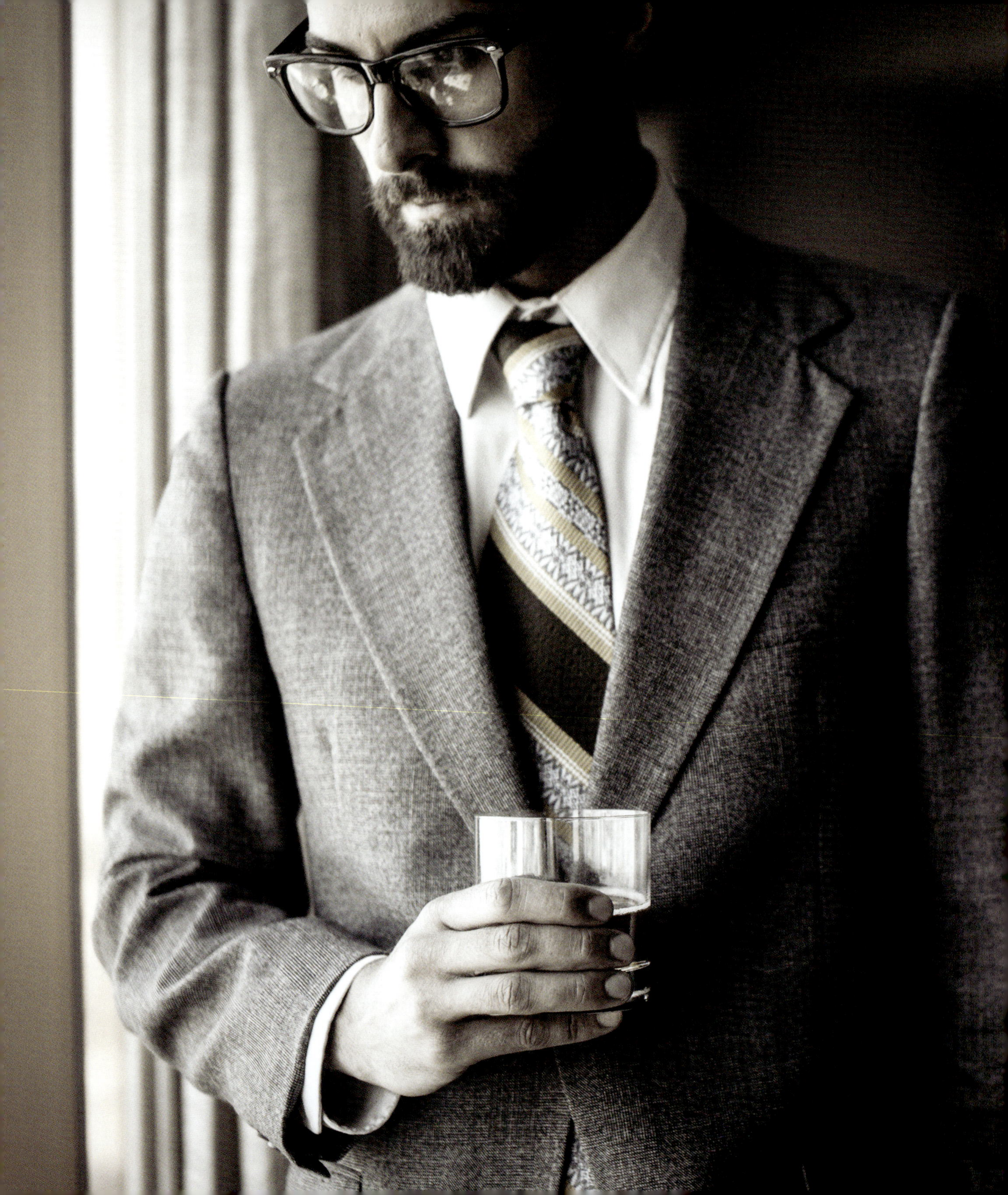

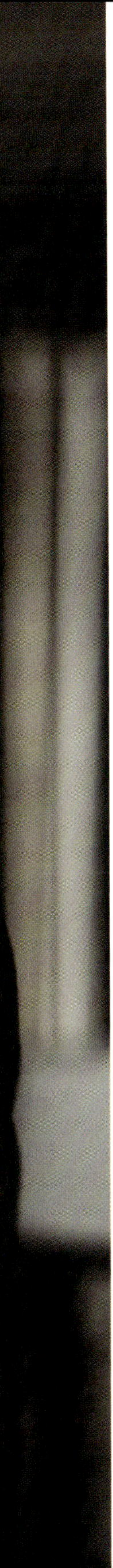

CHAPTER FOUR

Mixed Color Temperatures

A photographer, a model, and an assistant walk into a bar. It may sound like a bad joke, but it actually happens. What makes it a bad joke on the photographer is the mixed lighting that you'll find in many cool locations. Any room with a lightbulb and a window suddenly thrusts you into a juggling match of mixed color temperatures.

Consider the challenges you may face: You walk into a room and find nasty fluorescent light. You read Chapter 3, you know what to do—but wait. Besides that overhead fluorescent light, there's a big bank of windows letting in daylight. Now what? Your subject is half illuminated by light with a green tone (fluorescent) and half illuminated by light with a blue tone (daylight). Needless to say, the combination is not flattering for any portrait or event. What if a tungsten table lamp kicks some light into the scene? Now you are contending with blue, green, and orange light creating a big mess of your photo! So what do you do? How can you take charge of the light and make great images?

Survey the Scene

The very first thing you need to do when approaching a mixed lighting situation is to determine how many light sources you are contending with and where those light sources are located. Each type of light has a different color cast (or color temperature). Our eyes like to automatically white balance what we see, so look closely. In other words, when you walk into a fluorescent-lit room, you don't just see everything all in bright green; your eye auto-corrects for you. This normally helpful biological feature makes it more difficult for you to analyze mixed lighting situations. This is something you'll learn with practice and by careful examination.

Look around the room: Are there windows? What is the source of overhead light? Does the room have any decorative lighting, table lamps, or other mixed light sources? Understanding the scene and light sources will help you better conquer them. Next, ask yourself: What is the dominant light source in the scene? Is the room lit predominantly by window light? How much is that tungsten light from overhead affecting the room? Is the room illuminated by fluorescent overhead lights? What is that small daylight window in the corner doing? Understand your scene, and you'll be able to approach the problem with confidence. If you are having difficulty analyzing the mixed light in the scene, consider snapping a photograph and analyzing the image. This may make it easier to see! Once you know what you're up against, you can choose an approach for handling mixed lighting situations.

TAKEAWAY ACTION

For each scene you approach, take the time to analyze the light, including the number of light sources, color temperature, and direction of light.

Eliminate Conflicting Light Sources

Right off the bat, you may be able to eliminate one or more of the conflicting light sources. In the room with daylight and fluorescent light mixed, for example, you may be able to close the curtains over the windows to eliminate the daylight. For a portrait with tungsten lights and window light, you can turn off the tungsten lamp and focus on using only the daylight. Your first step is to figure out what you can do to reduce the number of conflicting light sources. The fewer color temperatures you have to contend with, the better!

After you analyze the light in the room, you will be able to analyze which light sources you can eliminate. Also, if you identify the dominant light source in the scene, you can use that to your advantage by trying to eliminate any secondary sources of light.

Move Your Subject

If you cannot eliminate any conflicting color temperatures, the next thing for you to consider is moving your subject. Try to move her into a part of the scene that reduces the mixed light. At minimum, ensure her face is illuminated by only one type of light.

Take a look at a practical example: You've been hired to photograph a model in a record store as a PR shot for the store. As you can see in **Figure 4.1**, very orange-yellow, overhead tungsten lights illuminate the entire store. A large window, however, allows in daylight at the front of the store. This creates undesirable mixed light on the subject when posing her in most areas of the room. You can't turn off the overhead tungsten lights because you're shooting during the store's operating hours, and you can't eliminate window light because there are no curtains. You must find another solution.

By moving the subject you can ensure that there is one predominant light source on the face. You move the model to the front of the store and turn her toward the window, lighting her entire face with daylight and using only a bit of tungsten light to illuminate the background. Finally, you switch your camera's white balance to Daylight to ensure accurate skin tones (**Figure 4.2**). Yes, the background stays orange in tone, but the subject is lit in flattering light.

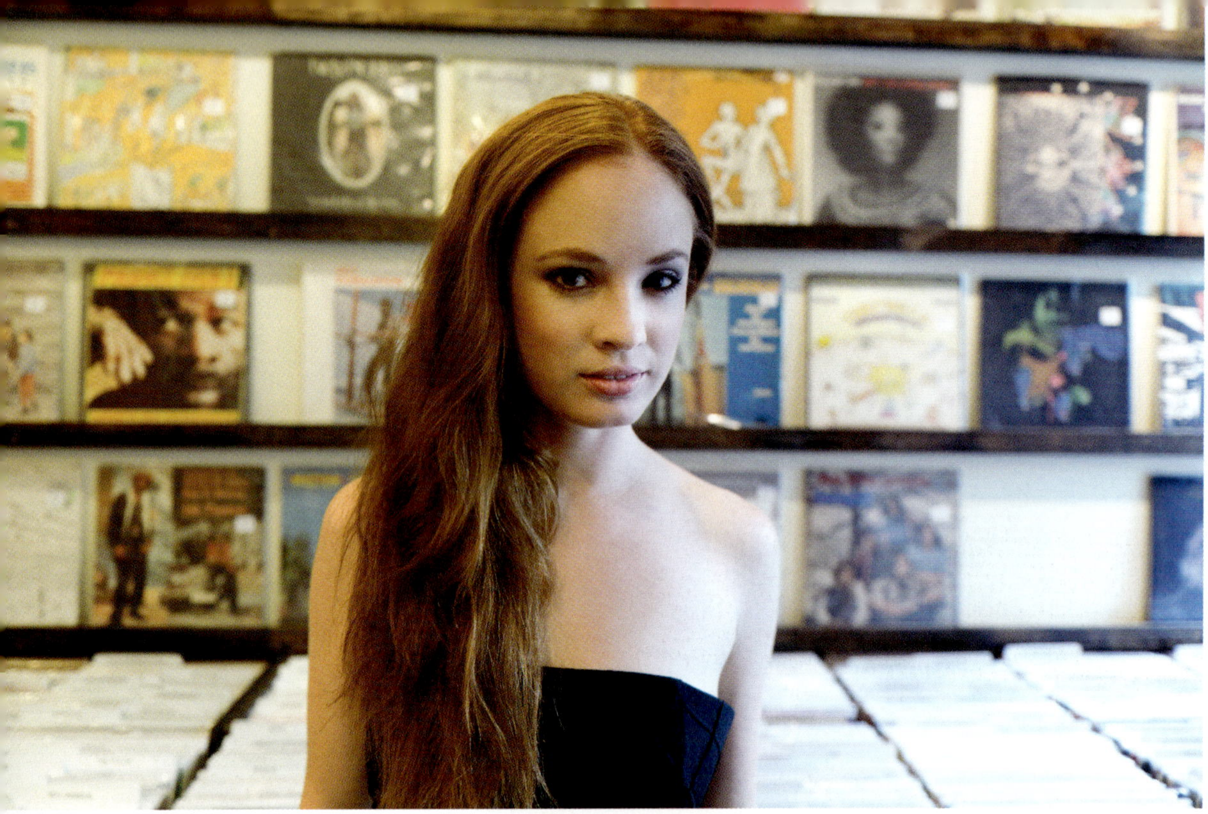

FIGURE 4.1

The subject is half lit by tungsten light, half lit by daylight through a window. This creates an unflattering mixed light on her face. The left side of the face is orange in tone, while the right side of the face is a cooler blue shade.

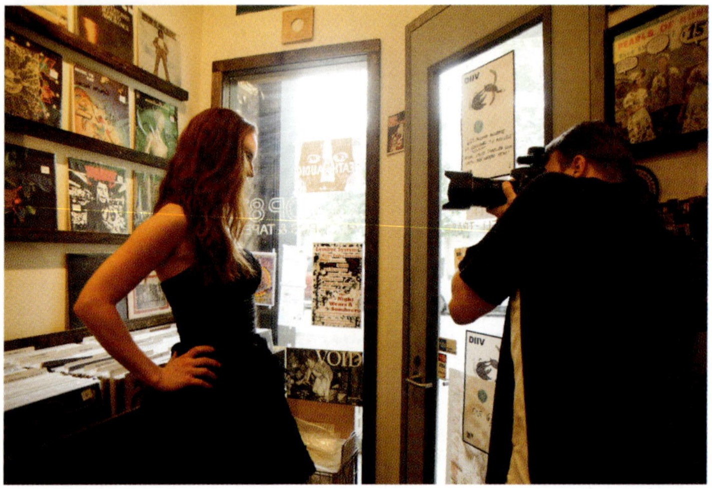

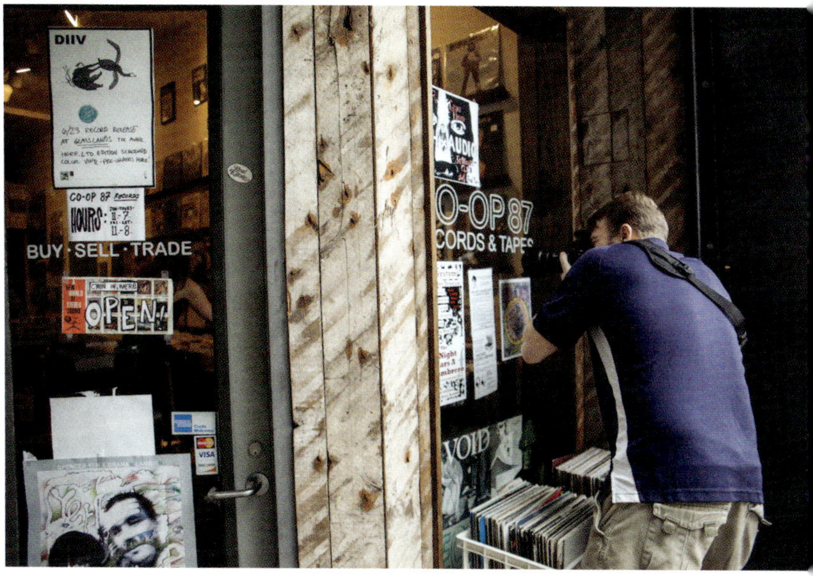

FIGURE 4.2
By moving the subject toward the window, you reduce the effect of the tungsten light on the face. While the background is still tungsten lit, the face is completely lit by daylight.

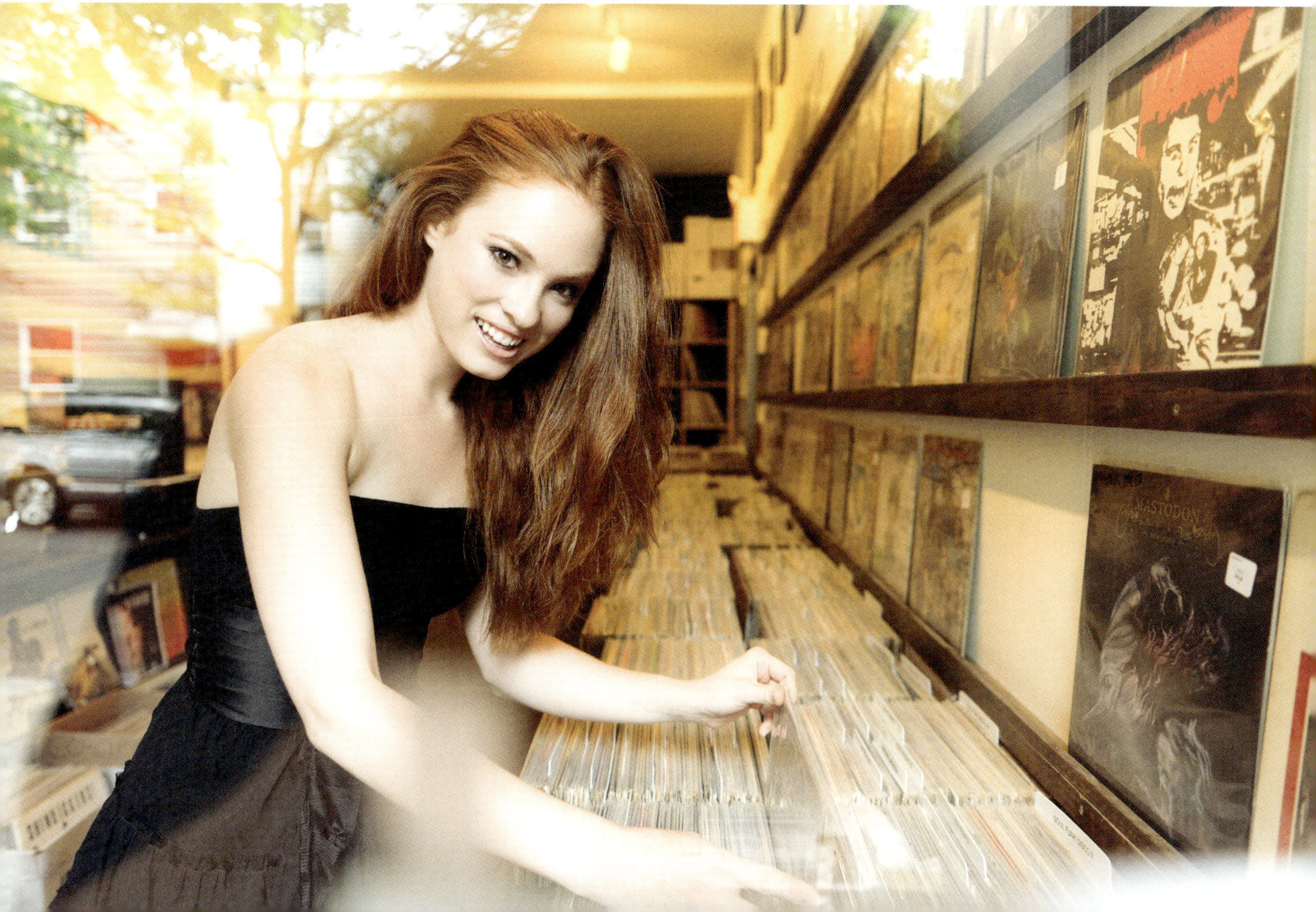

What if you don't want the subject near the front of the store or you can't move her into daylight for some reason? Your next option is to move her as far from the daylight as possible. Moving her toward the back of the store reduces the daylight-balanced light on her face and switches the predominant light source to the overhead tungsten. Change your white balance to tungsten (using white-balance presets, a gray card, or an ExpoDisc as discussed in Chapter 3), and you have a correctly white-balanced image. The quality of light may not yet be ideal, but the color in the image is much improved (**Figure 4.3**).

After you have moved your subject so there is only one dominant light source on the face or body, you can reduce the appearance of the mixed light source in the background by changing your frame. Instead of including the window in the background or including parts of the scene illuminated by window light (as in **Figure 4.4**), for example, try a camera angle that shows predominantly tungsten-balanced background elements.

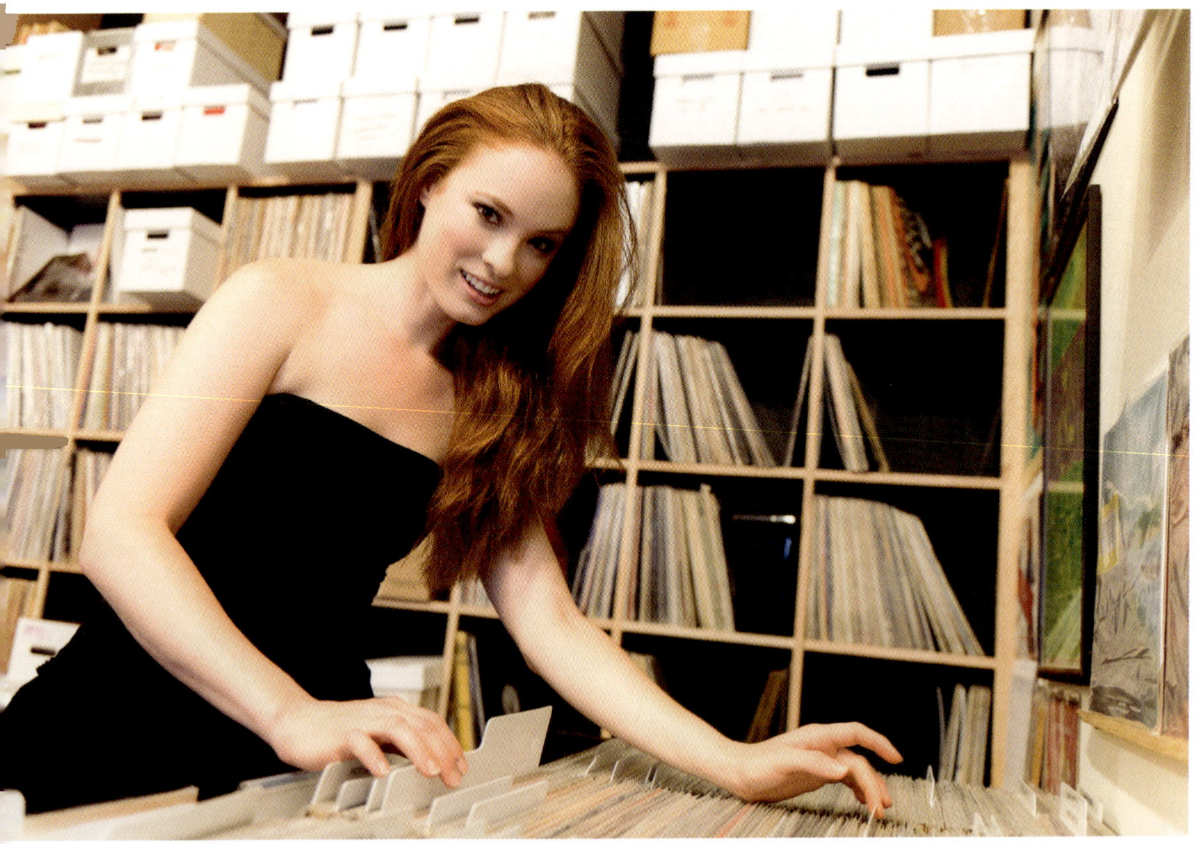

✔ FIGURE 4.3
If you move the subject away from the window, the tungsten light in the scene becomes dominant.

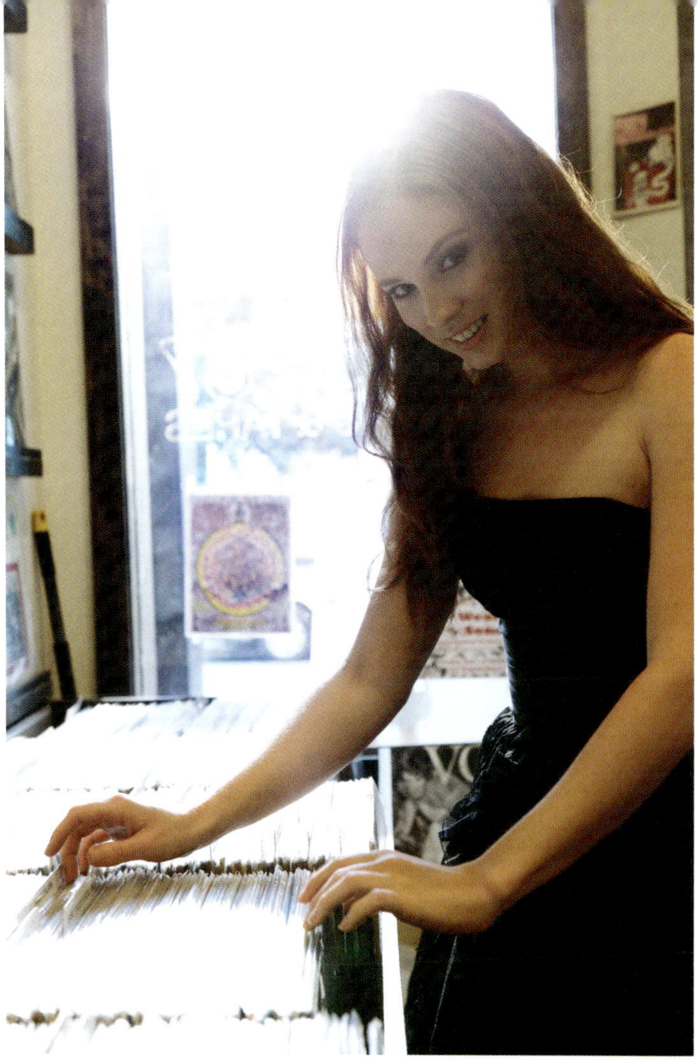

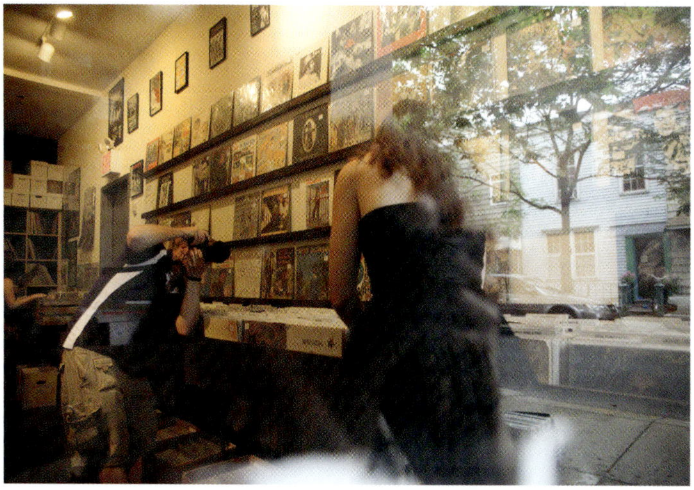

FIGURE 4.4
Your framing can help to eliminate conflicting light sources and white balances. Notice the conflicting light sources here; the light coming through the window is a different white balance than the light illuminating the subject's face.

WATCH IT! Remember your white balance.

In dealing with mixed lighting situations, the correct white balance is essential. For mixed lighting solutions, we highly recommended that you find a way to custom set your white balance. Use a color checker, a gray card, or an ExpoDisc as recommended in Chapter 3. An ExpoDisc will give you the most accurate custom white balance in mixed lighting situations because it accounts for all light sources and color temperatures affecting your subject (**Figure 4.5**).

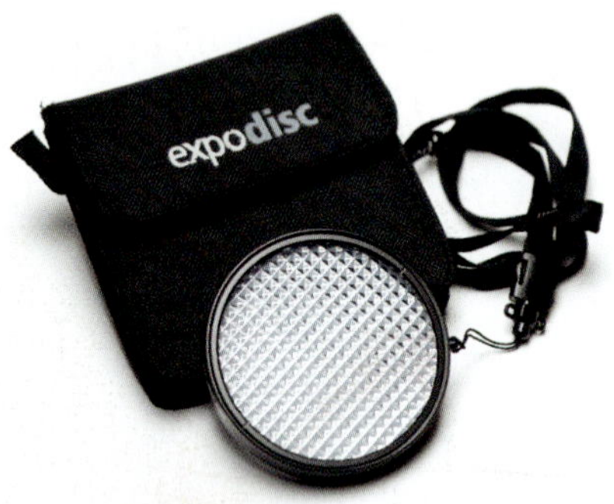

FIGURE 4.5
An ExpoDisc captures incidental light on a subject's face and therefore provides a more accurate reading of white balance.

Add a Gelled Flash

When you move your subject to reduce the number of light sources, you may have moved her into a poor lighting situation. Back at the record store, suppose you determine the ideal location of the model and the dominant source of light is tungsten. Yet this light is still quite unflattering, even after setting a good white balance. Because the room features overhead tungsten lights, you decide to add a flash to the scene to improve the direction of the light on the subject.

Fundamentally, you follow the same steps as you learned in Chapter 3: Set your white balance for the tungsten scene using a gray card or an ExpoDisc, then add a flash with a matching tungsten gel, sometimes called a CTO or color temperature orange gel. (Tungsten light is orange.) Notice the difference in the image before (**Figure 4.6**) and after adding the flash (**Figures 4.7** and **4.8**). The flash adds contrast and a better direction of light to the image.

If you do not gel the flash in this scene, you will be creating your own mixed-light scenario. While the scene is tungsten, your flash is daylight balanced. If you leave your flash ungelled, then you will have a tungsten environment with daylight flash on the face and body.

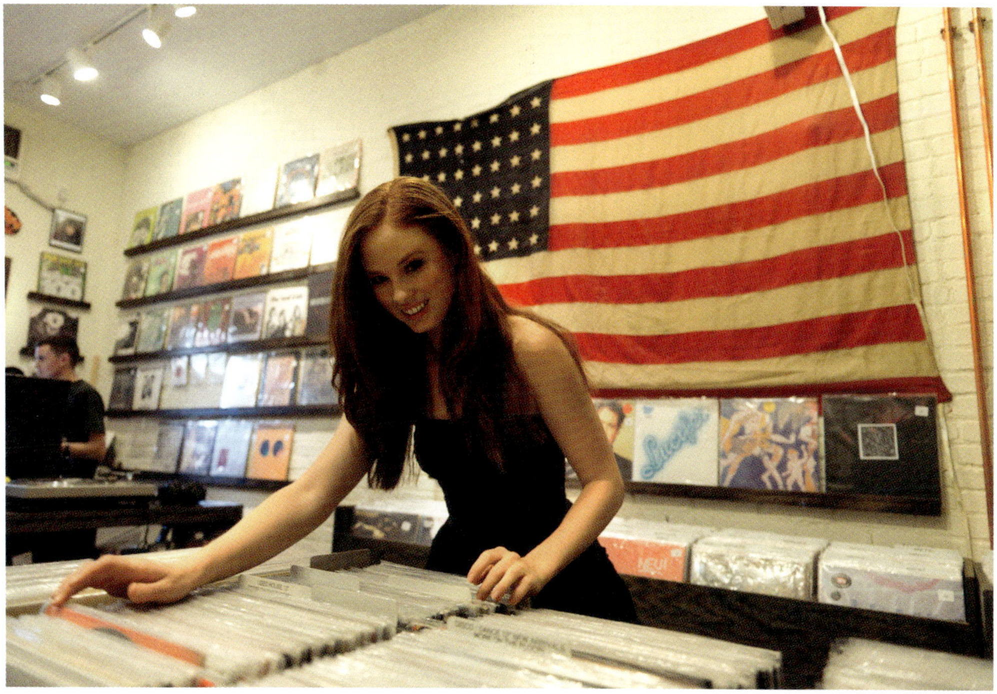

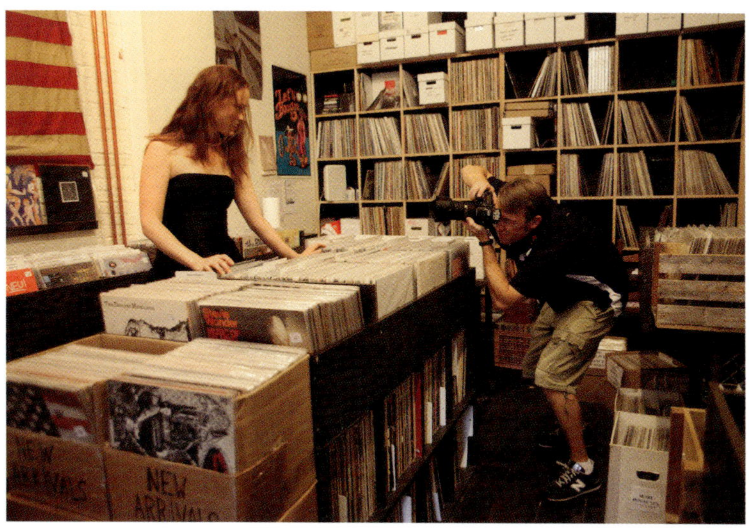

FIGURE 4.6
Here the tungsten-illuminated model has very unpleasant light on her face. There are shadows in her eyes, and she seems to blend into the background.

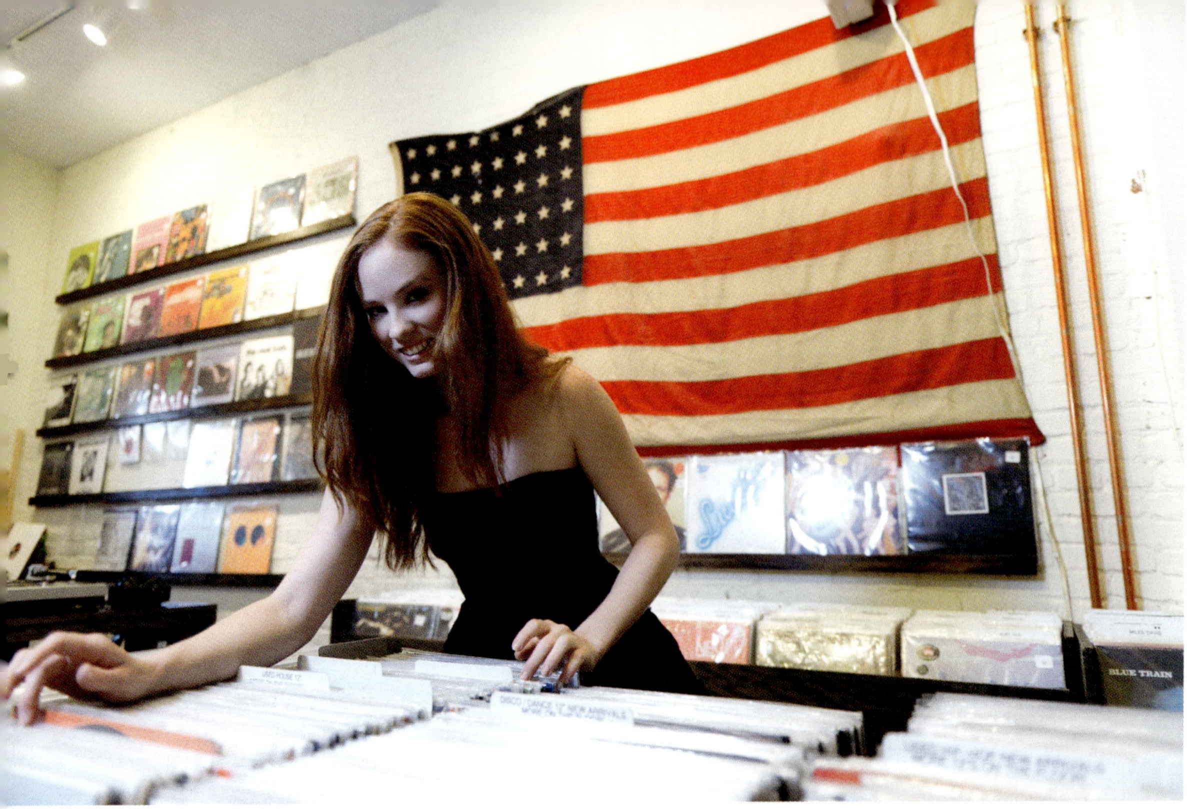

FIGURE 4.7
When you introduce a flash into the equation, the subject pops from the background and has a better quality of light on the face. With no gel, however, the light on her face is a different color temperature (daylight) compared to the ambient light (tungsten).

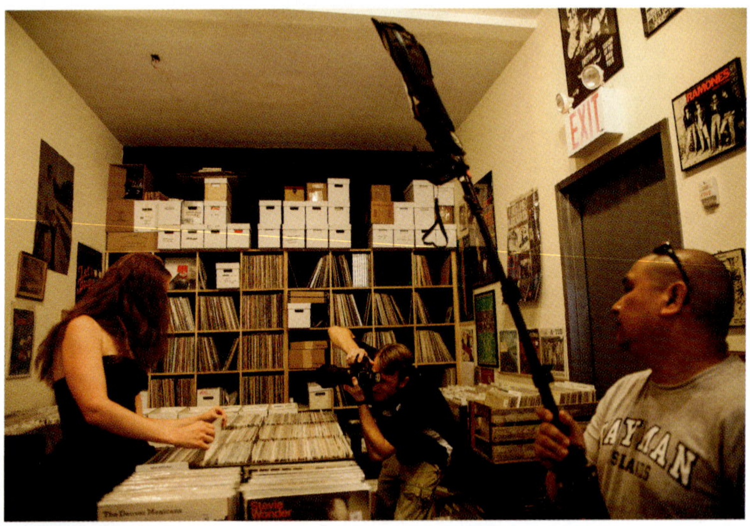

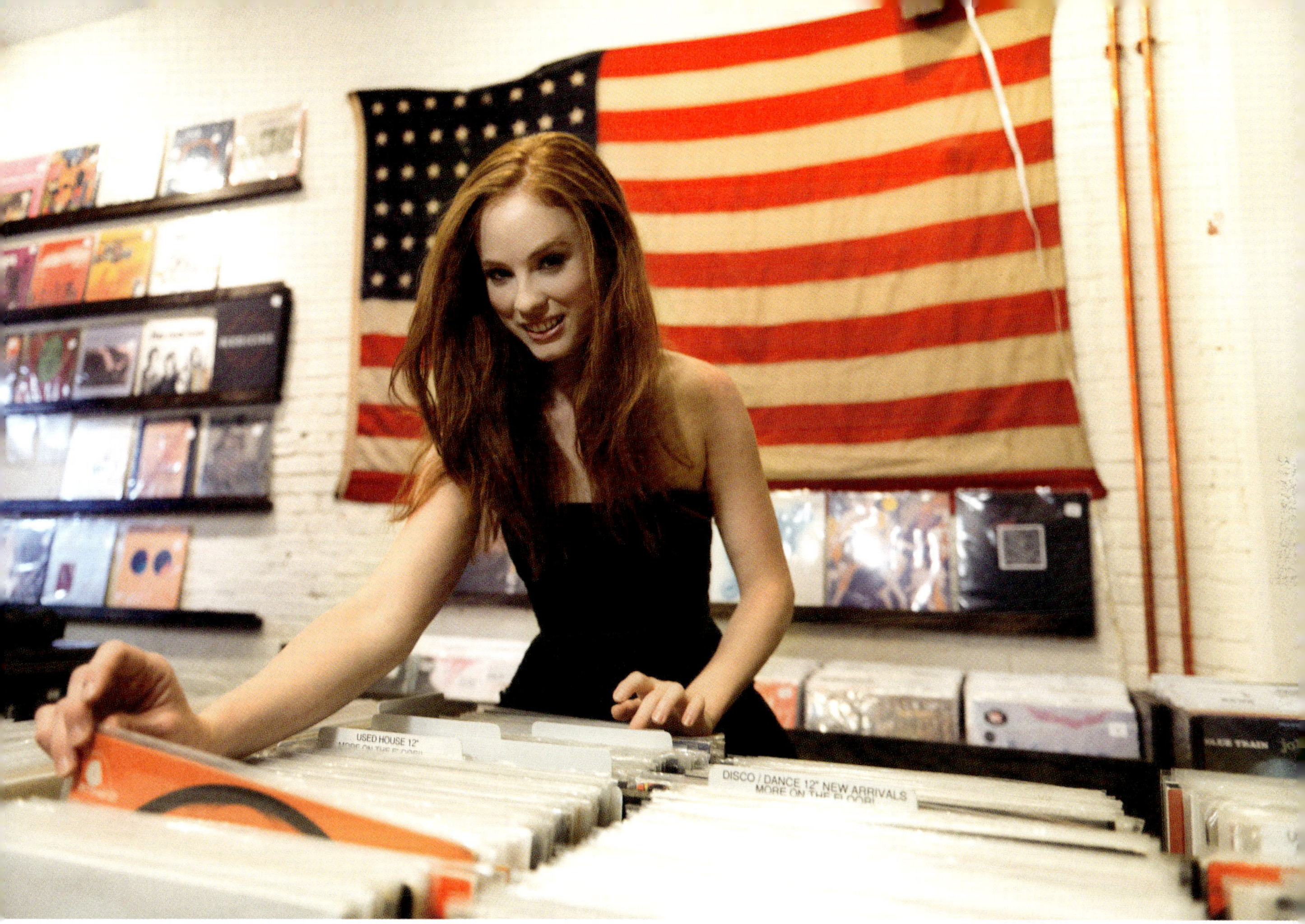

FIGURE 4.8

Add a tungsten (CTO) gel to the flash so that the flash color temperature matches the ambient light. Not only does the flash improve the quality of light on the face, but now you can neutralize the white balance for a balanced image.

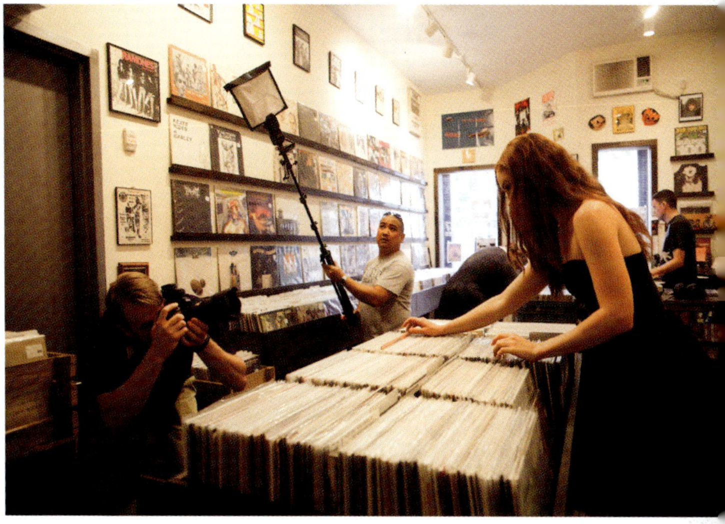

Overpower One Light Source

A final, very popular, solution for mixed lighting is to overpower one of the light sources. In short, you introduce a gelled flash into the scene and use it to overpower the weaker light source. In some situations, when you cannot turn off overhead light and cannot move your subject, overpowering at least one of the mixed light sources may be your only option.

In the record store scenario, for example, one option is to overpower the daylight window and white balance for tungsten light. Here are the steps to take:

1. **Set your white balance.** Set a custom white balance using an ExpoDisc. You could also use a gray card or use the Tungsten white-balance preset on your camera. This way, you are set up to capture the existing color temperature, plus the light you are about to add to the scene.
2. **Gel your flash.** Use an off-camera flash, and gel your flash with a CTO gel to turn the flash to a tungsten white balance. Now your flash white balance will match the white balance of the ambient light. (Under other lighting conditions, you may need to use different gels to match the ambient light.)
3. **Position your flash.** Place your flash near the light source that you are mimicking. At the record store, you're mimicking window light and therefore need to place the flash high and outside the window like the sun.
4. **Power your flash.** Be sure your flash overpowers the ambient light: in this case, the daylight from a window. Due to the contrasty nature of the scene, manually setting your flash's power will give you the most reliable results. You will also need a lot of light to overpower the daylight, so you may want to look at small flash options beyond the standard speedlights. The Qflash from Quantum (www.qtm.com) has a higher power output with many of the same features. If you are comfortable with studio flash on location, try a portable studio strobe.
5. **Shoot!** We think you will be pleased with the results (**Figure 4.9**).

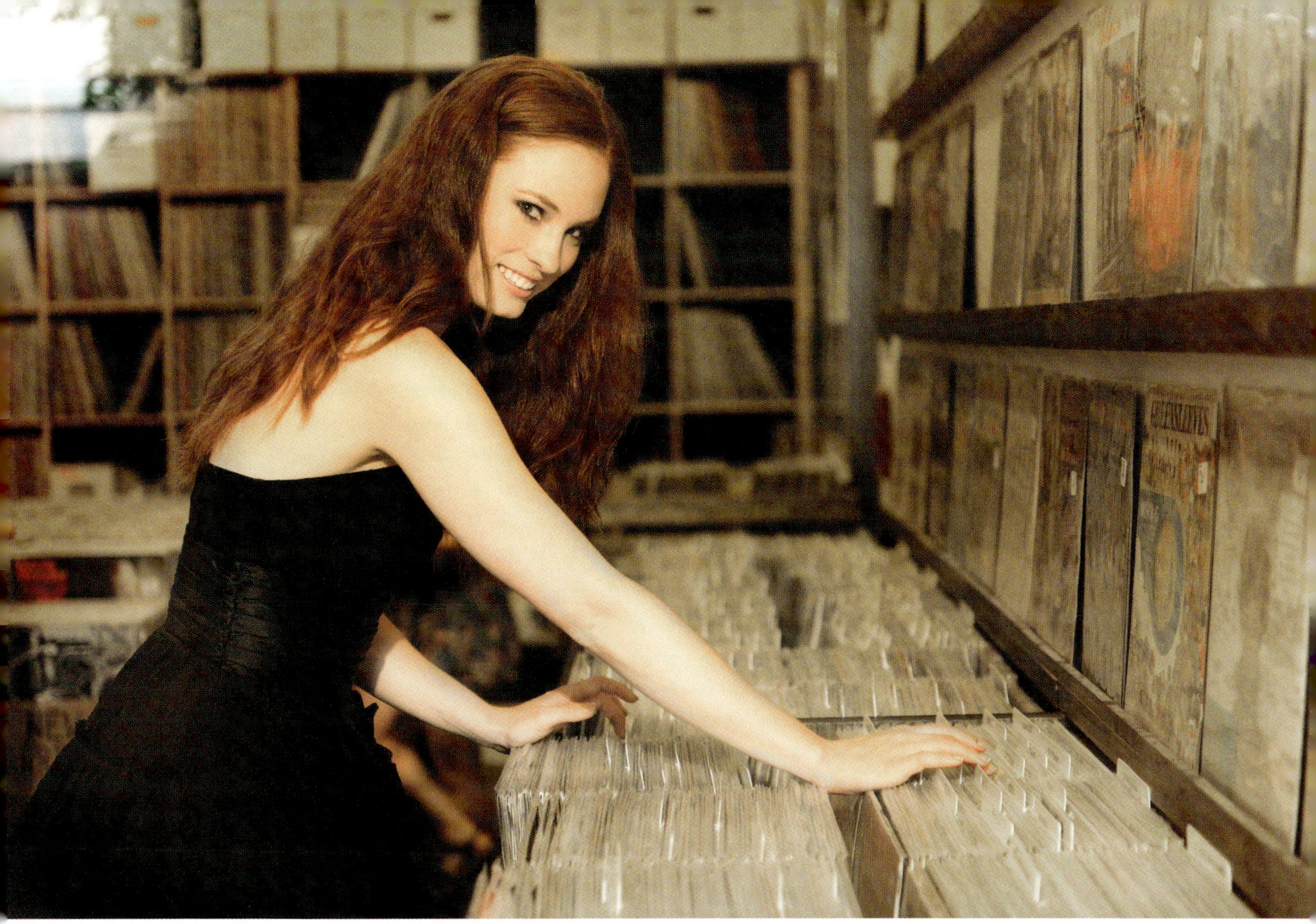

FIGURE 4.9
By turning the flash to a tungsten light source, you can match the ambient light indoors and overpower the daylight. The result is an even color balance!

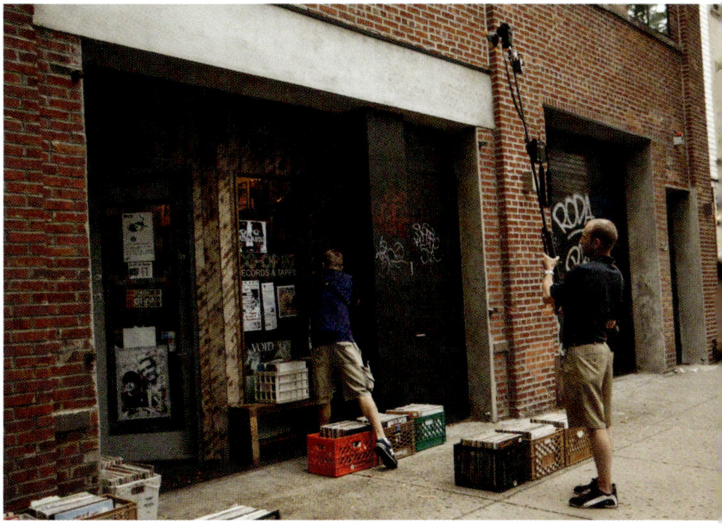

Another option for lighting this record store scene is to allow the daylight from the window to illuminate the subject and use a daylight-balanced flash to bounce off the ceiling or light the background, overpowering the tungsten light source. Now all lighting elements in the frame are daylight balanced. Ideally, you would turn off the tungsten lights in the room and use the daylight flashes to be the sole source of illumination. Remember the importance of white balance no matter which solution you choose. Stick a gray card in the scene to use as a reference in your post-processing, as seen in **Figure 4.10**.

Don't Wait for Post-Processing

To be honest, fixing mixed light scenes in post-processing is time consuming, painful, and less efficient than fixing mixed light in the field. You could process the same RAW file multiple times and combine the different color versions of the image together in Photoshop. The various versions of the image will have different white balance adjustments, however, and combining them will involve a lot of masking and attention to detail. If possible, why not just shoot it correctly in camera?

When you don't shoot it correctly in camera, and then find it too difficult to fix in post-production, what can you do? Many photographers resort to converting the images to black and white or desaturating them. Black and white is a strong medium to help focus the image on emotion and human interaction, but often it is used as a crutch to deal with bad white balance. What do you do if the client prefers images in color? Well... shoot it correctly in camera.

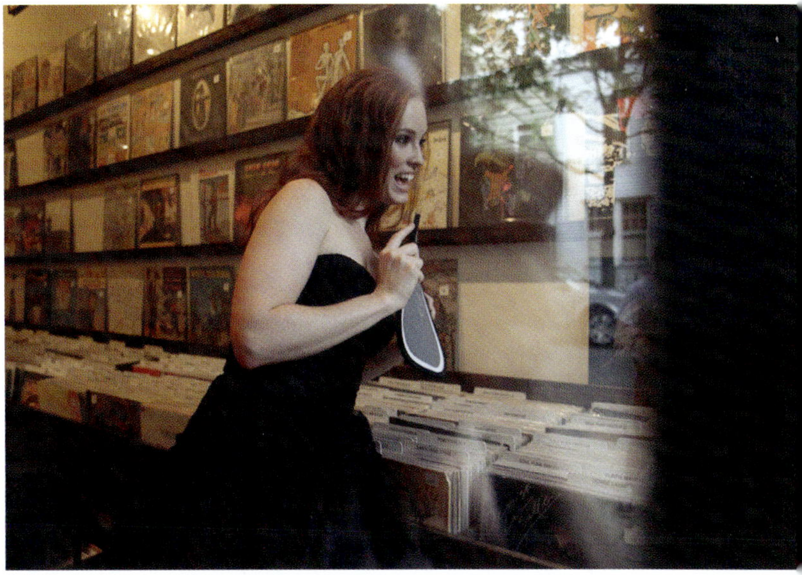

FIGURE 4.10
Don't forget the importance of white balance. You can use a gray card (seen here) to create a point of reference for correcting white balance in post-processing, shoot with an ExpoDisc, or use built-in white-balance presets.

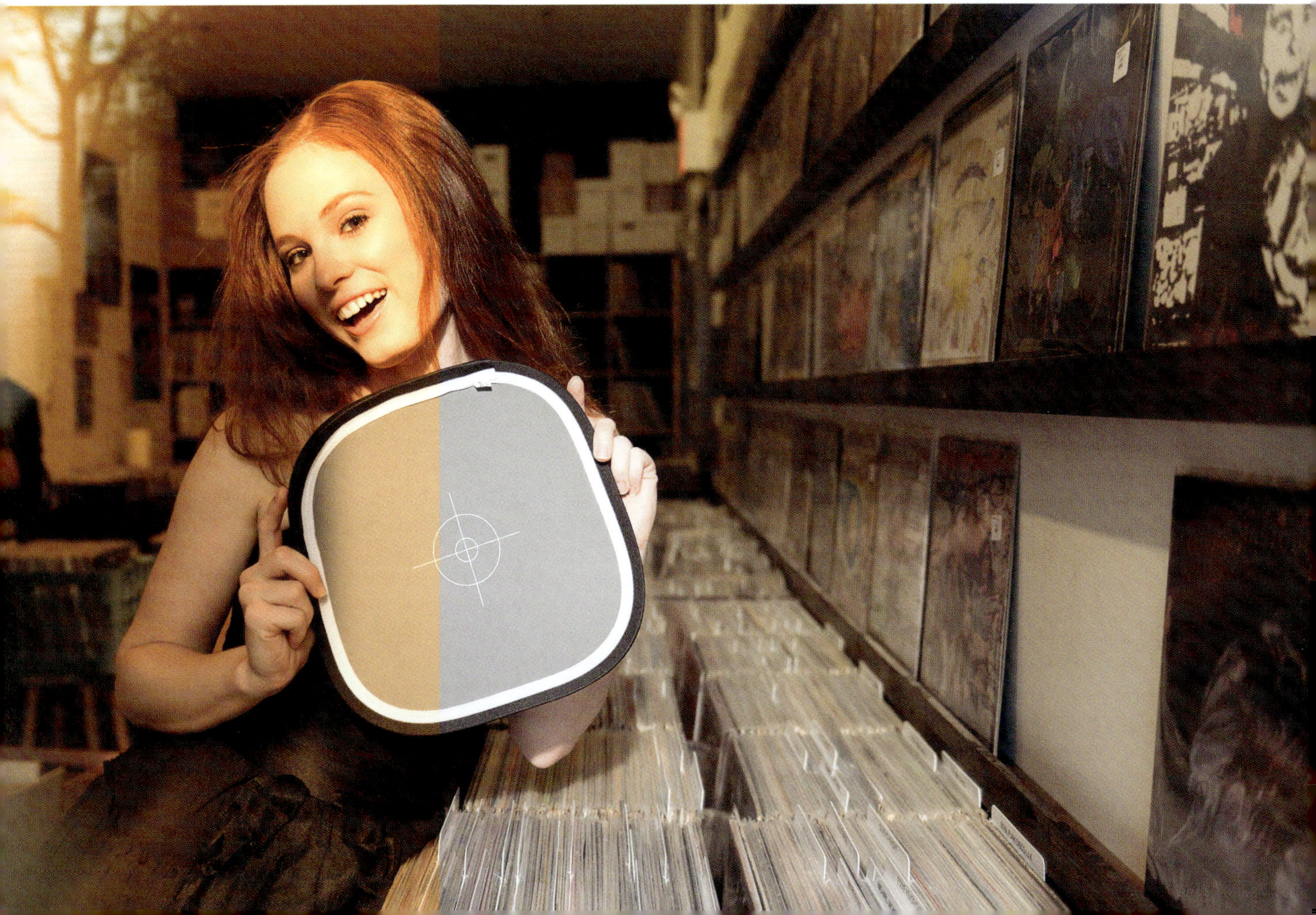

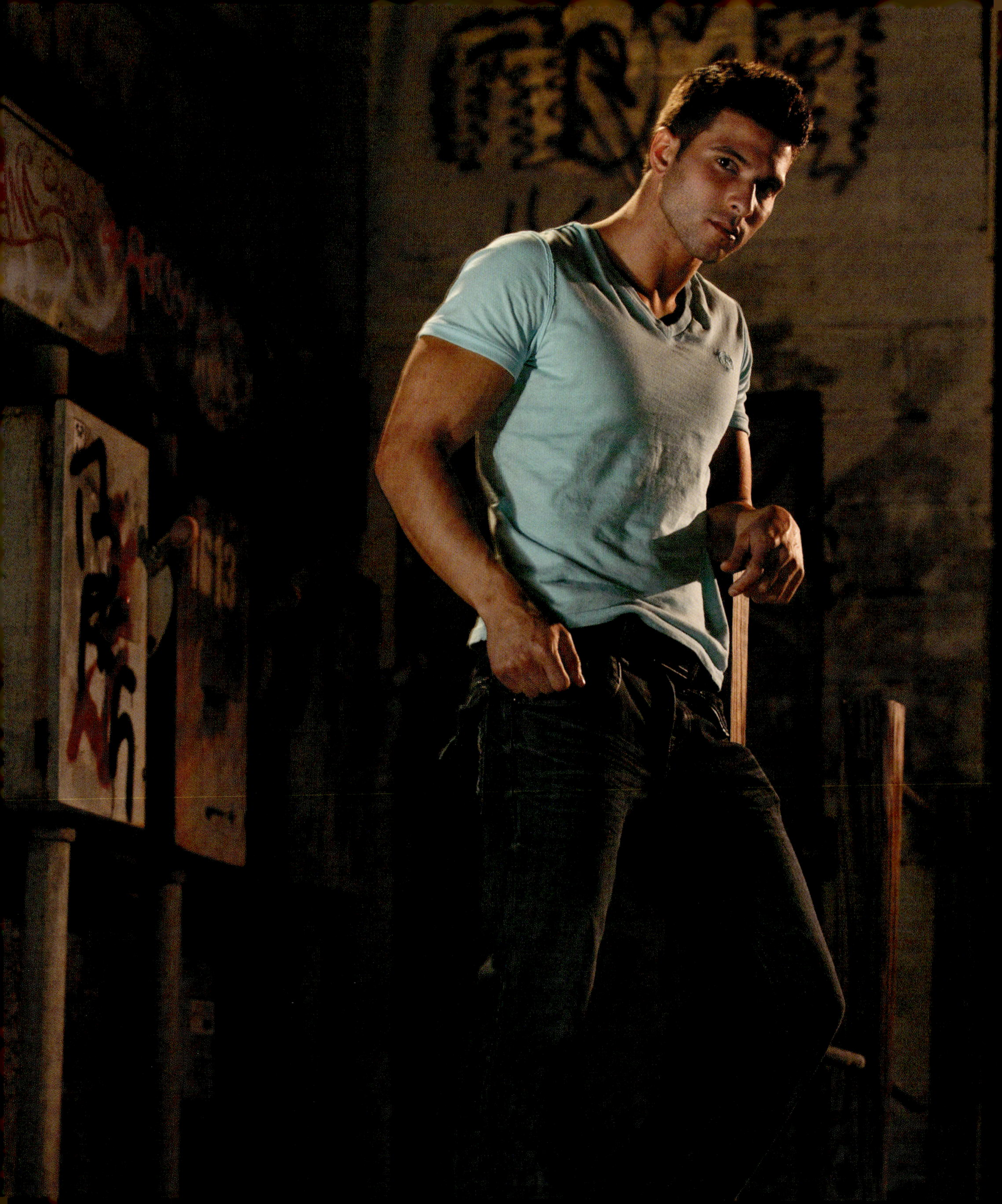

CHAPTER FIVE
Shooting at Night

Shooting at night can be a nightmare if you don't understand the tools available to you. It's difficult to focus, challenging to determine exposure, and you are stuck providing all the illumination for the scene. Yet you can work some of these same challenges to your advantage. The upside to this scenario is that when you walk into a night scene with no light, you have complete control! In this chapter, you'll learn how to overcome some of the immediate issues, as well as discover ways to exercise creative control with some added light of your own to create results.

Focus in the Dark

It's nighttime, and you must shoot in almost complete darkness. Maybe you're in an under-lit reception hall at a wedding. Or perhaps you're shooting your subject at night with a dimly lit street scene in the background. How on earth are you supposed to focus? You may not have noticed them in the dark, but several focusing tools are already baked into your camera and flash. As you'll see, a flashlight could be a great help as well.

AF Assist Illuminator

One of the first built-in tools to help you focus is your **AF Assist Illuminator light** (AF meaning auto-focus). You'll find this small light built into the upper-front part of your camera body, right next to the lens mount. It doesn't turn on all the time, as that would drain your battery substantially. To activate it, simply turn on the AF Assist Illuminator setting in your camera menu (check your manual for details, as it varies with each camera). Now when you shoot without a flash in the dark, the light will momentarily turn on to assist your camera in finding focus (**Figure 5.1**). If this doesn't seem to work on your camera, don't worry. In some cameras, you first must select your center focus point for the AF Assist Illuminator to engage. (If you need help with focus selection points, see Chapter 9, "Strong Backlight.")

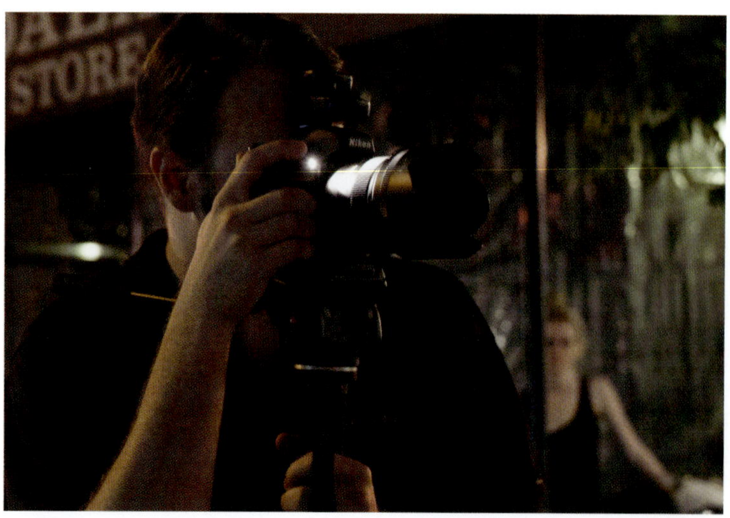

FIGURE 5.1
The AF Assist Illuminator shines a light on the subject to help the camera's auto-focus system in low light.

Wide-Area AF-Assist Illuminator

The next big help in your battle to grab focus is your flash's **Wide-Area AF-Assist Illuminator**. It works almost identically to your camera's illuminator and is a small infrared light within your flash. Once you turn it on, you never have to fiddle with it again. After you turn the beam on, your flash automatically projects a red, patterned beam of light onto your subject to aid your camera in finding focus. Again, this engages only when shooting in extremely low light, like the middle of the night, and the flash needs to be mounted on the camera for best results. To turn the beam on, you will find a prompt in your digital camera's menu options, but consult your manual for specific instructions because the terminology varies between cameras. Unlike the camera body's AF Assist Illuminator, the Wide-Area AF-Assist Illuminator is built into the front of the flash itself.

Flashlight

An alternative and somewhat obvious approach to shedding light on your scene is to use a good old flashlight (**Figure 5.2**). Why use a low-tech flashlight instead of the other techniques? Two reasons: camera battery life and pupils. If you use a flashlight, your camera doesn't have to drain its own batteries every time it tries to focus. Think about your subject's eyes, as well. When your subject stands in the dark, her pupils will dilate, becoming so big they dominate the eyes and hide that pretty eye color. When you illuminate your subject with a flashlight, the pupils contract for a more natural looking image, all the while making it easier for your camera to grab focus.

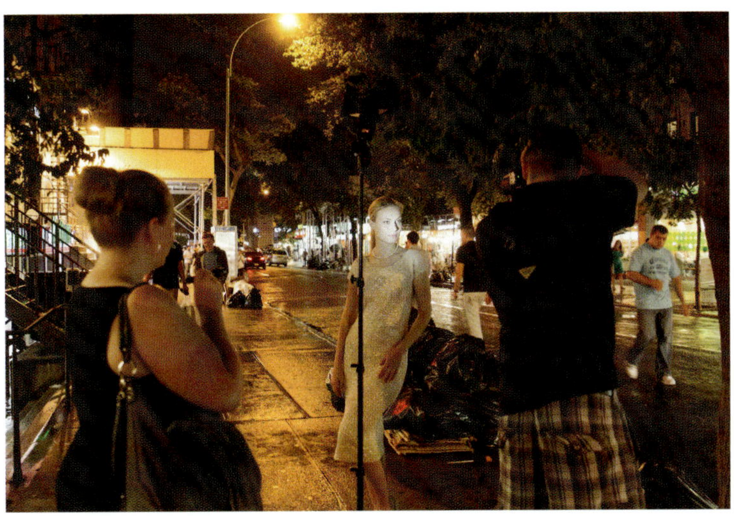

FIGURE 5.2
An assistant holds a flashlight to help the camera focus in low light. The flash creates an area of illumination and also contrast that enables your camera's auto-focus system to assist you in the low light. If you have no other solution, a flashlight may do the trick!

Depth-of-Field Preview

The final technique you can employ when trying to see in the dark is more about visualization than actual focus. As you read in Chapter 4, "Mixed Color Temperatures," moving your flash off your camera can yield major benefits. Unlike traditional studio strobes, however, your speedlight has no modeling light. When your flash is off the camera, you don't know what the light will look like until after you take the photo. A wonderful work-around to this dilemma is to trigger your flash wirelessly. Using the PocketWizard MiniTT1 and FlexTT5 system (www.pocketwizard.com), for example, you can activate a temporary modeling light from your camera. Simply press your **Depth-of-Field Preview button**; your speedlight will rapidly pulse, lighting your model and showing you what the image will look like *before* you pull the trigger (**Figure 5.3**). This button is typically located on the front of your camera body, near the lens. See your manual for specifics regarding your camera.

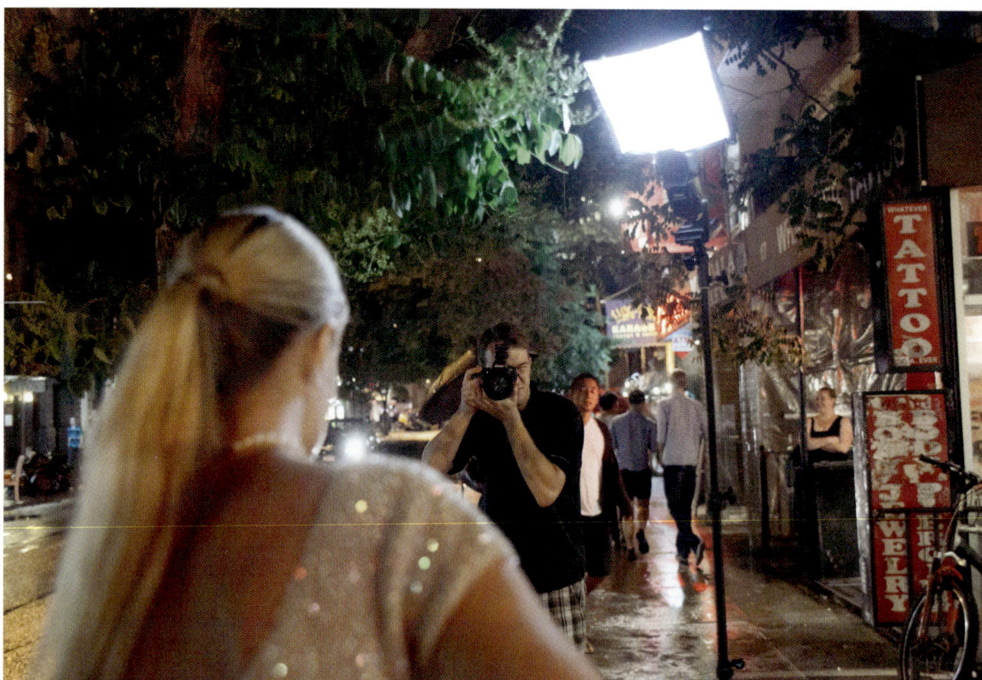

FIGURE 5.3
Pressing the Depth-of-Field Preview button triggers your flash to pulse rapidly, creating a mock modeling light. This button allows you to see how the light from a speedlight will look before you even take the photo and also helps you to focus in low light.

Find the Right Exposure

With your photo in focus, you now need to dial in the proper exposure. An underexposed picture is no good, no matter how sharp your subject may be. In brightly lit scenes, your camera does a pretty decent job of helping you with such features as **Program mode (P)** and **Aperture Priority mode (Av)**. At night, when there isn't much light for your camera's brain to work with, **Manual mode (M)** is definitely the way to go. When choosing your camera settings, put your emphasis on gathering the most light possible, as you are shooting in very little. Manual mode takes away the guess work, giving you all the creative control and consistent results.

The ISO Route

One fast and efficient way to emphasize light gathering is by turning up your **ISO** adjustment. The ISO setting determines your camera's overall sensitivity to light, which makes it a global modifier. It affects all light entering your camera, whether it's **ambient light** or light from your strobe. The benefits of increasing your ISO setting are several. Because your camera will gather light more efficiently, your flash will output less light for each photo. The less stress you put on your flash, the more you extend its battery life. A higher ISO also allows you to use a faster shutter, which reduces the chances of camera shake and blurry photographs.

Figures 5.4 through **Figure 5.6** were all shot at f/5.6 and a 1/125–second exposure. Notice the dramatic difference in the ambiance of the images as the ISO setting increases from ISO 200 (Figure 5.4) to 800 (Figure 5.5) to 3200 (Figure 5.6). To compensate for this extra senstivity, the power on the flash lighting the model was turned down at the same rate.

By cranking up the ISO like this, you can hand-hold a shot in the dark, and still walk away with a sharp image. Attempting the same shot at lower ISO settings would have required a much slower shutter speed and a tripod to stabilize it. Not only does this complicate the shot, tripods aren't always practical or even allowed in some venues. In **Figure 5.7**, you can see how the combination of high ISO and a fast lens allows you to get the shot, plus affords you the light sensitivity to brighten up your ambient exposure. By letting the ambient light bleed into the image near the same exposure as the light on your model, you create a more balanced photograph. This helps you to blend your subject with the surrounding environment.

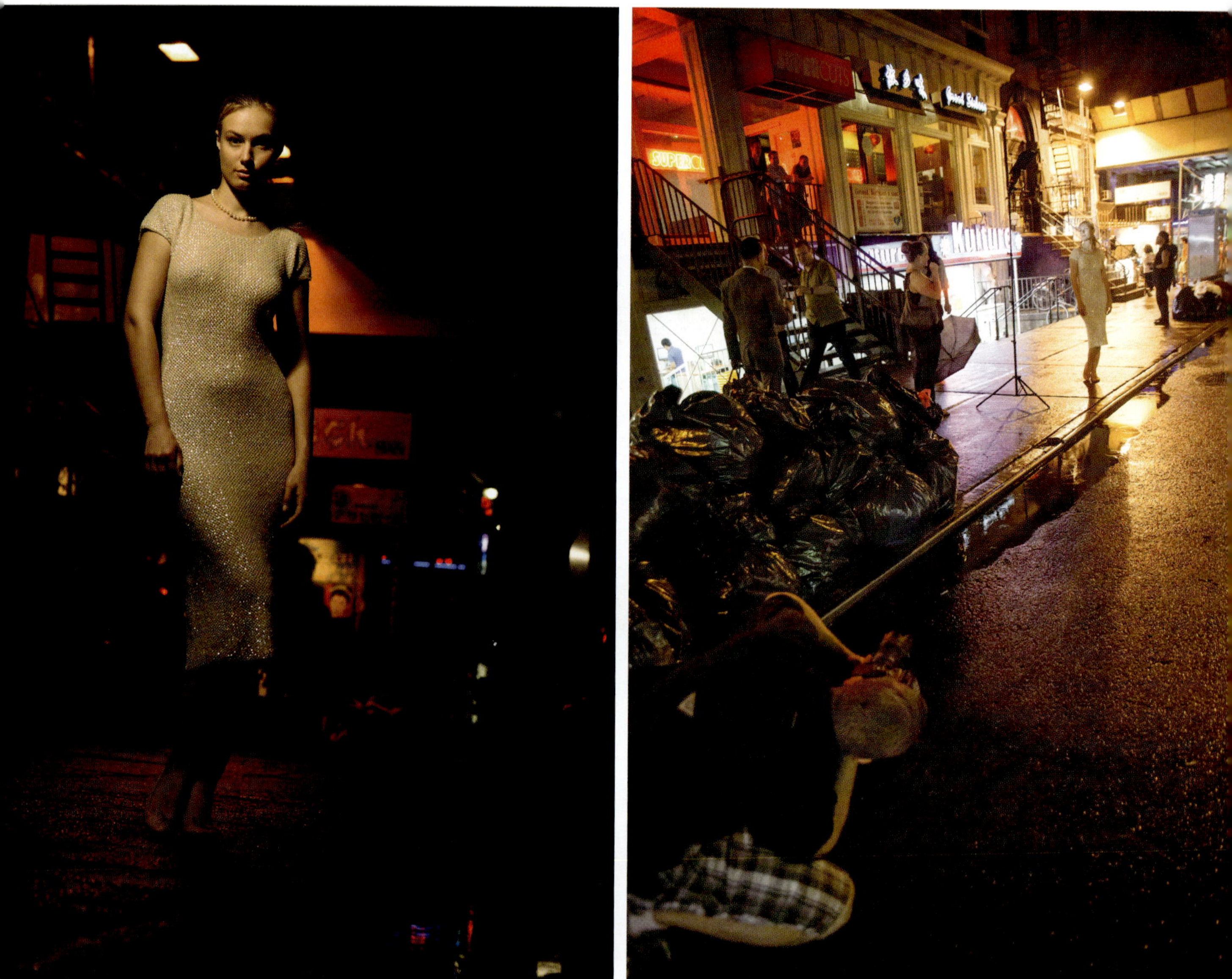

FIGURE 5.4

This is the first of three photos shot at f/5.6 and a 1/125-second exposure but with increasing ISO sensitivity. Here an ISO setting of 200 produces the darkest background.

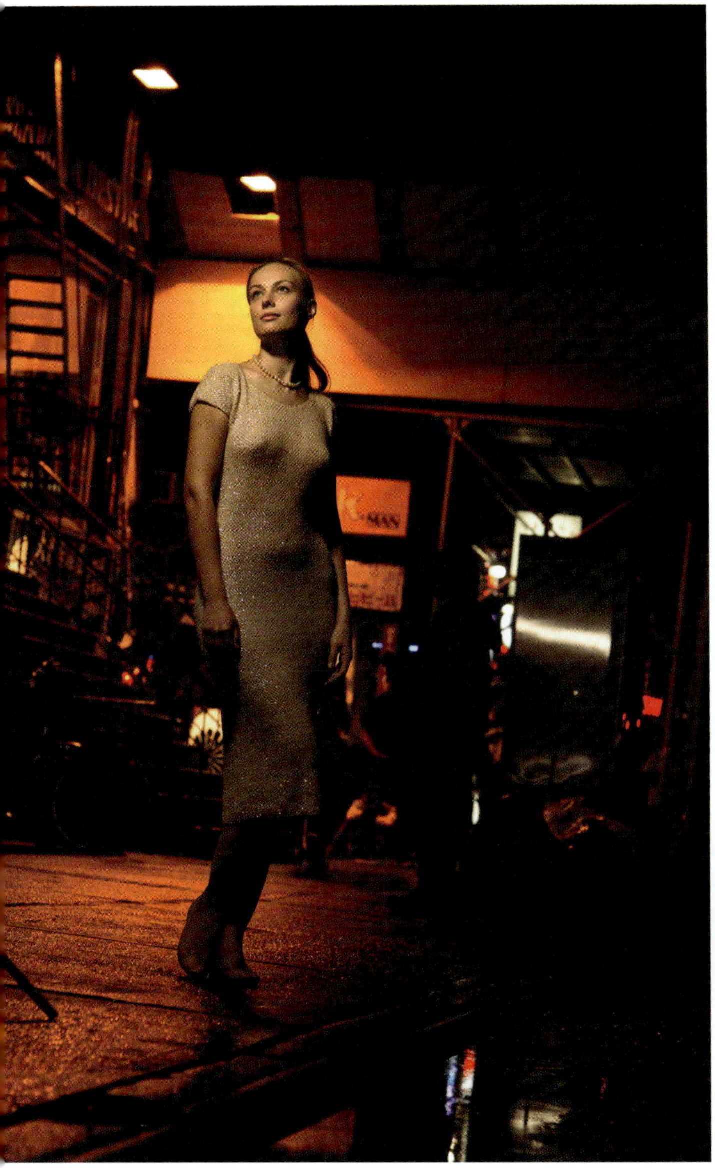

FIGURE 5.5
Increasing the ISO setting to 800 brightens the background compared to Figure 5.4. By increasing the ISO, you allow more ambient light into your exposure, and thus, more background detail is visible.

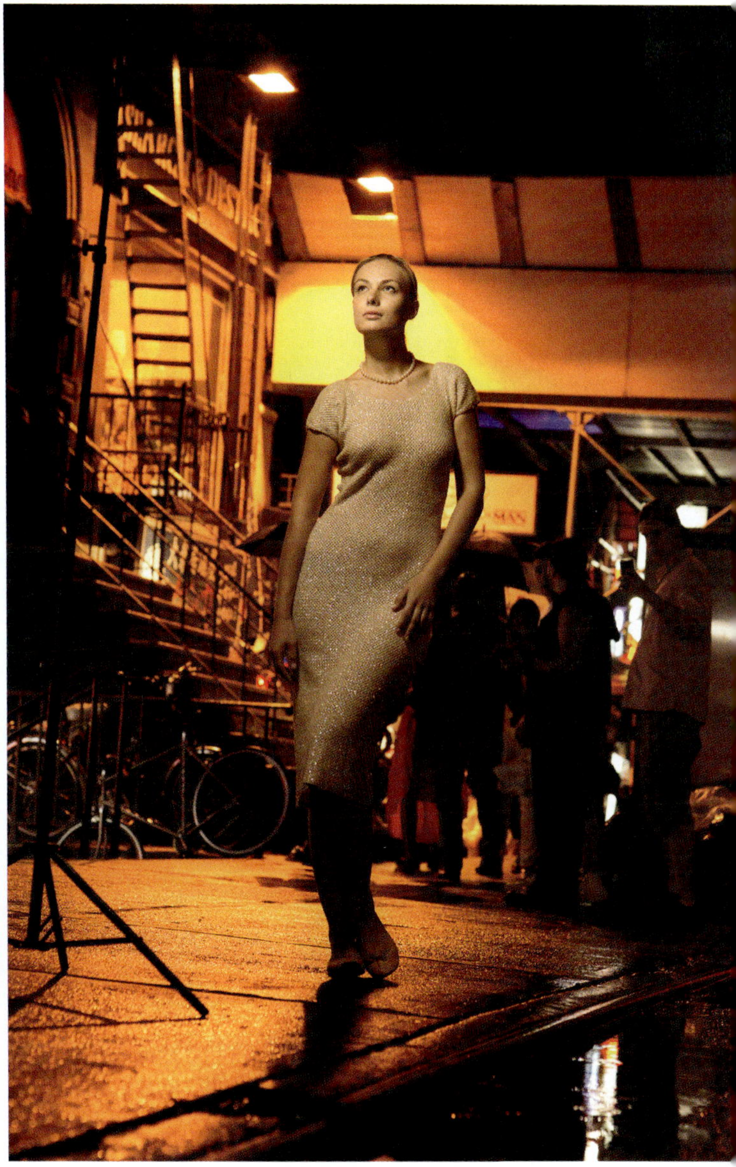

FIGURE 5.6
Stepping the ISO up to 3200 brightens the background even more.

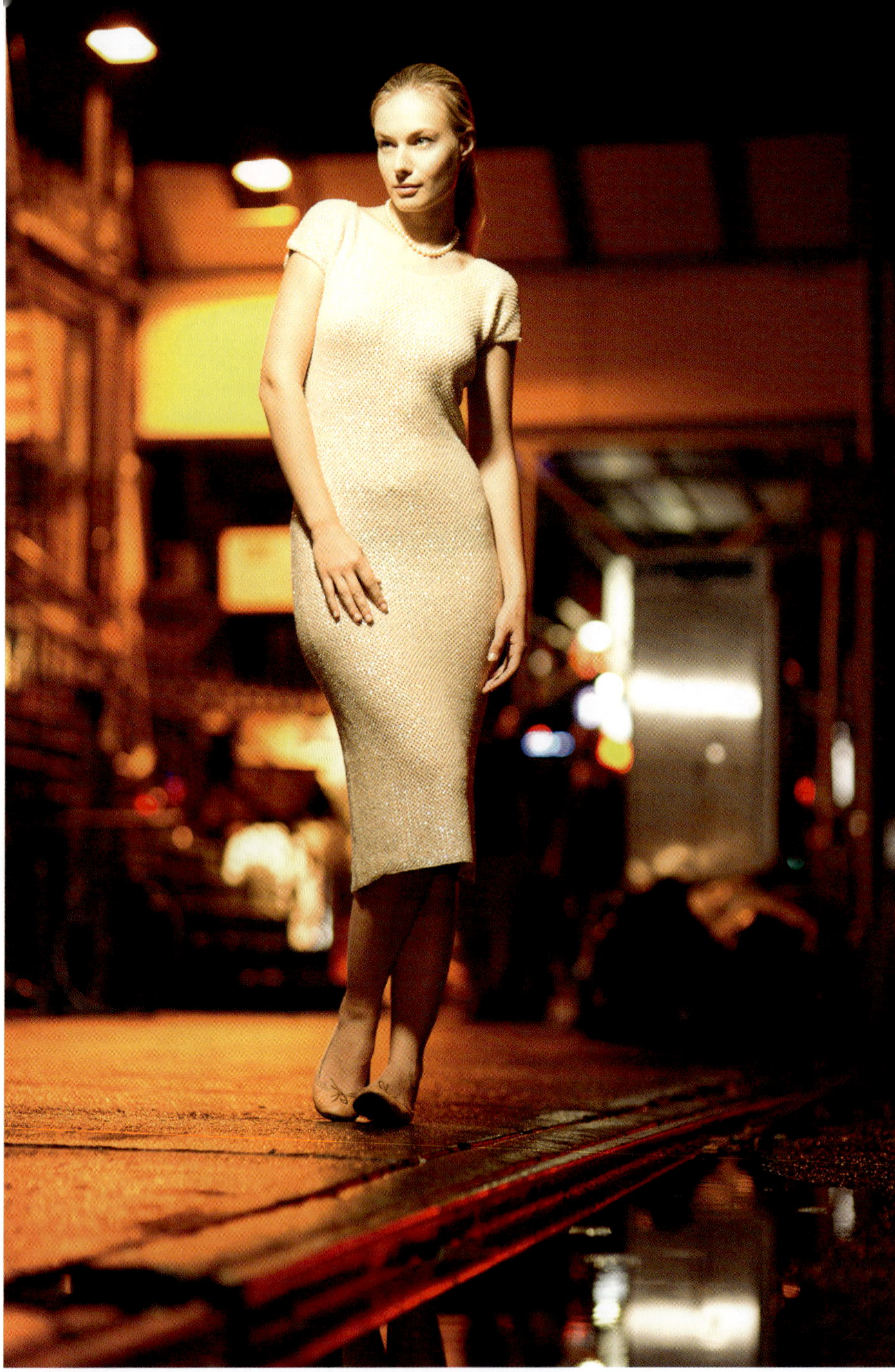

FIGURE 5.7
This image benefited from a high ISO and a prime lens with a wide aperture, letting lots of light into the camera in a dark scene. Not only were we able to take the photo without the aid of a tripod, but we also achieved a more balanced exposure by allowing more light from the background to register in our image.

Dragging Your Shutter

The second way to attack the low light of shooting at night is through adjusting your shutter speed. Lengthening your exposure by **dragging your shutter** allows more light into the camera. If you are at a location where using a tripod is viable, then the slow-shutter approach can lead to some really fun images. By adjusting your shutter speed (in Manual mode or even Shutter Priority mode), you are telling your camera to let in more ambient light and give you a brighter base exposure.

Consider a few examples. We shot **Figures 5.8** through **5.10** with a constant ISO 400 and f/5.6, but lengthened the shutter speed for each. There was no need to even adjust the flash power this time, because the shutter speed affects only the existing ambient light in the scene—another bonus to this approach! For Figure 5.8, we used a shutter speed of 1/60 sec. As you would expect, everything not lit by the flash is dark; it is still nighttime after all. If you want to see the environment and not just the model, you need to bring up the background light. For Figure 5.9, we slowed the shutter to 1/10 sec to allow the camera more time to gather light. Now the background is starting to come into play. In Figure 5.10, the camera shutter slowed down even more to 1/3 sec. See why a tripod is important here? This is where the fun factor kicks in. At really slow shutter speeds like this, you get light trails. Cabs flying by during the exposure created those streaks of light in the background. Definitely play around with this technique; you can create some surreal images by slowing time.

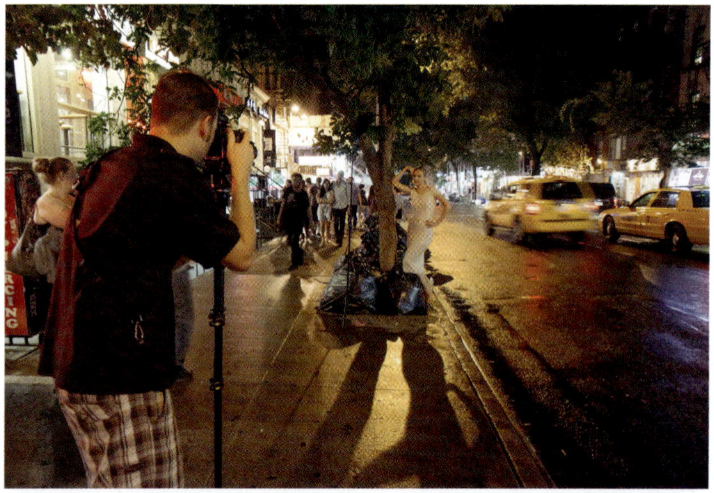

FIGURE 5.8
Camera settings of ISO 400, f/5.6, and 1/60 sec lit the model with the flash while leaving the rest of the scene in the dark.

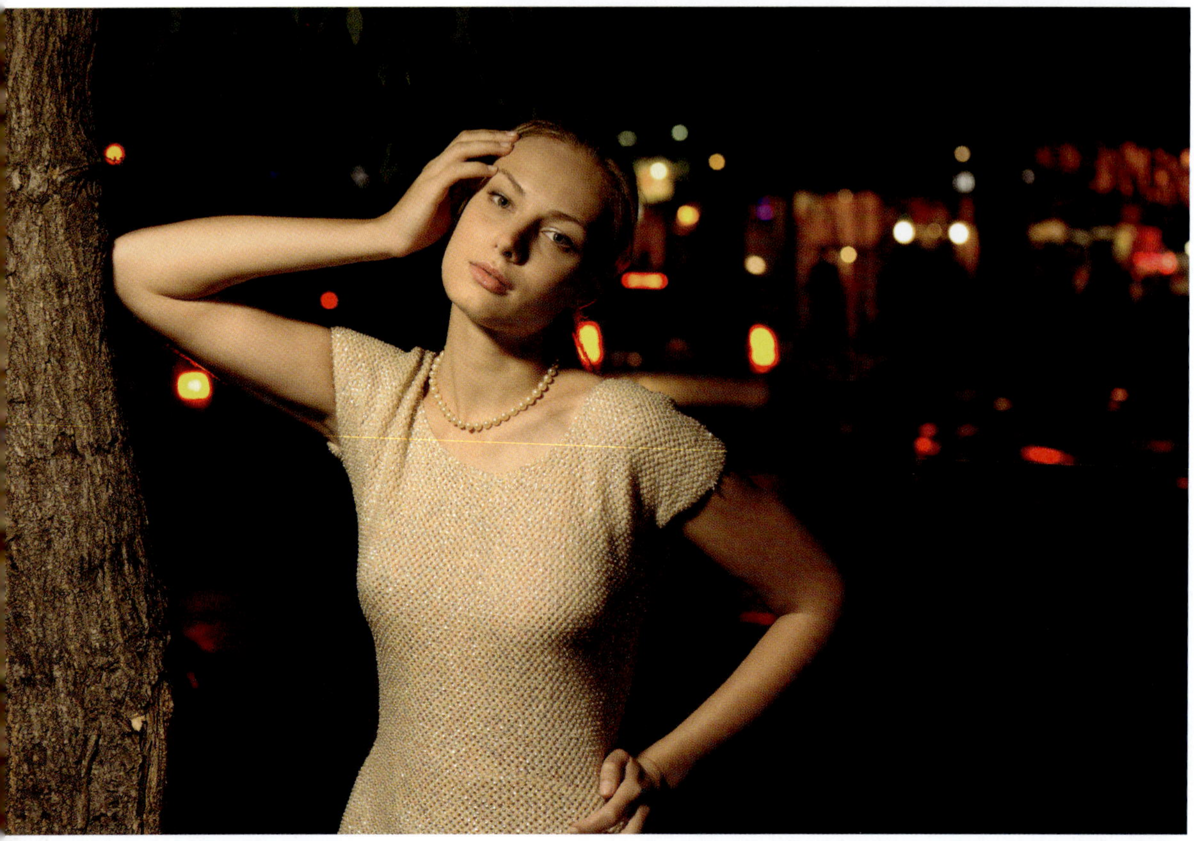

FIGURE 5.9

(right) Lengthening the shutter speed to 1/10 sec brightens the background. By having your shutter open longer, you allow more of the background to register in your frame and thus have more background detail.

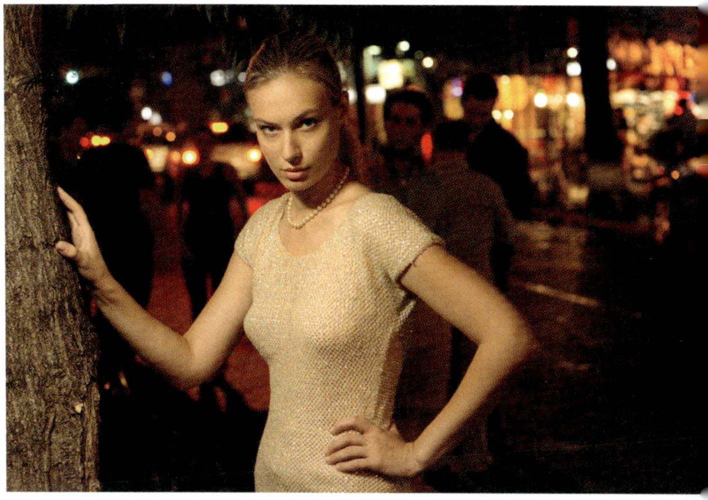

FIGURE 5.10

(below) At a 1/3-second exposure, the background is much brighter because you have allowed more ambient light to register during your long exposure. Because of the long exposure, the passing taxi cab tail lights create streaks as they pass, adding a sense of time and visual interest.

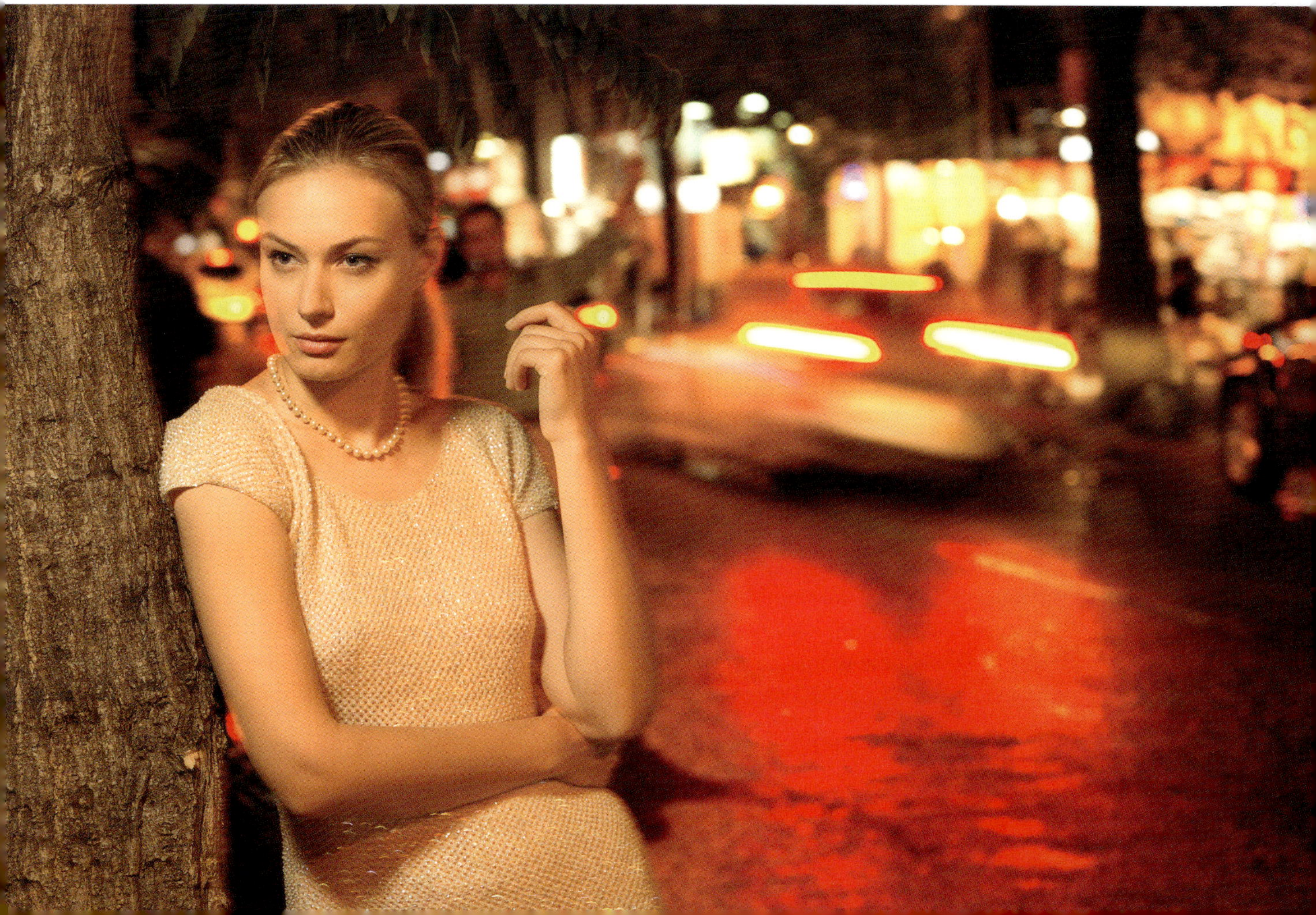

Use Light Modifiers

Shooting at night conveniently gives you a blank canvas on which to work, and a simple speedlight gives you plenty of power to paint it with. Now all you have to do is decide how to shape that light with various flash **modifiers**. A modifier is any tool that changes the color, quality, or direction of the light after it leaves the flash. When choosing modifiers, you must consider the quality of light as well as the mobility of your solution. Are you looking for a softer, more diffused solution? Or perhaps you want a more directional, constrasty solution. The various lights and modifiers you select will provide you with different brushes to illuminate your canvas.

You don't need to bring an entire studio on location to create flattering light on your subjects. When choosing your lighting solution and modifiers, mobility and quality are the deciding factors when walking out the door. Seen in Figure 5.3, the Rogue FlashBender (ExpoImaging, www.expoimaging.com) is one example of a compact solution that delivers quality results. This modifier acts like a miniature softbox on top of your speedlight, both diffusing and enlarging the light source. Dozens of companies create a variety of modifiying solutions for your flash, with everything from a snoot attachment (focuses the light) to a larger softbox attachment. As you saw in Figures 5.3, 5.4, and 5.8, mobility was key because the shoot was on a busy sidewalk in New York City. Anything larger would have obstructed pedestrian traffic and been difficult to manage on the street. A bare flash would have been too harsh on the subject and too focused. This modifier gives a more flattering light solution.

On the opposite end of the mobility spectrum are standard photo umbrellas. In **Figure 5.11**, the model is lit with a 60-inch Westcott bounce umbrella. This was the perfect modifer for the shot, because we were working in a large open space. A large umbrella also creates a big spread of even, soft light and can flatter a model's features from farther away. The FlashBender still provides a beautiful quality of light, but it works better when shooting more intimate, close shots that do not need full-body illumination as required in the setup for Figure 5.11.

The last variable to consider when modifying your flash is its color—not in the sense of a stylish Ferrari red housing, but the **color temperature** of the light. As you read in Chapters 3 and 4, most speedlights come with a pack of color corrective gels that can be attached to your flash to shift its color temperature. When you're out shooting at night, take note of the color of the existing light. For example, those overhead streetlamps have a very warm color temperature, very near that of the Tungsten white balance preset on your camera. By setting the proper camera white balance, you can neutralize this warm color cast, and by applying a CTO gel to your flash, you can bring both sources into a nice balance.

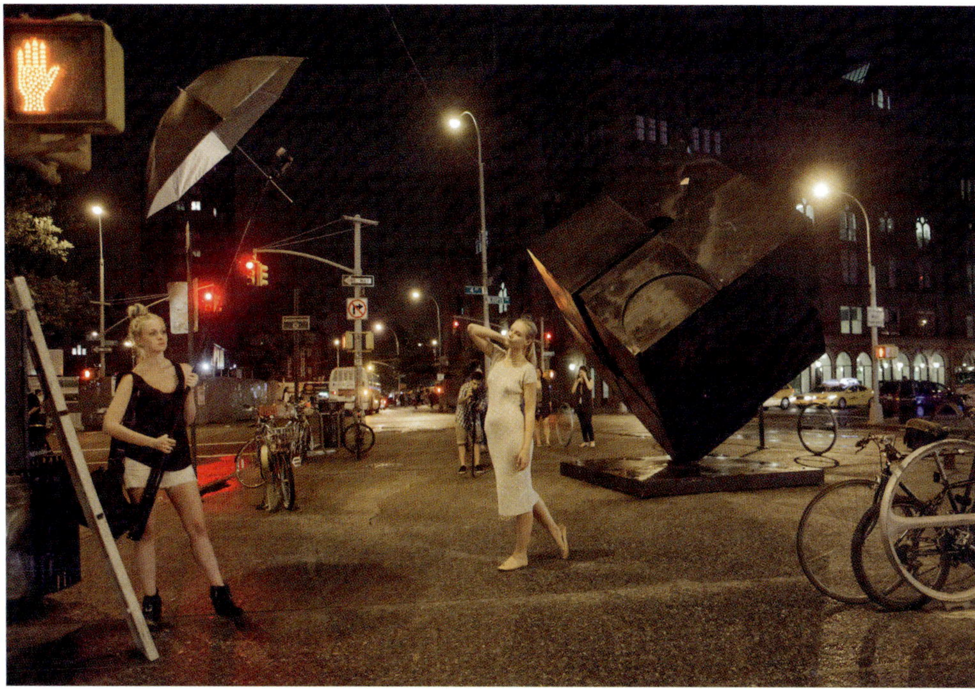

FIGURE 5.11
By using the Westcott 60-inch umbrella, we were able to create a much bigger light source that illuminated the scene with a larger spread of even light. This modifier turns our small flash into a larger, soft light source.

Try Stylistic Lighting

Now that you have all of the tools and techniques to paint the night with light, it comes down to how you want to apply them. When starting with night's black background, you can choose two basic approaches: contrast or balance. You can easily create an image that looks "lit," isolating the subject and building contrast. In other words, the settings you choose purposely make the subject stand out from the background and the scene. The opposite approach is to blend your subject and background together for a more natural look. In the end, the "right" answer comes down to your personal aethsetic and style.

Contrast

You can build contrast in a number of ways. By its very nature, lighting a subject on a black background creates a lot of contrast; everything is dark except for the subject, causing the person to stand out. You know how to brighten up the light in your backgrounds (using shutter speed and ISO), but the degree to which you do so, the **lighting ratio**, will set a tone to the final photo. The ratio basically compares the brightness of your subject to that of the background. For example, a lighting ratio of 1:1 means both are lit the same, while a shot with a 4:1 ratio means the subject is four times as bright as the background. The higher the lighting ratio, the greater the contrast. In other words, the subject will stand out more from the background with a higher lighting ratio. Don't worry about getting caught up in exact numbers and ratios here. What is important is undertstanding how the brightness of the background versus the brightness of your subject can affect the photograph.

You can also increase constrast by having contrasting color tempertures. As you read in Chapter 4, different types of lights emit specific color temperatures. Take a look at the color temperature imbalance in **Figure 5.12**: The background is lit by warm streetlamps, and the model is lit by a bare speedlight bounced off an umbrella. This means that the background is lit by orange light while the model is lit by cool blue light. To render her skin tone properly, we just set the camera white balance to the Flash preset.

To play off this color contrast, we used a fairly high contrast lighting ratio as well. Notice how dark the background is compared to the model. Both the color temperature imbalance and lighting ratio cause the subject to pop out of the image in strong contrast. The background has warm yellow tones, while the subject is daylight balanced.These constrasting color tempertures help provide separation between subject and background.

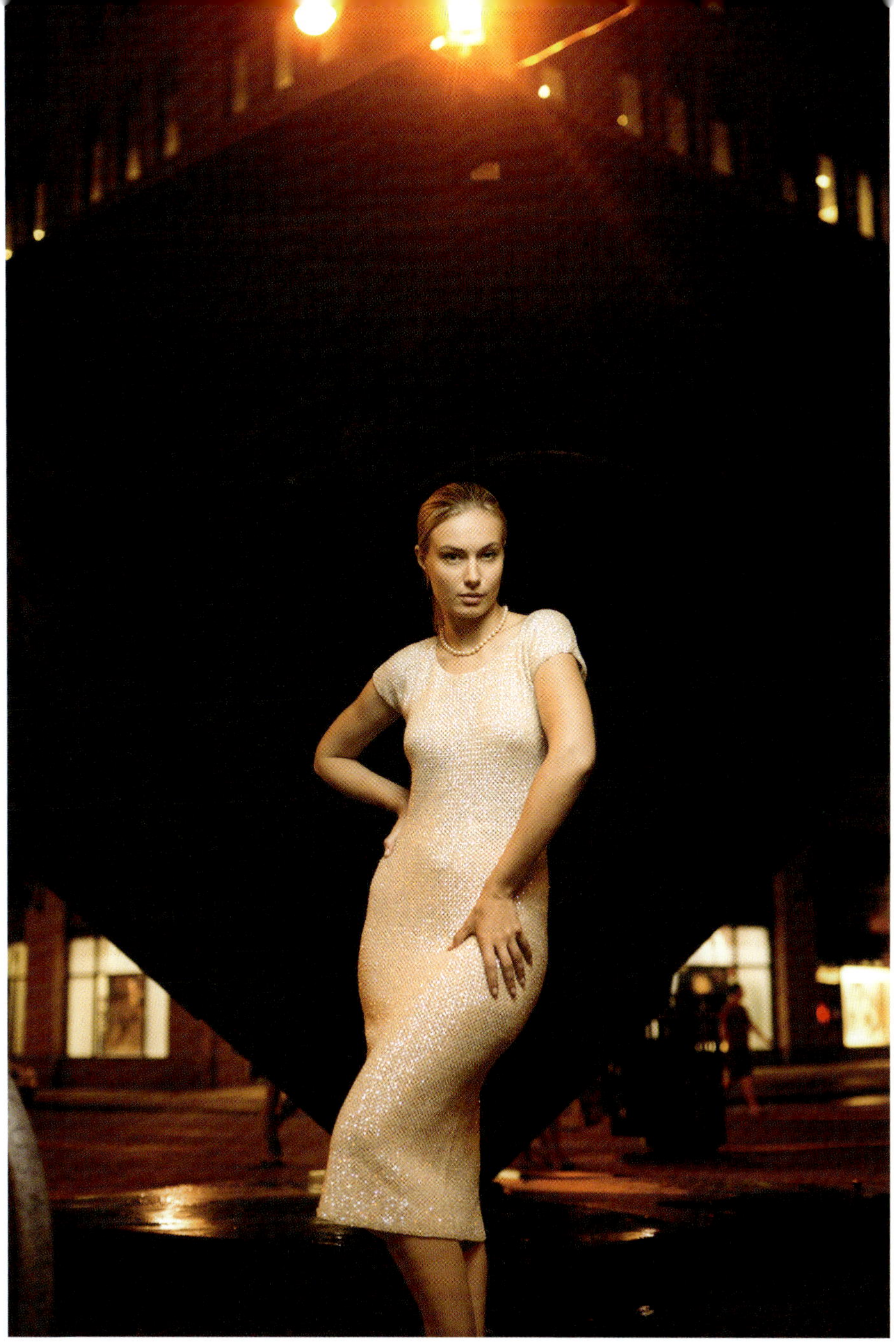

FIGURE 5.12
To create constrast, you can use exposure and lighting ratios, as well as color tempertures to separate the subject from the background. In this contrasty photo, the model is lit by an ungelled speedlight bounced into a Westcott 60-inch umbrella. Because the flash is ungelled, the background lights are warm and yellow, whereas the foreground is daylight balanced. Because of how we illumiated the scene, the background light is allowed to go dark to further separate the model from the rest of the scene.

Balance

If you prefer a more natural look to your photo, you'll really get to put this chapter's tools and techniques to work. The reward is a sublty lit image in which the light adds to the photo but doesn't draw as much attention to itself. **Figure 5.13** is a great example balancing things out a bit; compare it to the contrasty Figure 5.12.

The first step was to balance the color temperature of the image so that its cool tone didn't serve as a dead giveaway to the flash's existence. Because the streetlamps at this location were so warm, we applied a full CTO gel to warm up the speedlight. Next, we set the camera's white balance to the Tungsten preset. This way, both the ambient and the flash light became the same color and the camera was dialed in to represent them accurately. Notice how much more natural the result looks?

Finally, we addressed the difference in brightness between the background and the model. The flash was already balanced and exposed perfectly, so nothing needed to be changed there. To address the background light only, the best option was to adjust the shutter speed, because shutter speed doesn't impact your flash's output. By dragging the shutter, we gave the background light more time to burn into the exposure. As you can see in Figure 5.13, the results were a brighter background and an overall even feel to the photo.

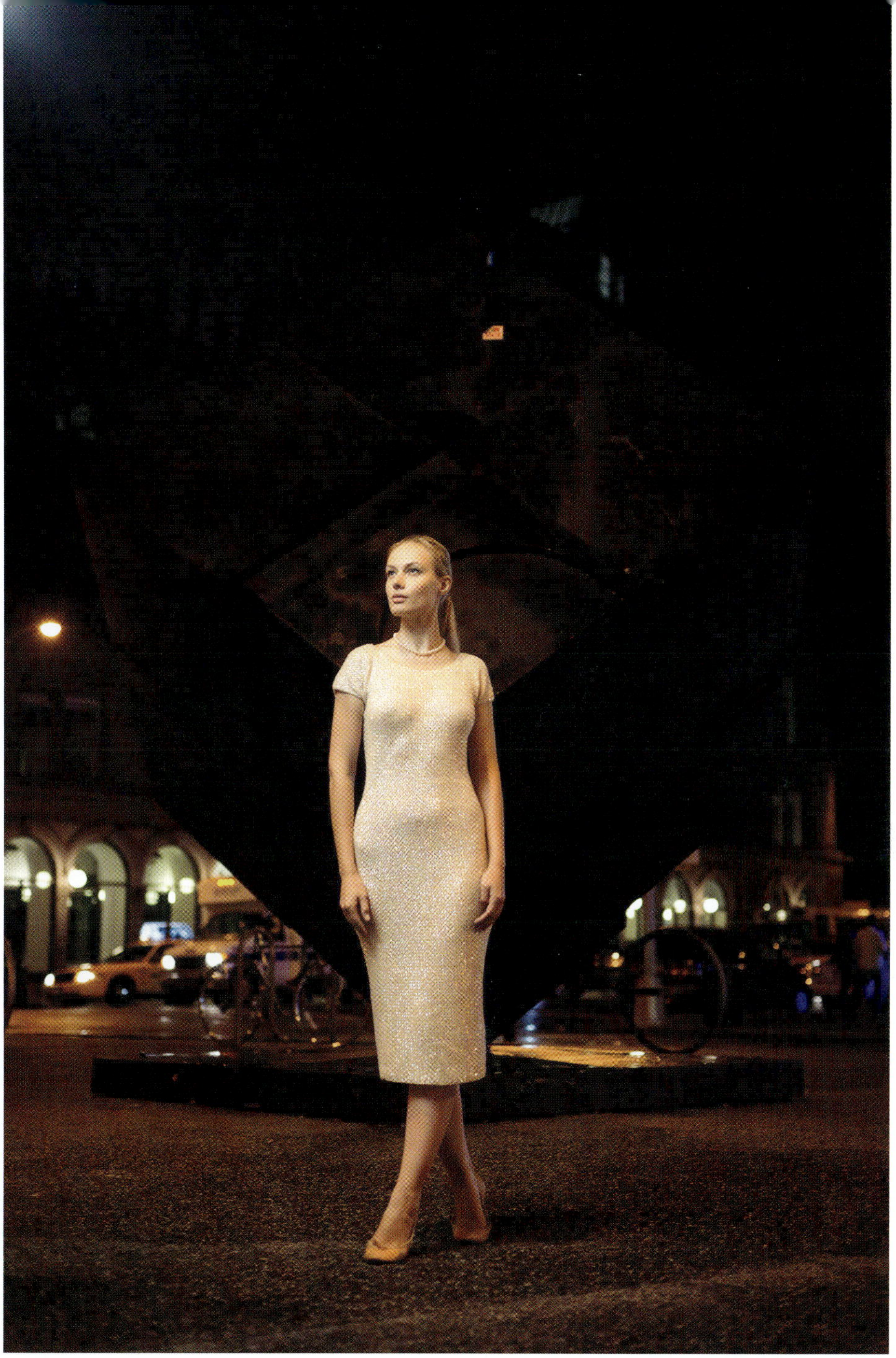

FIGURE 5.13
In this photo, the lighting ratio and color temperature are balanced to create a more even image. We gelled the speedlight to match the temperature of the streetlamps and slowed the shutter speed to allow more ambient light into the photo.

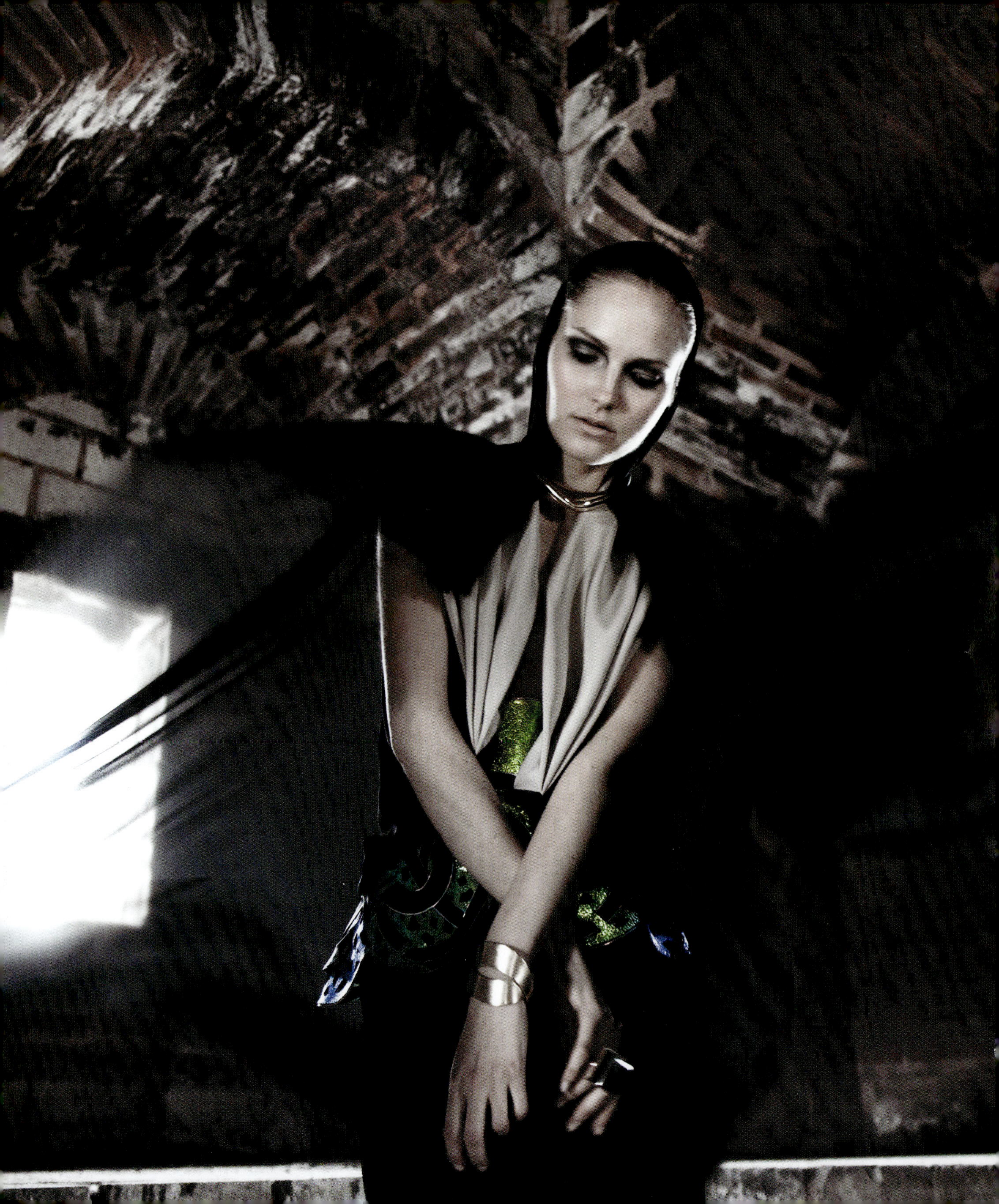

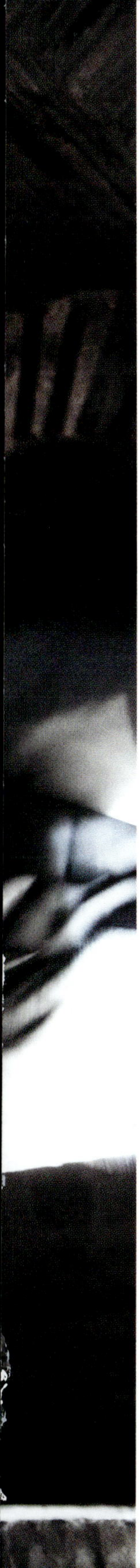

CHAPTER SIX
Extremely Low Light, No Flash Allowed

Does this sound familiar: The wedding is about to start. The church is dimly lit, with almost no illumination on the couple. The guests are ready with their point-and-shoot cameras with built-in flash, and you—the person being paid to photograph the wedding—were instructed not to use flash during the ceremony. The irony is painful, but what can you do?

Good photographs are often a combination of great light and a great moment. But how do you capture that great moment when it happens in low light?

Even if you are shooting in *extremely* low light, pay attention to the direction and quality of light. Just because there is minimal light doesn't mean you can't use your camera to make it appear striking! You have more options than you might think to help ensure your images are as remarkable as the moment.

Drag Your Shutter

You walk into the church after shooting outdoors, and your camera is set to manual exposure. Outside, settings of ISO 400, f/4.0, and 1/160-second exposure looked great. Yet in this dimly lit church, that exposure gives you almost no image at all, as seen in **Figure 6.1**.

The first step towards improving your exposure is to let in more light. To do so, try *dragging your shutter,* which simply means trying longer shutter speeds to correctly expose your image. Remember, "correct" exposure doesn't mean that the image needs to look the same in your camera as it does to the naked eye. Instead, you can overexpose according to what your in-camera light meter reads to create a more ideal representation of the light. For example, changing your shutter speed to 1/30 sec begins to let in more light, but the image is still too dark (**Figure 6.2**). Unfortunately, long shutter speeds make you more vulnerable to blurry photos from camera shake. Approaching a shutter speed of 1/10 sec vastly improves the exposure but starts to reveal camera shake (**Figure 6.3**). At a shutter speed of 1/4 sec, the exposure is great, but everything else is a blurry mess (**Figure 6.4**). You need to stabilize the image by adjusting a few other components to perfect the shot.

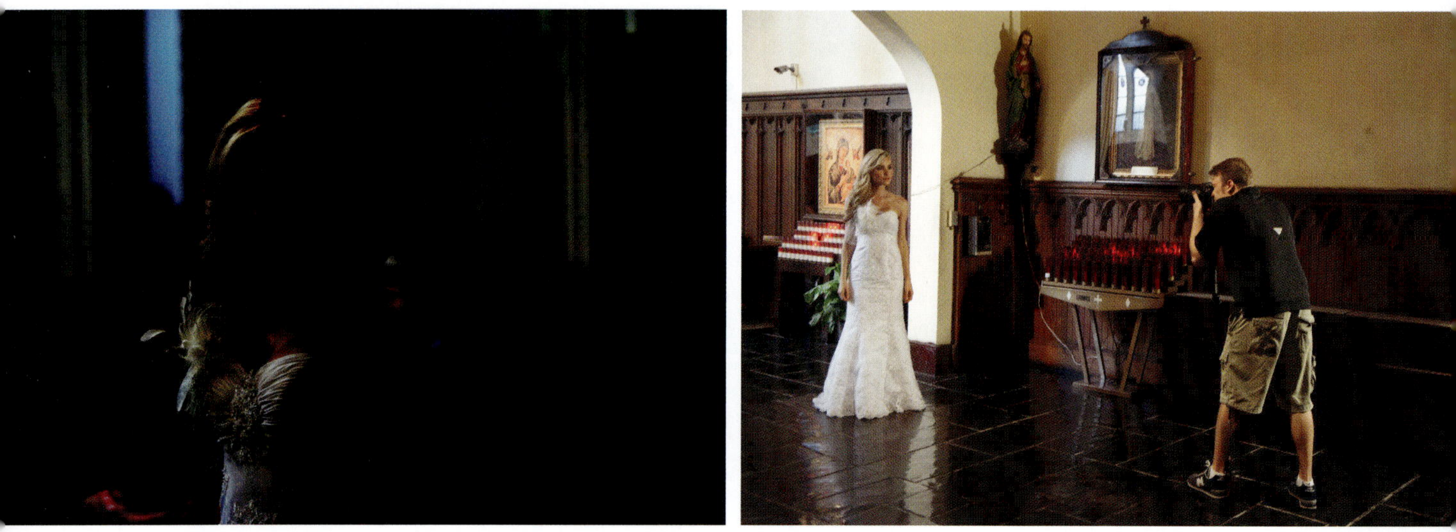

FIGURE 6.1
If you come indoors with your camera on manual shooting and the same settings as you used outside for the wedding (ISO 400, f/4.0, 1/160 sec), your image will be almost nonexistent.

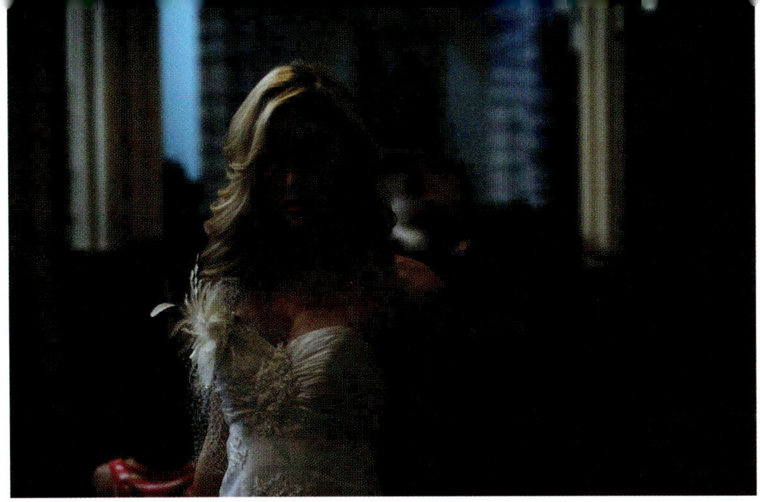

FIGURE 6.2
To improve the exposure, use a slower shutter speed to let in more light. You will have a longer exposure. Here 1/30 sec is still not sufficient for a correct exposure.

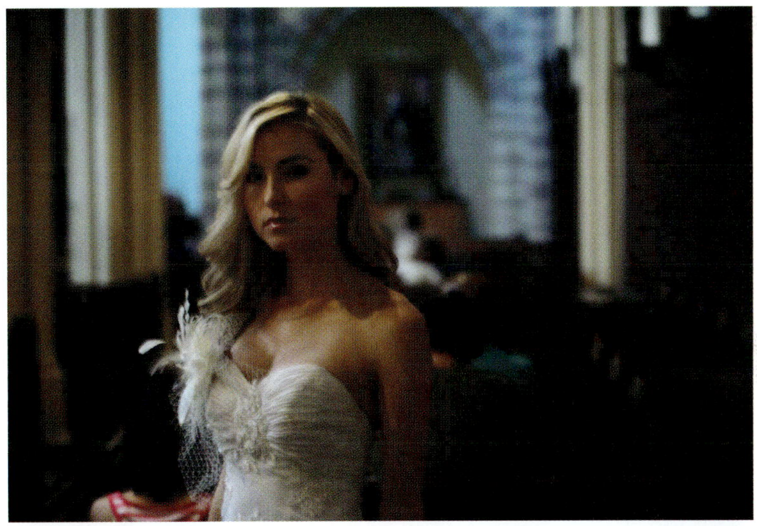

FIGURE 6.3
At a shutter speed of 1/10 sec, the image is not quite light enough and slightly out of focus from camera shake.

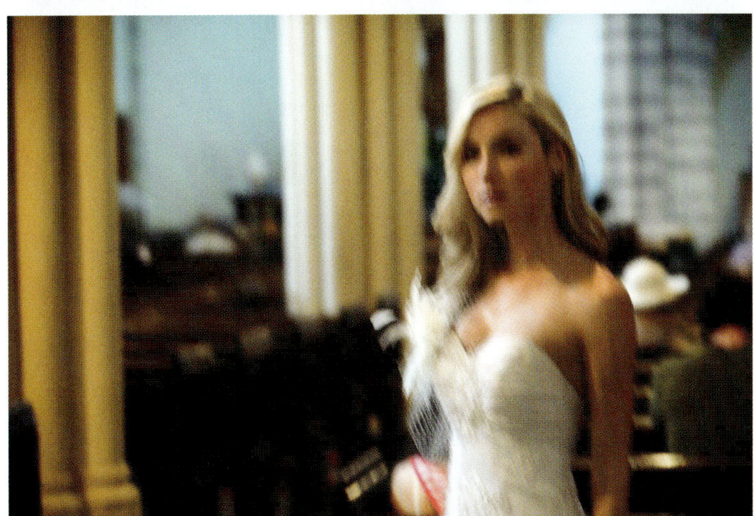

FIGURE 6.4
A setting of 1/4 sec finally achieves an ideal exposure, but the image is extremely blurry due to camera shake. You need to employ a few more techniques to produce a correctly lit, focused image.

Try an Image-Stabilized Lens

No matter how steely your resolve, holding a camera perfectly still by hand is practically impossible, especially for long exposures in low light.

As a general rule, you don't want to shoot slower than 1/focal length of lens. For example, if you shoot a 24mm lens, don't hand hold shots for longer than 1/24 second. Remembering this rule becomes even more critical when you're shooting at longer focal lengths. You should be extremely careful when trying to hold a 70–200mm lens by hand, when shooting at 200mm, because any camera shake becomes amplified. In this case, you'll not want to shoot slower than 1/200 sec.

If you are forced to hold your lens for longer exposures than desired, consider using an IS (Image-Stabilization) or VR (Vibration-Reduction) lens to help reduce blurring caused by camera motion. Some manufacturers have different names for this, as seen in the Canon and Nikon variations, but the function stays the same. The lens itself helps to compensate and correct for camera shake to provide you with a better image. These lenses do cost more than their nonstabilized counterparts, but if you shoot in low light often, an image-stabilized lens might be a great investment. For **Figure 6.5**, Erik used a 70–200mm VR lens to vastly improve the sharpness in the image.

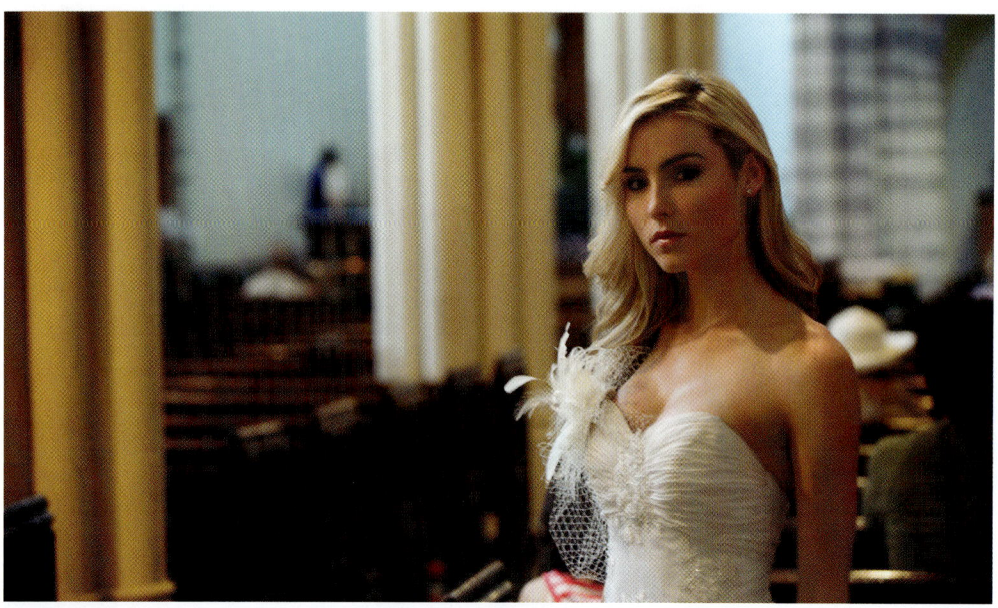

FIGURE 6.5
When shooting at a very slow shutter speed (here 1/4 sec), using an image-stabilized lens will help you achieve critical focus.

Use a Tripod

Another way to avoid camera shake is to use a tripod. Pick one that is sturdy while still light and easy to transport, such as a carbon-fiber tripod. Compare **Figures 6.6** and **6.7**, both shot at ISO 400 f/5.6, 1/3 sec. As you can see in Figure 6.7, attempting to hold this long exposure by hand results in blur, but switching to a tripod for **Figure 6.8** achieves a tack-sharp image. When using a telephoto lens, consider mounting the lens to the tripod using a lens collar instead of the body of the camera. By mounting the lens to the tripod, you are changing the balance point and therefore increasing the stability of the lens. Most telephoto lenses come with a lense collar already attached.

Tripods, however, are not a cure-all. They can get in the way, particularly at crowded events. When space is limited, consider using a monopod to help give you that steadier hand, while creating a much smaller footprint on the ground. Also, if your subject moves during a long exposure, your image will still be blurry even if your camera is stock-still on a tripod. In other words, tripods are most useful when you have a lot of space and your subjects aren't moving around too much. Individual or group portraits in lower light will benefit from a tripod.

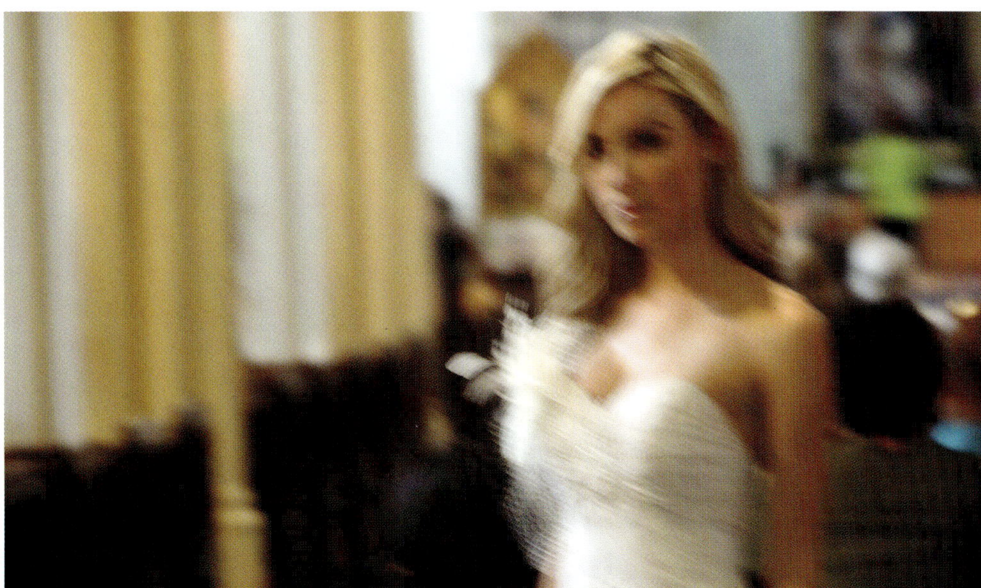

FIGURE 6.6
The image requires a long, 1/3-sec shutter speed to achieve the right exposure, and is out of focus when shot with the camera in hand.

FIGURE 6.7
Switching to a carbon-fiber Manfotto tripod for the 1/3-sec exposure prevents camera shake.

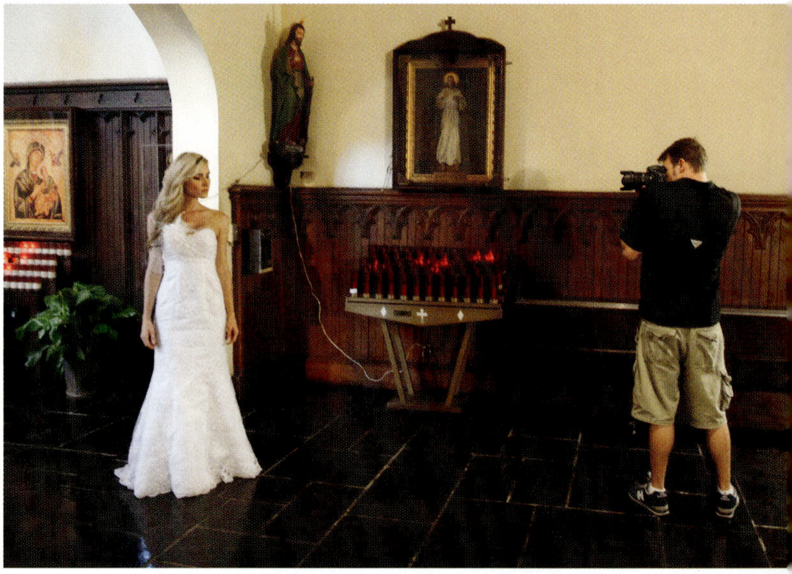

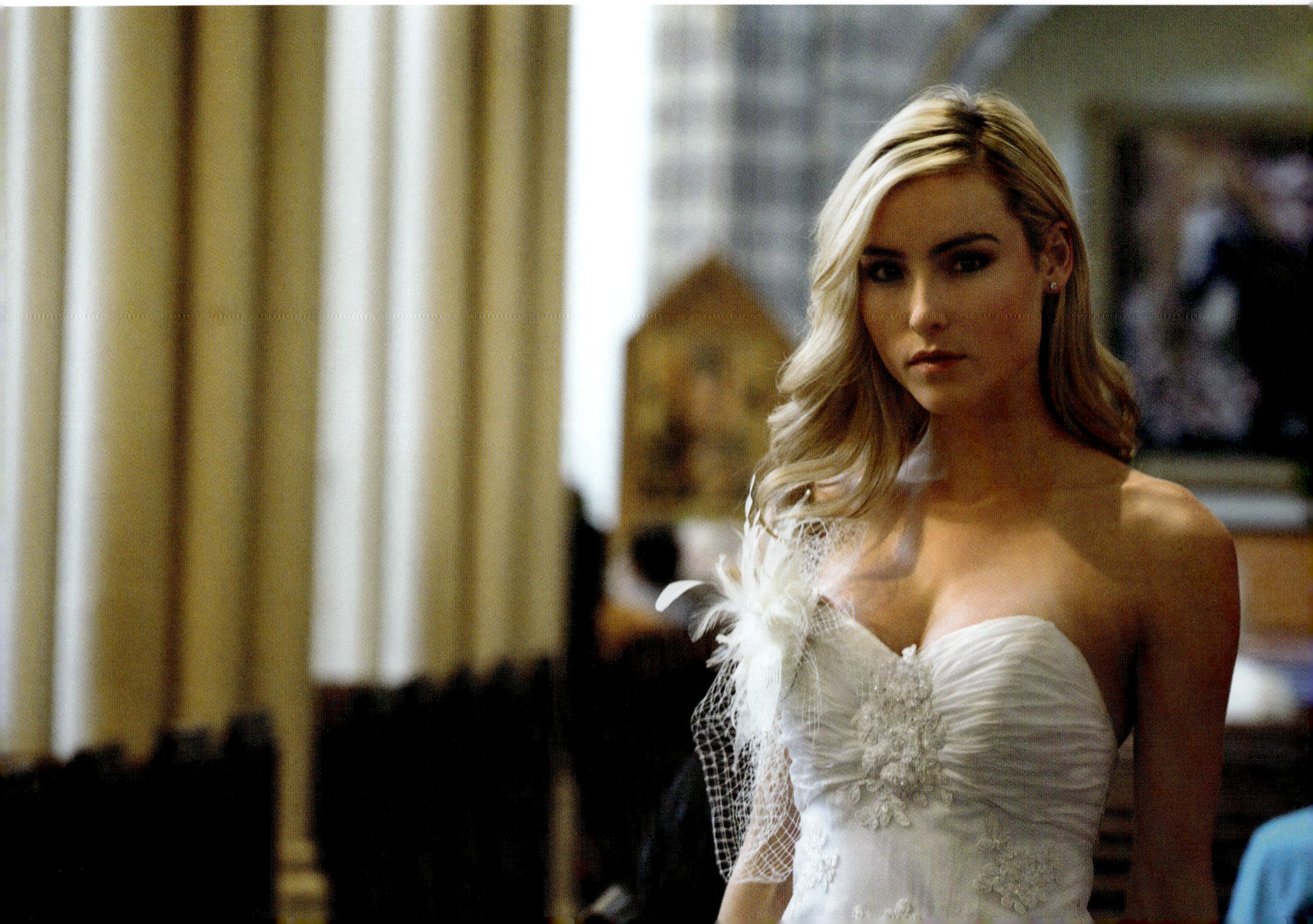

TAKEAWAY ACTION

When taking photographs in a low light situation, stagger your legs, bend your knees, and keep your elbows firm to your sides. A solid stance like this reduces the opportunity for camera shake. Exhaling slowly and squeezing the trigger—instead of stabbing at it—will minimize camera shake at slow shutter speeds as well.

Shoot with a Fast Glass

When shooting in low-light situations, a lens with wide aperture capabilities, also called **fast glass**, is a must have. Using lenses with larger apertures enables you to let more light into the lens. This means you can use faster shutter speeds than you would with a standard lens, thereby reducing the chance for camera shake and the resulting motion blur. When choosing a lens for a low-light situation, try to shoot with as wide aperture as possible. Often this means shooting at f/2.8 or wider. Shooting at a wide aperture produces a narrower depth of field, which will help you to simplify busy backgrounds by letting them fall out of focus. Figure 6.8 features the correct exposure but against a static and uninspiring background. Switching to an f/1.4 lens minimizes the background and downplays distractions, as you can see in Figure 6.8.

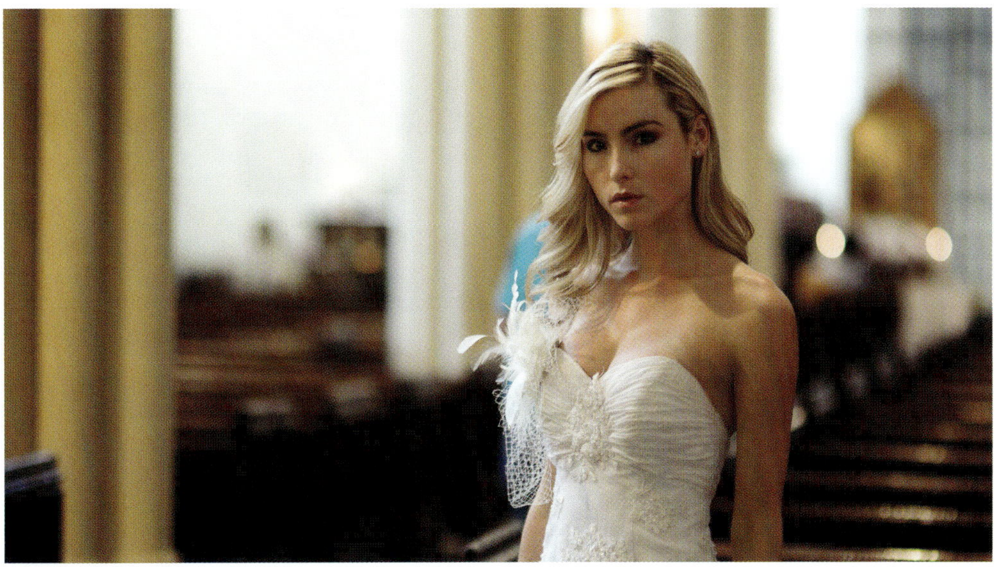

FIGURE 6.8
Shooting at a very wide aperture (f/1.4) and ISO 400 enabled us to achieve a sharp image at a shutter speed of 1/30 sec, higher than usual for this light.

Increase to a High ISO

To create well-exposed images in low-light situations, you can also try increasing your ISO setting from the common 200 or 400 (**Figure 6.9**). ISO is the measurement of film's or a sensor's sensitivity to light. The higher the ISO number, the more sensitive the sensor is to light, and therefore less light is necessary for the same exposure.

With the earliest digital cameras, you didn't want to increase your ISO above 400 because you would begin to see noise in your image, which is digital photography's equivalent to film grain. **Noise** is unwanted texture or detail in an image caused by electrical fluctuations from a camera's sensor set at high sensitivity. In recent years, however, camera sensor technology has improved drastically, meaning you can now shoot at ISO 1600 and above without a ruinous amount of noise (**Figure 6.10**). In fact, the newest cameras enable you to shoot astronomically high ISOs, near 200,000—almost enough to shoot in complete darkness!

Yet just because you *can* do something doesn't mean you *should.* As you increase your ISO, you enable yourself to shoot at faster shutter speeds, but you also increase the noise in your image. It's all a trade off. Keep in mind that final file output and use will help determine how essential perfect focus and minimal grain are. For example, an image that will be displayed as a four-foot-wide print on a wall will require significantly less grain than an image that will appear in an online gallery only.

A noisy image is better than a blurry image or not getting the shot at all, but at what point is the noise too much? The answer is a matter of taste, and we recommend you do a bit of testing and research. Check out reviews online to see at which ISOs noise becomes noticeable. Do tests for yourself. Shoot in low light at various ISOs, and compare the images side by side at 100% zoom. You'll quickly be able to make judgments about what is acceptable noise for your purposes.

TAKEAWAY ACTION

Try a tripod, higher ISO, fast glass, or image-stabilized lenses to achieve tack-sharp focus in low light.

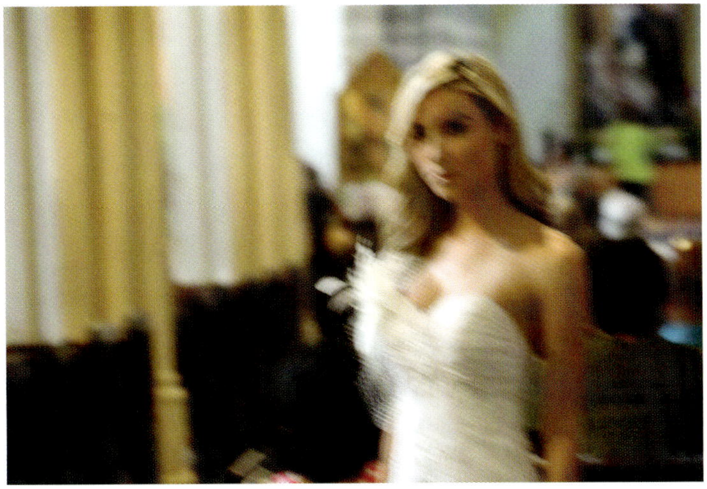

FIGURE 6.9
Shooting at a low ISO like 400 shown here means that the sensor is not very sensitive to light. Although the image has minimal noise, the low ISO combined with an f/4.0 aperture and 1/4-second exposure makes the shot difficult to hold steady by hand.

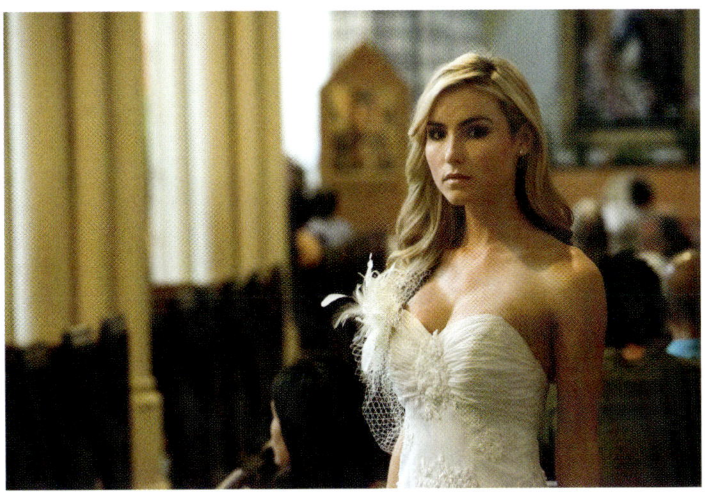

FIGURE 6.10
Nowadays, you can use extremely high ISOs to improve your camera sensor's light sensitivity. Although the noise level in this image is not ideal, ultra-high ISOs, like the 25600 ISO used here, are now acceptable with certain shots. This will depend on your camera quality and also the final output use of the image.

EQUIPMENT TIP Try noise reduction software.

Many software companies offer solutions for reducing noise in your images during post-production. Starting with version 3, Adobe Lightroom, for example, includes some phenomenal noise-reduction tools that enable you to significantly decrease the appearance of noise in your images. Noise Ninja (Picture Code, picturecode.com), Topaz DeNoise (Topaz Labs, www.topazlabs.com), and Noiseware (Imagenomic, imagenomic.com) offer similar capabilities as well. If you feel like experimenting, you can find free downloadable trials of all four online.

Combine It!

When shooting in low-light situations, use all the tools at your disposal (**Figure 6.11**). If flash isn't permitted, you can increase the ISO setting, use a fast lens, set up a tripod, or try an image-stabilization lens. Which option do we recommend? Combine them all!

Move or Re-enact

Sometimes lenses and settings can do only so much in low light. When all else fails, you can try manipulating your subjects instead.

If possible, move your subjects near some sort of light source. Even if the window is only dimly lit, move them closer to the window or an open doorway with light. Do your best to give yourself a little more light to work with.

Although you always want to do your best to capture the moments while they happen, sometimes extenuating circumstances take over. In these cases, consider re-enacting the scene. For example, wedding photographers frequently re-enact the exchanging of rings after the ceremony so that they can get additional angles and better light. Re-enacting a scene is certainly not your go-to solution, but it is another option when no flash is permitted.

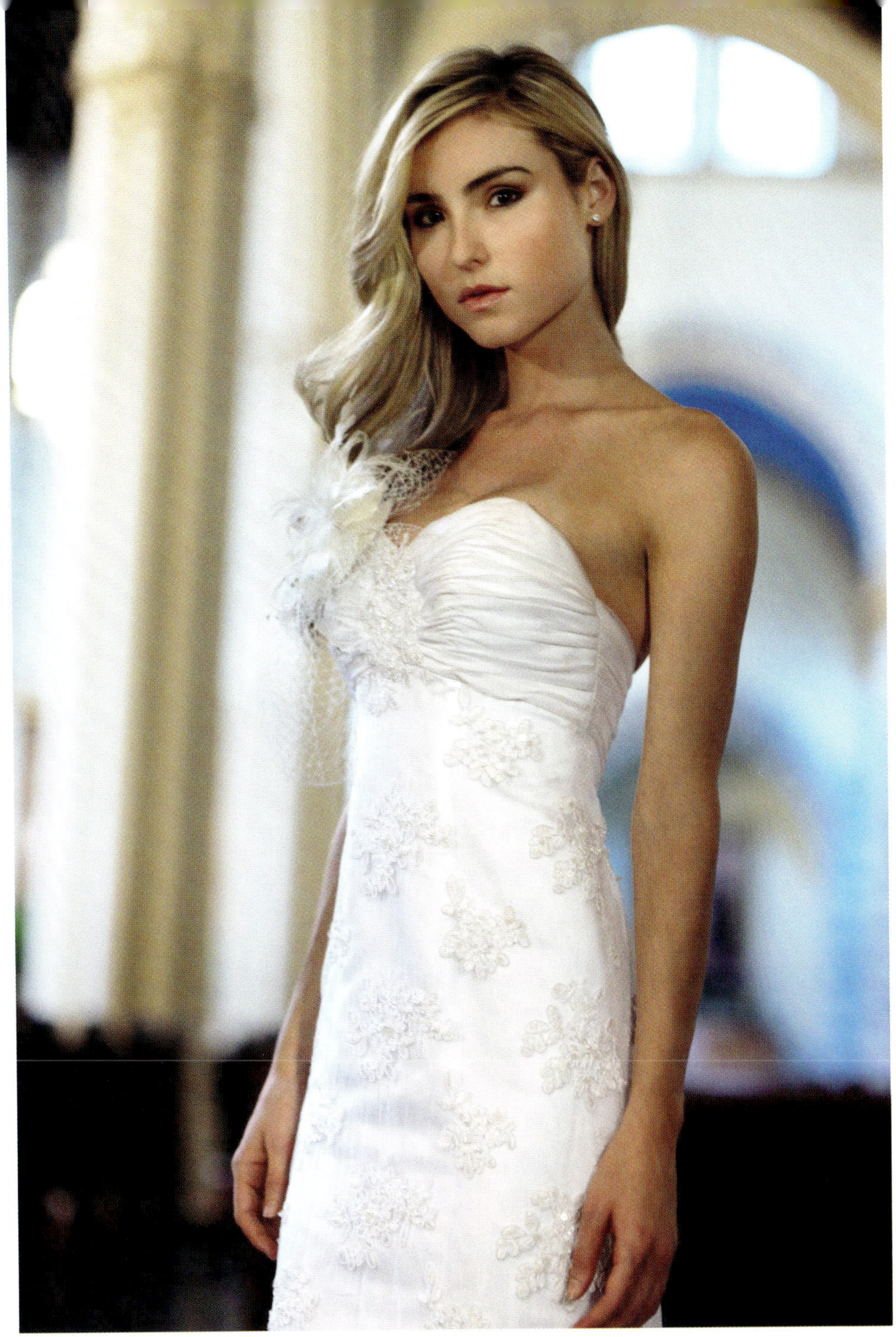

FIGURE 6.11
Combining fast glass and a high ISO setting, you can achieve in-focus images, even in low light. Here, Erik used an ISO of 800, aperture of f/2.2, and exposure of 1/20 sec.

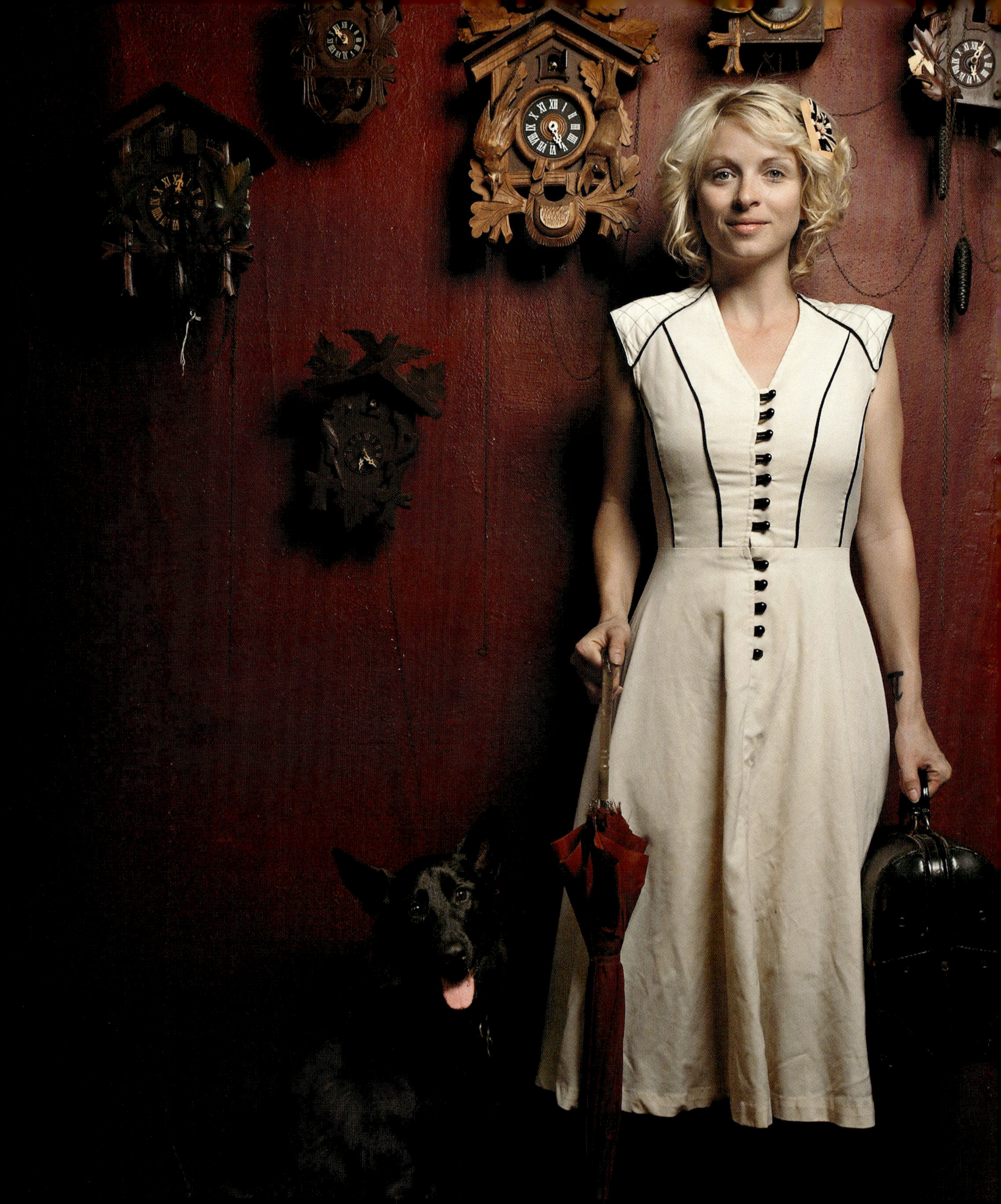

CHAPTER SEVEN Low Light with Flash

Whether shooting indoors or in the evening, low-light situations seem to be the rule rather than the exception. When you walk into a room to photograph an event or a wedding reception, you are almost certain to be walking into the dark. Event coordinators love candlelight and dim house lights to help create an ambiance within a space. Unfortunately, this doesn't give us photographers much light to work with—unless we bring our own. With the proper flash and a few techniques, you'll be able to overcome this lack of light to create captivating images in any kind of room.

Try On-Camera Flash

Think of your speedlight as a fancy headlight for your camera. The default placement for it is on top of your camera, connected via the hot shoe, and firing dead ahead. Unfortunately, this placement usually leaves your subjects looking like a deer in the headlights as seen in **Figure 7.1**.

The solution is to ratchet the head of your speedlight around to a more advantageous direction. Rather than blasting your subject with a hard, direct beam of light, you can angle the flash head to bounce light off things around the room. As the light bounces, the originally small beam of light spreads out. By the time it hits your subject, the light will be similar to the light of a large softbox.

In **Figure 7.2**, for example, we turned the flash head 90 degrees to the left. All the light now hits the wall then bounces back to illuminate the model. Notice the incredible difference in the quality of light from this small redirection.

What if it's not always possible or practical to drag your subjects near a wall? Apply the same bouncing technique, except fire the flash straight up and turn the ceiling into a large softbox. **Figure 7.3** demonstrates this technique. Notice the widespread, soft quality of the light shining down. In many event halls for receptions or parties, this is an easy and effective solution.

Although this overhead light is much more flattering than the harsh direct flash, it isn't quite perfect. Now that the light is shining down from directly overhead, it creates shadows in the model's eyes. See how lifeless they became in Figure 7.3? Because no light hits the model's eyes, they have no **catchlight**; there's no spark to them. With a bit of bounce help, however, you can achieve the best of both worlds.

Some speedlights have a built-in bounce card. When you aim your flash up towards the ceiling, this bounce card sticks up and redirects a small amount of the flash forward, hitting the subject directly. This direct light creates a small sparkle in the eye and fills in some of those shadows under the eyebrows.

Although they're a step in the right direction, built-in bounce cards are too small to do much good. Instead, try a modifier like ExpoImaging's Rogue FlashBender (www.expoimaging.com). Attached to your speedlight, it acts like a super-sized bounce card, while still letting the majority of the light shine up to bounce off the ceiling. In **Figure 7.4**, you can see the perfect combination of ceiling bounce with a push of soft on-camera flash from the Rogue FlashBender. You get the soft overhead light and plenty of fill around the eyes, along with that all-important sparkle. The FlashBender is one of our preferred solutions, but there are dozens of modifiers available on the market.

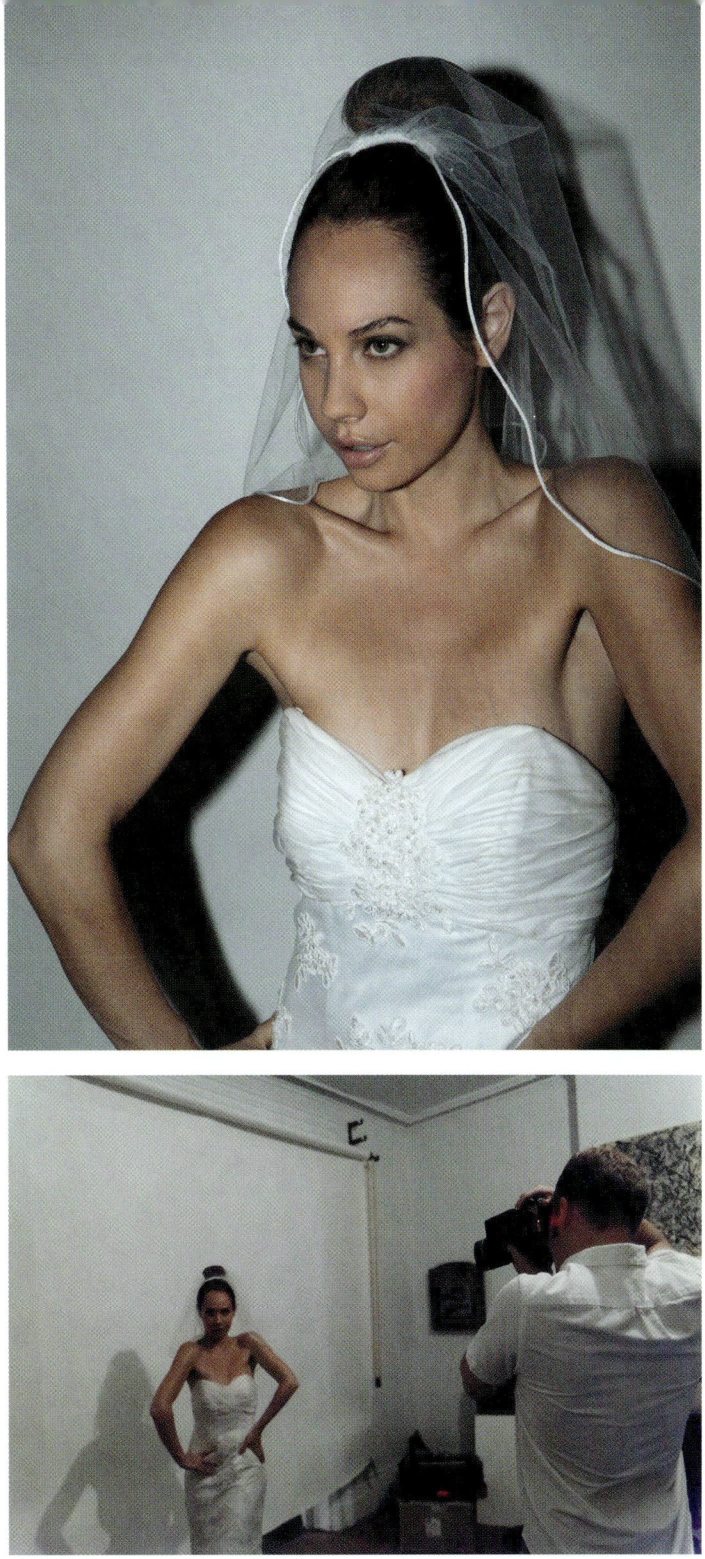

❌ **FIGURE 7.1**
Placing your speedlight on top of the camera does not produce optimum results. The light is harsh and unflattering. Instead, you will want to bounce your flash off the walls or ceiling, or add a flash modifier.

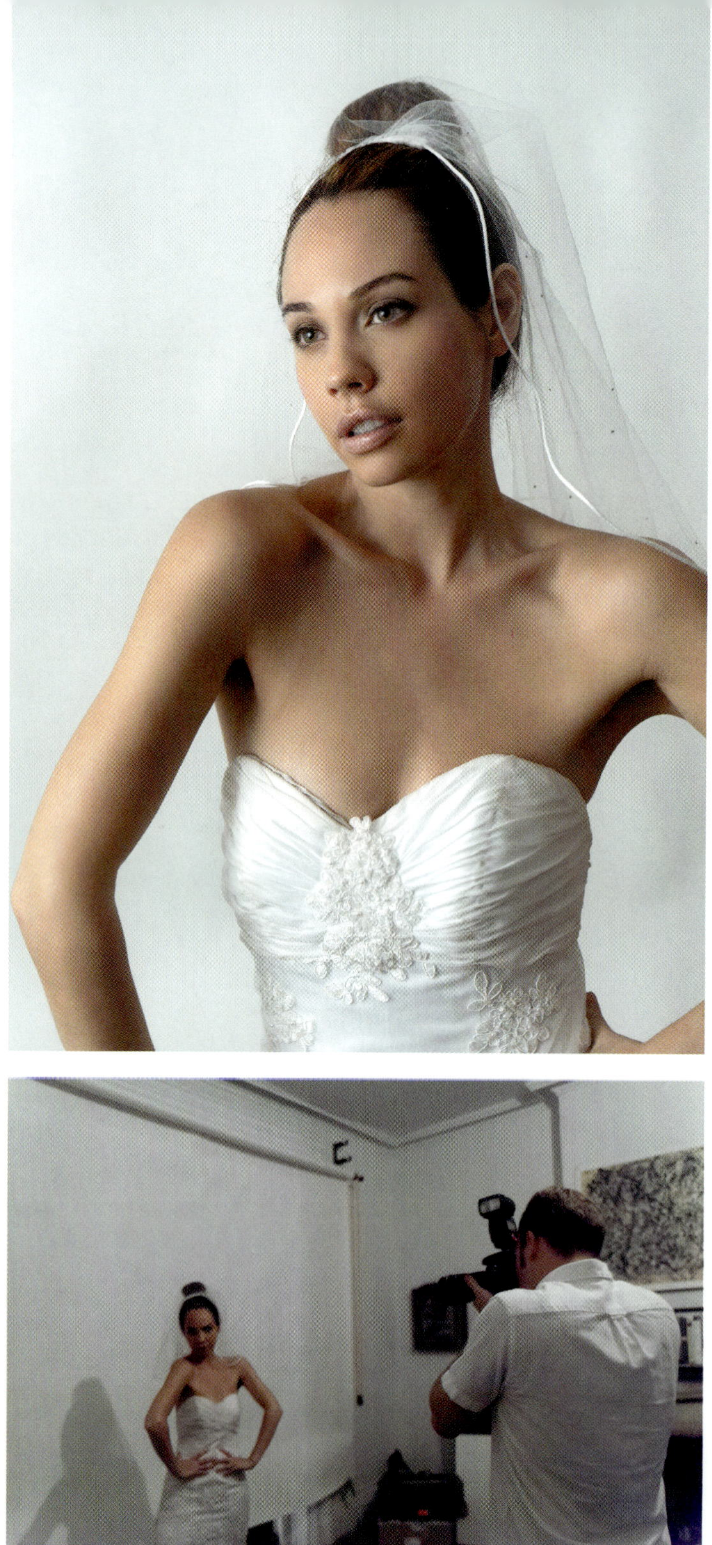

FIGURE 7.2
When you take control of the exposure in a backlit situation, you can correctly expose for your subject. To create a soft side light, aim the speedlight to the left at a white wall, which bounces the light back onto the model. This turns the wall into a large, soft reflector of light.

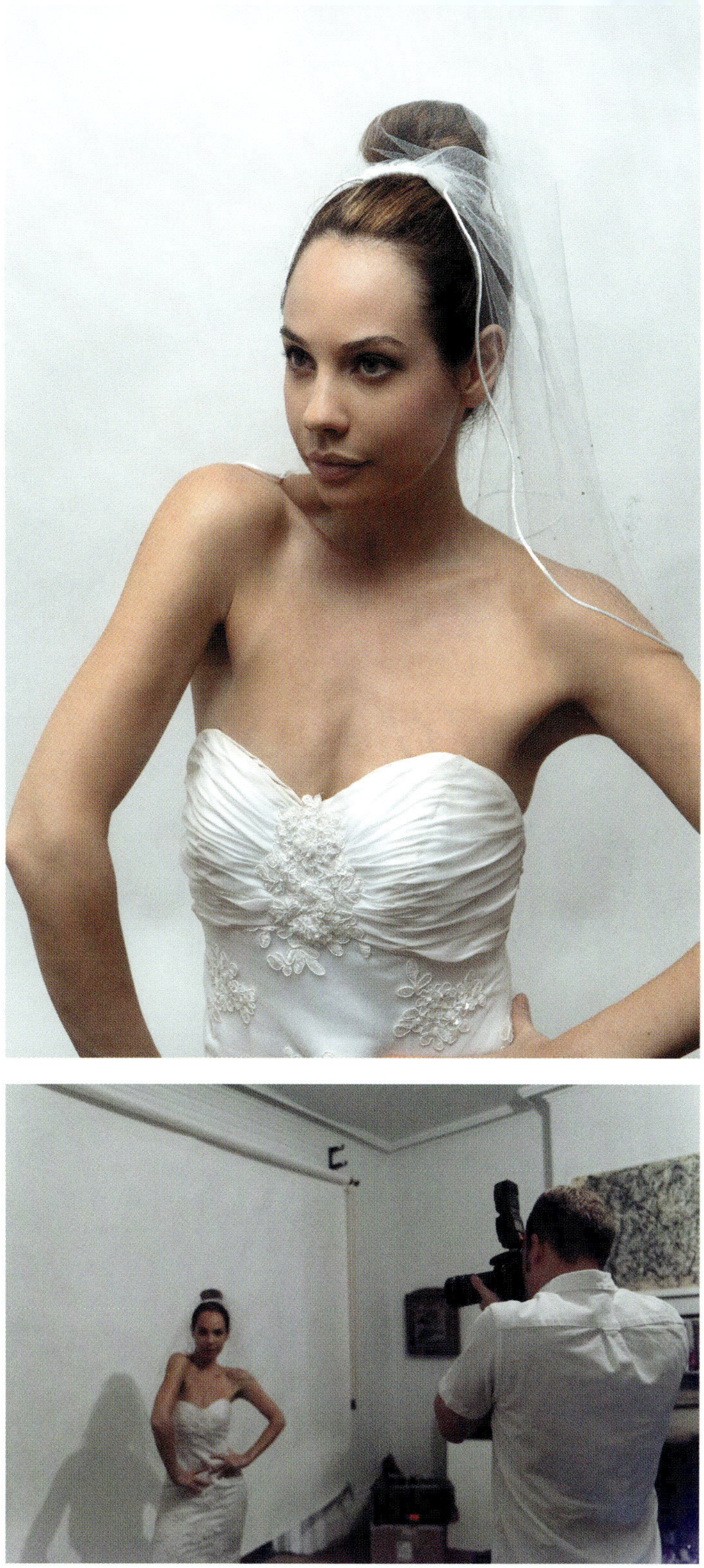

FIGURE 7.3
Try firing your speedlight straight up into a white ceiling. The light will bounce back down onto the model, creating soft, overhead lighting.

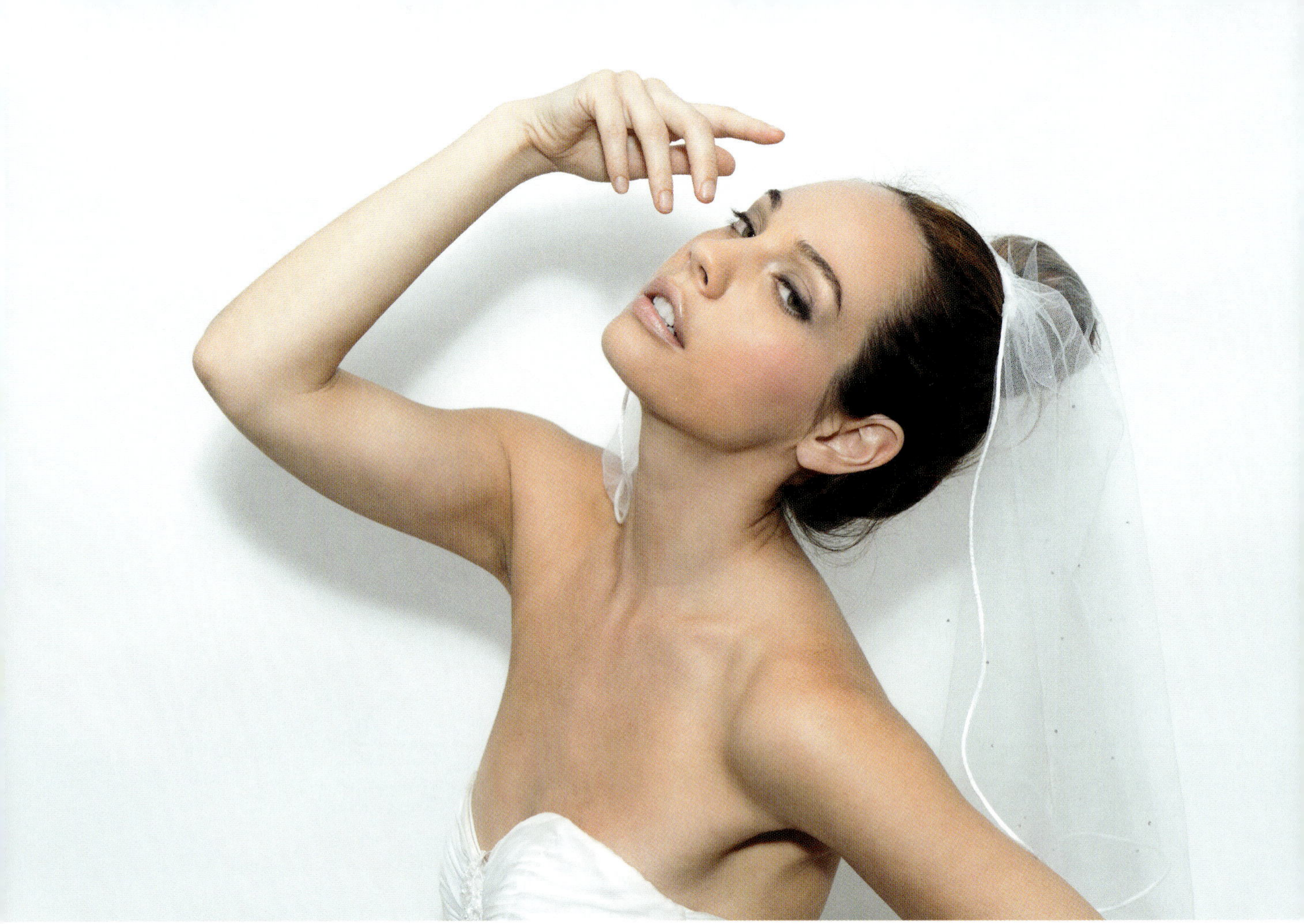

FIGURE 7.4
When you take control of the exposure in a backlit situation, you can correctly expose for your subject. The speedlight in this shot fires straight up onto a white ceiling. Helping to bounce and fill simultaneously, a Rogue FlashBender redirects some of the light towards the model to fill in shadows under the brows and to spark the eyes.

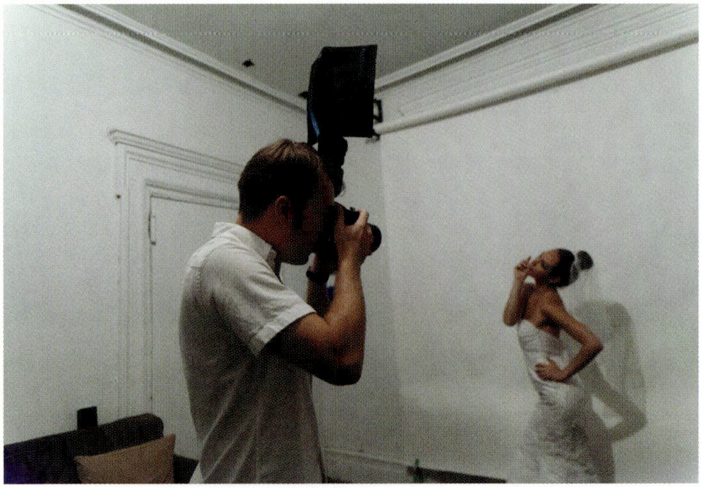

WATCH IT! Bounce off neutral surfaces only.

Bouncing is a great tool for softening the light and improving the direction of light, but choose your bounce surfaces carefully. Bouncing off colored, non-neutral surfaces will create a color cast in the image—not the effect you want. Bounce off neutral or white surfaces only.

The success of these bounce techniques has to do with the qualities of soft light. The soft wrapping quality of light is ideal for portraits and photographing people in general. The larger and closer your light source is in relation to your subject, the softer that light will be.

You may not be able to raise or lower the ceiling to vary the softness of the light, but you can move your subject closer to a nearby wall for better results. Notice in **Figures 7.5**, **7.6**, and **7.7** how the shadows become more pronounced as the model gets farther away from the wall. In Figure 7.5, the model is right next to the wall and the light bouncing off it is powerful, so the light quality becomes very soft with minimal shadows. In Figure 7.7, the model is five to seven feet away from the wall. Because she's farther from the wall, the light quality is harder with more contrasty shadows on the side of her face.

Which setup you use depends on your taste. Understanding how the distance affects your light quality gives you the knowledge to paint with the light you want; no longer will you be at the mercy of a room's existing light.

TAKEAWAY ACTIONS

- When bouncing light off a wall, the closer the subject is to the wall, the softer and broader the light source.
- Try not to use direct flash on camera. Ideally, you would either bounce your flash off a neutral wall or ceiling, or use a modifier to soften the light.

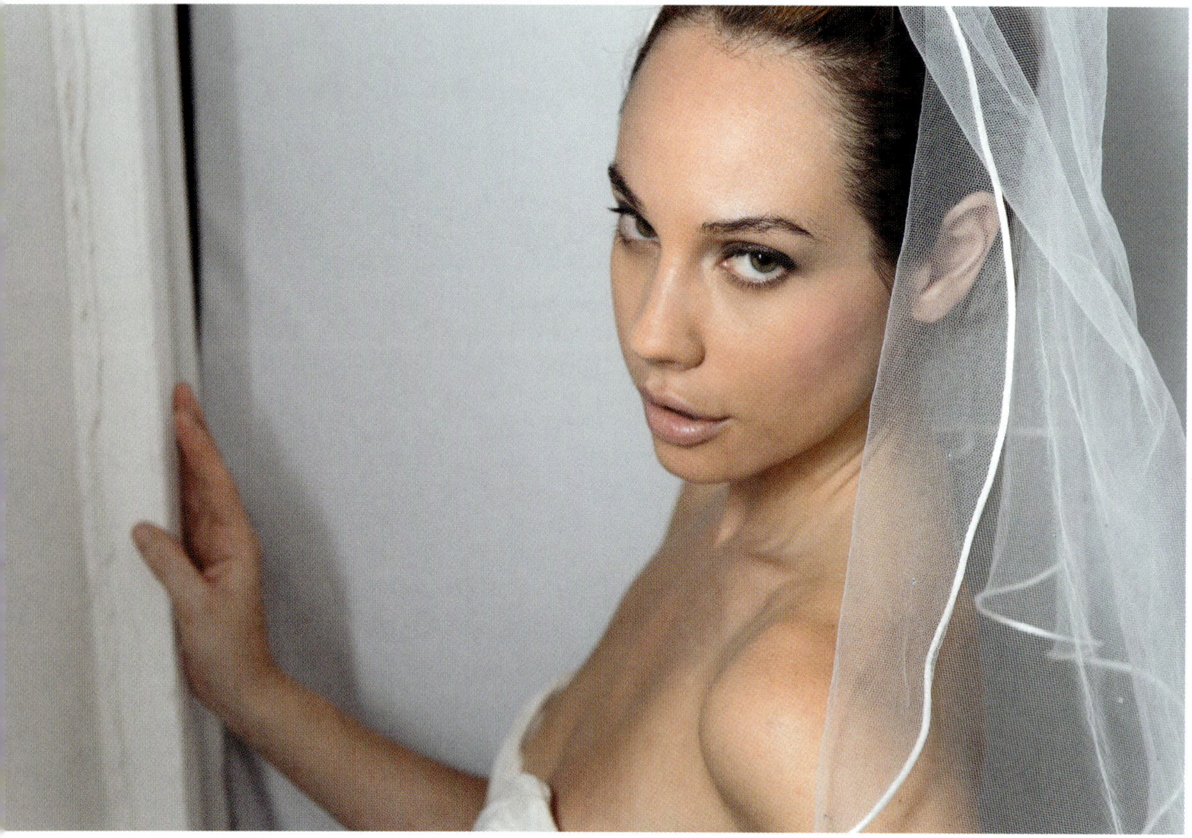

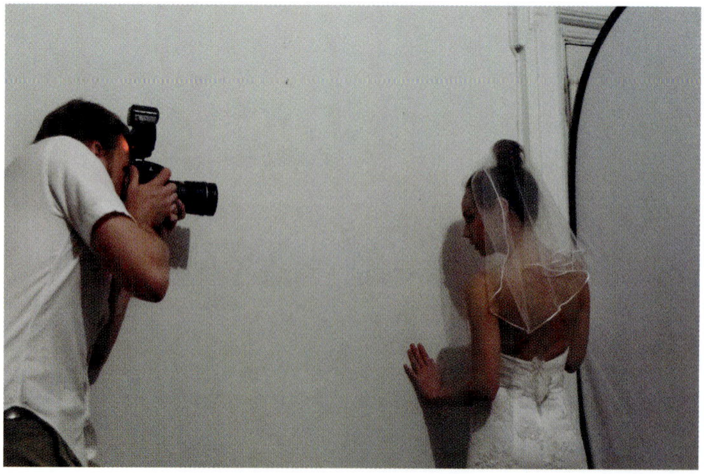

FIGURE 7.5
Here a bare speedlight aims at the wall, which bounces light back at the model. The model is standing right up against the wall, so the resulting light quality is soft and wrapping.

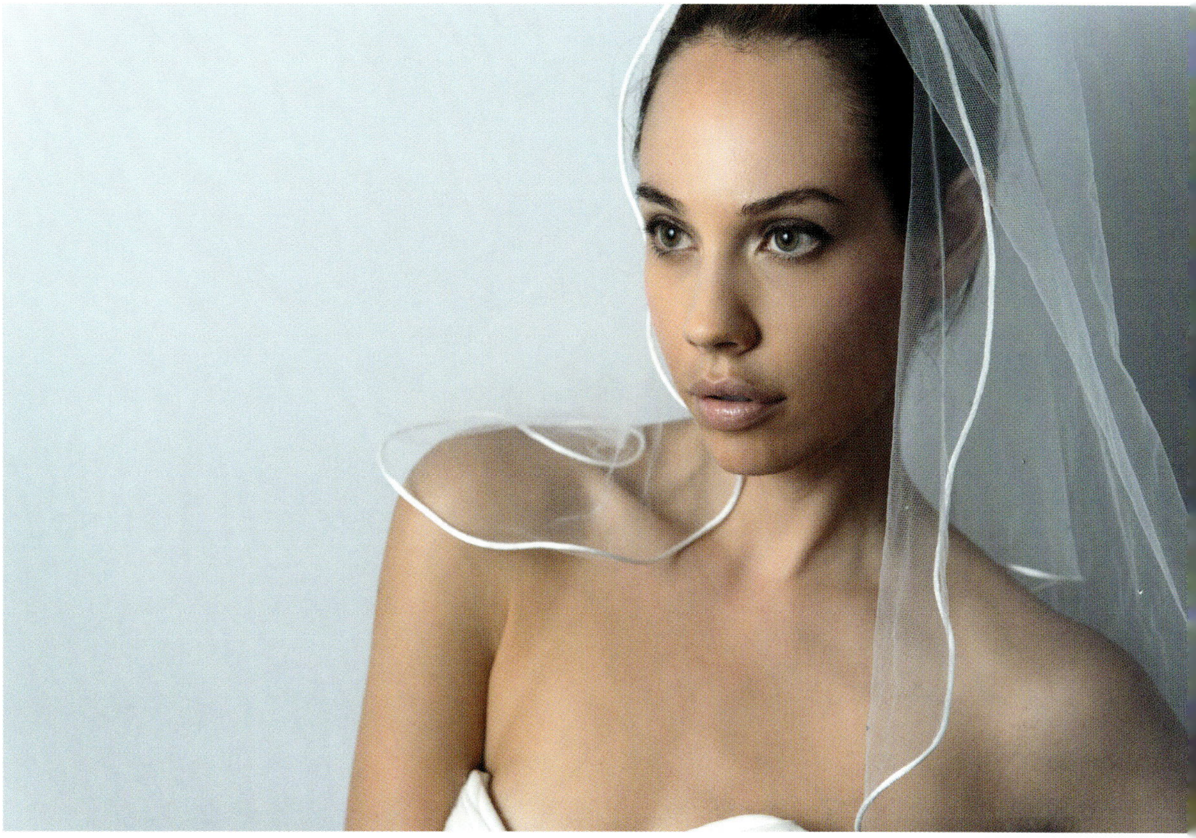

FIGURE 7.6

With the model now a few feet away from the wall, the light source (the wall) is now farther away and the resulting light quality is less soft. This can be seen in the shadows appearing on the model's cheek.

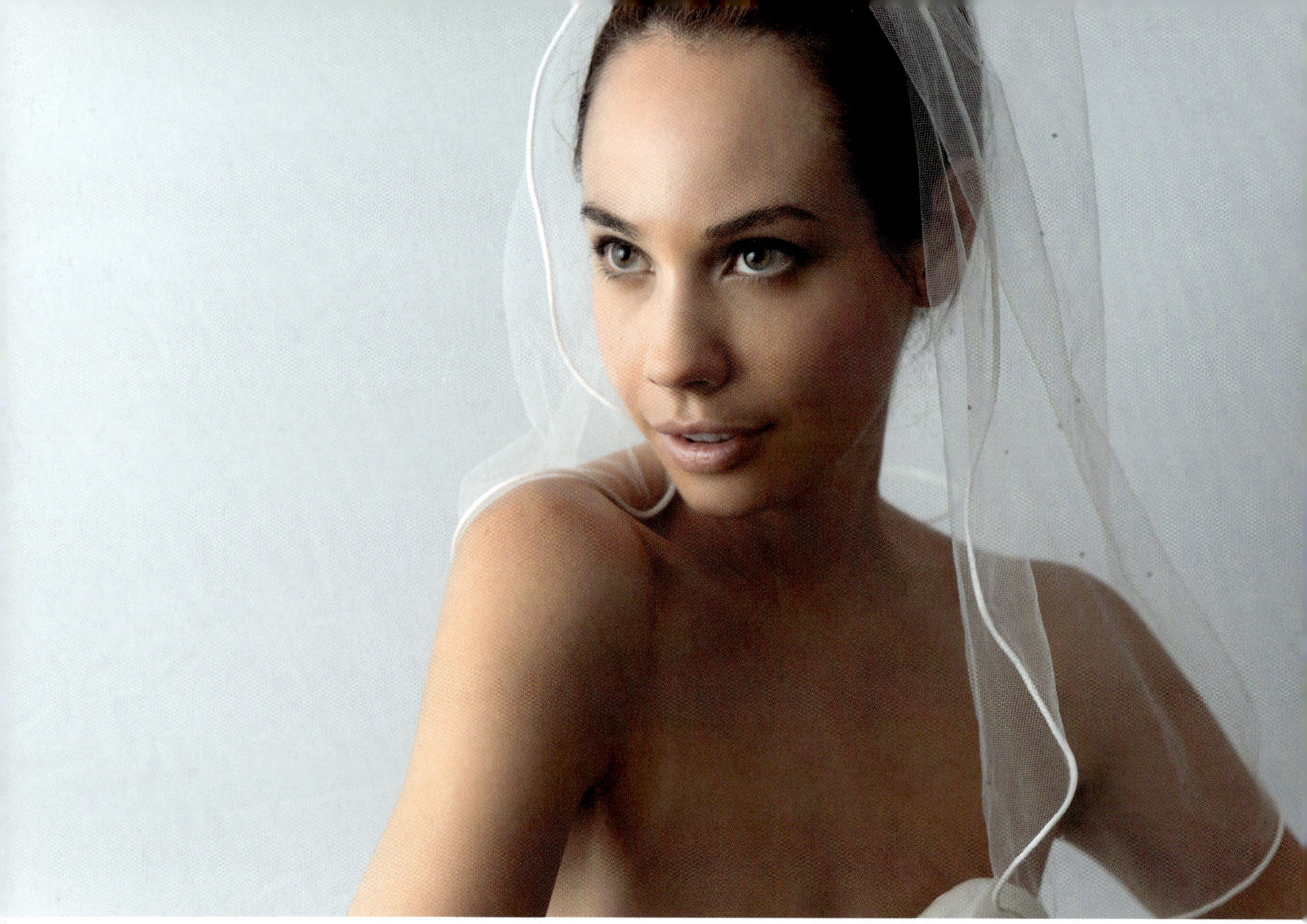

FIGURE 7.7
Stepping into the middle of the room moves the model a good distance from the wall (at least 7 feet). The light quality is now much more harsh and creates more contrast on the model's face, sculpting her cheek with a darker shadow. The final quality of light is your preference, but knowing how distance affects the quality of light gives you control.

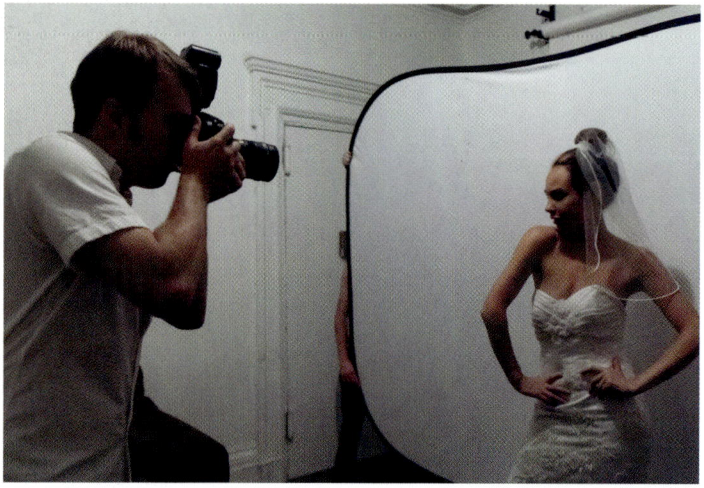

Modify on Location

All of these techniques are great tools to have in your belt, but someday you may be asked to take pictures outside of your white-walled comfort zone. Consider an extreme worst-case scenario: The location seems picturesque at first glance, with bright red walls accented by bold patterns—a visually interesting background to say the least. Unfortunately, you have little to no ambient light to work with (**Figure 7.8**).

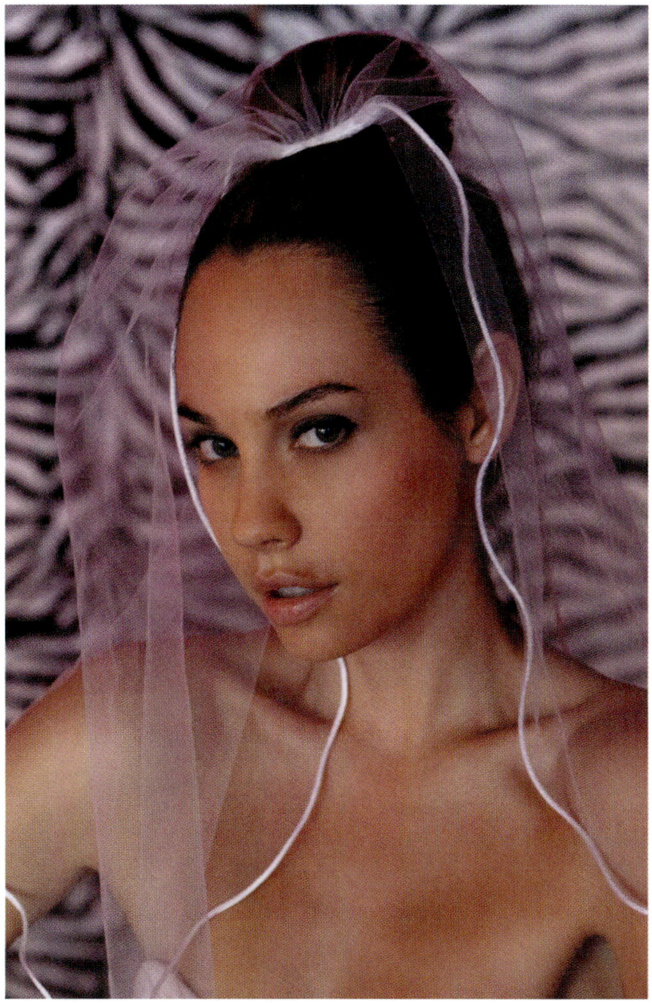

FIGURE 7.8
This image was taken using only the ambient light in the room. The room is extremely dark with nothing but a dim lamp and intermittent party lights to illuminate the image.

The first step is to bring out that speedlight and shed some of your own light on the model. As you saw earlier in this chapter, that direct blast of light is not the most flattering approach and produces that "bad snapshot" look (**Figure 7.9**).

Bouncing the flash off the ceiling and the wall is a great way to change the direction and quality of the light, but it is not the best technique in certain situations. If you bounce your light off a colored surface, for instance, it will pick up that color cast and bounce it onto your subject. In **Figures 7.10** and **7.11**, notice how bouncing the white light of a speedlight off a red wall and ceiling lit the model with red light as a result. Creative, yes, but less than ideal when documenting an event. To avoid unwanted color casts, bounce your flash off only white or neutral colored surfaces.

What do you do if, after analyzing a room, you realize you can't resort to bouncing the light? Fortunately, you can find a number of modifiers to help you soften the blow of your harsh speedlight. For example, the Rogue FlashBender is designed to spread out and take the edge off a direct flash for more pleasing shadows. You can bend the Rogue FlashBender to reflect light in a specific direction, which is great when a room offers no options for bouncing. In addition, if you add the FlashBender's Rogue Diffusion Panel attachment, you can effectively transform your harsh speedlight into a small on-camera softbox, as demonstrated in **Figure 7.12**. Notice the softer transition in the shadows as well as smoother highlights on the model's face.

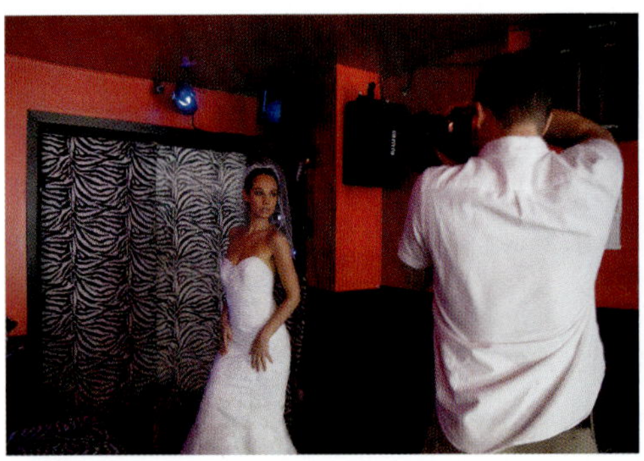

FIGURE 7.9
When you photograph the subject with a flash on the camera pointed directly at the model, the light is harsh and unflattering.

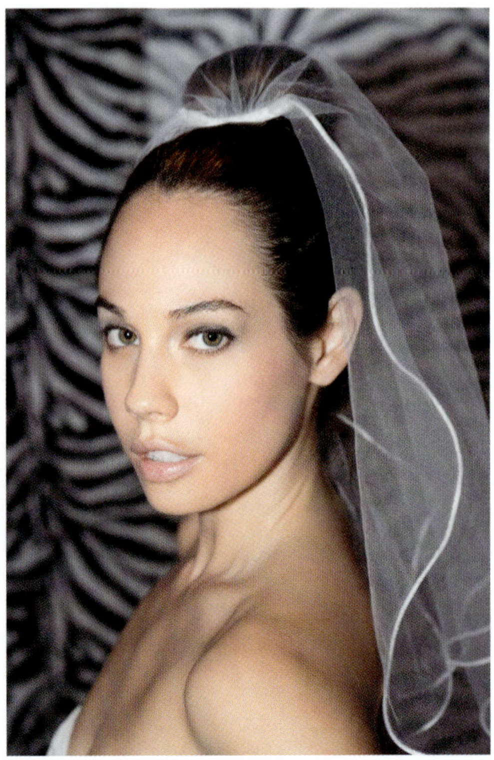

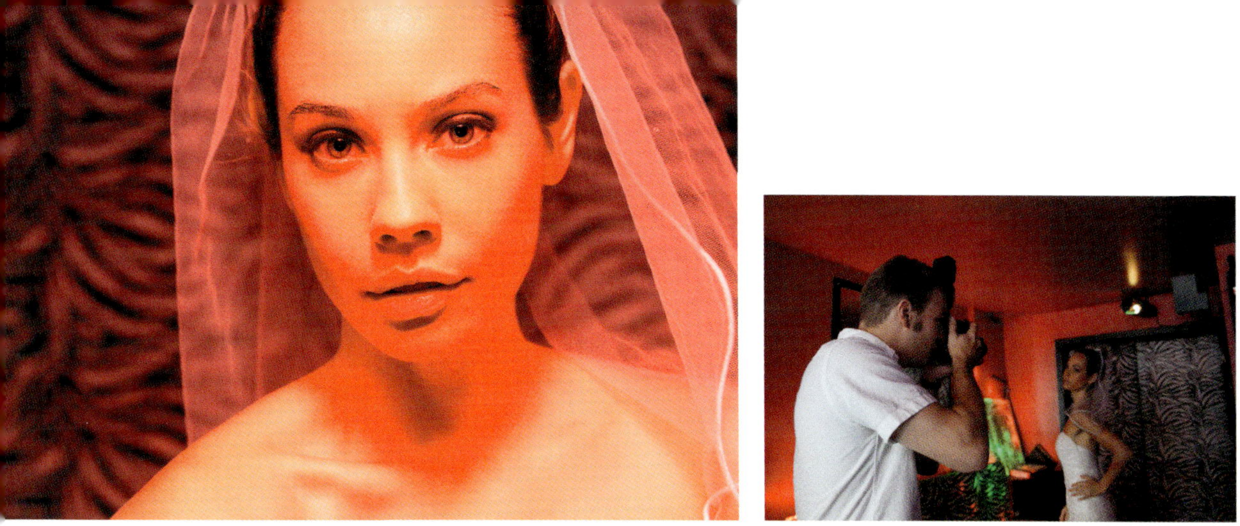

FIGURE 7.10
Beware of bouncing an on-camera flash off a colored ceiling. Here the light picked up the color cast of the ceiling and turned the model red in the process.

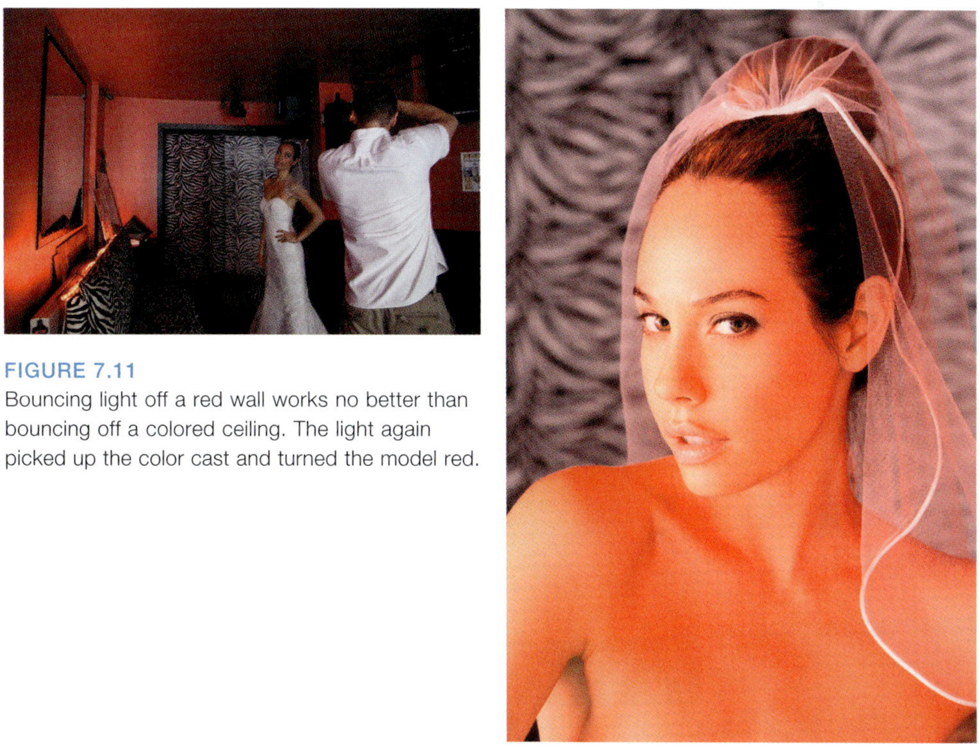

FIGURE 7.11
Bouncing light off a red wall works no better than bouncing off a colored ceiling. The light again picked up the color cast and turned the model red.

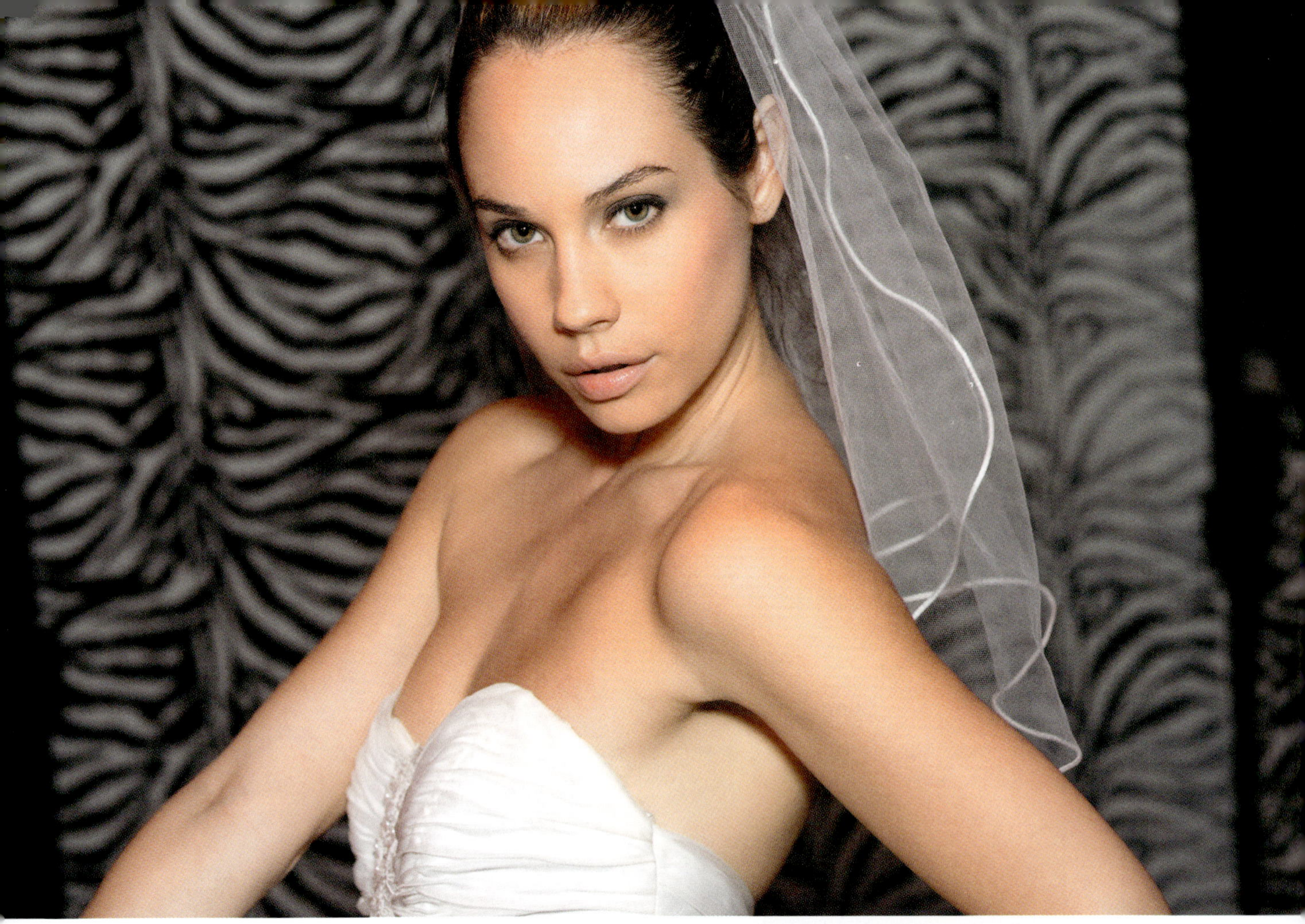

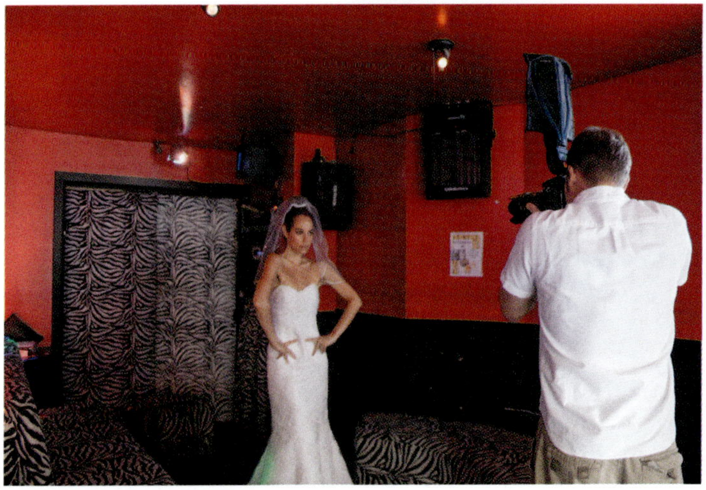

FIGURE 7.12
Here a Rogue FlashBender and optional Diffusion Panel soften a speedlight aimed directly at the model, creating softer shadows and smoother highlights. Be sure the FlashBender is no longer bouncing light off of the ceiling to illuminate the subject, and instead is pushing all light forward.

Move Your Flash Off Camera

If bouncing the flash isn't an option and you want more than that relatively flat on-camera flash, then take your flash off camera. There are a wealth of advantages to be had once you free your flash from its hot shoe. One way to do this is to simply connect your flash back to the hot shoe on top of your camera via a TTL cable. With this easy and reliable method, you retain all the functionality of your flash while gaining the ability to move it around anywhere within arm's reach.

By moving the flash off camera, you now have the flexibility to attach an actual softbox to the speedlight. For **Figure 7.13**, we used a PocketBox from F.J. Westcott (fjwestcott.com). Westcott offers a kit of these small softboxes designed to work specifically with your speedlight.

The light quality in Figures 7.12 and 7.13 is very similar due to comparable size and placement of the Rogue FlashBender with Diffusion Panel and the Westcott PocketBox, used respectively in each shot. The real advantage of off-camera lighting becomes more visible when you start to move your flash around your model's face. In **Figure 7.14**, look at the difference in the shadows created by the PocketBox when you move the light **off the camera axis** by about 25 degrees. Moving the light over 45 degrees to the side of the model's face in **Figure 7.15** adds even more contrast. This ability to sculpt your subject's face by creating shadow enhances your photography and makes your subjects appear more three dimensional in the final image.

If you replace the TTL cable with a set of wireless triggers, the options for where you can place the flash become infinite. Simply place one trigger on top of your camera and attach a receiver to your speedlight. Now when your camera fires, the flash will fire too, after receiving the signal wirelessly. There are a variety of triggering tools from companies such as PocketWizard (www.pocketwizard.com), RadioPoppers (radiopoppers.com), and more.

For **Figure 7.16**, we placed the speedlight with PocketBox all the way behind the model and triggered the flash using PocketWizard wireless radio transmitters (specifically the MiniTT1 and FlexTT5 models). Just like in the previous photos, the farther the flash moves off the camera's axis, the more shadows are created. By placing the speedlight behind the model, we captured a very dramatic image with a lot of shadow. After all, the drama lives in the shadows.

TAKEAWAY ACTION

If you want to create more drama and give more dimensionality to your subject, take your flash off camera using a TTL cable or radio trigger.

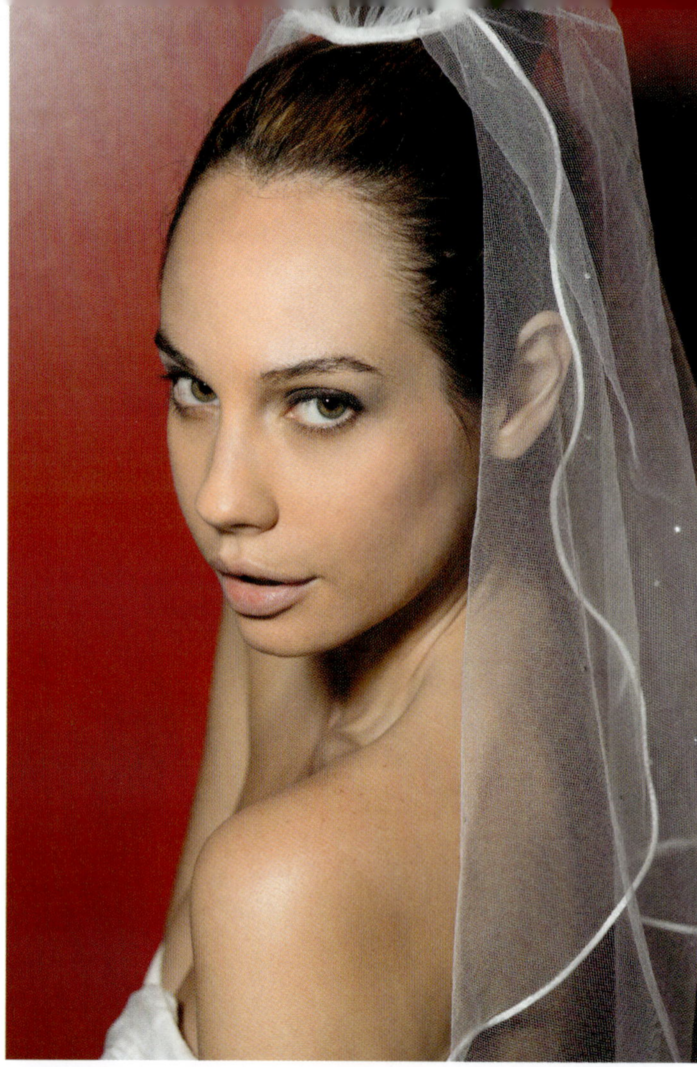

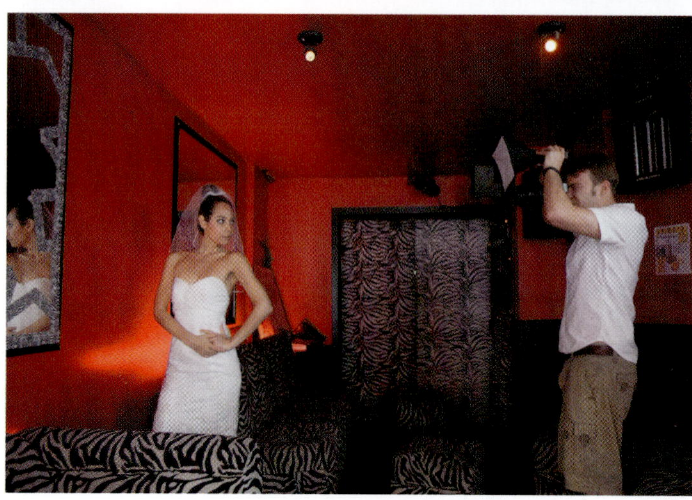

FIGURE 7.13

For this image the speedlight was moved slightly off camera and triggered via the attached TTL cable. Using a Westcott PocketBox with this setup, we achieved a soft and directional light.

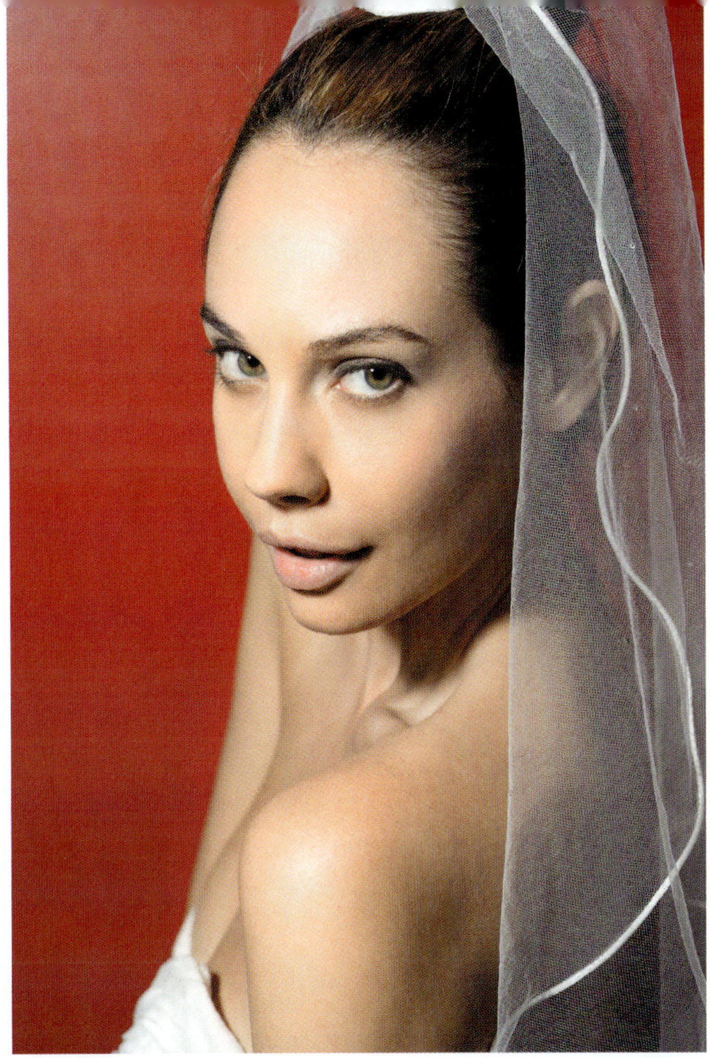

FIGURE 7.14
The model is still lit by a speedlight, connected via a TTL cable to the camera, and modified with a PocketBox. The difference is that we moved the light 25 degrees to the side of the model's face. As a result, shadows are beginning to appear on the side of her face.

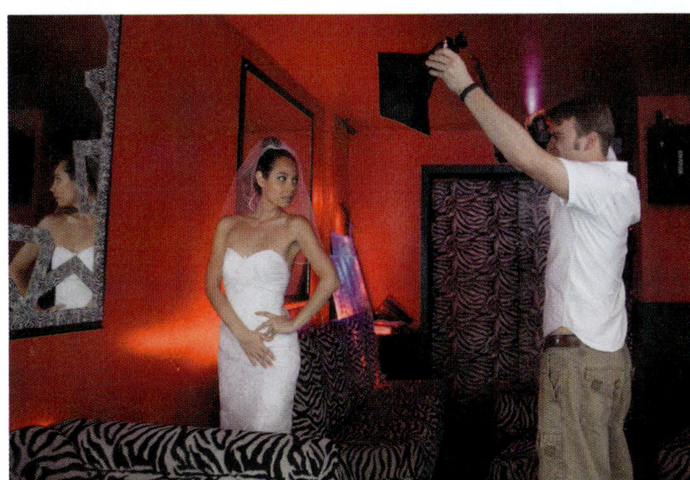

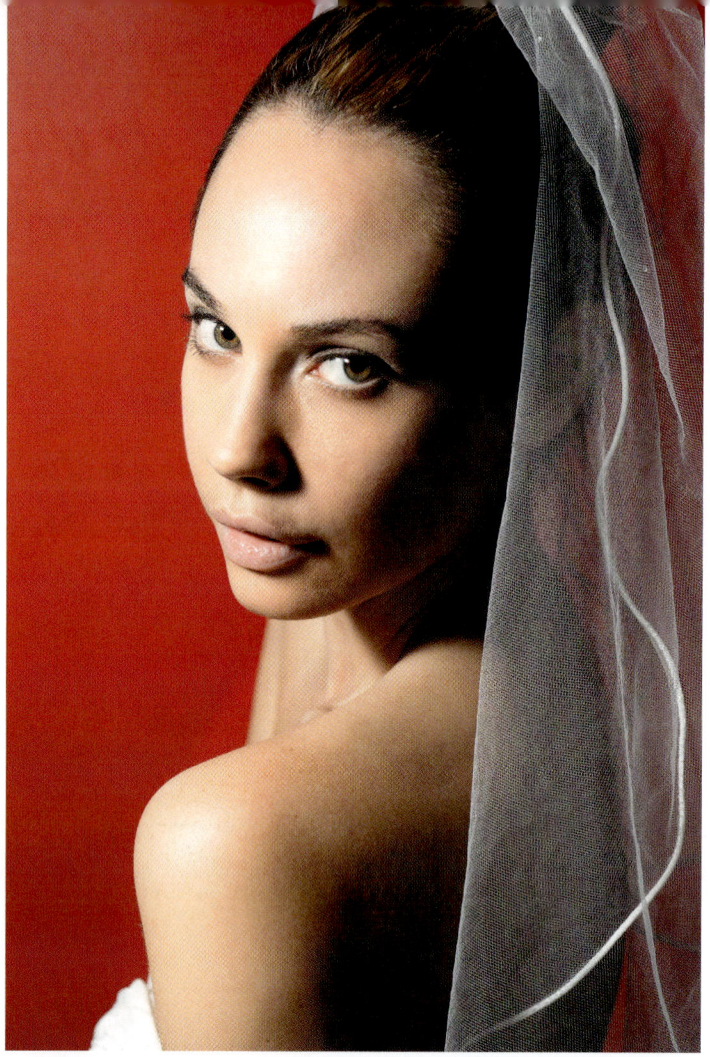

FIGURE 7.15
Moving the light 45 degrees to the side of the model's face results in more pronounced shadows that begin to sculpt her face and create a contrasty, three-dimensional look to the photo.

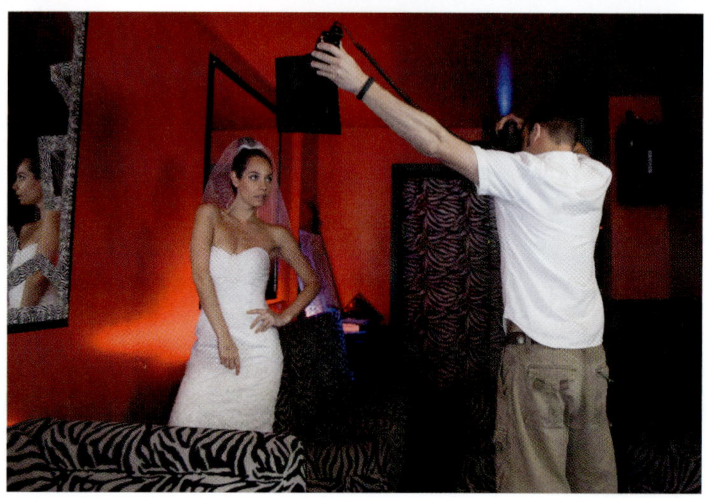

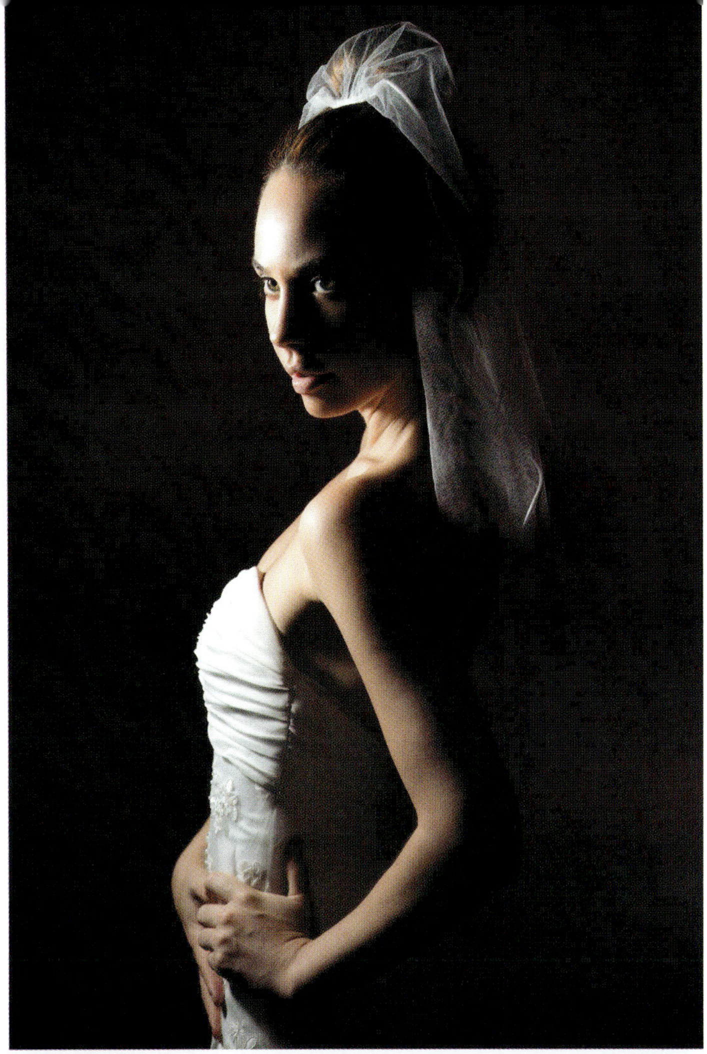

FIGURE 7.16
A PocketWizard wireless radio trigger enables you to place your flash far away from the camera. Here we placed the speedlight and PocketBox behind the model to create a lot of shadows and drama on the model's face.

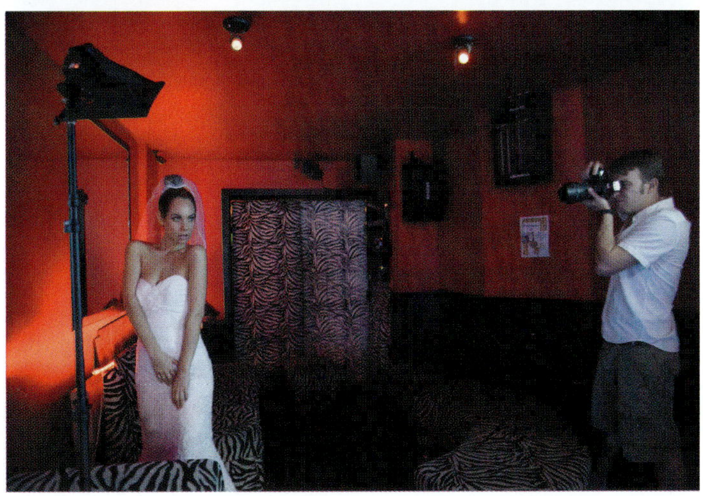

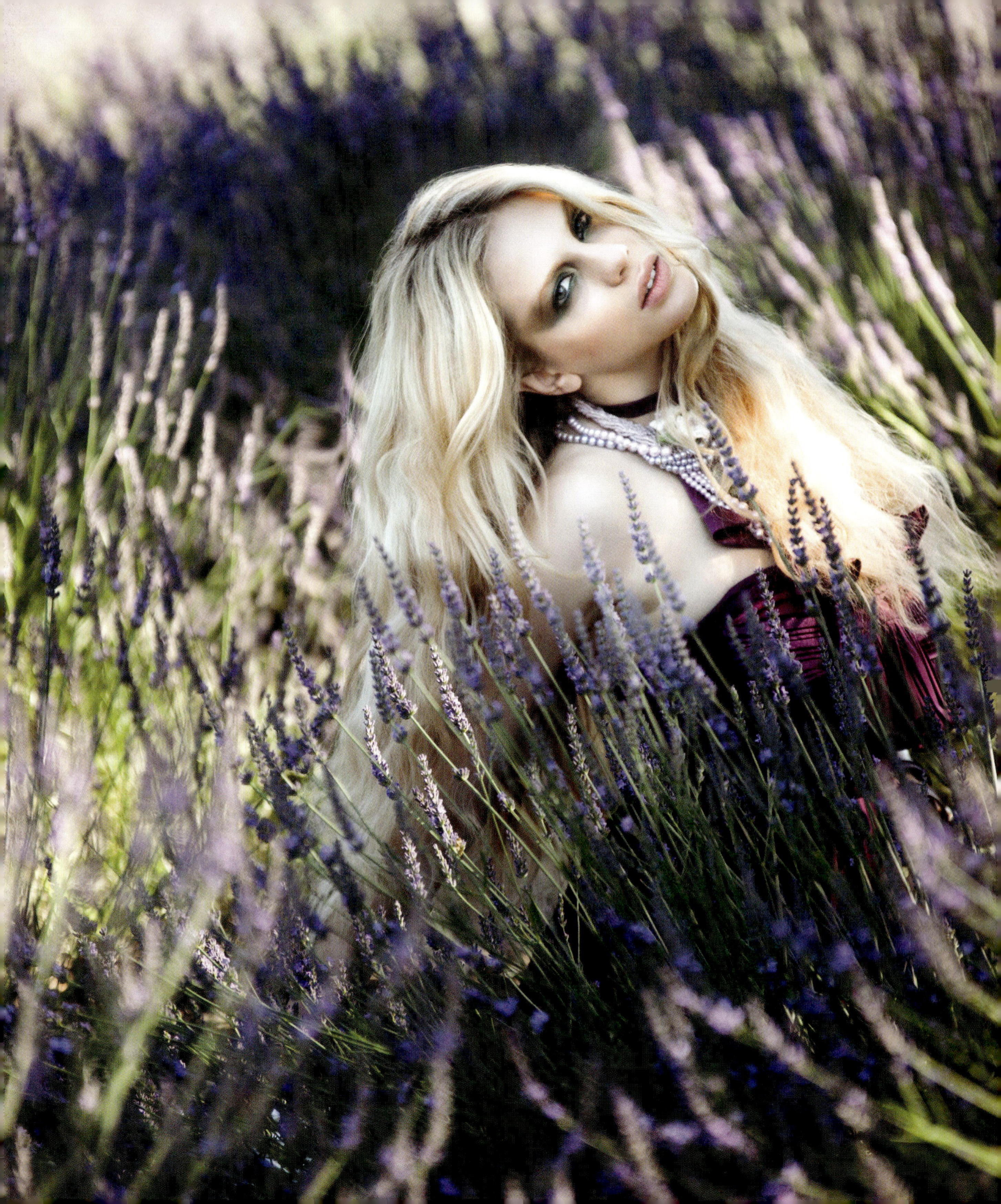

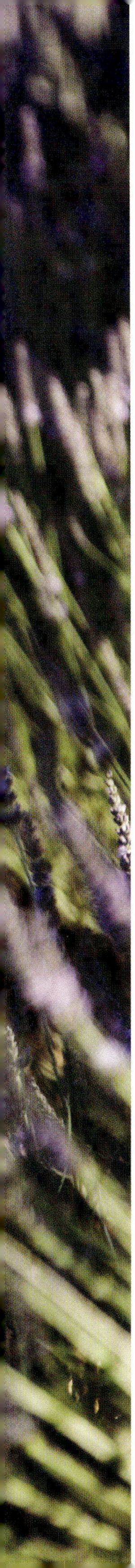

CHAPTER EIGHT

Dappled Light, High Contrast

Sometimes you may encounter a scene with extreme contrast. One area of the frame may be in deep shadow, while other parts are in direct sunlight. Other times, there may be unsightly highlights and shadows mixed on a subject's face: a brightly lit nose, a streak of light across the face, or shadows cast by the branches of a tree. Even with today's technology and cameras, this is a difficult scene to conquer. Combine a black suit with a white dress at a wedding, and it seems impossible to capture all the tonalities even if the light is flattering. Although scenes like this are not always the easiest to manage, you can actually come away with powerful images if you know how to use the light to your advantage.

This chapter will show you how to tame these unruly scenes and offer techniques for bringing the dramatic lighting under your control.

Choose What's Important

In some situations, you simply cannot capture the entire **tonal range** of the scene. You may find a highlight is too bright for you to expose properly while still capturing the detail in the totally shadowed background. In this instance you must make an executive decision: What part of the scene is most important to you? Is it okay to blow out the highlights? Or are the highlights the most important part of the scene? Suppose, for example, you are photographing a wedding late in the day and you pose the bride in a beam of light. The background is in dark shadow. If you split the difference and expose for a middle exposure, nothing will be exposed correctly. The highlights will be blown out, and the shadows muddy. Instead, you will want to set your exposure for the highlights in the image, which will be on your subject's face, the most important part of the scene. You can achieve this by using Manual exposure (M), Aperture Priority mode with Exposure Compensation, or by spot metering in your camera.

BEGINNER TIP Pick an exposure mode that works for you.

Make time to understand how to guide your camera to the correct exposure. Erik prefers to take total control by using the manual camera settings (M). Lindsay prefers to use Av mode, letting the camera arrive at a setting then tweaking it through Exposure Compensation. Refer to your camera's manual and practice to see which approach works best for you!

Allowing your camera to select the average exposure gives you an average exposure for the entire image, meaning the camera overexposes the highlights while bringing back some detail into the shadow areas. Alternately, you could also use spot metering to set the exposure for the highlights on the subject's face, as we did in **Figure 8.1**. Notice how the most important element of the image, the model, is exposed correctly while the rest of the image falls to shadow.

If the entire scene is important, you may need to try another approach.

TAKEAWAY ACTION

You don't always have to have all the detail in the highlights and shadow areas of an image. You can selectively set your exposure of specific highlights or shadow detail of the photo, which can result in dramatic images.

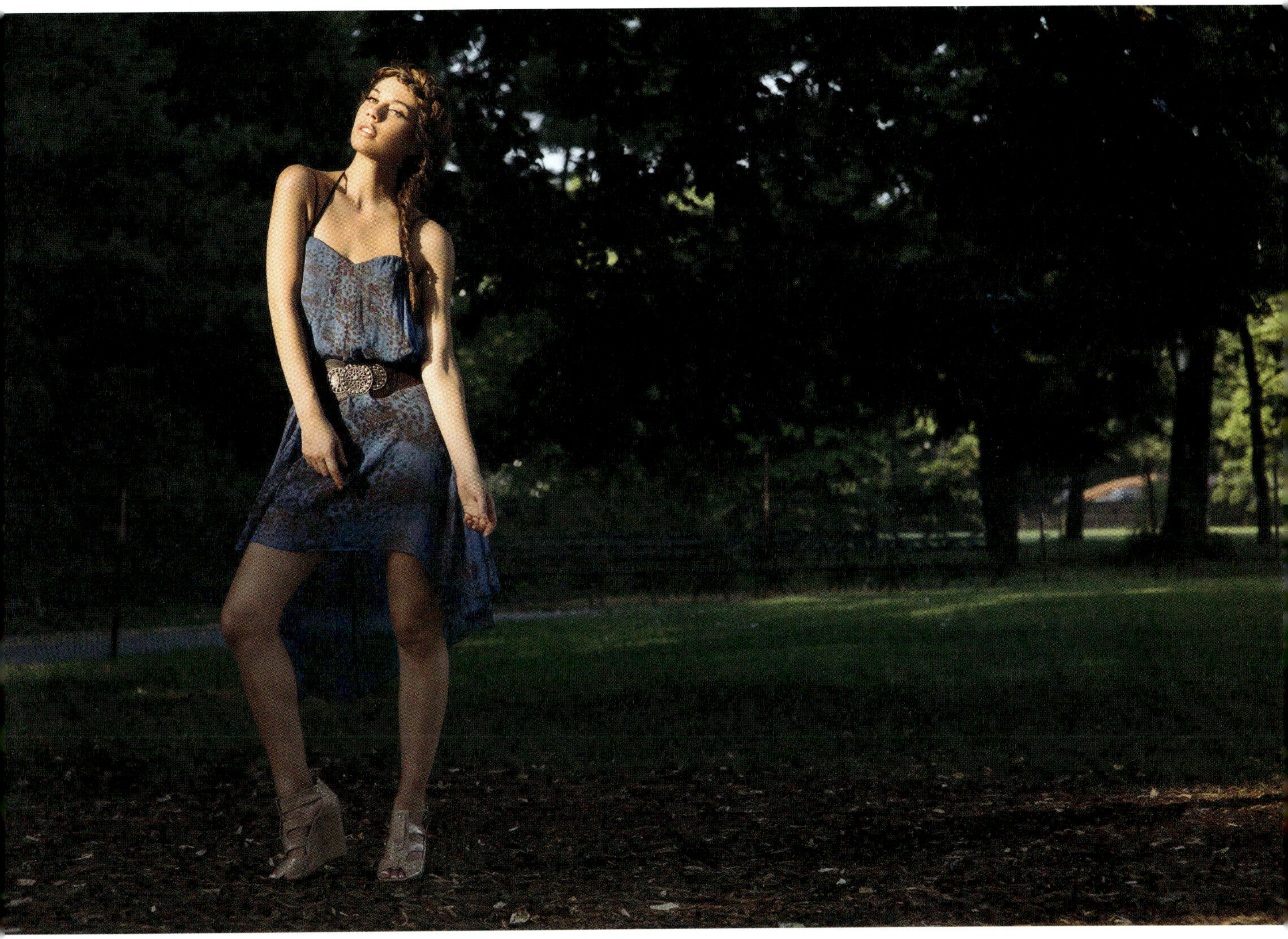

FIGURE 8.1
After setting the camera to spot metering, we metered for the highlights on the model's face. This produced a more accurate exposure, preserving the detail in the most important part of the image.

LINDSAY IN ACTION

Men's Fashion Editorial in Direct Sunlight

I was shooting a fashion editorial in direct, midday light, and there was nearly a five-stop range in exposure in the scene. In other words, the brightest highlights were nearly five stops brighter than the darkest shadow. On the surface, it looked like an impossible scene to capture.

I decided, of course, that my model was the most important element of the scene. He would be correctly exposed, and I would allow the shadow areas to fall to black. I used the highlights and shadows in the scene to create visual elements that resulted in a very successful, high-impact image! I analyzed the scene, decided which elements should be correctly exposed, and then composed the shot to make use of the high-contrast elements.

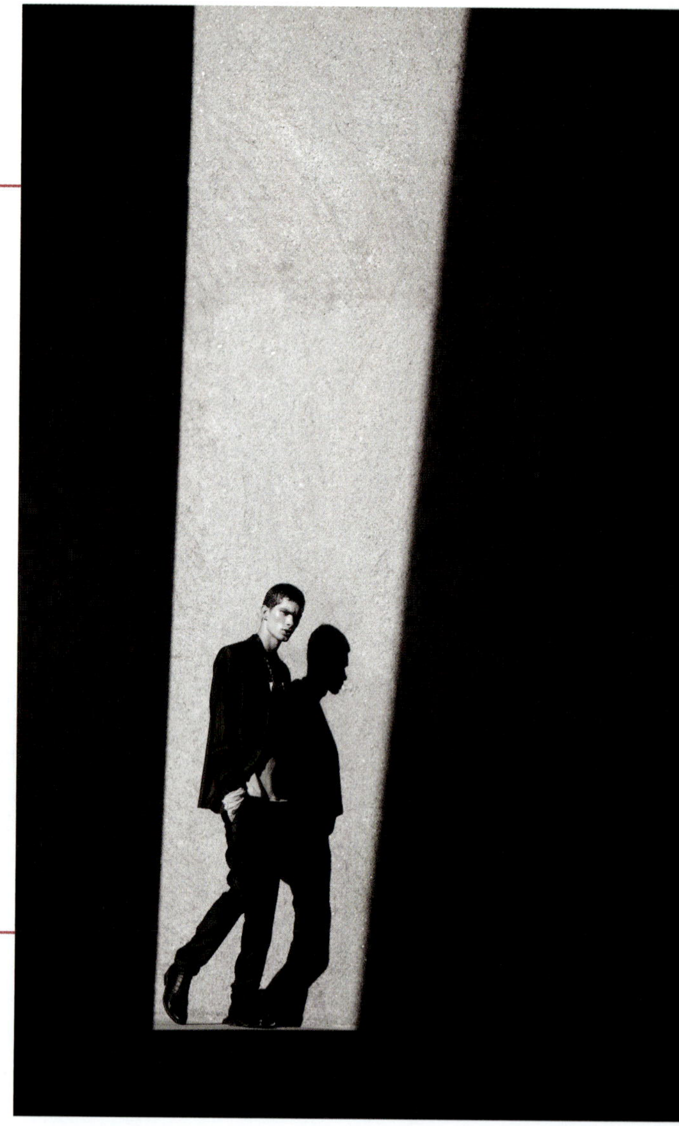

Purposefully Place Highlights

One way to handle dappled light or a scene with a large range in light is to use it to your advantage. Don't fight it! Embrace it! In the video and cinema world, as well as on high-end fashion shoots, photographers actually use patterns to create dappled light and shadow to add depth and interest to a scene.

Use this uneven light to create drama and focus the eye. If there is a beam of light in the darkness, put the subject in the beam of light. Or place the highlight of dappled light on her eye. If you are very purposeful with your highlight placement, you can produce truly striking results.

ERIK IN ACTION

Female Fashion in an Open Field

When shooting on location, you need to stay on your toes. For example, I began my shoot around midday, so I was shooting in direct, harsh sunlight. Seeing as we were in the middle of an overgrown field, with no trees or shade in sight, the last thing I had to worry about was dappled light.

As the sun began to set, however, those tall strands of grass and brush suddenly started to come into play. Rather than asking my assistant to start gardening for us, I decided to somehow work the foliage into the frame. With careful placement of the shadow I was able to draw attention to the model's eye, rather than let the shadow become a distracting, negative feature. By exposing for the highlights, I was able to properly expose the model's skin, and the shadow from the foliage nearby almost looked like a tattoo on the her face.

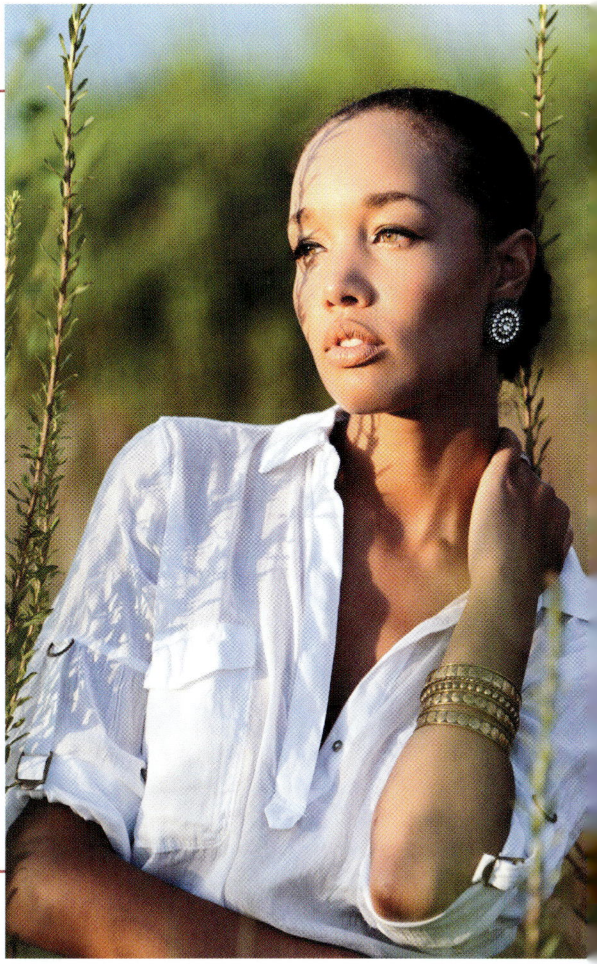

Even Out the Light

If the dappled or uneven light is just unpleasant or undesirable, your next option is to even out the highlights and shadows. There are two main approaches:

- Add light to fill in the shadows
- Find a way to block off the highlights

Shot in dappled light, **Figure 8.2** is an example of unsightly highlights on the face. The highlights on the forehead and nose in particular are what we need to fix. You can remedy this problem by filling in the shadows with a reflector or flash or by evening out the scene by blocking off or diffusing highlights. Take a look at a few options for improving this shot.

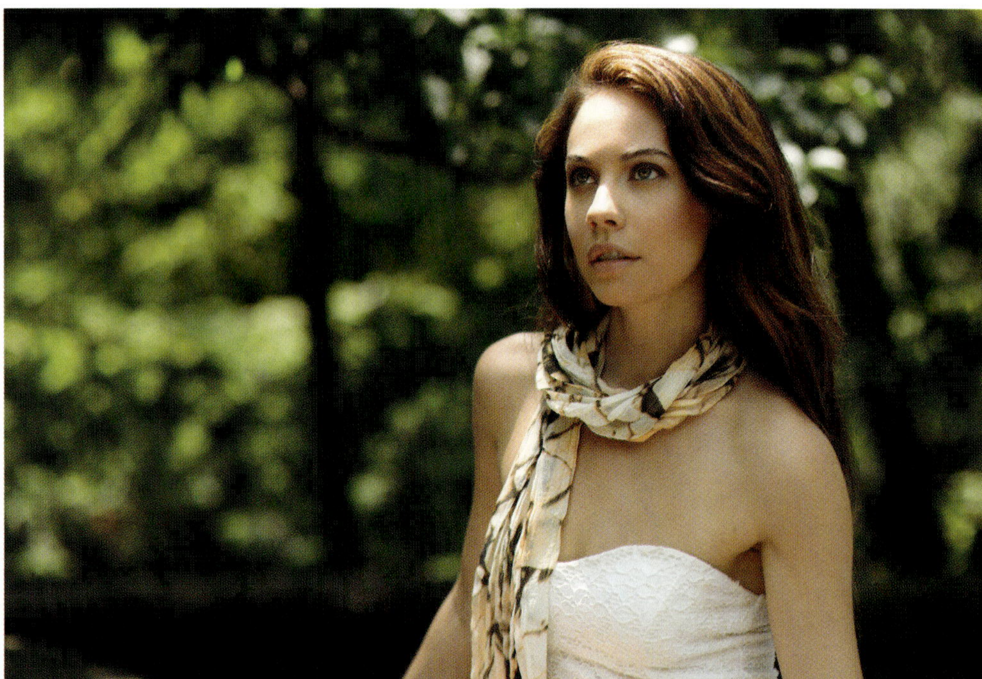

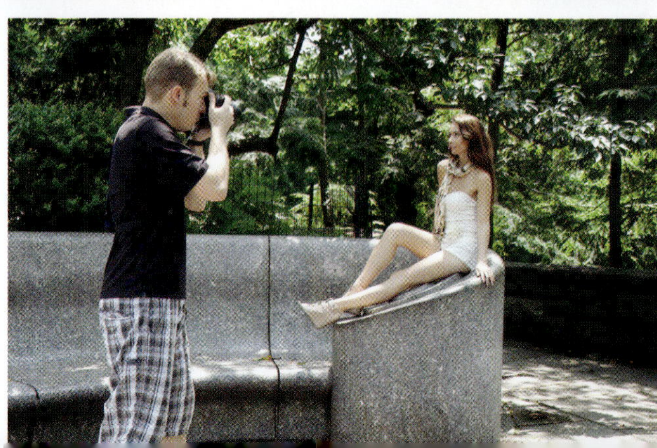

✗ **FIGURE 8.2**
The light illuminating the face is uneven and creates undesirable contrast and hot spots.

Fill with a Reflector

First, you might try a reflector to even out the range between the highlights and shadows. If you have enough ambient light, consider using a large reflector to bounce light into the scene. You may be able to overpower the uneven light and provide sufficient illumination to fill in the shadows. Starting with **Figure 8.3**, we next kicked a great deal of light onto the subject with a silver reflector for **Figure 8.4**. Because we added so much extra light to our model (and only our model), after adjusting to the appropriate camera settings, we ended up with a darker background. The effect's success is a matter of taste; either you like the way the subject pops from the background, or you feel the darkness is unrealistic to the scene.

Unfortunately, if you are attempting to even out the light, you may have to use a great deal of reflected light to overpower the highlights or fill in the shadows. For this reason, the light on the subject's face might be too strong and unflattering.

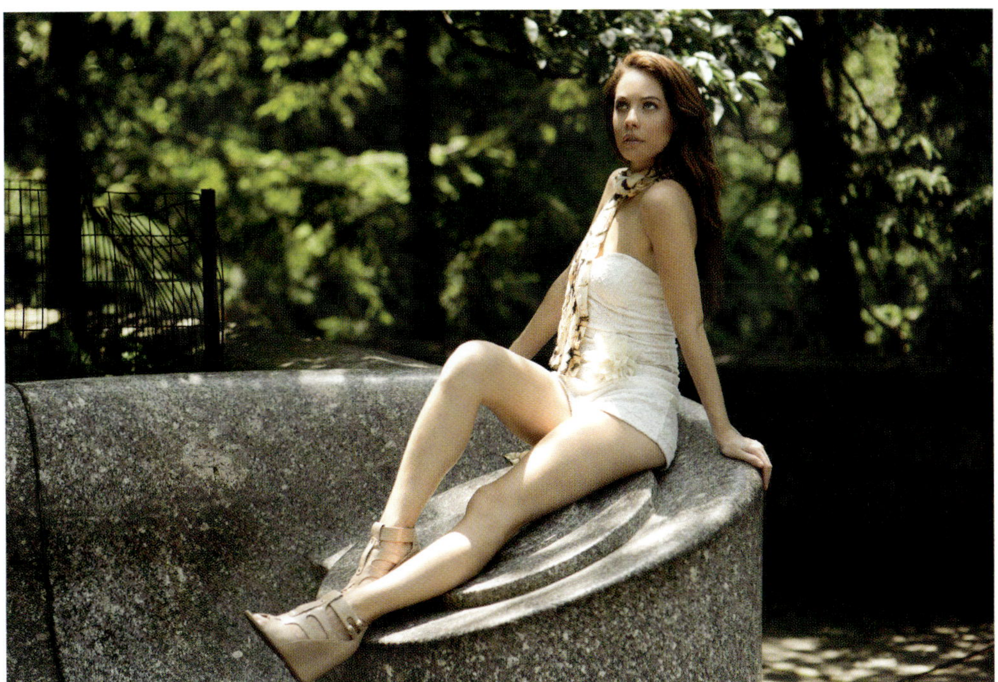

✗ FIGURE 8.3
The original image has unpleasant highlights on the face and forehead. The highlights draw attention to undesirable elements of the frame.

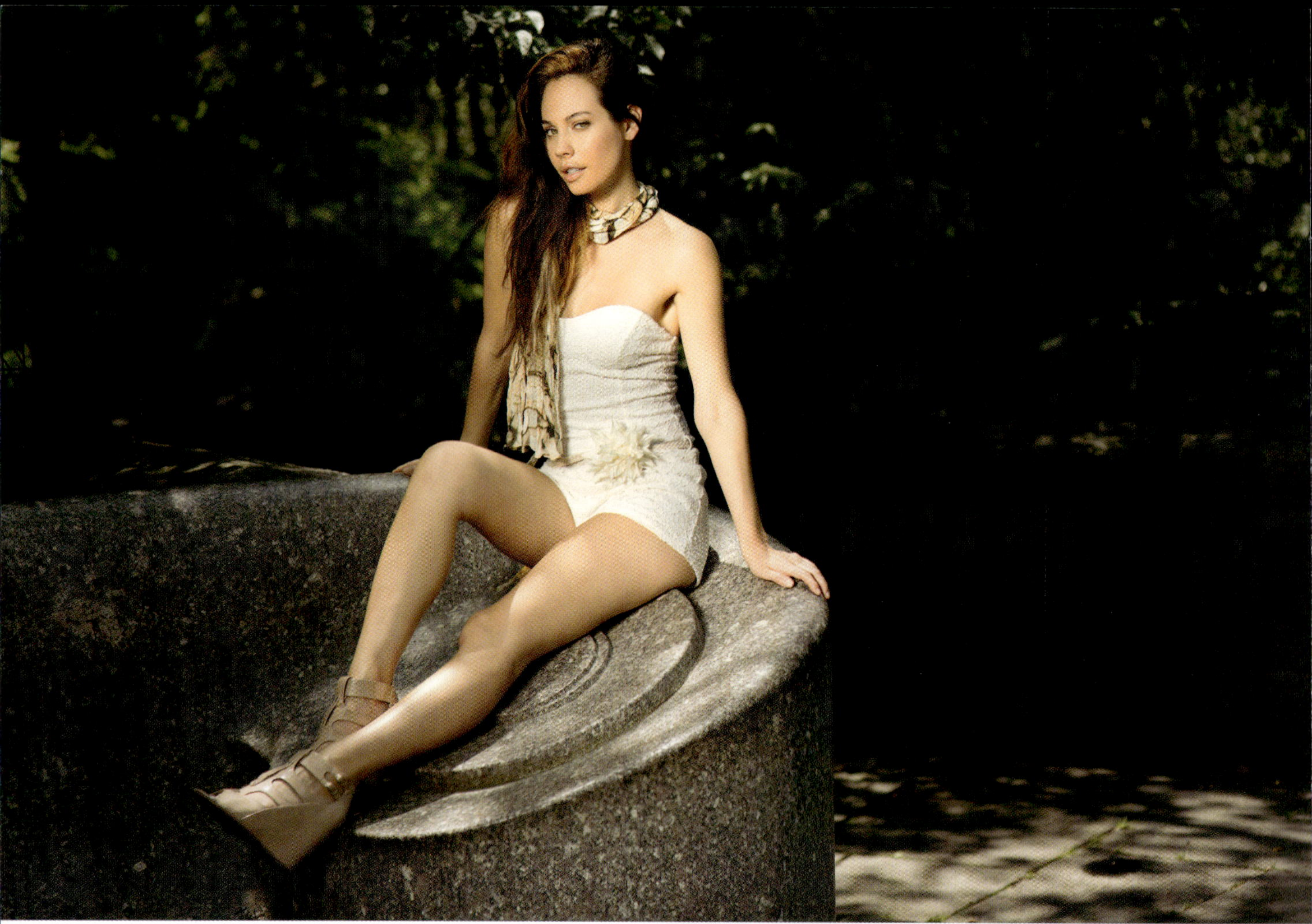

FIGURE 8.4
By adding a reflector into the scene, you can fill in the shadows and even out the exposure. Because we made the subject brighter and exposed for the highlights here, the background appears darker in comparison.

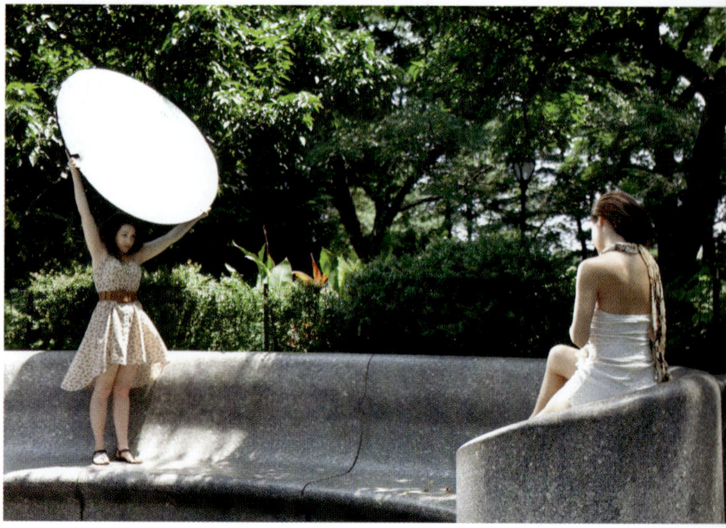

WATCH IT! Mind the reflector angle.

Be aware of the angle of your reflector. Reflecting underneath your subject can create bottom light and unflattering shadows. When you are using a reflector to fill in the shadows in a high contrast scene, be sure that you are not creating opposing light sources. For example, if your main light source is to the far left and you are filling from the right, be sure that you are not creating a dead spot of shadows in the center of the face or scene. Your reflector fill should be just that: fill. It should not look like a second light source in the scene. Vary the angle of your reflector and **feather** the light to modify its intensity. For more advice on using reflectors, see Chapter 1, "Direct Sunlight."

Block Off Highlights

Your next option for bringing the scene's exposure to a more even level is to block off, or *flag off*, the bright highlights. (The item you use to block light is called a **flag**.) Blocking the brightest highlights leaves you with an even exposure and reduces the contrast in this area of the scene.

When you flag off the light on the subject, you eliminate all overhead light. Again starting from Figure 8.3, for **Figure 8.5** we eliminated light on the hair as well. If you want to include some additional dimension to your image and perhaps retain more shape to the face and highlights on the hair, consider using a diffuser instead.

EQUIPMENT TIP Create flags resourcefully!

Several companies create "professional grade" flags, but basically these are just frames with black cloth stretched across them. Instead, consider constructing a frame of coat hangers and stretching black pantyhose over them. Really, anything will do as a flag if you can find a way to get it in between the subject and the light. You can use a stand with a boom arm and a black board, or you can just hold up cardboard. If you can't reach the correct angle to eliminate the unwanted highlight, try rigging something that will allow you to reach unusual angles. Sometimes a recipe of mop handles and gaffers tape can do magic.

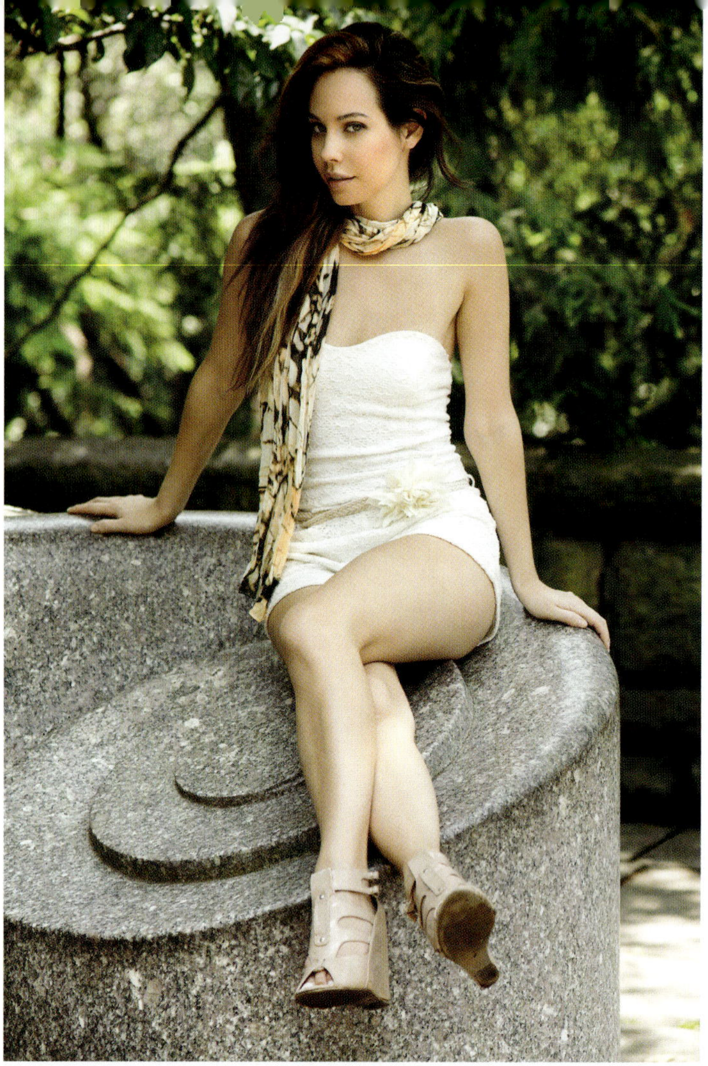

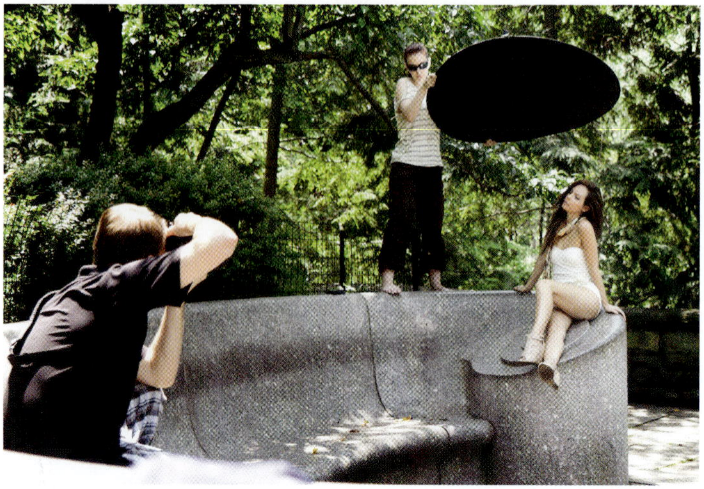

FIGURE 8.5
Using the black side of a reflector, we blocked off overhead light. Completely eliminating the overhead light source eliminated the unpleasant highlights. Notice that we even eliminated light on the top of the head and hair.

Diffuse the Light

You can also fix dappled light by using a diffuser to soften the highlights and provide more even illumination. Instead of completely flagging off and eliminating highlights, try making them softer and reducing contrast. By using a diffuser, you still allow light to illuminate your subject, but it will be much more even. If the dappled light is subtle, diffusing can effectively eliminate highlights without drastically darkening the light on your subject. In **Figure 8.6**, we maintained highlights in the hair because we did not eliminate overhead light. (To learn more about diffusers, see Chapter 2, "Direct Sunlight, No Shade in Sight.")

TAKEAWAY ACTION

Remember, a diffuser does not eliminate ambient light, but instead acts as a way to even out the highlights and shadows on a subject's face.

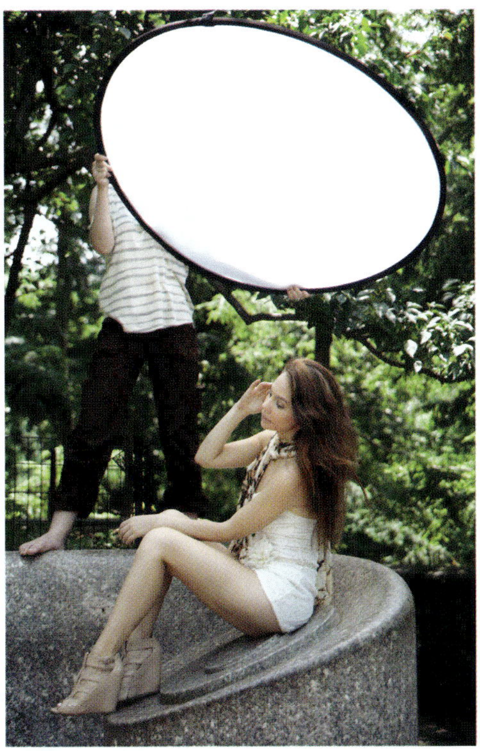

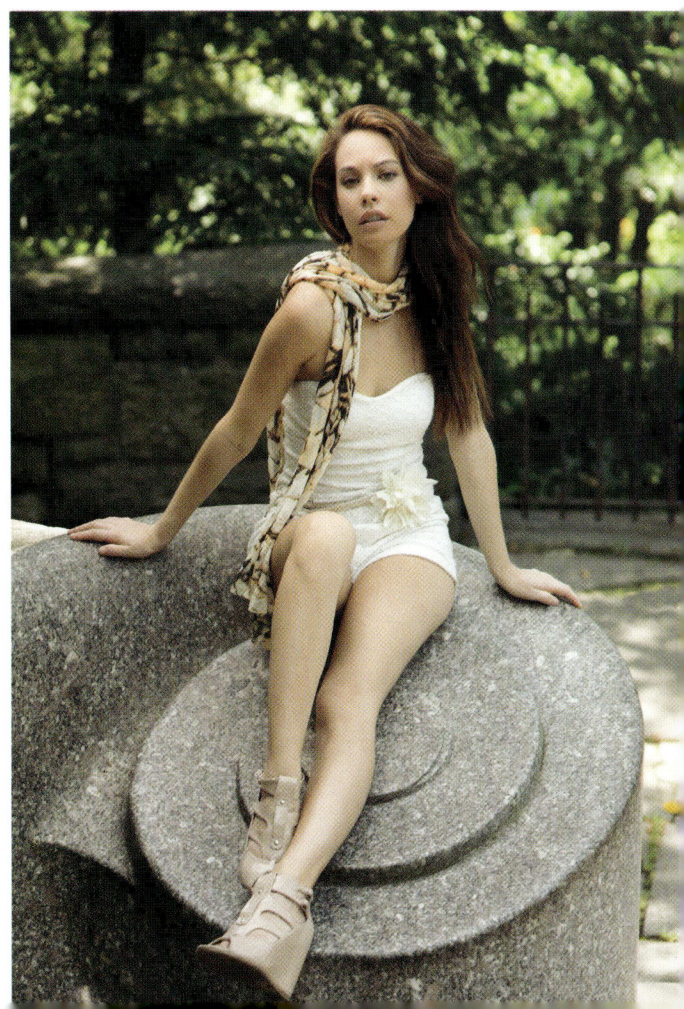

✔ **FIGURE 8.6**
Adding a diffuser above the subject's head softens the overhead light and makes it more even. Notice how you can still see light on the hair and a bit of shape to the face—the result of using a diffuser instead of a flag overhead.

Diffuse, Then Add a Reflector

After you eliminate and reduce unwanted highlights, you can then build light back into the image by adding a reflector. In short, you first eliminate bright highlights, then fill in the shadows to bring the image to a manageable range of highlights and shadows. The resulting light on the face will be crisp and flattering, as in **Figure 8.7**. If you have the ability to both diffuse and reflect, this is likely the most visually pleasing option!

FIGURE 8.7
Eliminate overhead light, then add a reflector to kick light back into the eyes. This gives a direction of light and contrast to the face.

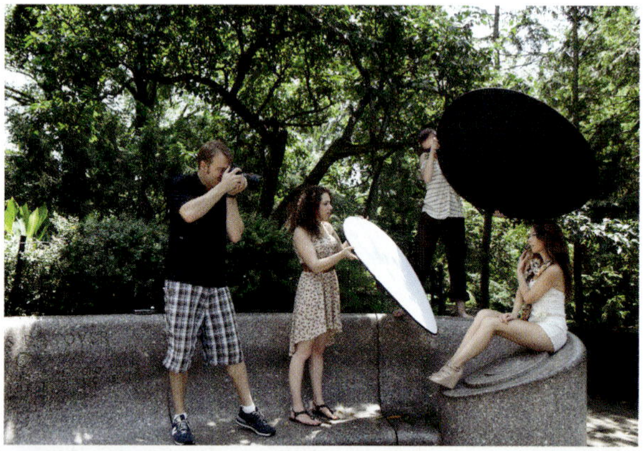

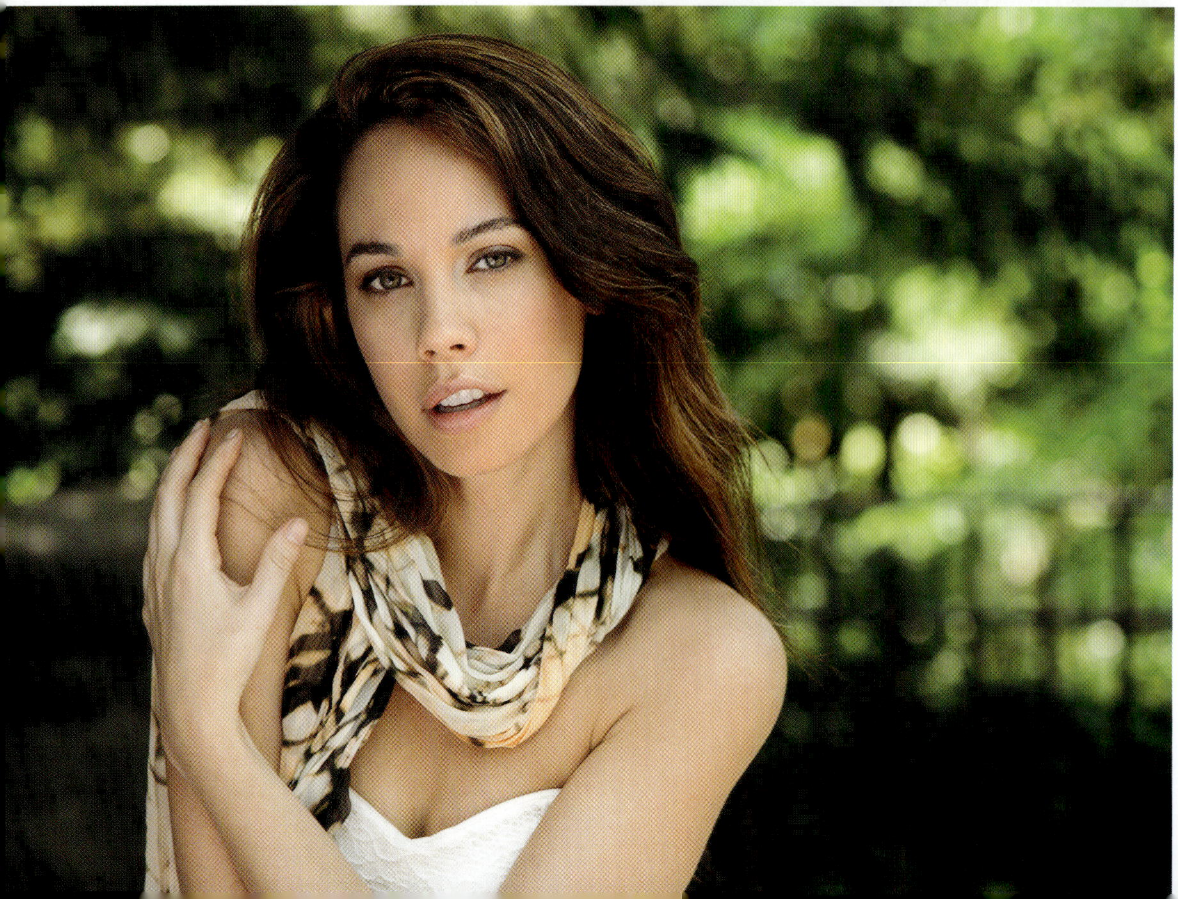

Use Fill Flash

Lastly, you may consider using fill flash to fill in the shadows or at least provide a bit of detail in the shadow areas of a scene. Also, don't use your flash on full power. Doing so may overpower the ambient light of the scene, which likely helps to set a mood. Instead, use a lesser power setting or TTL mode to allow you to just fill in shadows without overpowering the scene. Sometimes all you need is a few drops, not the entire bucket.

In **Figures 8.8** through **8.11**, you can see how varying the flash output can allow some of the ambient light to show through the image. In general, you'll be wisest to take your flash off camera. This helps you to avoid that on-camera party flash look. Because we are subtly filling in the shadows in this series of images, the flash is not our primary light source and on-camera flash at a lower power output is sufficient. Getting the flash off camera, however, is usually a better approach because it creates more directional light that helps to shape the face and add depth to the photo.

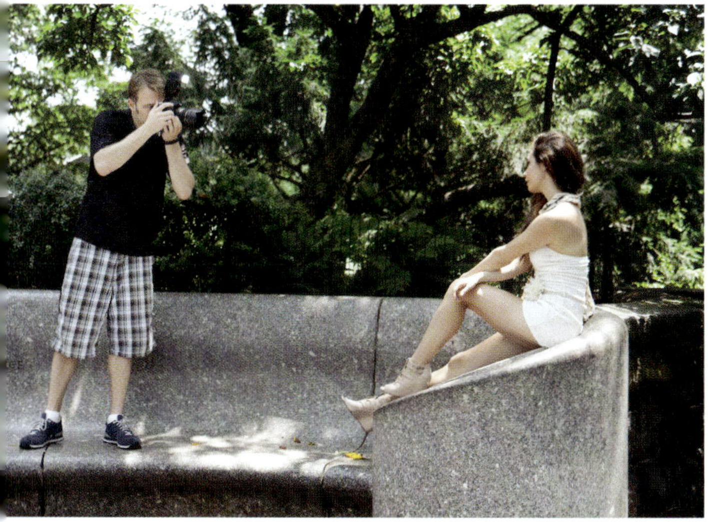

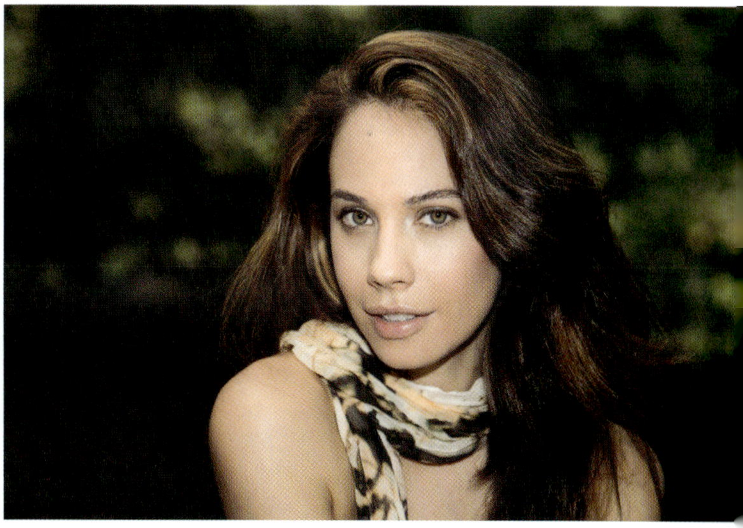

FIGURE 8.8
As a baseline, we used a flash on the camera at full power to balance with the ambient light. This image has too much of a flash-on-camera look to it. Not only does the flash overpower the ambient light, but it also lacks shape, quality of shadows, and direction of light. The on-camera flash effect at full power creates a flat, over-lit image.

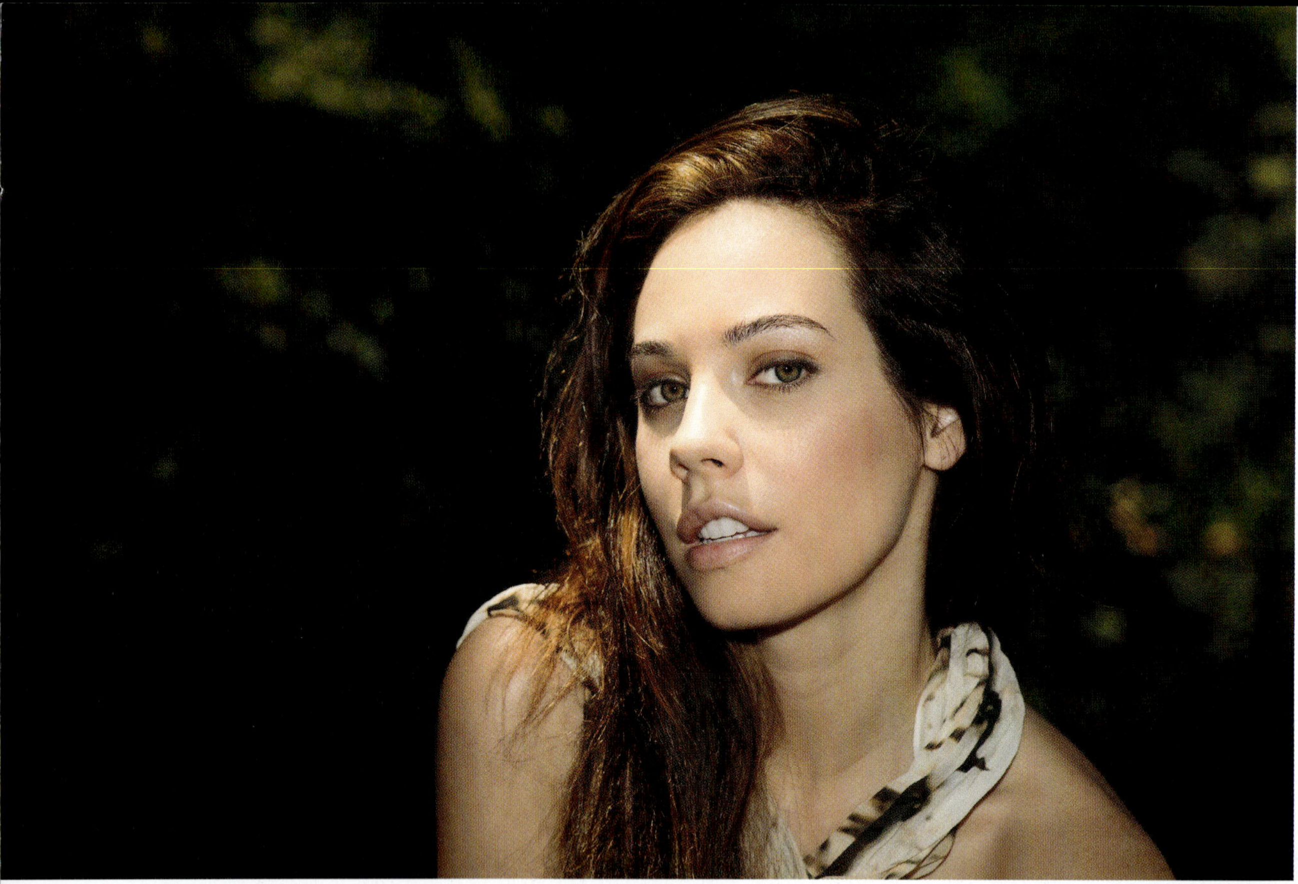

✔ FIGURE 8.9

Setting the flash at half power allows some of the ambient light to show through. The image has more depth because we did not completely overpower ambient light on the face, but still helped even out the exposure. Notice the added contrast and quality of light.

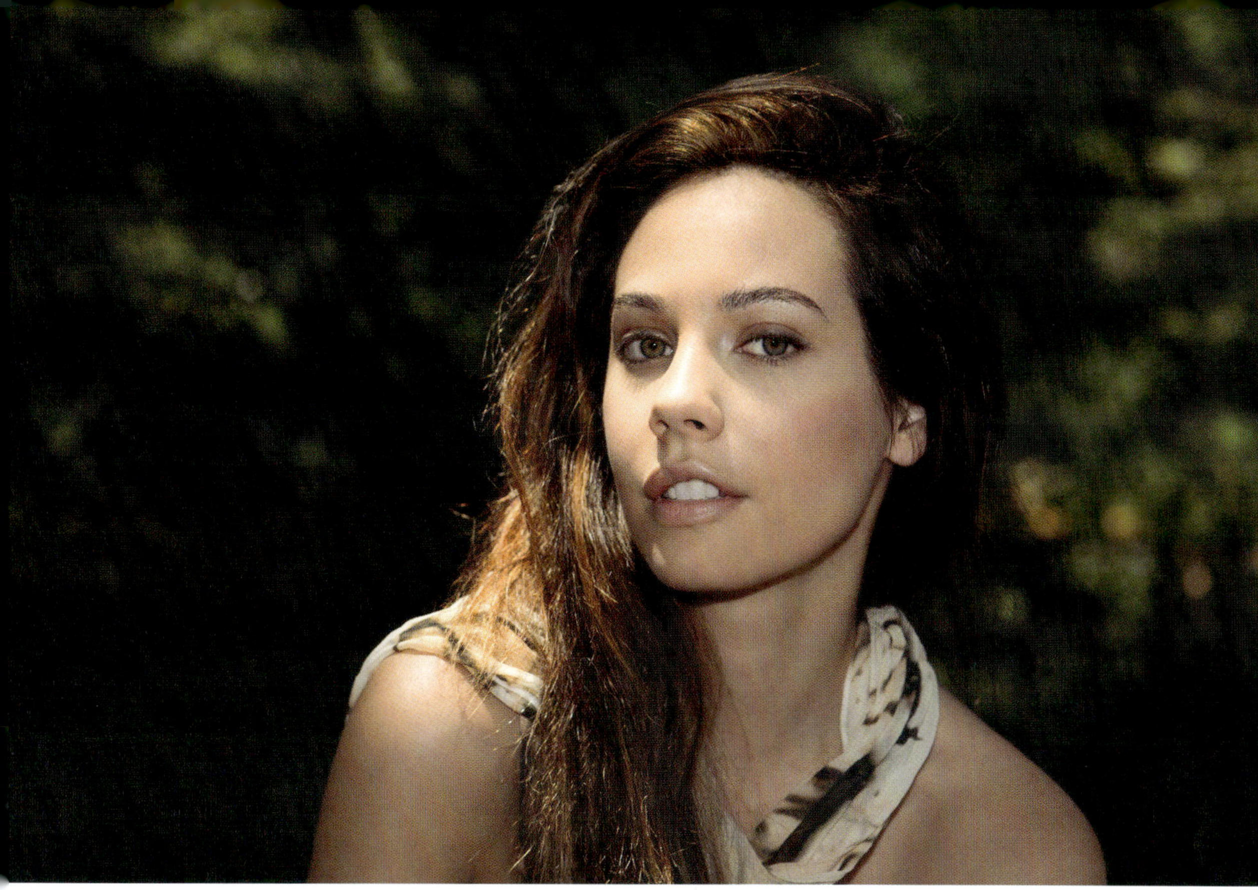

✔ FIGURE 8.10
On 1/4 power, the flash still allows the ambient light to register on the face and hair, while helping to fill in the shadows. This is a very subtle fill, but it evens out shadows and adds a sparkling catchlight to the eye.

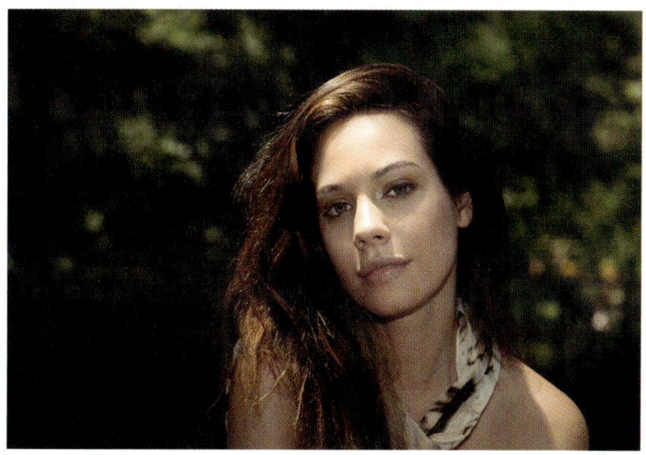

✘ FIGURE 8.11
With the flash on 1/8 power, many of the original problems with dappled light return. The uneven light on the face becomes more noticeable because the power of the fill flash is too low.

Remember, you can combine approaches. Try blocking off overhead light while also using a flash to illuminate the face. Here, basically the flash would replace the roll of the reflector we discussed earlier. The diffusion helps to reduce bright highlights, while the fill flash acts to build back in the shadows and add contrast to the face. **Figures 8.12** and **8.13** demonstrate this technique with different flash powers.

TAKEAWAY ACTION

Although fill flash may be a useful tool for evening out dappled ambient lights, stay away from using the flash at full power in order to prevent overexposed or flat flash-on-camera results.

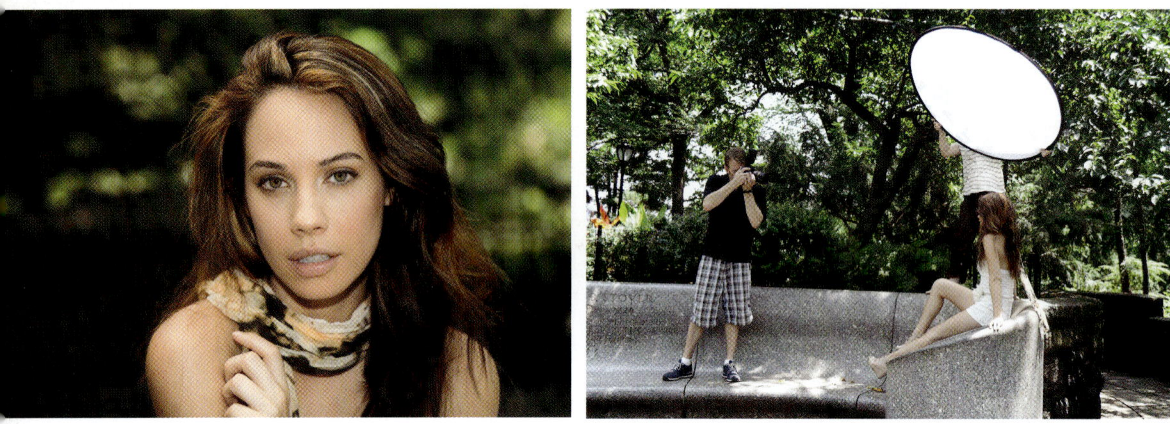

FIGURE 8.12
Use a diffuser to reduce the brightness of highlights, while filling in light on the face with a flash. Here the full-power flash is too much illumination, however.

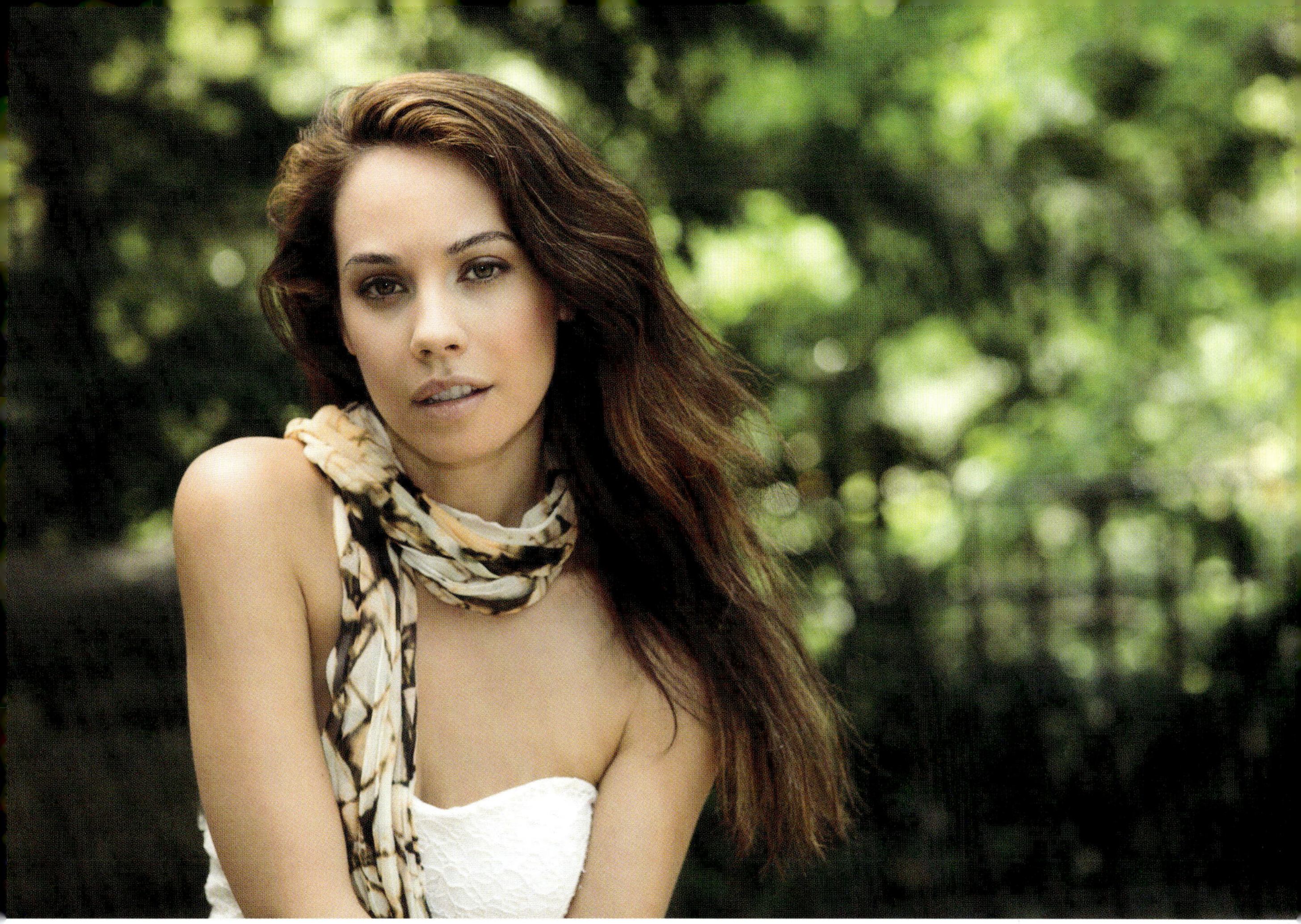

FIGURE 8.13
Using a diffuser helps to even out the quality of light on the face, while the flash at 1/4 power gives a pleasant fill and contrast.

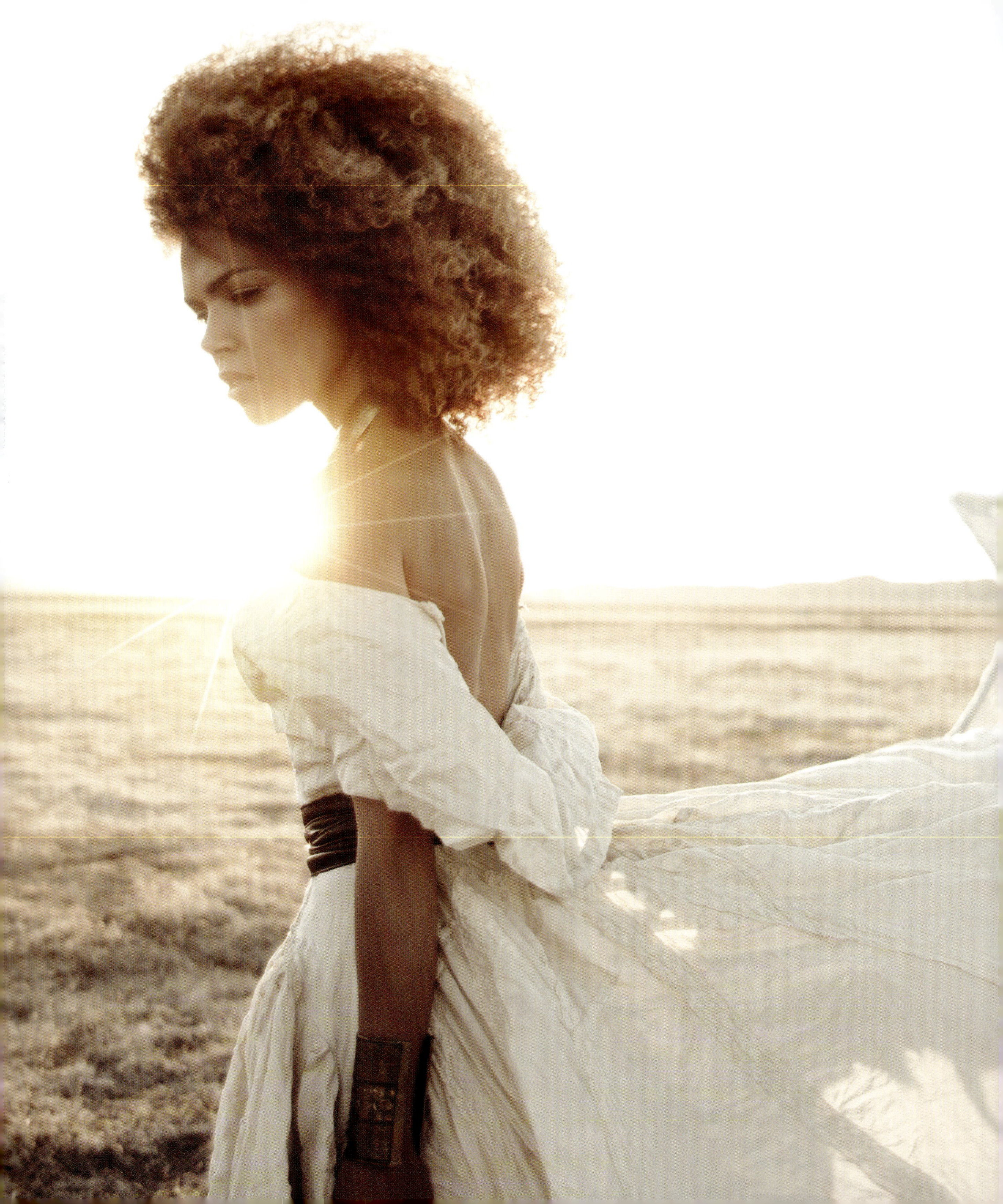

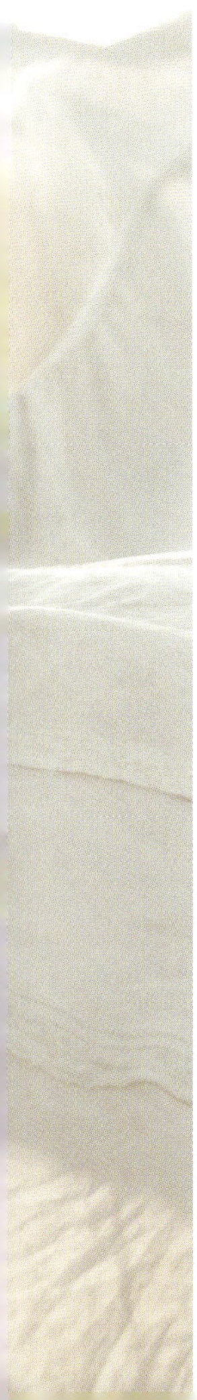

CHAPTER NINE
Strong Backlight

Your client's event is scheduled right at sunset, meaning you are stuck shooting directly into the sun. There's no need to curse your bad luck; heavily backlit shots can be some of the most beautiful and dramatic images out there! When you take control of this situation, you can turn the sun into a radiant glow or striking hair light for your subject. The keys to cracking the backlight challenge are:

- Harnessing lens flare
- Overcoming difficulty focusing
- Achieving correct exposure

This chapter outlines the strategies you need to turn heavily backlit scenes into photographic gold.

Harness Lens Flare

Lens flare is caused when light enters through the front of the lens and scatters through the internal optical elements. This extraneous light often degrades image quality and drastically reduces contrast. That technical speak means lens flare has the potential to create very distracting highlights and can make your images look muddy from low contrast. In backlit scenes, lens flare can totally dominate an image if you don't control it properly. We shot **Figure 9.1** directly into the sun. You can see how the light imparts a glowing lens flare to the portrait and decreases the overall contrast.

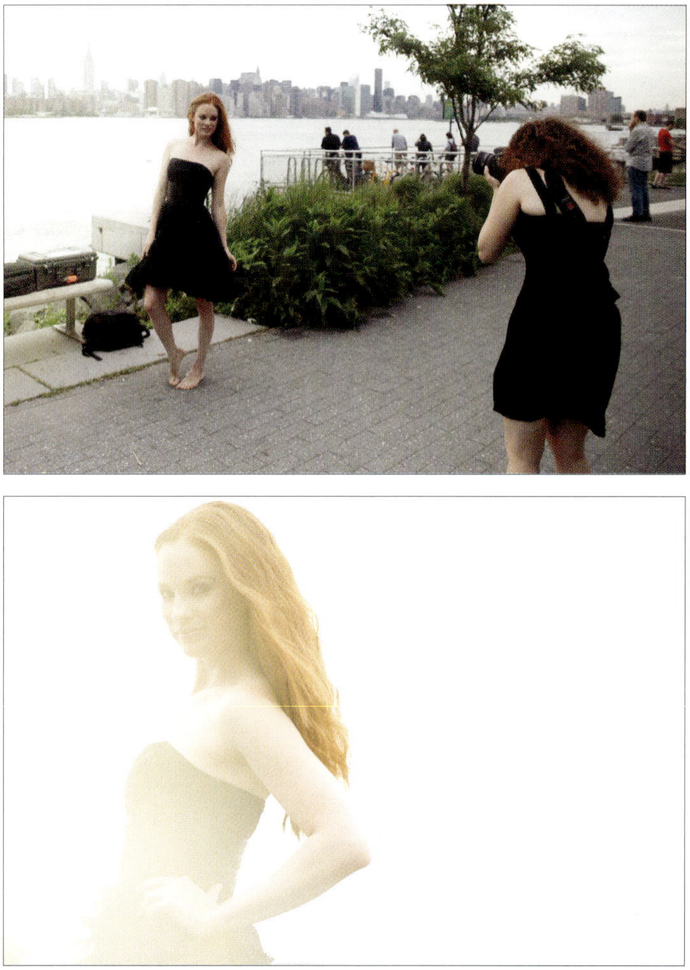

FIGURE 9.1
Shot directly into the sun, this portrait suffers from lens flare and an overall muddy look of decreased contrast.

To cut down on lens flare, you can try using a lens hood, also known as a lens shade, to block out undesirable sources of light (**Figure 9.2**). Most lenses already come with a basic hood, but a number of vendors offer larger shades to make shooting into the sun even easier.

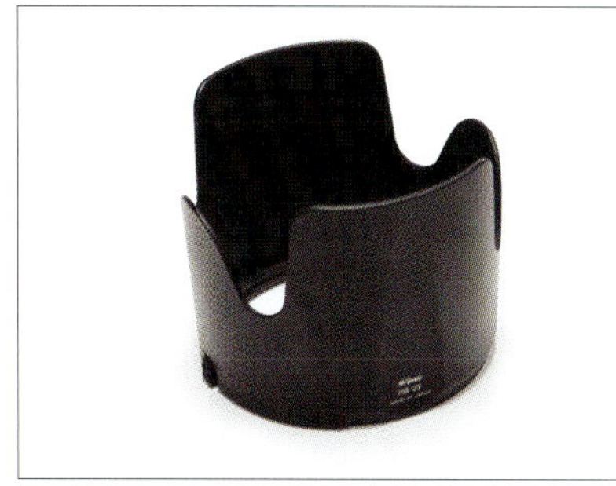

FIGURE 9.2

When shooting on location, use a lens hood, especially for backlit scenes.

If you don't have a lens hood available or are still experiencing lens flare even with a hood, you can try some additional blocking strategies. Simply hold your hand in front of the sun to block off light, while leaving your subject unobstructed. If the sun or light source isn't actually in your frame, you should be able to position your hand (or other **flag**) to block some of the light refracting within the lens. You could also have an assistant hold something above the lens to block excess light. In **Figure 9.3**, we used a reflector with the black side towards the camera to block excess sunlight from hitting the lens, cutting down lens flare significantly. Finally, you can stick your subject in front of the sun to block off the direct rays, reduce lens flare, and make focusing easier.

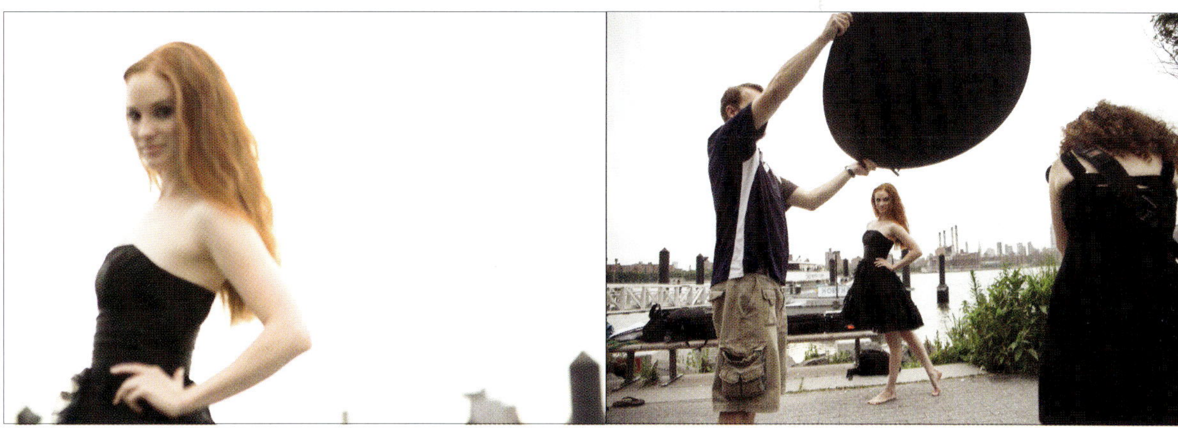

FIGURE 9.3

With its black side toward the camera, a reflector helps prevent direct light from hitting the lens and causing flare. You can see the resulting image has more contrast and a better quality of light. Instead of a reflector, you could also use a piece of cardboard or other foam core to block the light.

A completely different approach to lens flare is to embrace it. Don't block it, rock it! In fact, backlit images with lens flare can set a whimsical or romantic mood, lending drama and emotion to your images. Lens flare is often more flattering at wider apertures when the background becomes a softer flare or blur (think f/1.4 to f/2.8). Your biggest challenge is to vary your shooting angle to prevent the lens flare from obscuring your subject's face. When you get comfortable with lens flare, it can be a great creative tool. In **Figure 9.4**, we used a silver reflector as well as purposeful lens flare to create a striking image. (You'll learn more about using light modifiers later in the book.)

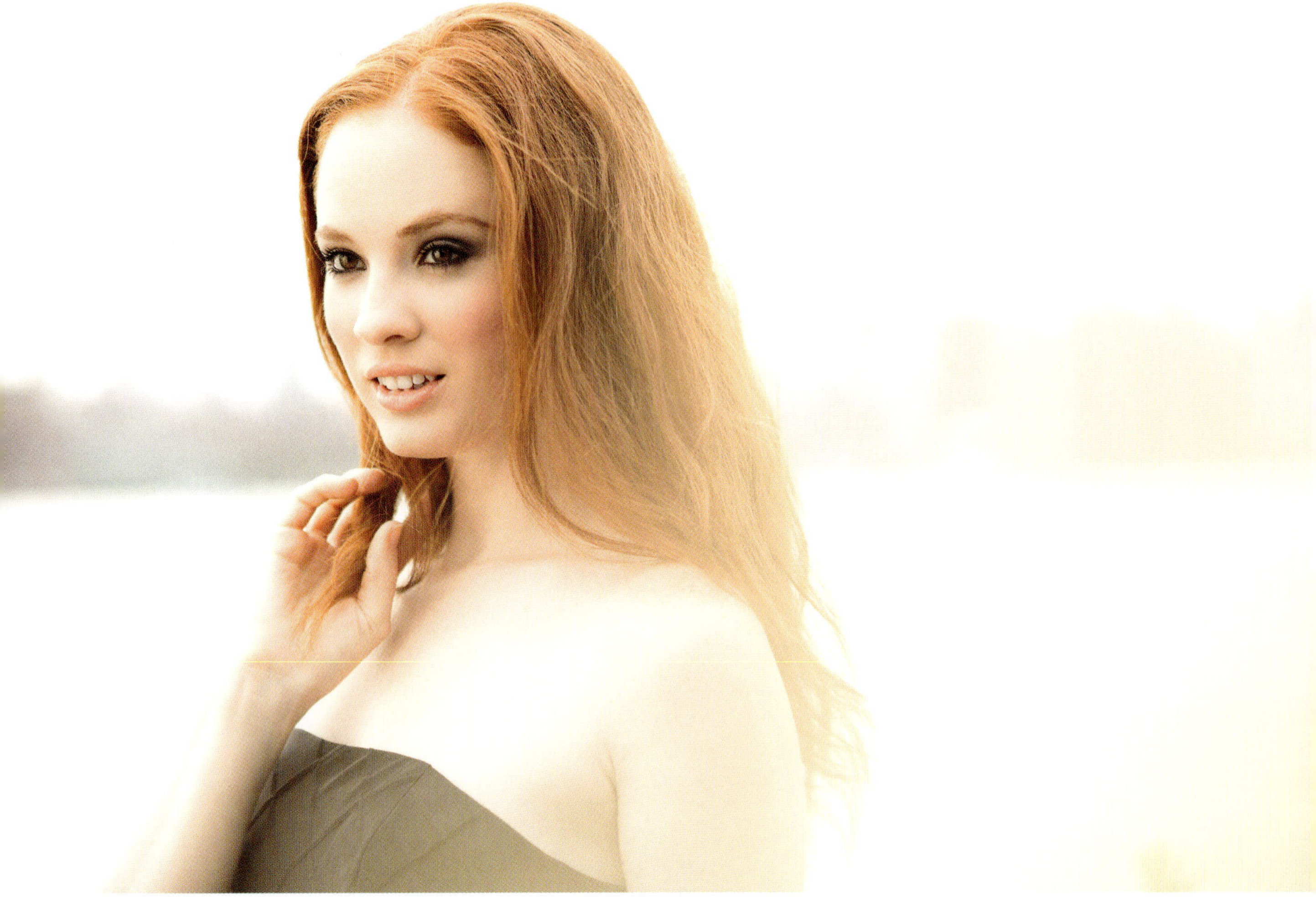

✔ FIGURE 9.4
Lens flare doesn't always have to be an enemy, but instead can be a great visual tool when controlled correctly. Here lens flare adds ambiance and a light mood.

Overcome Difficulty Focusing

Shooting into heavy backlighting can confuse your camera, especially if you have an older digital camera with more a primitive auto-focus system. The camera searches for areas of high contrast and often will select something in the background or an area of contrast around the edge of your subject. This may result in a slightly misfocused image or even a strongly back-focused image. Many beginning photographers find this to be the most challenging part of backlit portraiture. In fact, even experienced photographers suffer from misfocused images when dealing with heavily backlit situations (**Figure 9.5**).

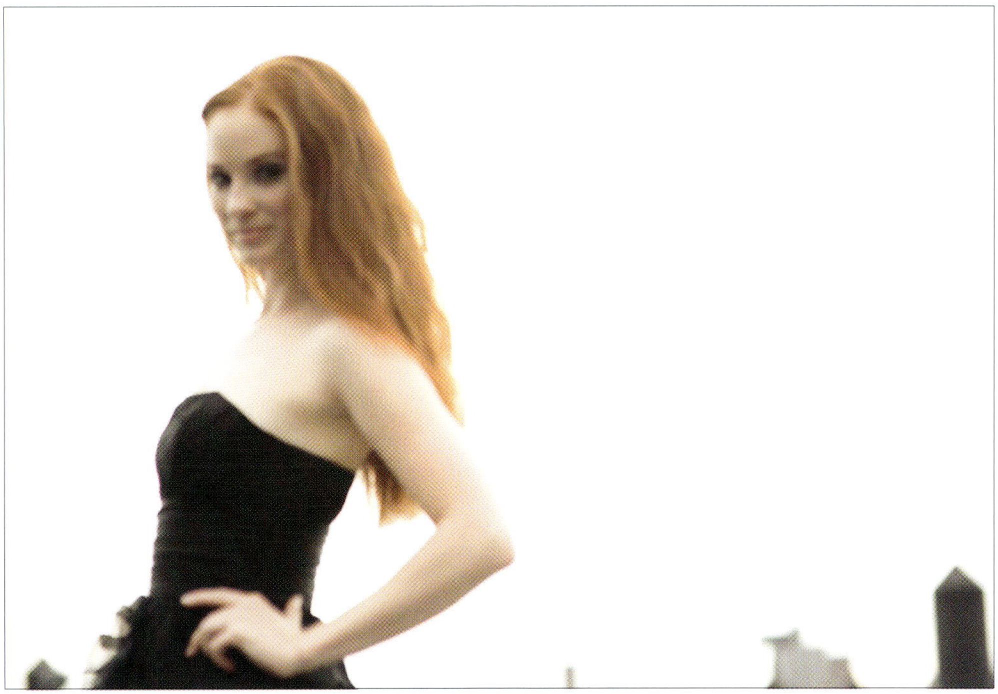

FIGURE 9.5
Heavily backlit scenes are a challenge for auto-focus systems. Often you end up with misfocused images like this one.

Your first option for limiting this focusing dilemma is to decrease lens flare. The direct or refracted light entering into your lens decreases contrast and makes it difficult for the camera to decipher the intended area of focus. Block off the sun, put on a lens hood, do anything to cut down on direct backlight. In fact, if you can, align the sun directly behind your subject (hide it from the camera's view) and then lock the focus. Reducing light into the lens makes finding focus easier for your camera. When you hide the sun behind your subject (or other object), you can depress your shutter button half way to lock the focus, and then recompose your frame as desired.

Finally, take control of your auto-focus by selecting a specific focus point. Choosing a focus point is a great way to tell your camera the most important element in your frame, instead of allowing auto-focus to simply select the area of the frame it *thinks* requires focus. Refer to your camera's manual for specific information on setting selective focus points on your camera. Newer (and also higher-end cameras) usually have more focus points and more mode choices.

Obviously, you want your subject's face to be in focus, but when shooting up close with a narrow **depth of field**, you're working with only a few millimeters of space that'll be sharp. In this case, you'll want to be sure that the eye of your subject closest to the camera is the one that you focus on. Focusing on the back eye or ears just looks funny.

BEGINNER TIP Separate your focus and shutter.

By default, your camera's focus button is also its shutter. In other words, you focus with the same button that you push to take a photograph. You have the ability, however, to separate these two buttons by activating the focus button to the back of your camera. Doing so gives you more control over your focus and helps to lock focus in a backlit situation. Because each camera system is different, you'll need to consult your camera's manual for the specifics of how to adjust back-button focus. Back-button focus also helps you when tracking focus with moving subjects, which comes in handy when shooting sports, weddings, and events.

Achieve Correct Exposure

When you shoot a heavily backlit image, achieving the correct exposure can be challenging. If you leave the decision up to your camera's metering system, the images will often be dramatically underexposed. The meter detects the highlights in the background and exposes for these highlights, resulting in a nearly silhouetted or underexposed image (**Figure 9.6**).

Because there is such a wide range in exposure between the highlight area of the photograph and the shadow areas, you must find a solution for exposure. You must either expose for the highlights, expose for the shadows, or find a way to compress that wide exposure range. Compressing the exposure range means darkening down the highlights and brightening up the shadows so that there isn't such a great difference between the two. You can solve your exposure dilemma with natural light or by introducing off-camera flash. Consider your natural light solutions first.

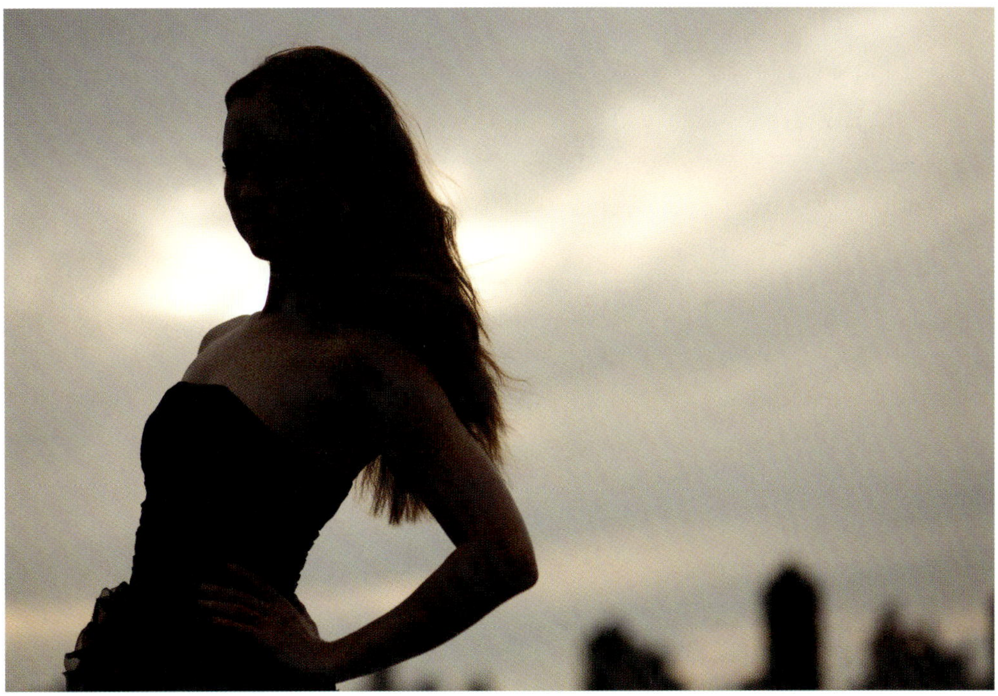

FIGURE 9.6
When you leave your camera up to its own devices, backlit scenes can be quite tricky. Often the camera will expose for the bright sky, leaving your subject in silhouette or drastically underexposed.

Natural Light Solutions

The best approach when shooting in a backlit situation is to meter for the face of your subject. Your subject's face is the most important element in the frame, so this is where you need to ensure the best possible exposure. There are a few ways you can go about this.

First, you can set your camera to **Manual (M) mode**. This allows you to dial in all of the settings for a precise and consistant exposure as seen in **Figure 9.7**. If you are comfortable with it, this approach can help you coax out the most accurate exposure settings. Erik prefers this method because it is straight to the point and doesn't involve tweaking the camera's auto-exposure values; it bypasses them altogether.

FIGURE 9.7

When you take control of the exposure in a backlit situation, you can correctly expose for your subject instead of allowing your camera to dictate the exposure.

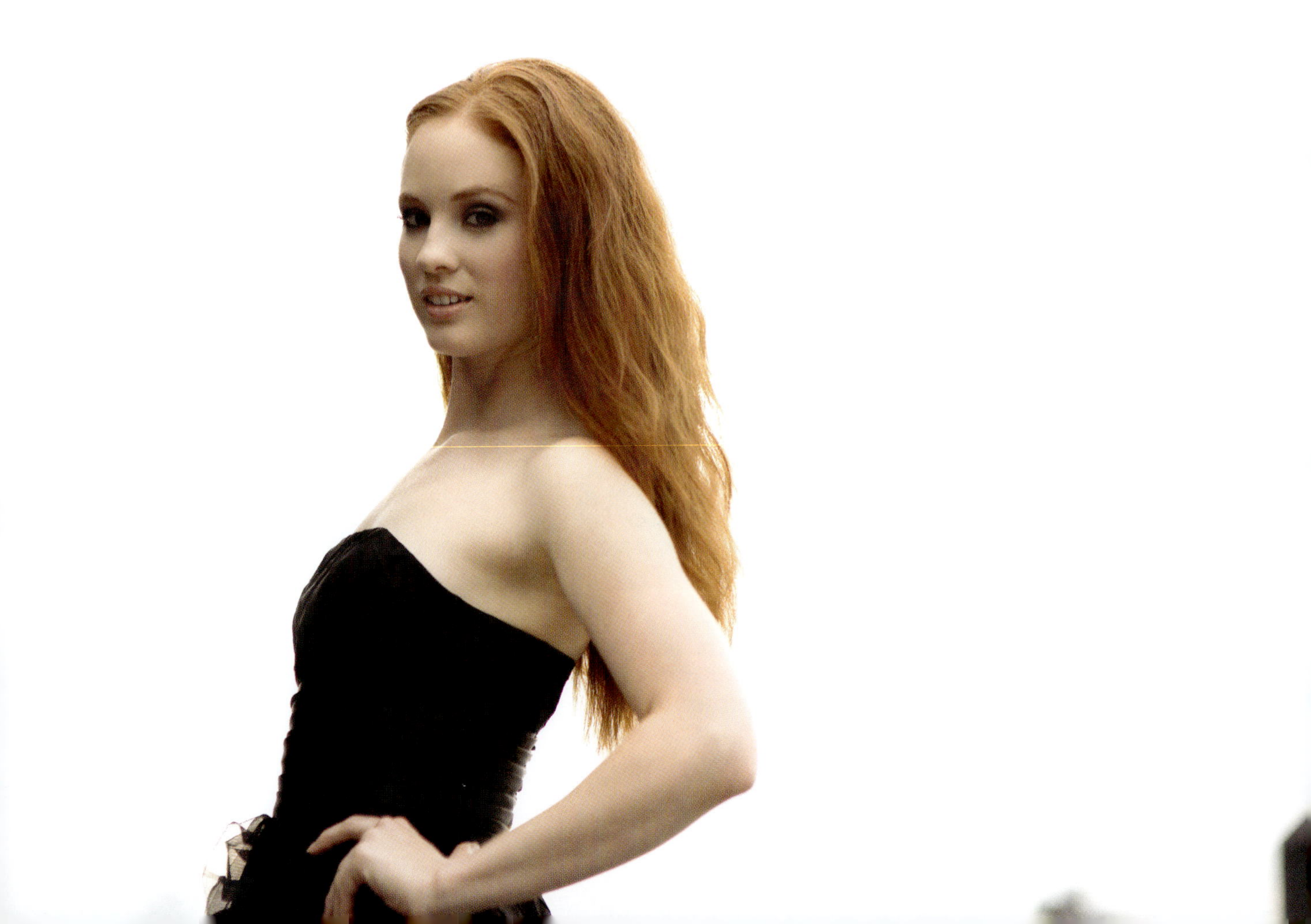

Next, you can use **Aperture Priority mode** with added adjustments from **Exposure Compensation**. Yes, it's a big name, but basically you are allowing your camera to set the shutter speed based upon the aperture you selected. From there, you tell your camera whether the exposure should be lighter or darker by dialing in the Exposure Compensation button. This option enables your camera to adjust to changes in lighting automatically while still giving you power to steer your camera's auto exposure.

In Aperture Priority mode, you set the aperture of the exposure. This allows you to control your depth of field. As the lighting in the scene changes, your camera is automatically adjusting the shutter speed (and your final exposure) to increase or decrease the light in the image accordingly (**Figure 9.8**). For example, suppose you have a backlit image. You want your f-stop to be f/2.8, so you set your camera on Aperture Priority. The camera then reads "ISO 100, f/2.8, 1/125 sec." If the image is too dark, you can dial your exposure compensation to +1. This will make the exposure one stop brighter by decreasing the shutter speed. The camera will now read "ISO 100, f/2.8, 1/60 sec."

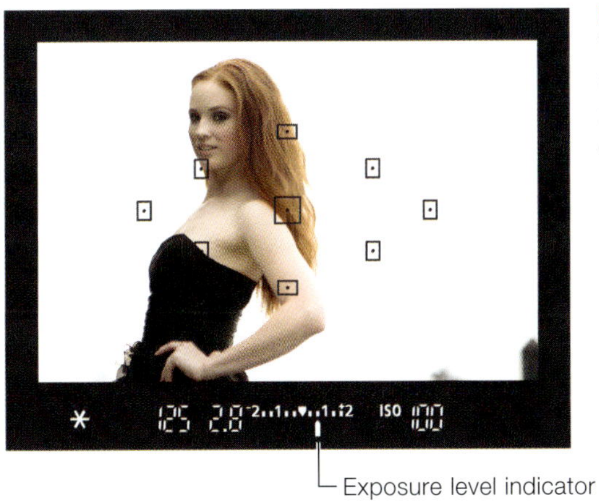

FIGURE 9.8
While manual metering is often a great option for correctly exposing backlit scenes, Aperture Priority mode with Exposure Compensation is another commonly used exposure approach.

WATCH IT! Beware of slow shutters.

In Aperture Priority mode, when you adjust the exposure compensation, you're automatically changing the shutter speed to let in more light. The slower the shutter speed, the more difficult it is to hold the camera steady by hand and retain crisp focus. Avoid taking hand-held shots with exposures longer than 1/focal length of your lens. If your shutter speed is getting too slow, start to increase your ISO. Many newer digital cameras can handle much higher ISOs with minimal noise.

Finally, you can use your camera's selective focus and Spot-Metering mode to expose for your subject's face. Instead of allowing your camera to take an average exposure reading for the entire frame, spot metering enables you to set exposure based upon a specific area of your photo, such as the subject's face.

In effect, you are telling your camera what the most important area of the photograph is and setting the exposure accordingly. In a heavily backlit situation, you are exposing for the shadow, and your background highlights may become overexposed. Be sure that these highlights are carefully placed so they are not distracting to the eye. For example, overexposing a bald sky can help create a clean background for your subject, whereas an overexposed highlight on a car can be a loud distraction.

Another approach is to compress the huge exposure range between very bright highlights and relatively dark shadows by using a reflector. A backlit scene is a perfect opportunity to use a reflector because you can easily catch the light behind the subject and bounce it back onto the face. Put the sun at the subject's back, and hold the reflector at an angle to catch the light. This, of course, is ideal when dealing with sunlight (as opposed to some odd-colored light source that will create discoloration if used to illuminate the face). White or silver reflectors are ideal. Gold and a silver-gold mix are often too warm when the sun is lower in the sky and already warm in tone. After the lackluster shot in **Figure 9.9**, notice how we not only lightened the face with a silver reflector, but also improved the contrast on the face in **Figure 9.10**. The quality of light is improved, and catchlights appear in the eyes. (Check Chapters 1 and 2 for more tips on reflector use.)

WATCH IT! Avoid too much fill.

Particularly in backlit situations, you very easily can have too much reflection. Because the sun is at an ideal angle to reflect, a common misconception is that you should reflect as much light as possible to brighten up the subject and to more closely match the exposure of the sun backlighting the subject.

When reflecting with evening light, try feathering the light past your subject, but not bouncing it all back squarely onto the model. If you try to reflect at full power, the light will be harsh and unflattering on the face, as mentioned in previous chapters.

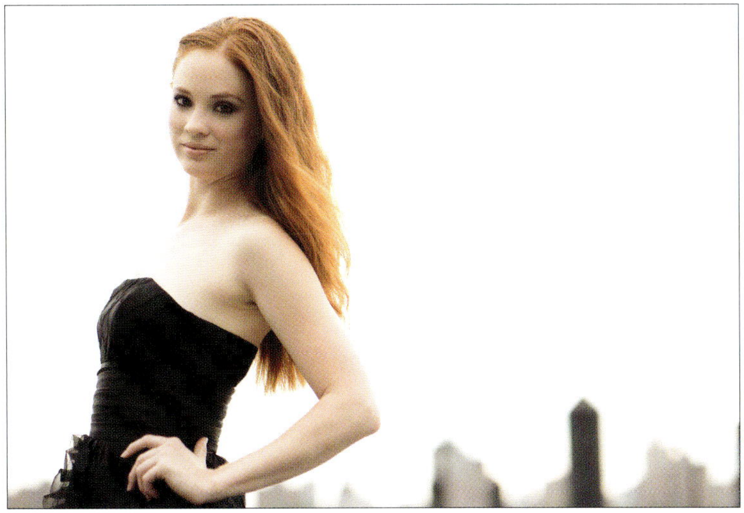

FIGURE 9.9
Without a reflector, the light on the face is dull with shadows in the subject's eyes.

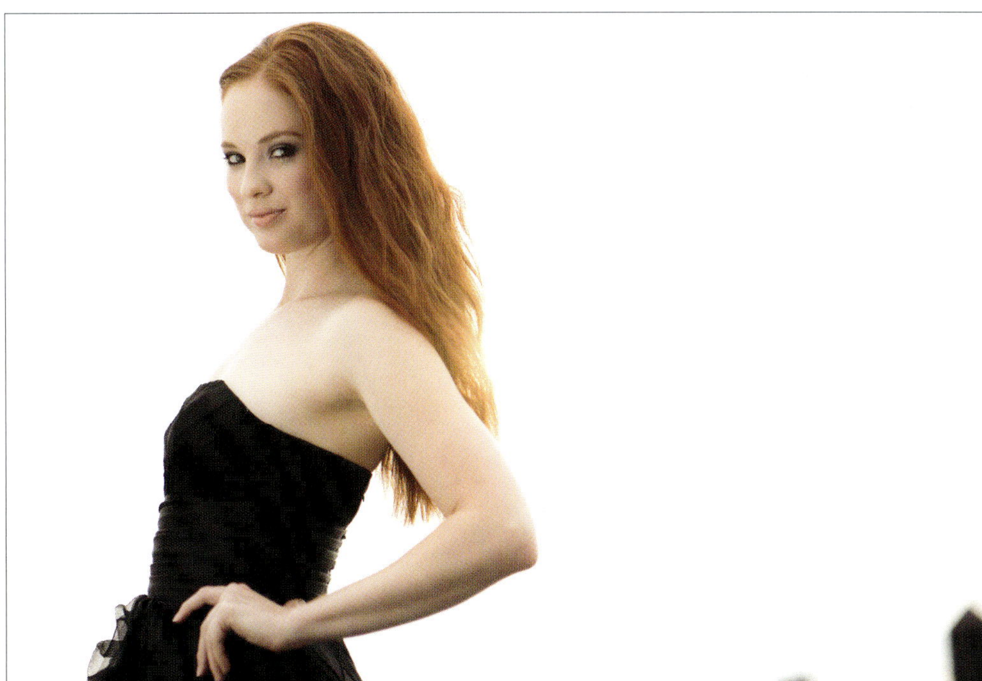

FIGURE 9.10
A silver reflector significantly improves the image by adding a direction of light, filling in shadows in the eyes, and increasing contrast on the face.

Flash Solutions

The advantage of using an off-camera flash in heavy backlight lies in your ability to expose separately for your model and bright background. With a reflector, you're just bouncing around the light that's already there, as opposed to a flash where you have complete control over the quality and amount of light hitting your subject. This control gives you creative freedom to adjust the lighting ratio between your subject and the background.

The first step in the process of using a flash for fill is the same for any other photo you would shoot. Without even turning on the flash, take a photo of the existing ambient light. From this photo, determine the necessary camera settings to produce a background with the exposure that you want. As seen in **Figure 9.11**, your subject will be dark but you will have established a base exposure from which you can build in your flash.

Now to turn on that flash! There is no magic flash power setting, but by manually setting the flash power, you can dial it up and down until your subject is properly exposed. For **Figure 9.12**, we triggered a speedlight with PocketWizard wireless radio triggers. To create a softer, more pleasing light on the model's face, we added a 60-inch Westcott umbrella (F.J. Westcott, www.fjwestcott.com) to create a larger light source.

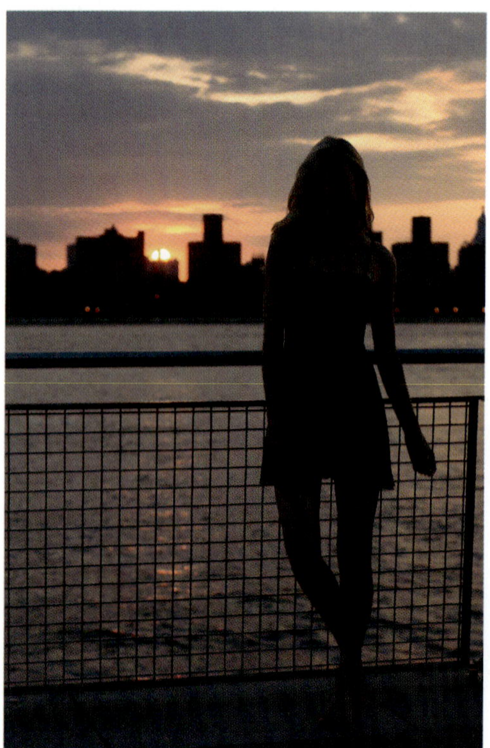

FIGURE 9.11
When shooting with flash to balance with backlight, shoot a starting image (before the flash) to determine the correct settings for the ambient exposure. We recommend you shoot in Manual mode to lock in this ideal exposure.

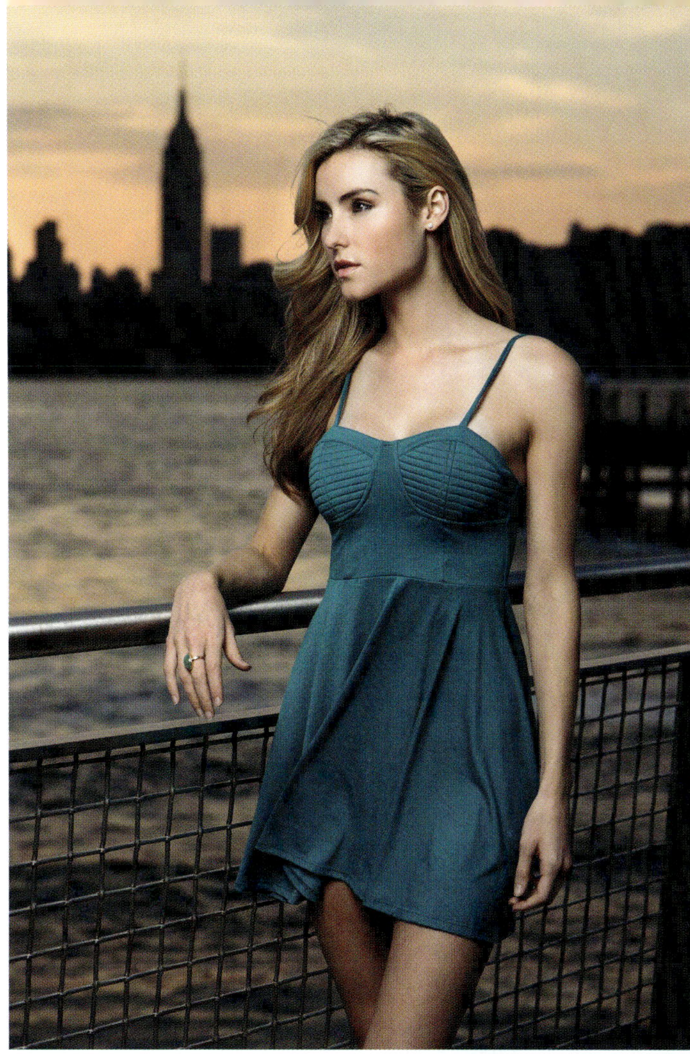

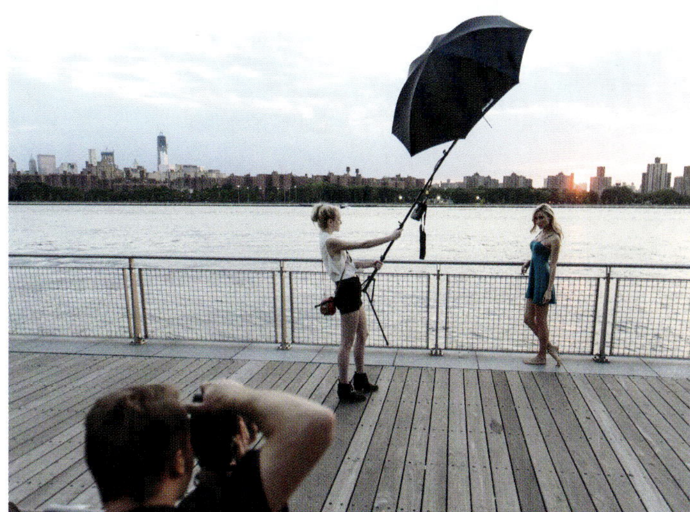

FIGURE 9.12
To properly expose the model and create a softer light, we used a bare, off-camera speedlight modified by a 60-inch bounce umbrella.

WATCH IT! Monitor your flash sync speed.

When using your flash off camera, make sure to keep your shutter speed slower than 1/200 of a second. Check your camera's manual for the specific Flash Sync Speed or X-Sync Speed setting. This is the fastest shutter speed that you can shoot at while using a flash. If you exceed this speed, the resulting image will not be properly illuminated by the flash. Try adjusting your aperture or ISO to compensate for this cap.

Late afternoon when the sun has just set is often referred to as the Golden Hour, because right around sunset, the temperature of the light becomes very warm. In fact, the color temperature becomes very near that of a tungsten lightbulb. Beautiful as the light is, it creates an imbalance in color temperatures between the Daylight temperature of your flash's light and that of the sunset. Fortunately, you can attach CTO (Color Temperature Orange) gels to your speedlight to shift it to a warmer temperature, just like you saw in Chapter 4, "Mixed Color Temperatures." The result can be seen in **Figure 9.13**, where the quality of the light is the same, but now the model and the rest of the scene are the same **color temperature**.

With the flash exposure and color temperature dialed in, you can start to tweak the image in other ways. Because the light from your speedlight travels at such high speeds, it is not affected by your camera's shutter speed. This means that you are free to adjust your shutter speed, up to your camera's X-Sync speed, and all the while the flash exposure on your model will remain constant. Notice how much lighter the background is in **Figure 9.14**, yet the model is still lit the same. No settings were changed except for the shutter speed. By drastically dragging, or slowing down, the shutter speed, more ambient light was allowed into the final exposure.

This ability to alter the **lighting ratio** between the ambient-lit background and the flash-lit subject gives you immense creative control over the final exposure. **Figures 9.15** and **9.16** demonstrate even more variations of this lighting ratio, and the results range from a very natural looking scene to a more dramatic contrasty photograph. Make sure you experiment with this balance to match your own specific style.

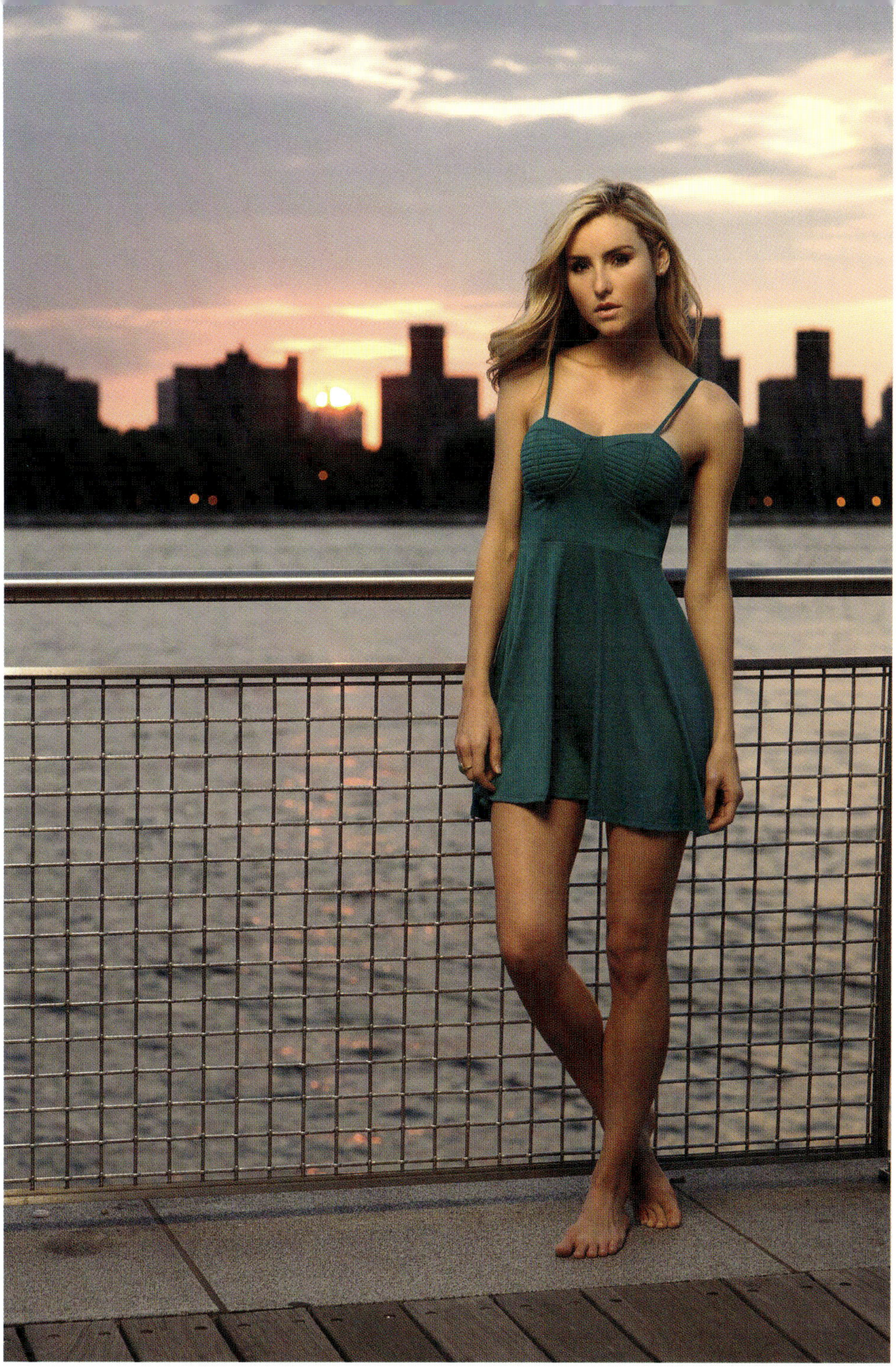

FIGURE 9.13

The model is lit by a single speedlight warmed up in color temperature with a CTO gel and modified by a 60-inch bounce umbrella.

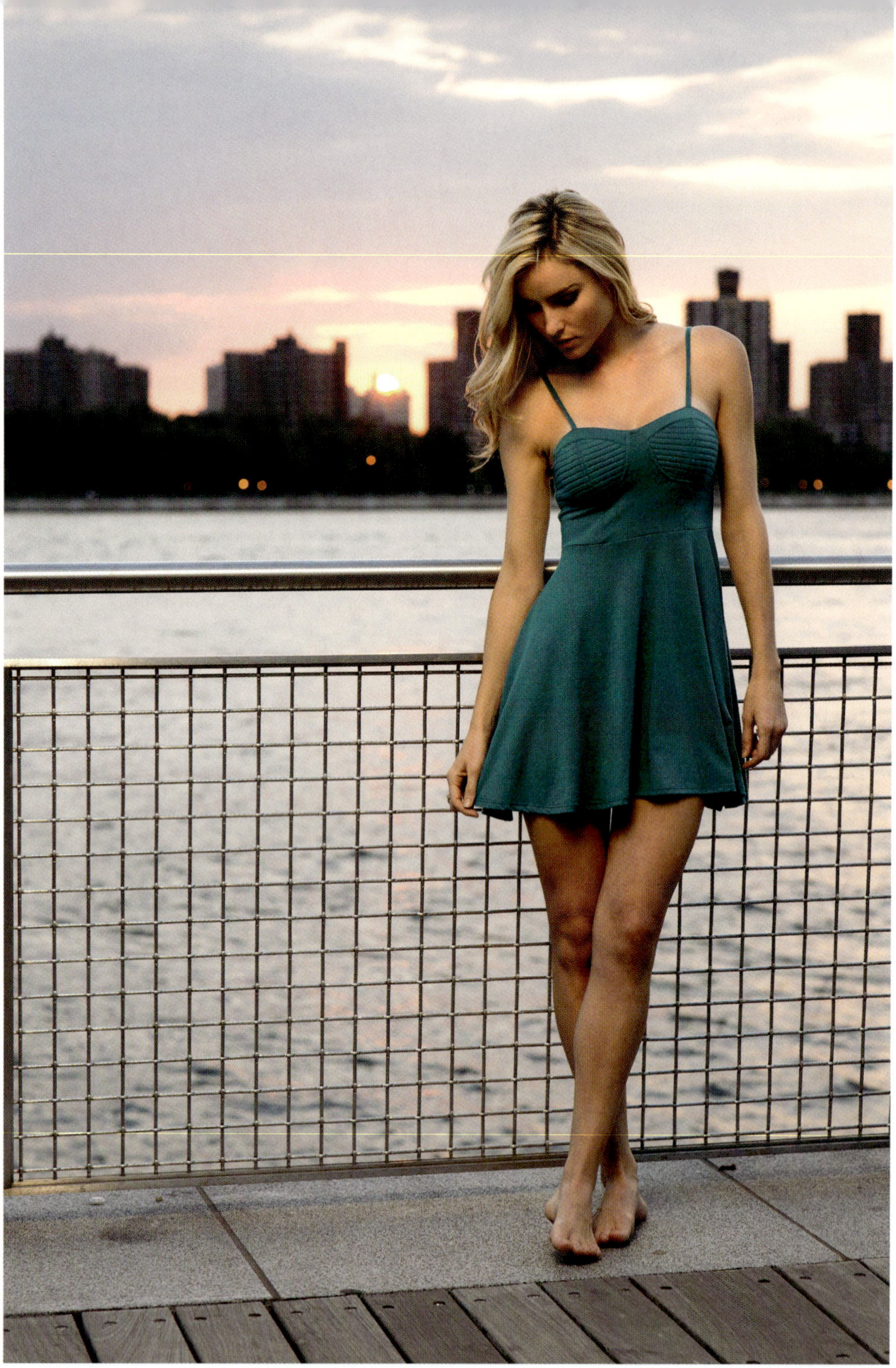

FIGURE 9.14
Doubling the shutter speed lets in more ambient background light.

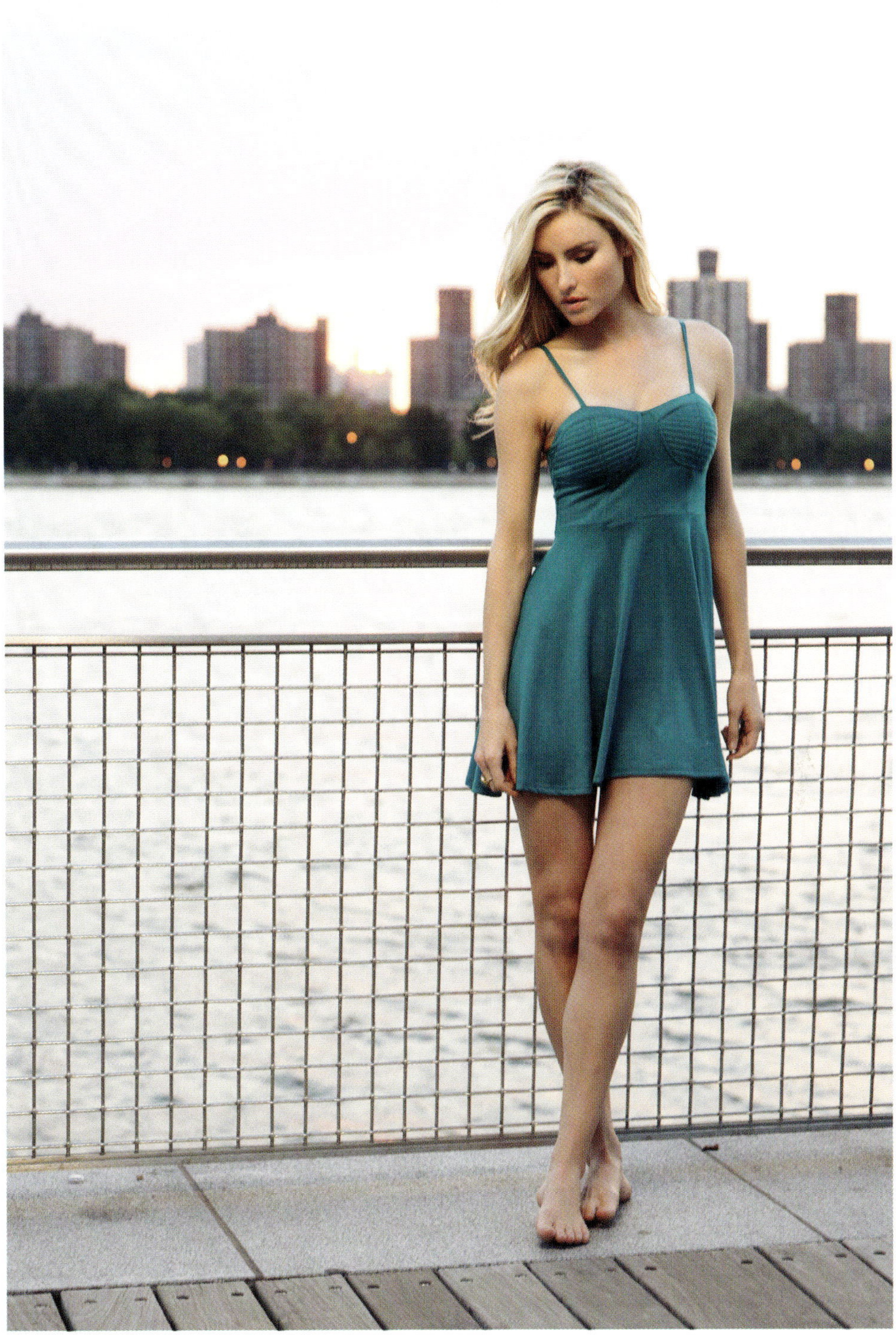

FIGURE 9.15

Here the shutter speed was slowed down two more stops to let in even more ambient background light.

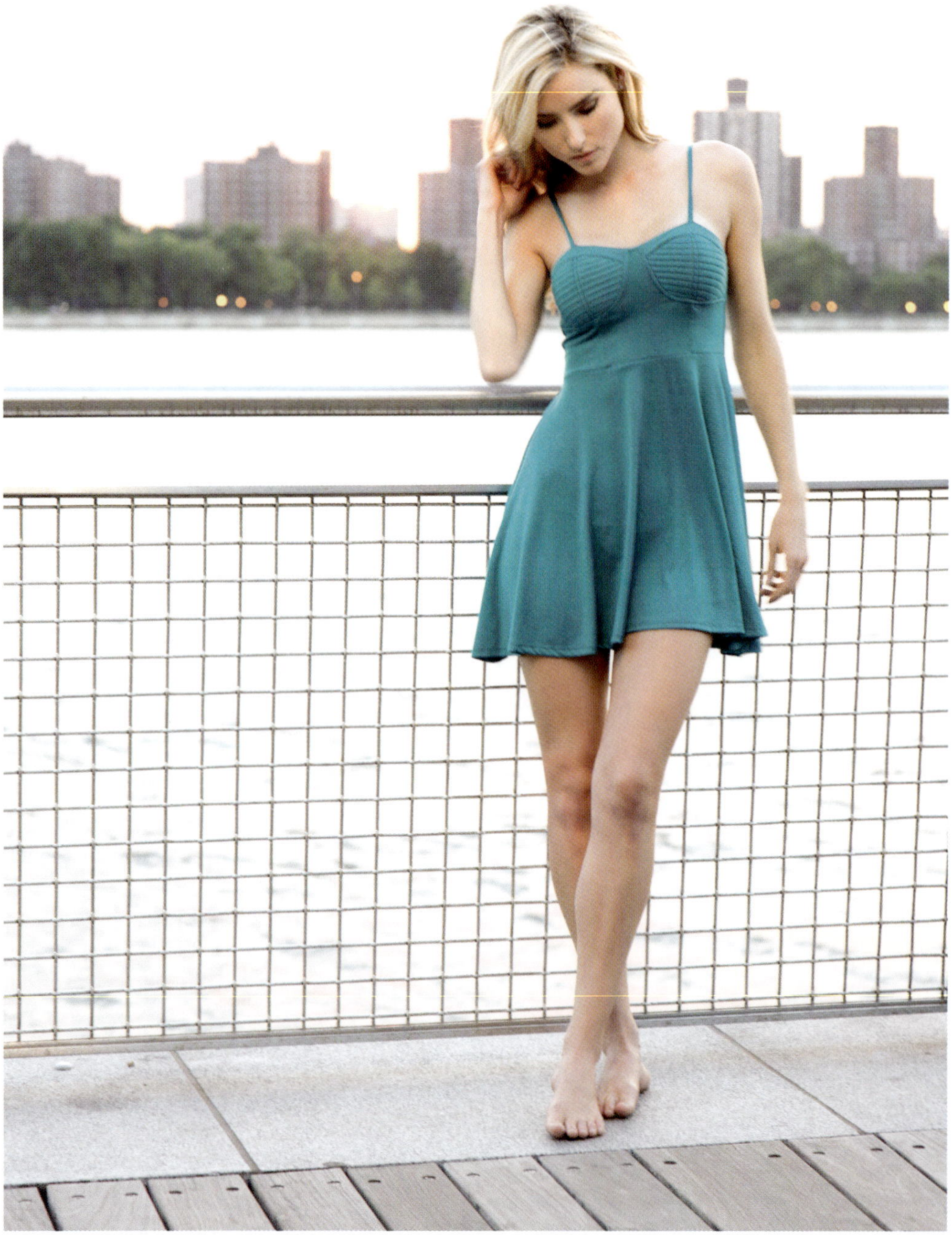

FIGURE 9.16
For an even more dramatic effect, the shutter speed was slowed down enough to match background exposure with the flash exposure on the model.

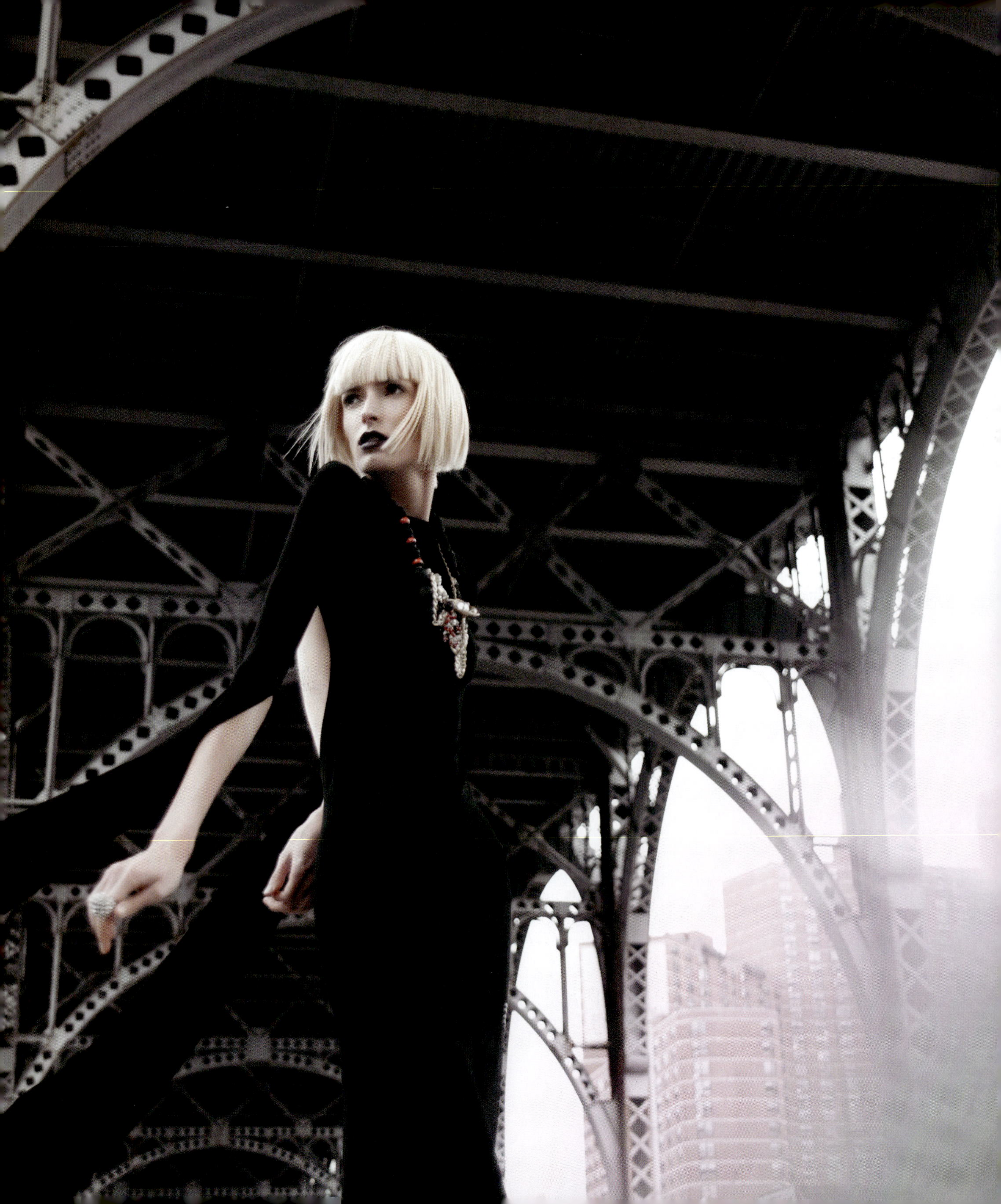

CHAPTER TEN
Overcast Day

Eventually, we all face a drab, overcast day during a shoot. Although many photographers cringe at the thought, these seemingly adverse conditions often present great opportunities, like high-impact backgrounds! For example, Lindsay created **Figure 10.1** on an overcast day. The detail in the clouds is what made for an eye-catching image.

On dark and rainy days, the clouds hang low in the sky, imparting a foreboding tone to your images. While these skies make for dramatic backgrounds, unfortunately, they often throw unflattering light on your subject's face. Some people think, mistakenly, that an overcast sky creates a good quality of light because it is soft and even. Unfortunately the light lacks contrast and can cause that undesirable raccoon-eyes effect. So how do you capture the drama without this?

Using reflectors, flash, and innovative posing in natural light are just few great ways to make flattering, well-lit portraits on the most miserable of overcast days.

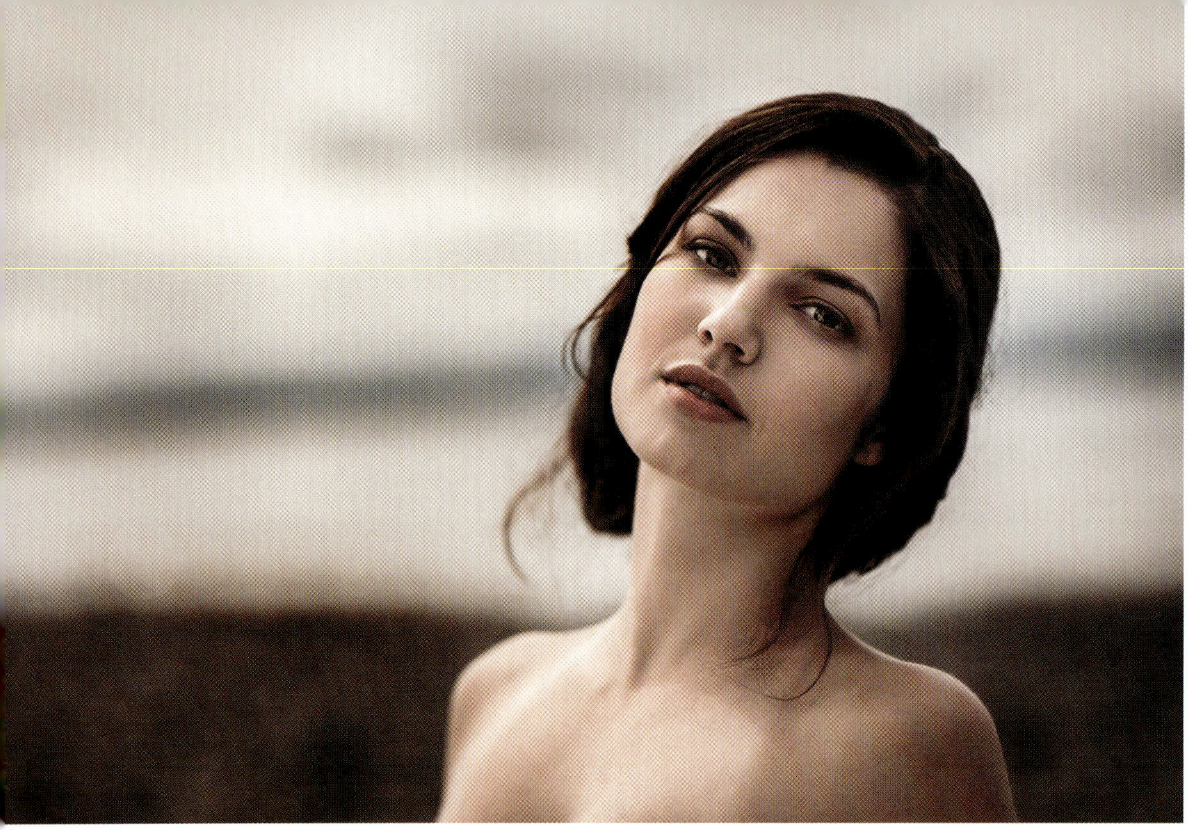

FIGURE 10.1
By shooting on a cloudy day or with bad weather, you can make use of the added sky detail to create drama in your images. This dramatic cloud image was created during one of Lindsay's fashion engagement sessions.

Watch Your Angles

The simplest thing you can do to improve overcast light is to physically move your subject to face different directions. Even on an overcast day, the light is not the same from all angles. In fact, moving your subject can completely change the direction of light and significantly improve the quality of light on the face. Examine the light on the subject's face, and slowly rotate the person. Watch to see which angles give more contrast and flattering light.

Take a look at **Figures 10.2** and **10.3**. In Figure 10.2, the subject has miserable light on her face, deep shadows in her eyes, and a completely unflattering direction of light. When the model is turned 180 degrees to face the opposite direction, the light improves markedly (Figure 10.3). Keep this in mind when working with your subjects under any condition: Even a slight change in position can completely change the light on their faces.

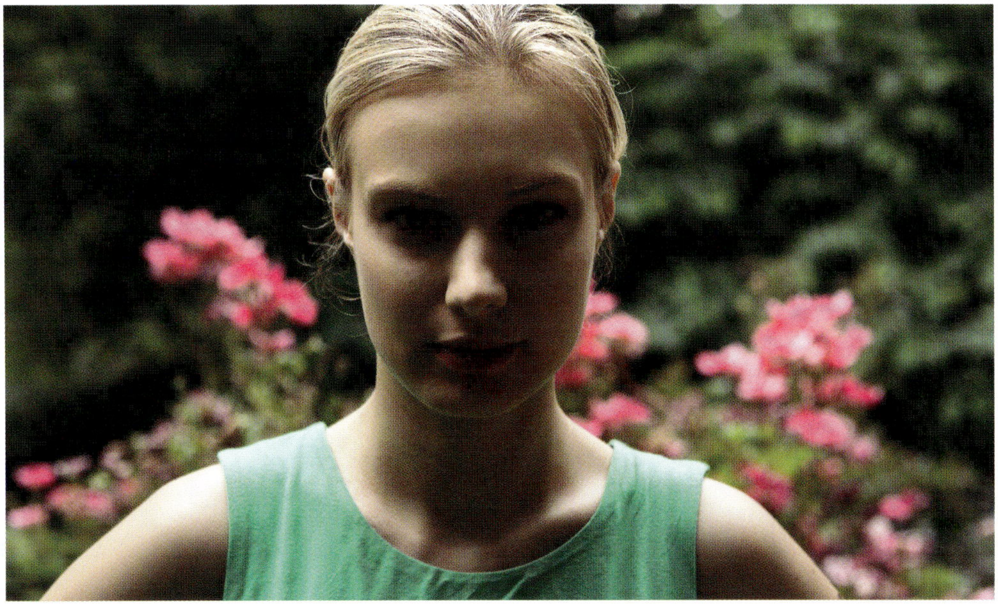

FIGURE 10.2
The light on this girl's face is awful with unusual highlights and deep shadows.

FIGURE 10.3
By rotating the subject 180 degrees, you can completely change the quality of light. Even on an overcast day, the direction and angle of your subject makes a massive difference in the image.

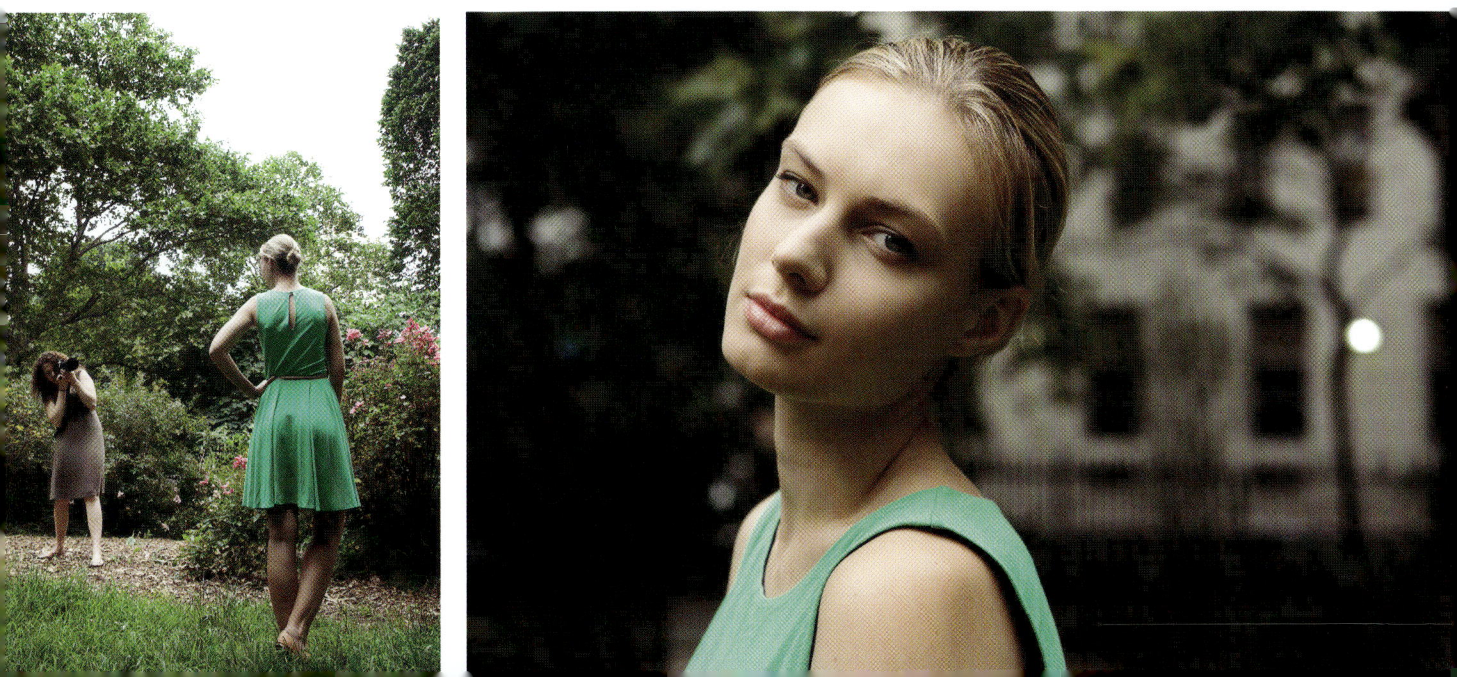

TAKEAWAY ACTION

Try rotating or moving your subject to drastically change the quality of light on the face on an overcast day.

Try Reflectors

The most common solution to an overcast day is to use a reflector to fill in the shadows and add contrast to the light, similar to the techniques you learned in Chapters 1 and 2. You'll want to do a few things differently on an overcast day, however. For example, you may need to get closer to your subject to fill in the shadows. On a *very* dark day, you may even want to put the reflector directly under the chin to kick light back into the eyes. Other times you may want to back off a bit and use a silver reflector. There is no right answer because overcast days are not all the same.

EQUIPMENT TIP Try a 5-in-1 Reflector for maximum versatility.

Because you want versatility, you may want to choose a reflector that contains a variety of reflecting surfaces like the 5-in-1 Reflector. Most have a combination of black, white, silver, silver-gold mix, and a diffusion material like the one in **Figure 10.4**. You can use the white to subtly fill in shadows up close. Silver can provide a cool or neutral fill when you need more light or are working at a distance. Silver-gold warms up the image a bit without over-saturating warm tones (like gold would do). Black is used to build in shadows to create contrast. Finally, the diffusion material is used to soften the light even more.

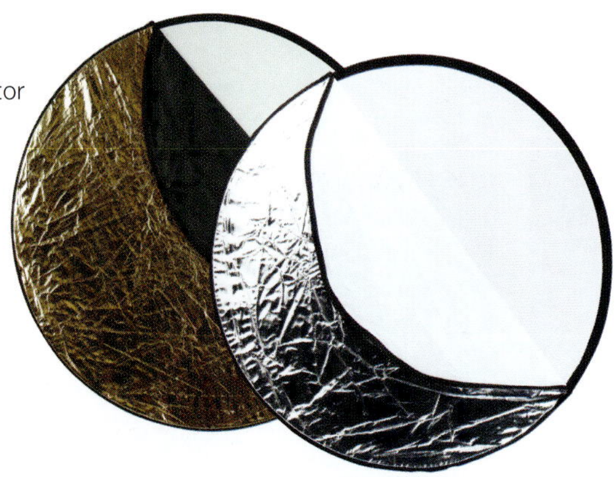

FIGURE 10.4
Choose a reflector that allows you versatility, such as this 5-in-1 Reflector that provides black, white, silver, silver-gold mix, and diffusion.

You'll need to experiment with the conditions you encounter, but here are a few guidelines for using three types of reflectors. Compare the results of using each with an original shot like in **Figure 10.5**.

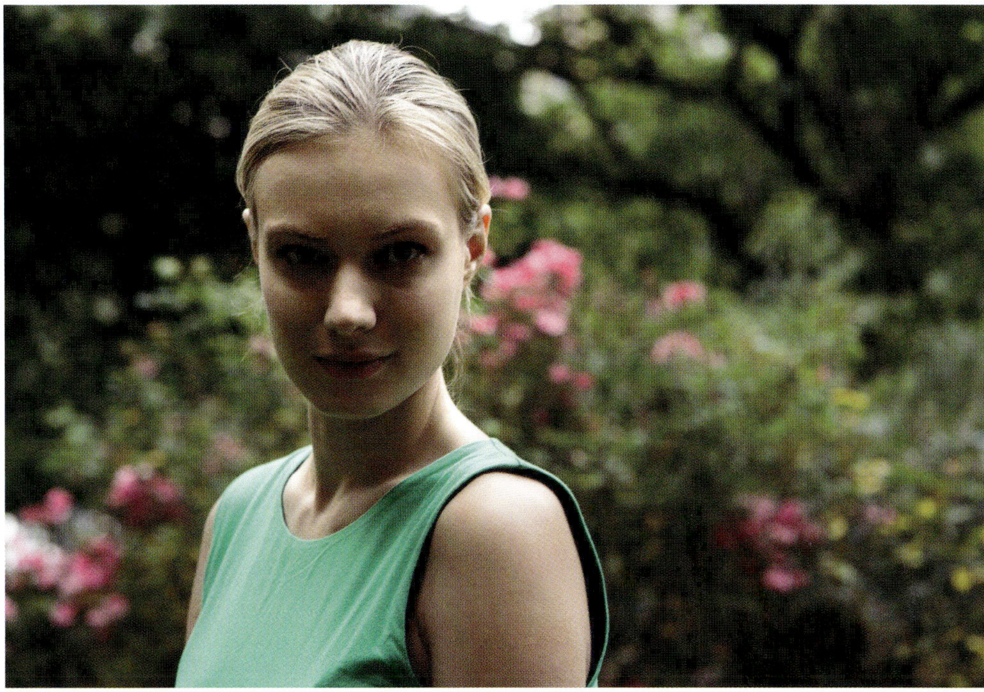

FIGURE 10.5
Again we have very undesirable light on the face. The majority of the light is at the back of the model's head and hitting her shoulders, with a small highlight on the nose.

- **Soft White:** A white reflector or white piece of foam-core board helps to give a soft and subtle fill to your image. You will have less **specular highlights** and a gentler fill, as shown in **Figure 10.6**. This is great for adding a touch of fill or just a bit of light into the eyes.

TAKEAWAY ACTION

White reflectors are best used in close to your subject. Their output isn't as efficient as a silver reflector, so offset this by really working them in there. The reward is a much softer fill light.

- **Silver:** A silver reflector will give your image more contrast and also a stronger fill, which is great for particularly dark days. With a silver reflector, you do not have to be extremely close to your subject. Instead, consider backing up and changing the reflector's angle to imitate a direction of light. For **Figure 10.7**, the reflector is very close to the subject; in **Figure 10.8** we backed up, thus dialing down the intensity of the fill light. Even on an overcast day, you do not need to have the reflector extremely close to the subject to get a pleasant fill.

TAKEAWAY ACTION

To imitate the existing direction of light, raise that reflector overhead. You'll find that tilting the bottom of the reflector towards your subject will maximize the output as well.

- **Silver-Gold Mix:** A reflector with a silver-gold mix will add a bit of warmth to your image to help combat the cooler color temperature of an overcast day. This hint of gold is also great during the winter months to warm the skin tones of people who haven't been out in the sun for a while. (**Figure 10.9**).

WATCH IT! Avoid gold reflectors.

Some photographers gravitate toward a warmer toned reflector on an overcast day, but there are very few times, if any, when an all-gold reflector is a good tool. Gold, typically, is unflattering because it is too warm and yellow in tone and looks unnatural. Also, using a gold reflector may cause uneven warmth in your image, creating areas that are golden and warm, while other areas are more blue and cool tones. Instead, try a silver-gold mix to warm up your images more subtly.

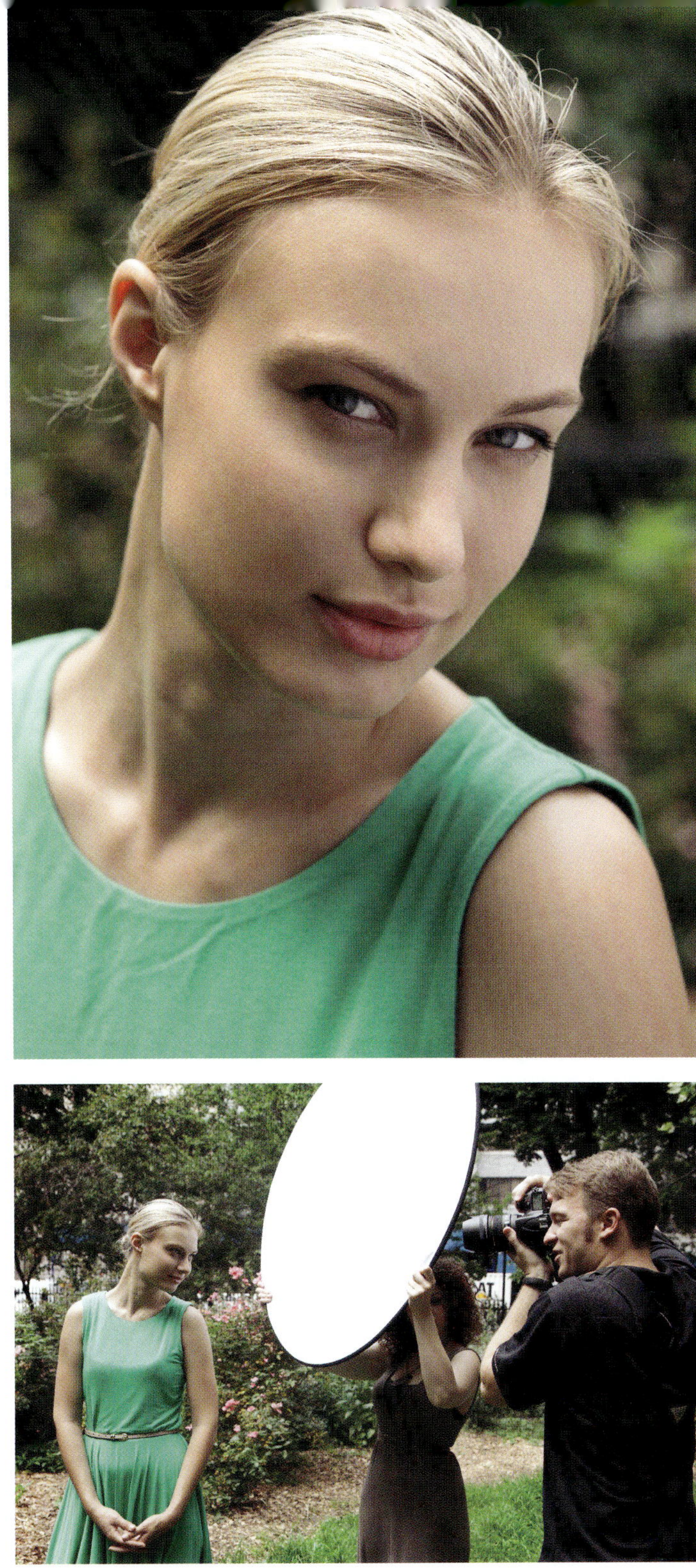

FIGURE 10.6
A white reflector is a great tool for filling in shadows when you want a soft and subtle effect. It is best used when very close to the subject.

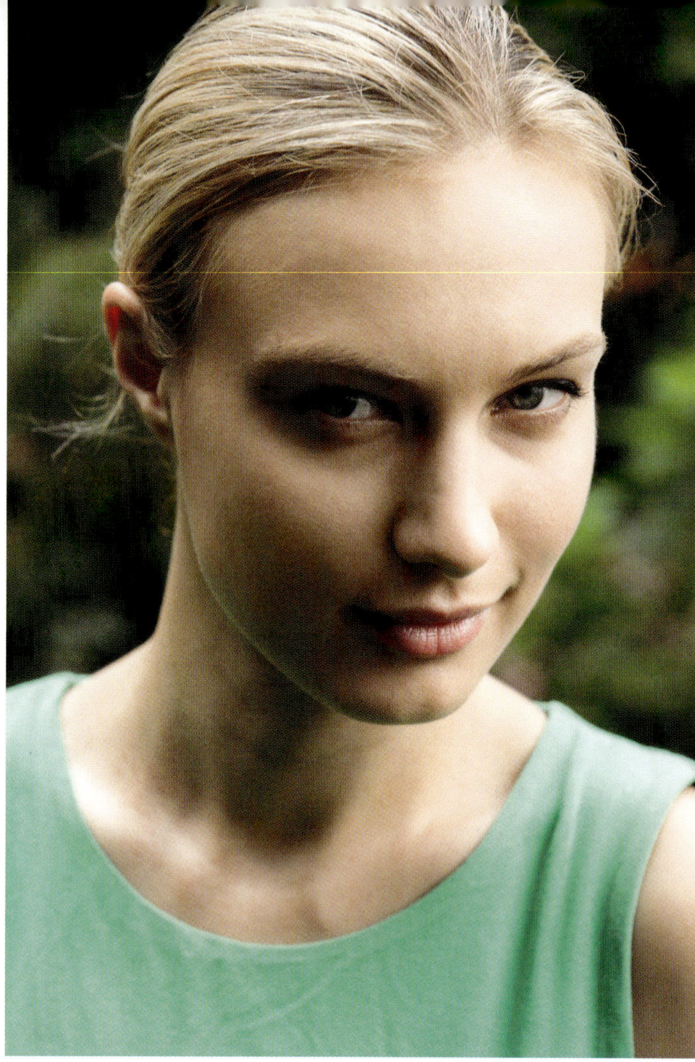

FIGURE 10.7
On an overcast day, a silver reflector is a great tool for filling in shadows. Because silver reflector is more specular, it creates more contrast. Here we used a silver reflector very close to the model's face. In fact, the reflector is a bit too close to her face.

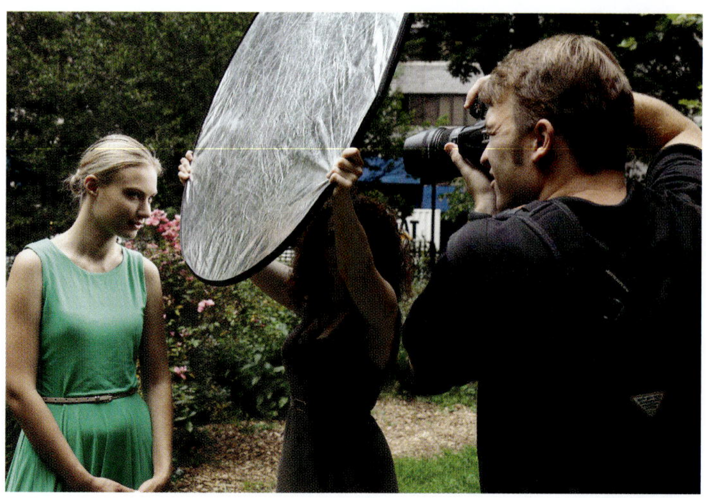

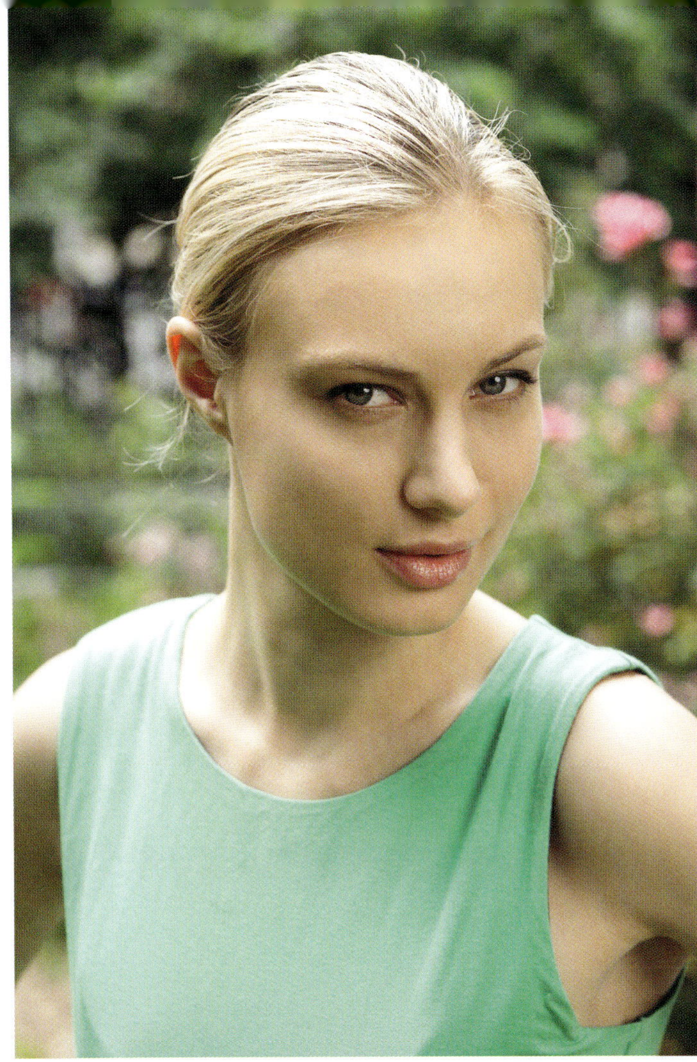

FIGURE 10.8
Backing the reflector away from the model creates a much more even and pleasing light on her face. The optimum distance of the model to the reflector will vary from shoot to shoot. If you're not happy with the results in close, put some distance between the reflector and your model and try again, as seen here.

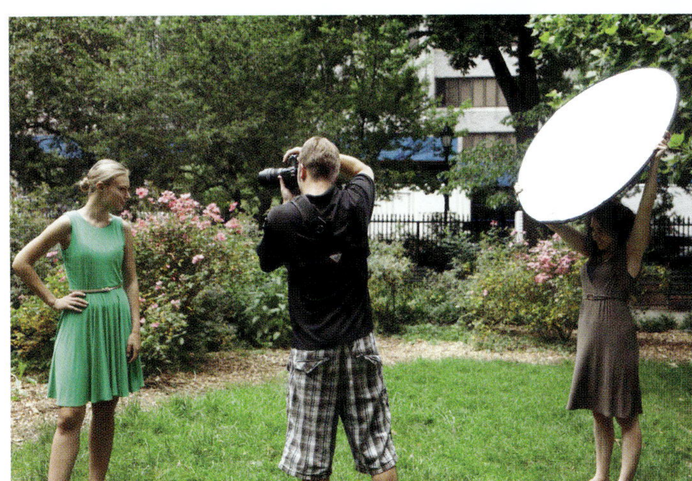

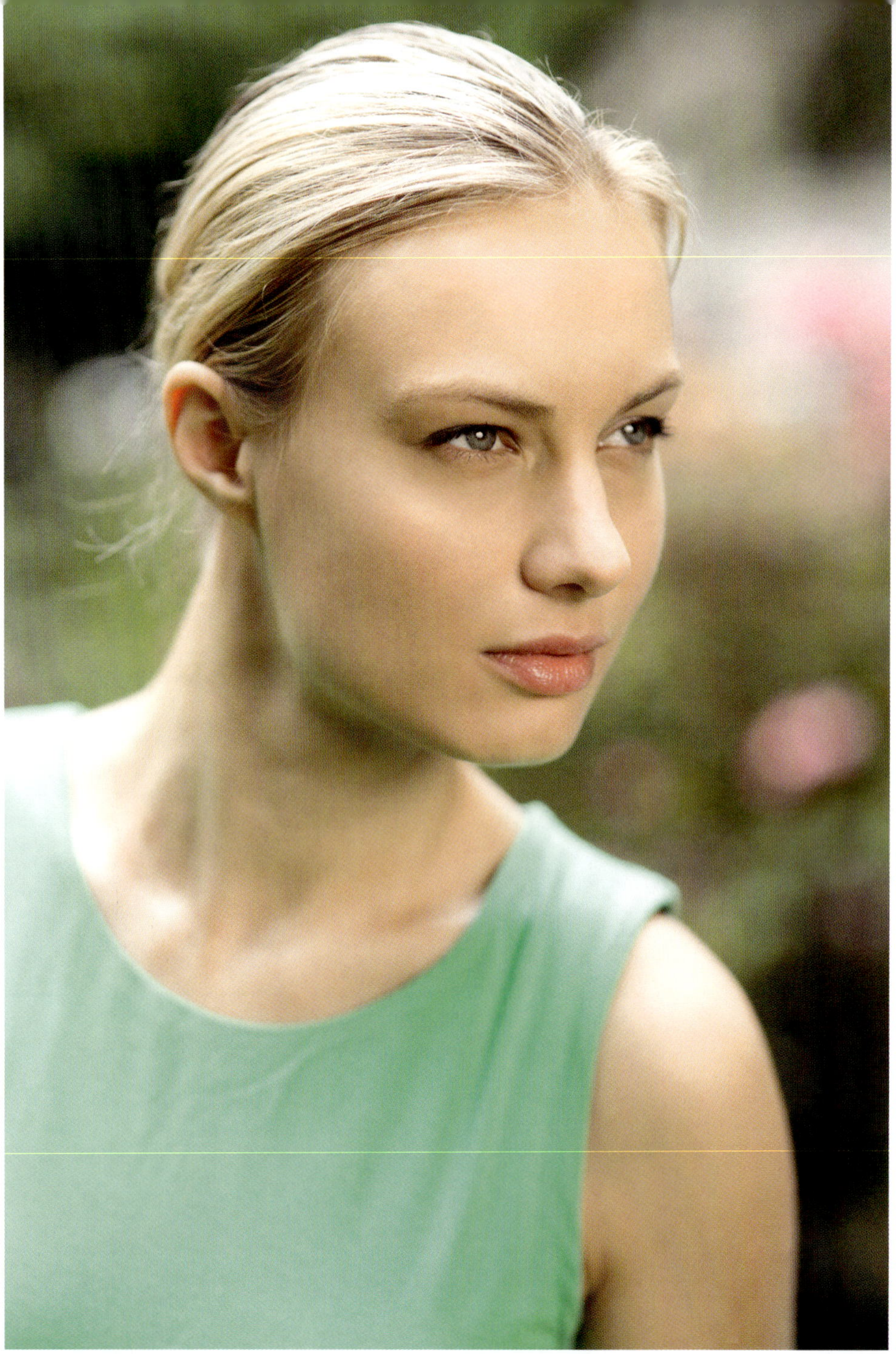

FIGURE 10.9
On an overcast day, you may want to add a bit of warmth to your image. Consider using a silver-gold mix reflector to add just a touch of warm tone to your fill light, without overdoing it.

Eliminate Overhead Light

One of the biggest problems on an overcast day is overhead light. The sky becomes a large, diffused light source. Inexperienced photographers often think that this soft light equates to good photographs. This is not always the case, at least not right out of the box!

Think of it this way: In the studio, if you put a giant softbox directly over your subject's head, would that be good light? No! The light would be soft, but it would cast shadows in the eyes and put highlights on the nose and forehead. These same undesirable effects occur outside on an overcast day.

So what can you do? One option is to follow Chapter 1's advice and eliminate overhead light by blocking it off. Put the subject beneath an overhang of some sort—under a tree, under a porch roof, or in a doorway. If the setting provides nothing useful, create your own shade by using a **flag**, which is another name for a tool that blocks light. Consider using a dark piece of foam core or the black side of your reflector.

Blocking off overhead light reduces the problems associated with the wrong direction of light. It puts your subject in the shade and sheds even light, but often it lacks that "pop" of light that you desire. Take a look at this in practice. **Figure 10.10** shows the straight shot without any reflectors or a diffuser. Notice the deep shadows in the eyes and highlights on the nose.

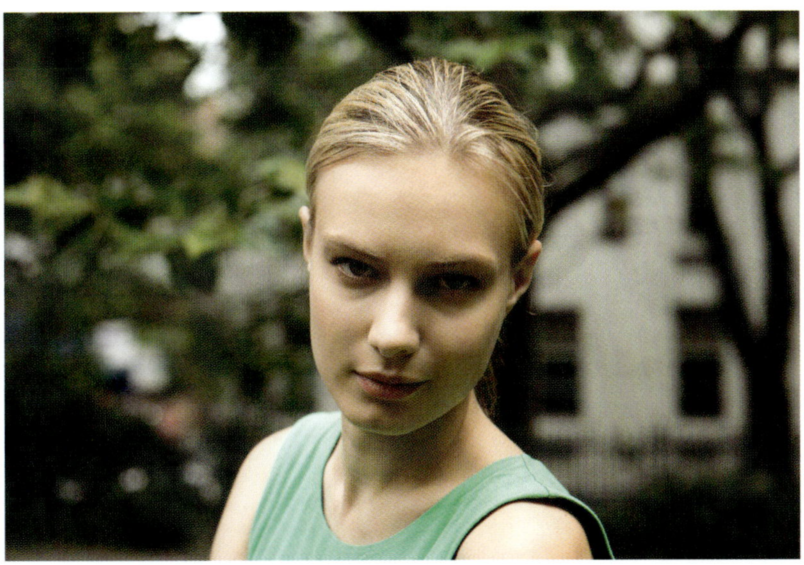

✗ FIGURE 10.10
Here is the unmodified ambient light, which creates unpleasant shadows in the eyes and highlights on the nose.

Putting a piece of dark foam core over the subject's head does a lot to even out the light, as you can see in **Figure 10.11**. The light is still less than ideal, but at least the direction of light is better.

Consider creating a sandwich with your subject as the middle. Use a black reflector or foam core above the head, and a white or silver reflector beneath. This setup evens the light while giving a sparkle to the eyes and a bit of kick to the image. Notice how adding a white piece of foam core underneath the model's chin in **Figure 10.12** lightens up the face and also adds **catchlights** to the eyes.

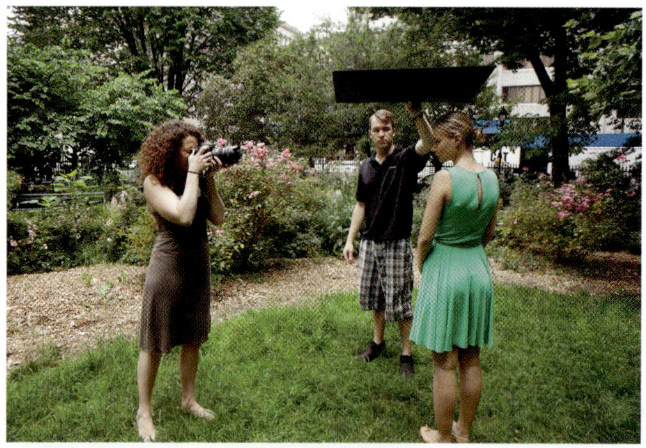

FIGURE 10.11
Placing a black piece of foam core over the model's head blocks off overhead light. This is by no means great light, but it does change the direction of light so that it isn't severely overhead.

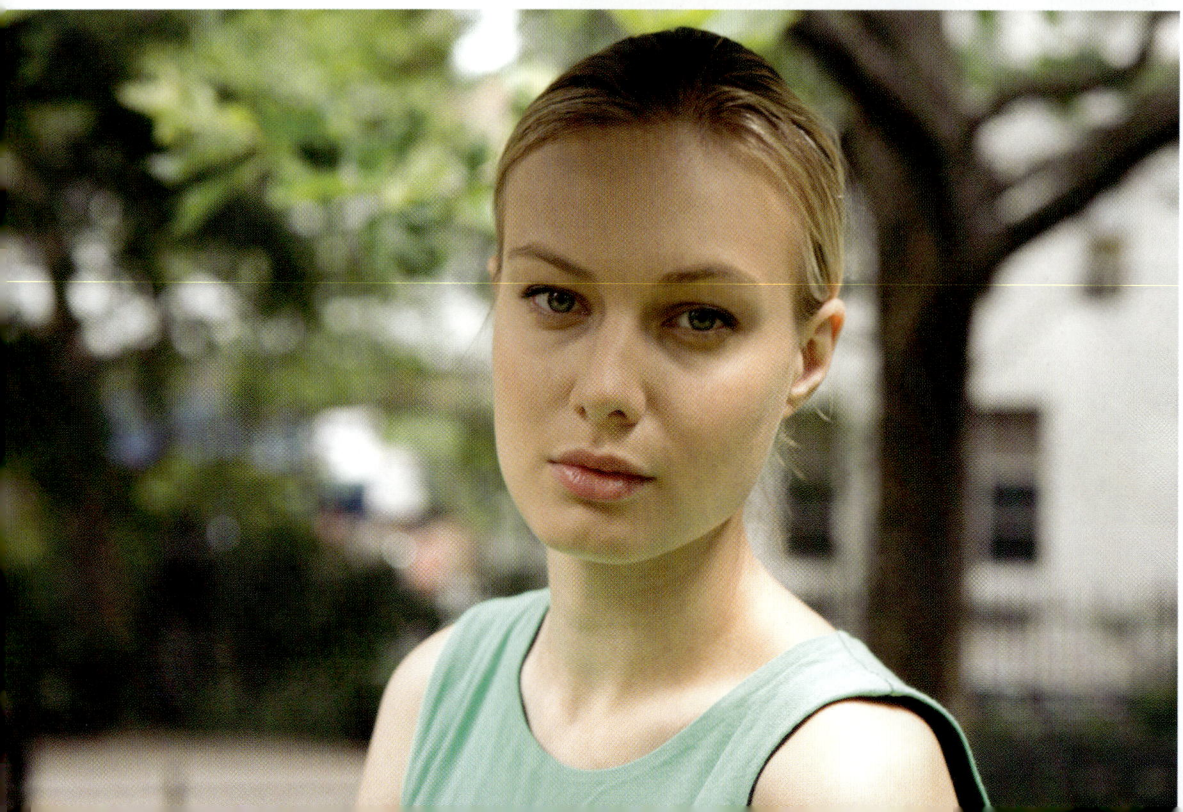

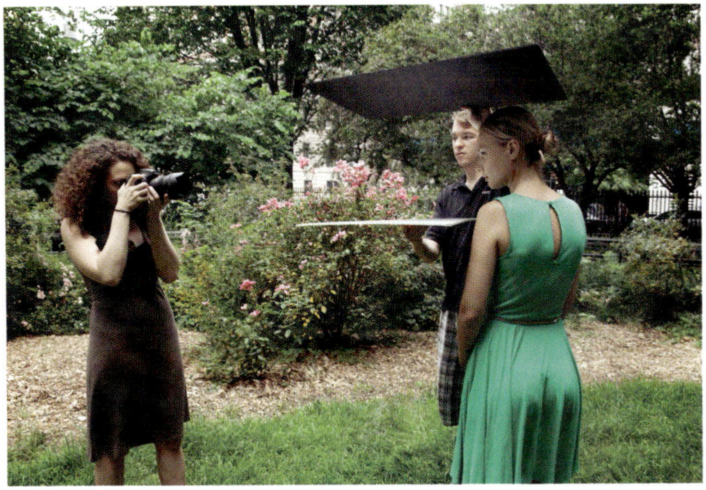

✔ FIGURE 10.12
To add that extra "pop," place a white piece of foam core under the model's chin to lighten up the image and create flattering catchlights in the eyes.

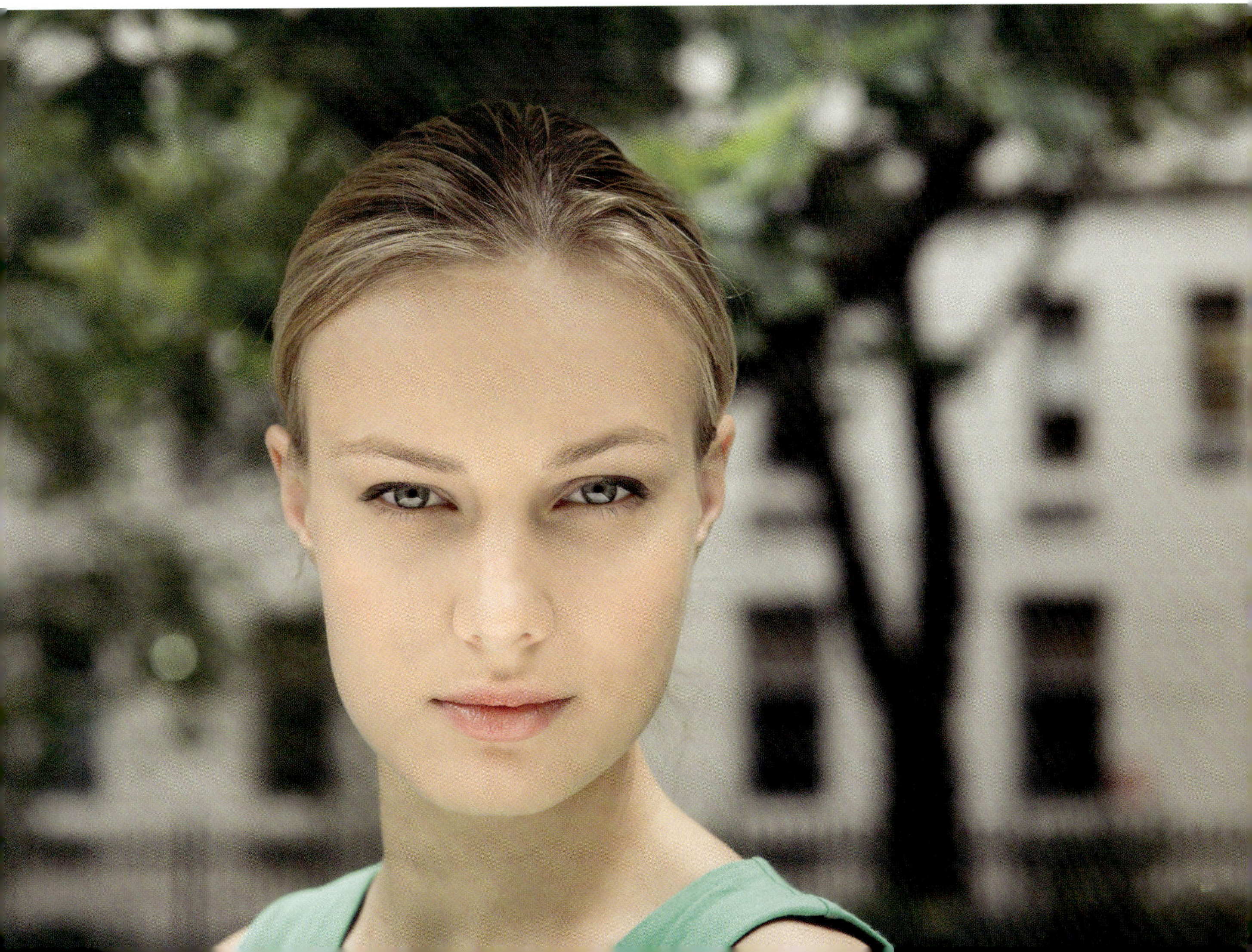

Another variation on the sandwich approach is to replace the overhead foam core with a diffuser to make the overhead light softer. Then you add the reflector beneath. Notice the different quality of light using a diffuser creates (**Figure 10.13**). So in the end, what is the correct combination? Whichever you prefer! Or whichever modifiers you have available!

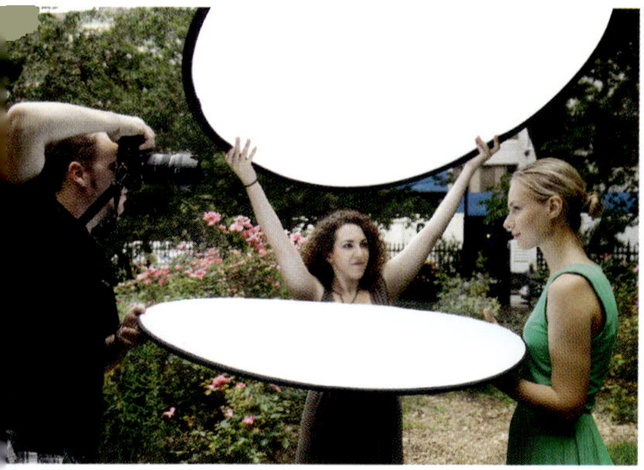

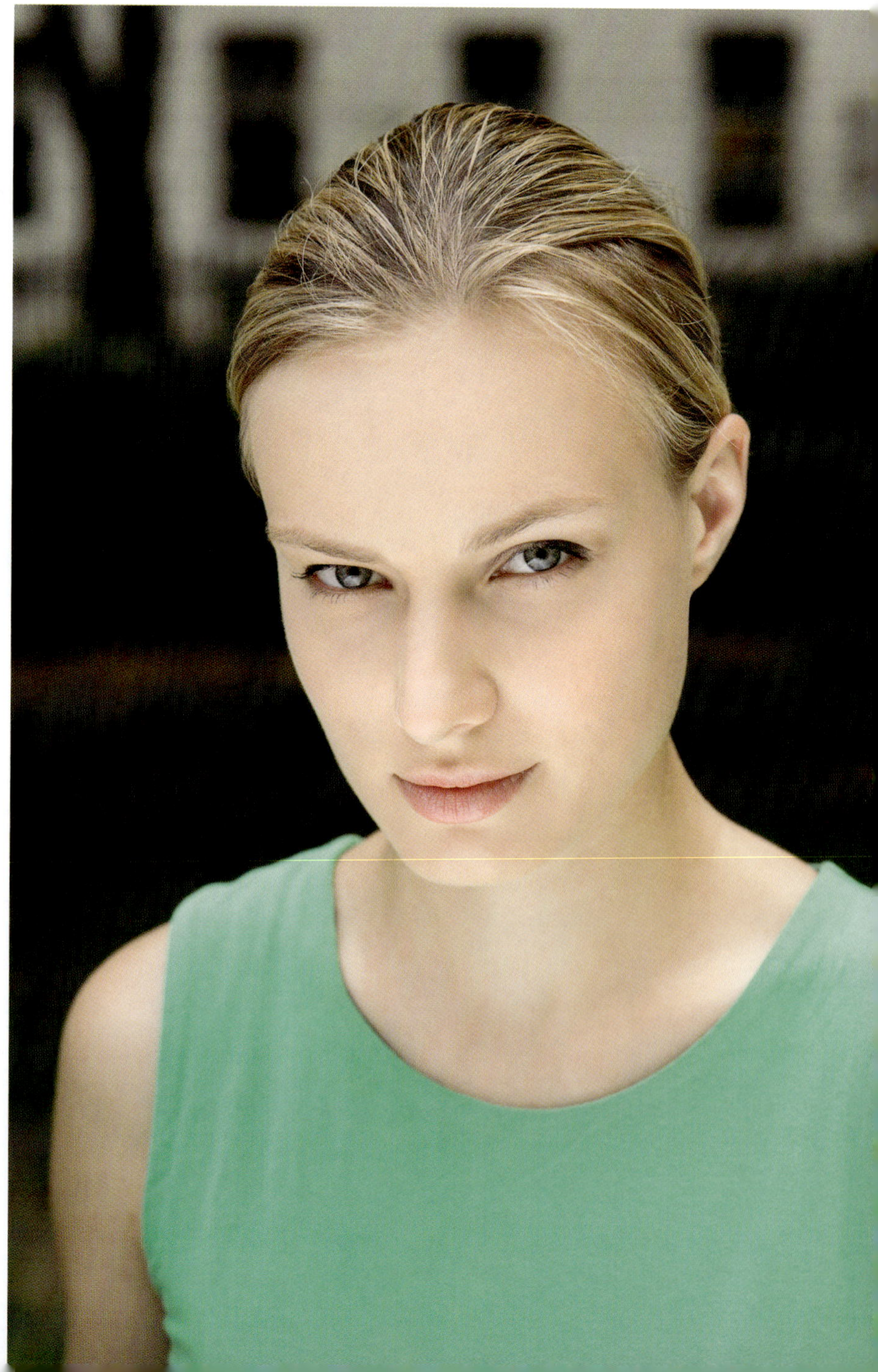

✔ FIGURE 10.13
Take control of the light by softening overhead light using a diffuser and adding a kicker or fill light by placing a reflector beneath the face.

BEGINNER TIP **Use neutral flags.**

If you are using something as a flag to block off overhead light, be sure that it is neutral in tone like a black or white. If you use something colored, such as a colored piece of cardboard, to block off the light, then chances are your subject will have an unpleasant color cast to the face. The reflected color cast might be subtle, but it will still throw off the color balance of your image.

Turn Their Eyes to the Skies

On overcast days, try posing your subjects so that they turn their faces and eyes to the sky. By lifting the eyes or changing your level of shooting, you can actually have the subjects lift their faces to catch the light from the sky.

The basic tactic is to stand elevated above your subjects. Simply sitting them down will do the trick. When they lift their chins to look at you, they are allowing their eyes to catch the light from the sky. **Figure 10.14** was shot straight on at eye level; notice how her eyes are dark with almost no light. In **Figure 10.15**, however, Erik elevated himself above the model, and therefore, she had to look upwards. Notice the light now catching in her eyes and the drastically different light on her face.

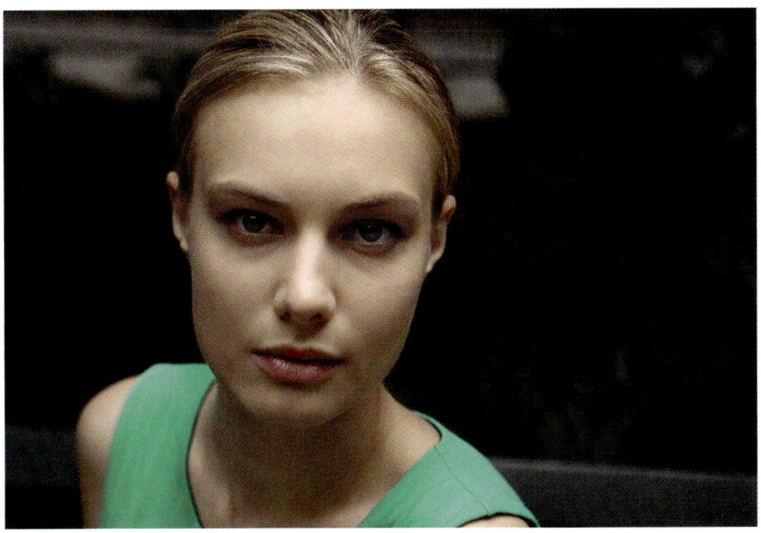

✗ **FIGURE 10.14**
When the model is looking straight ahead and we are shooting from her eye level, her eyes have dark shadows and the light is unflattering.

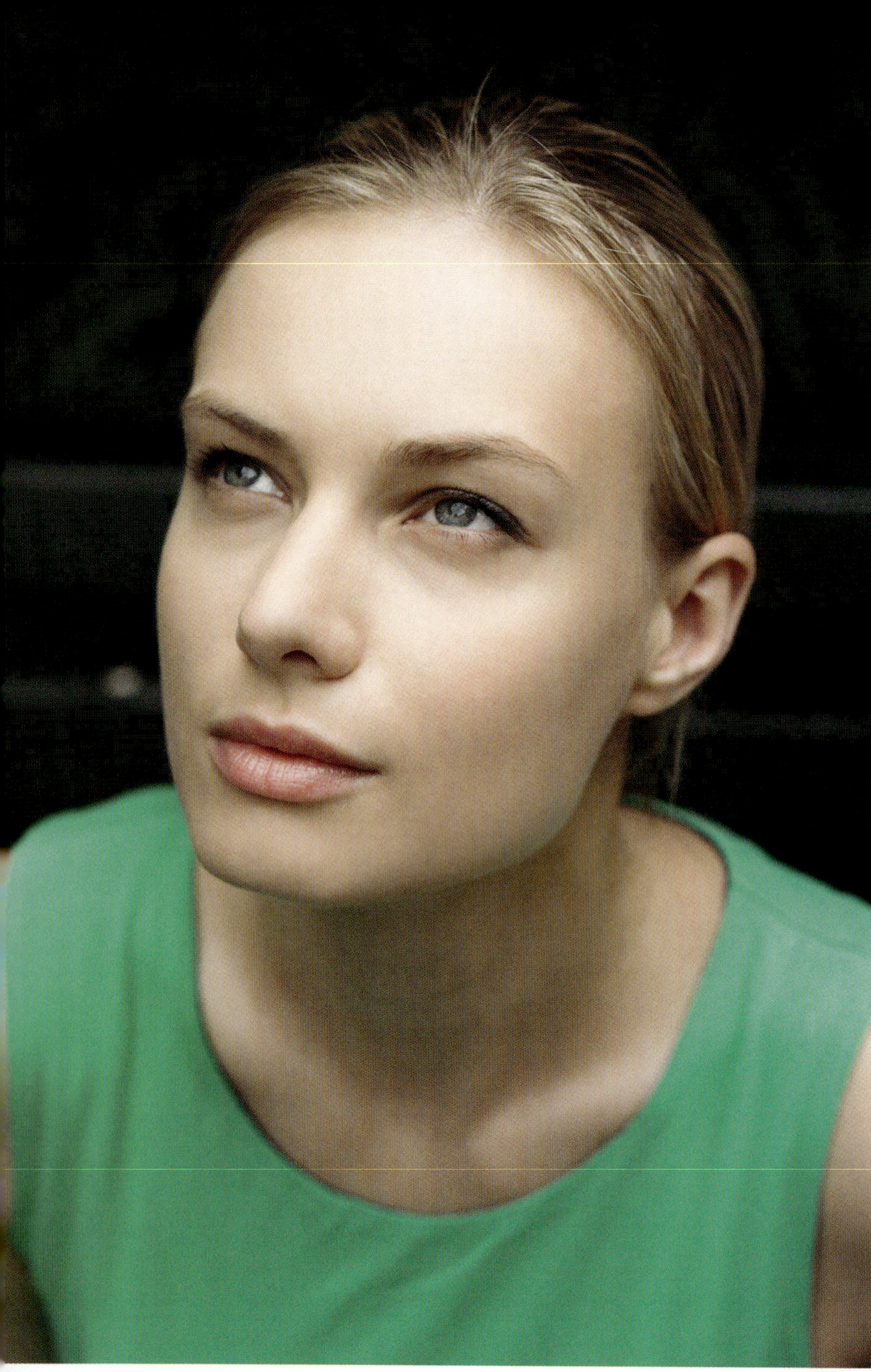

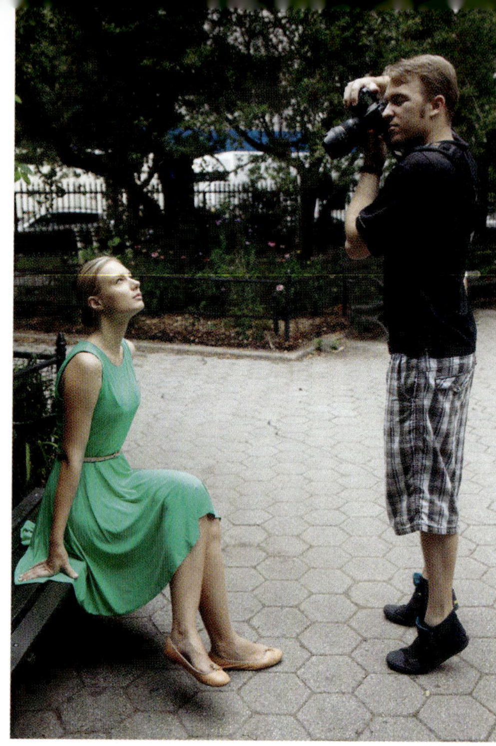

FIGURE 10.15
Because Erik was shooting from a very high angle, the model just raised her chin up and, therefore, her eyes caught the light of the sky.

Another approach is to lay your subjects on their backs, putting them parallel with the overcast sky as in **Figure 10.16**. This is one of Lindsay's go-to solutions for an overcast day. Remember how an overcast day is like a big softbox above your subjects? By changing the angle of their faces or laying them on their backs, you are now facing them toward the light source! This creates an even light source and fills in shadows in the eyes. You'll gain not only a beautiful quality of light on the subject, but also make an unusual angle. What's great is that you don't even need to introduce a reflector or diffuser—just make use of what's available!

FIGURE 10.16
This image was shot during one of Lindsay's fashion editorials. Placing the model on her back created a flattering and even source of light on the model.

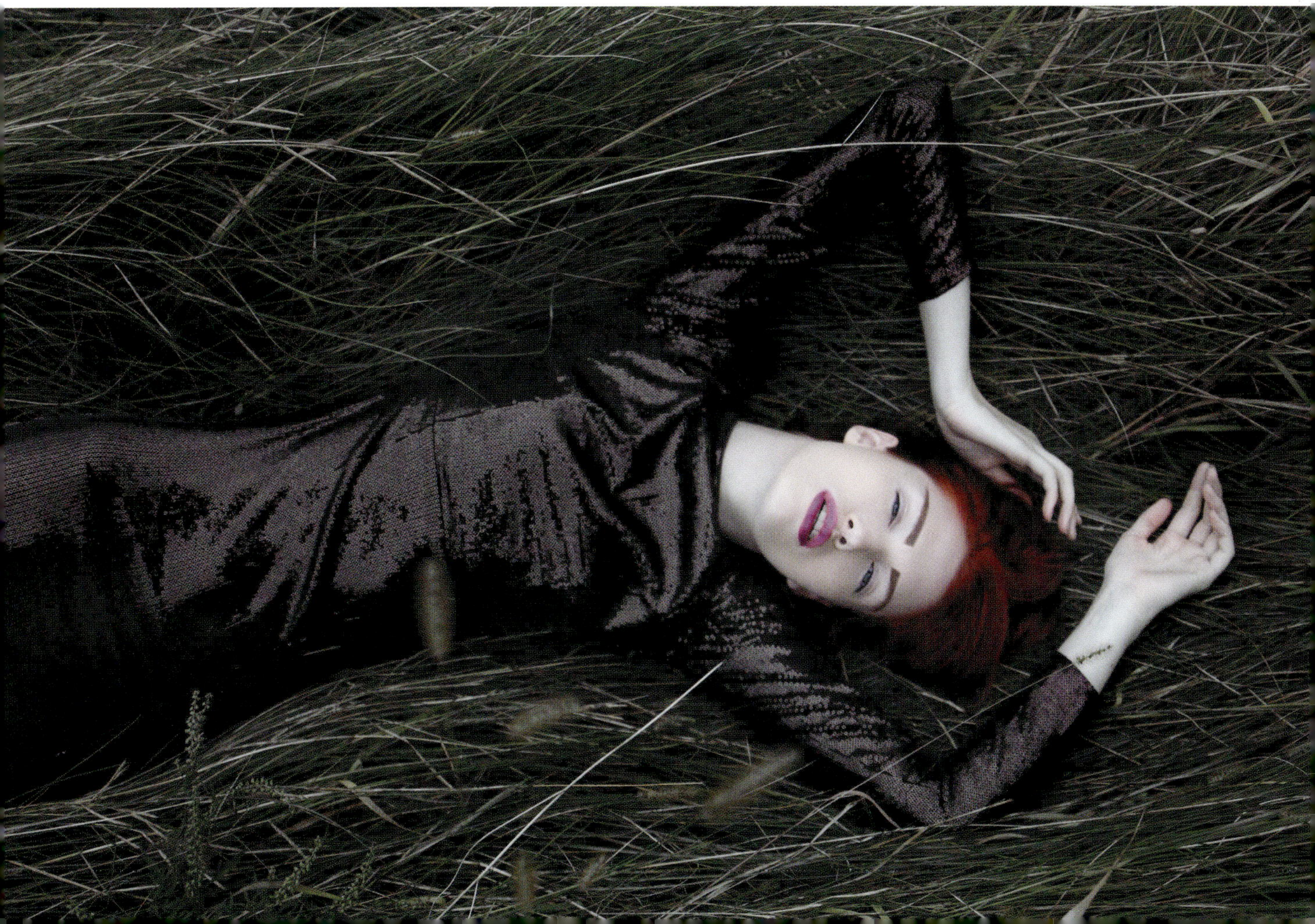

Use Flash

Using reflectors and changing the angle of your subject will help you through most cloudy days. Yet some very dreary days offer minimal light to reflect, or light that is flat and undesirable. Or perhaps you're photographing a group that needs equal illumination, and a reflector won't do the job. What if you simply can't find a way to block overhead light? In all these instances, you may need to try the next option: Use a flash! When used correctly, a flash can give a bit of punch to your images and help you conquer many overcast woes!

Compare **Figure 10.17**, which we shot with no flash, to **Figure 10.18**, which we took using a basic setup of a single off-camera speed light with an umbrella modifier. Notice the quality of light created by using a flash. The flash does not overpower the image, but instead adds a direction of light and creates contrast. Furthermore, with a group of people, you could back the umbrella away from the subjects to create a broad, even illumination across the group. In the figures you can see the drastic difference we achieved by adding a flash. Notice that you can still see the ambient light on her hair and shoulders. A flash image does not need to look like a "flash photo." The flash can be used to augment the ambient light without overpowering it.

Another useful benefit of using a flash is that you can vary the ambient exposure for creative control. In other words, you can make the environment and background look lighter or darker depending on your desired effect. You can, for example, darken down the ambient light to help the subject stand out from the background, *or* you can increase the exposure of the ambient light to give it the appearance of a brighter day.

Figures 10.19 through **10.22** illustrate how varying the ambient exposure while keeping the flash constant can alter the look of a scene. As a benchmark, Figure 10.19 shows the results without a flash. For Figure 10.20, we used a flash with the ambient at an even exposure. Figure 10.21 drops by 1 stop, while Figure 10.22 increases exposure by one stop. For all three figures, we used the same basic setup behind the scenes. Again, there is no right answer for flash exposures. In the end, the "best" visual solution will depend on the mood you want to set.

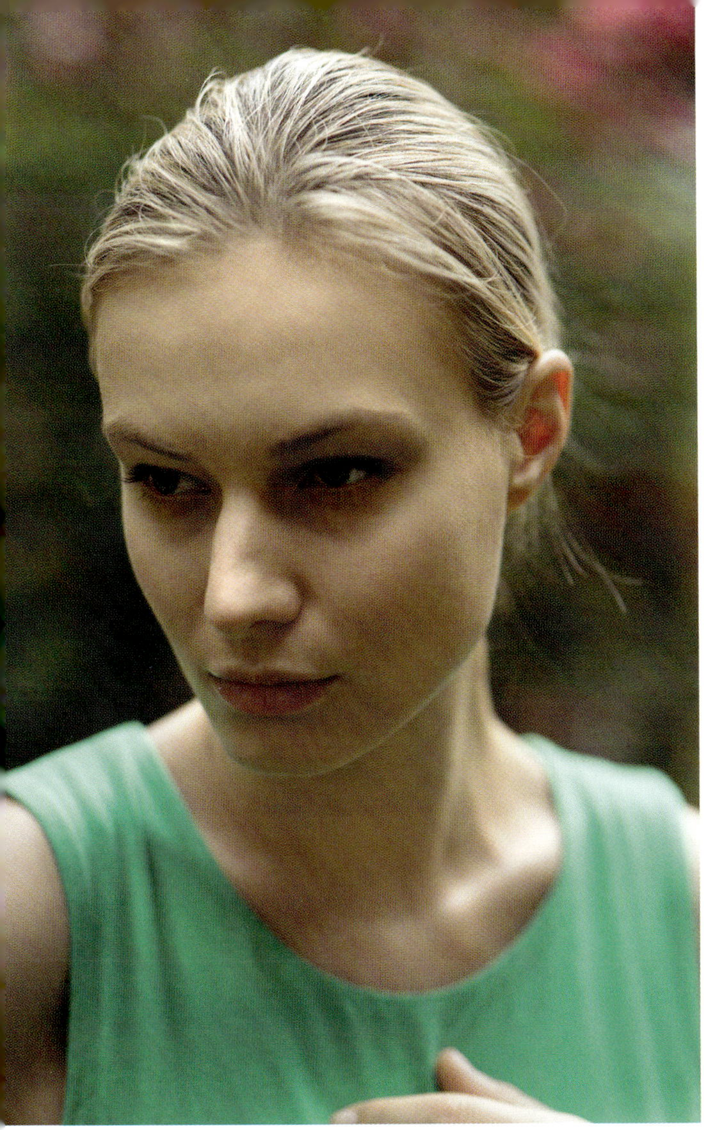

FIGURE 10.17
Without a flash, the light on the face is unpleasant and unflattering.

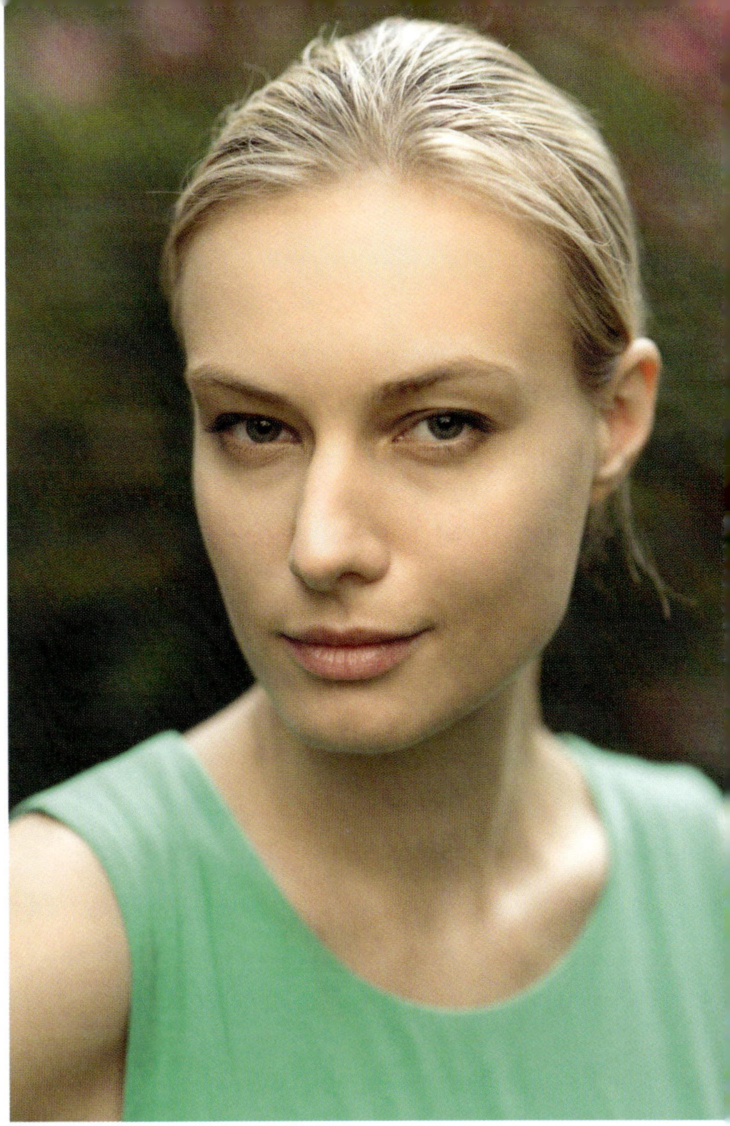

FIGURE 10.18
Add an off-camera flash with an umbrella modifier, and the quality of light becomes very flattering without overpowering the ambient light.

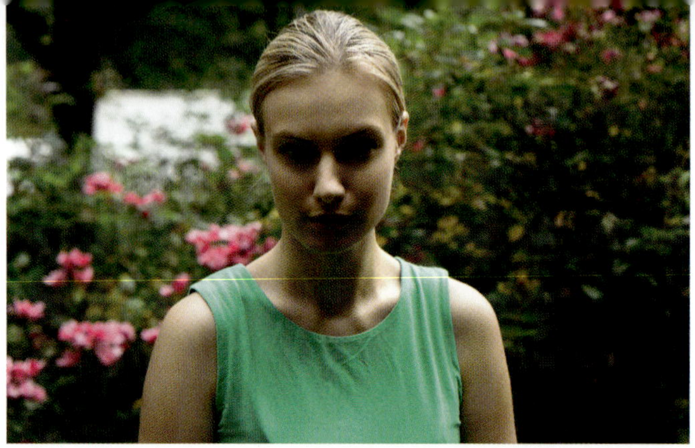

FIGURE 10.19
Here we photographed the model without modifying the ambient light.

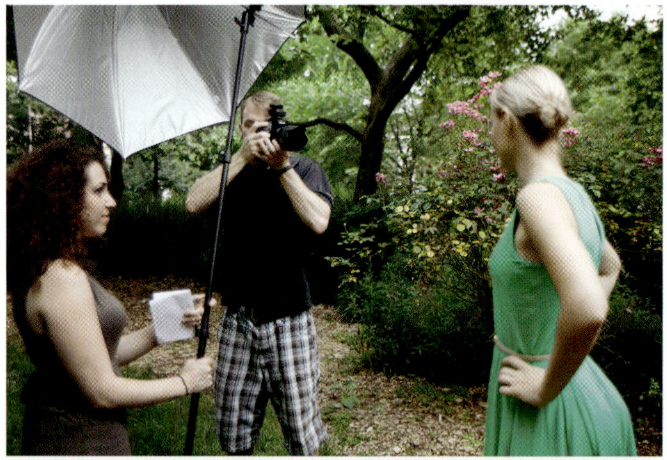

FIGURE 10.20
Using an off-camera flash and umbrella modifier, we kept the ambient at the original exposure. Shoot with the ambient exposure at 0 compensation, and the ambient light appears closest to reality.

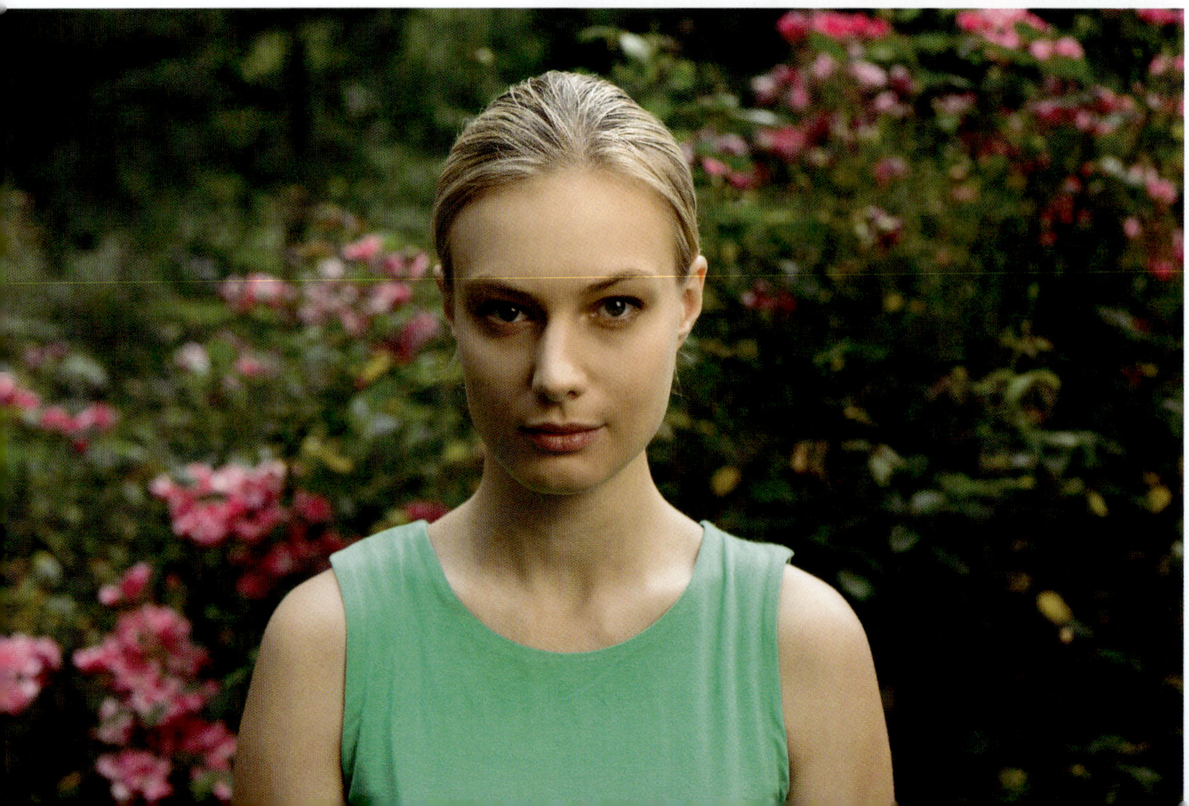

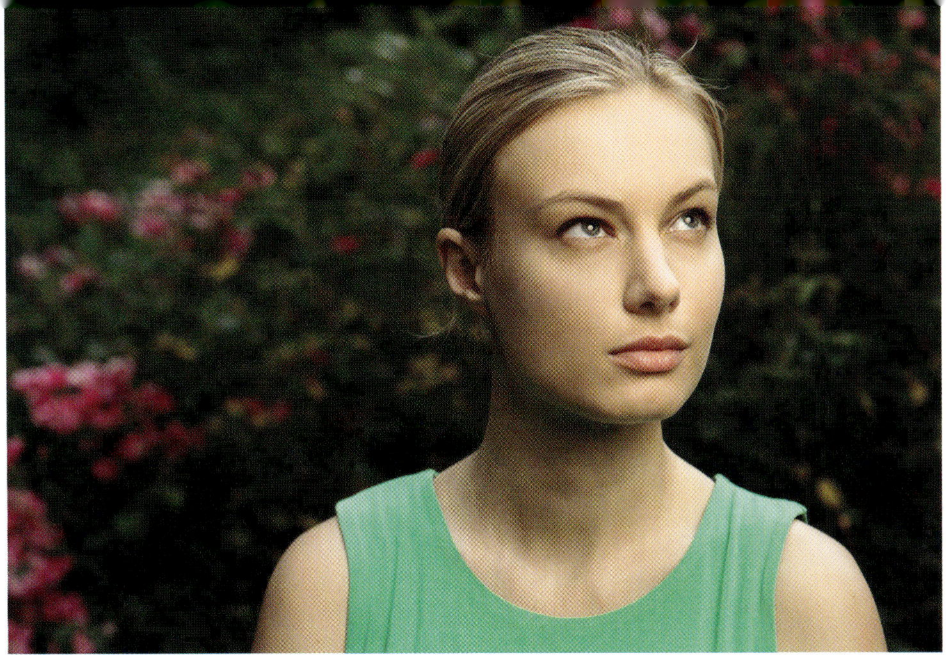

FIGURE 10.21
By underexposing the ambient by 1 stop of light, the subject now stands out more from the background, yet the background looks darker and more foreboding.

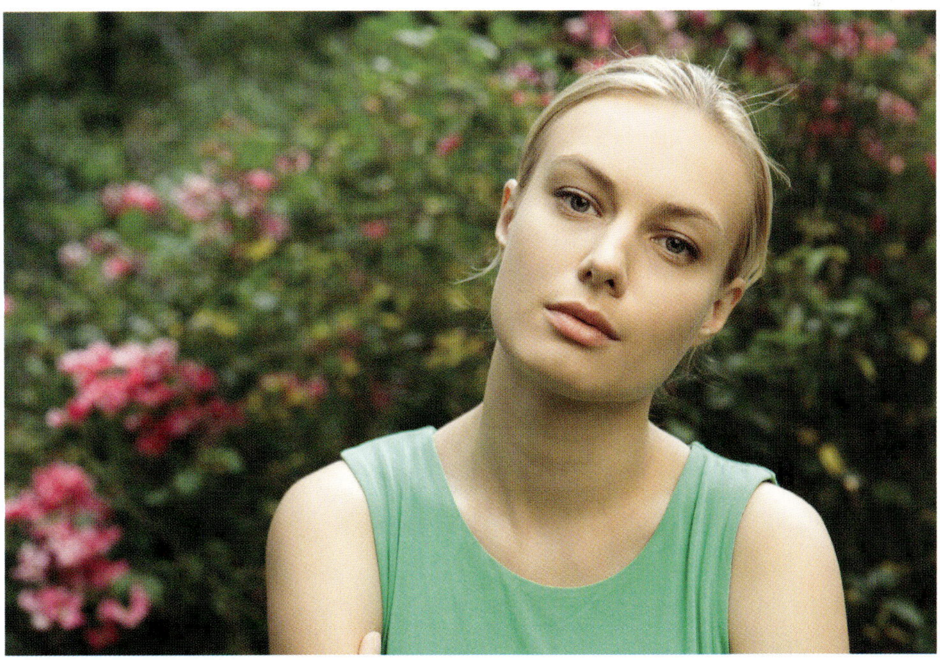

FIGURE 10.22
By bringing up the ambient exposure to +1, we lightened the scene and used flash to simply fill in the shadows on the subject's face.

APPENDIX A
Glossary

AF-Assist Illuminator light This light on your camera will pulse to cast illumination on your subject in low light. This small light makes it easier to see and focus on your subject. This option is not always enabled in your camera, so check your manual for more information.

Ambient light Ambient light is produced by light sources that already exist in a scene, as opposed to those introduced by the photographer. Ambient light can be natural (sun, window light) or man-made (street lamps, neon signs).

Aperture Priority (Av) mode In Aperture Priority mode, you set the aperture that you want to shoot at, then the camera adjusts the shutter speed to achieve appropriate exposure.

Bokeh This term refers to the way a lens renders out-of-focus light. Put simply, the bokeh of a lens determines the pattern and quality of the blur in a photo's background (the area behind your subject when you use a narrow depth of field).

Catchlight This is another name for the specular highlight (see specular highlights) in a subject's eyes. Taking the shape of the light source that creates them, catchlights help draw attention to a subject's eyes and are frequently used to add energy and connection with the subject.

Color cast A color cast refers to an unwanted tint of a color in a scene. For example, a fluorescent light may create an underlying (and undesirable) green tone in a scene. Generally, you want to eliminate or combat color casts.

Color temperature Color temperature literally means the temperature in degrees Kelvin of light in your scene. Typically, the actual number values are not of importance. Instead, knowing the color temperature in the scene allows you to set your white balance so that the light appears neutral to your camera sensor.

Covered shade Covered shade is the result of a covering or obstruction (a porch, an overhang, a tree) blocking the light over your subject's head. Covered shade often produces a better quality of light on the face than open shade (see open shade).

Depth-of-Field Preview button When you press the Depth-of-Field Preview button on your camera, the camera closes down your aperture to the actual aperture you will be using when creating the exposure. This enables you to view the aperture and depth of field as it will appear in your image. When you shoot images with flash, the Depth-of-Field Preview button causes your flash to pulse, enabling you to preview the illumination and focus in your image.

Depth of Field The depth of field of an image is the area of focus in an image. A narrow depth of field implies that only a very small portion of the frame is in focus. Depth of field helps control the eye in a scene.

Diffuser A diffuser is typically a neutral, semi-translucent material (like a white bedsheet) that is used to even out and soften the light in a scene. Diffusion material is often sold in "stops" to indicate how much exposure it is reducing while softening the light.

Dragging your shutter This phrase refers to using a longer shutter speed to allow ambient light to register in your frame. When shooting at night, your flash freezes motion and illuminates your subject. By dragging the shutter and using longer exposures, you can expose the environment for ambient light.

Exposure compensation Most frequently used in Av or TV modes, exposure compensation allows you to adjust your image's exposure by adjusting the camera's meter. For example, if an image is too dark, you can set the Exposure Compensation dial to +1 to increase the exposure of your image by 1 stop of light. Similarly, if you have a blown-out highlight in a scene, you can dial the exposure compensation to –1/3 to decrease the overall exposure of your scene by 1/3 of a stop. This is a useful tool for refining exposure when using Aperture Priority mode.

Fast glass This term refers to a lens with a wide aperture. A lens with an aperture of f/2.8 is faster than one with an aperture of f/3.5. Fast glass is typically considered f/2.8 or wider.

Feather To feather is the act of creating a gradient of an effect. When you feather a reflector, for example, you are rotate it away from the light, so your subject receives only part of the reflection instead of its full force. This tends to give a more subtle and flattering illumination.

Feathering light To feather light, you rotate it away from your subject so the full illumination is not hitting your subject. Feathering creates a transition between direct light and no light when a light source is rotated away from a subject.

Flag A flag is any tool used to block light. Flags come in a wide variety of shapes and sizes, but could be as simple as a piece foam core.

Image noise Noise is the digital sensor's equivalent to film grain. It is a random color/luminance variation that appears in your image typically when shooting at higher ISOs.

IS (Image-Stabilization) Image stabilization helps to counteract involuntary camera shake to give you a more stable, focused image. In Nikon it is referred to as VR, and in Sigma it is called OS. This is typically built into lenses, though sometimes camera bodies have IS features.

ISO (International Organization for Standardization) ISO measures the sensitivity of the image sensor or film to light. Lower ISO settings mean your sensor is less sensitive to light, and you can usually achieve a finer grain and less noise. Higher ISO settings are great when dealing with low-light situations or fast-moving subjects because they make your camera more sensitive to light. High ISOs, however, lead to more grain and a noisier image.

Lighting ratio This term typically refers to the values of areas of highlight to areas of shadow in a photo. For example, a lighting ratio of 2:1 means one side of the face is twice as bright as the other side of the face. A higher lighting ratio creates greater drama to a scene.

Manual (M) mode This is a camera setting in which a photographer must select both aperture and shutter speed. Manual mode gives you the most control over your image exposure.

Off the camera axis When your flash is on the camera on the hot shoe or directly above, this is considered on the camera axis. Moving the flash from this position is referred to as moving it off the camera axis. Taking the flash off the camera axis helps to create more shape and direction to the light.

Open shade Open shade is produced by structures of objects that are not in direct sunlight, including large buildings or trees. An overcast day also counts as open shade. With open shade, there is no direct covering over a subject's head.

Program (P) mode This is a camera setting in which your camera selects both the aperture and shutter speed. This is generally used by beginning photographers.

Scrim Used to help diffuse the light in a scene or on your subject, a scrim is a frame covered by a large piece of diffusion material to cut out different amounts of light. Scrims make the light softer and more even in the frame.

Specular highlights A specular highlight is a contrasty highlight in a scene, typically caused by the reflection of the light source on the subject.

Tonal range The tonal range of a photographic scene refers to the exposure difference between the highlights and shadow areas of the photograph. A large range creates a contrasty scene, and often a single frame cannot capture the entire range of exposures.

VR (vibration-reduction) This is Nikon's name for optical image stabilization (see above).

White balance Both a camera setting and a process, white balance adjusts the light source in the scene to appear neutral. In real life, our eyes naturally adjust white balance to perceive light sources as neutral, yet this is not how light is recorded by camera sensors. In photography, you must compensate for the camera sensor's intepretation of light by using white balance presets, custom white balance, or by selecting a neutral area of the frame in post-production.

Wide-Area AF-Assist beam Your flash unit will emit an infrared beam of light when focusing in low-light situations. This light makes it easier to focus in low-light conditions.

APPENDIX B
Equipment

Fancy equipment doesn't a good photographer make. Equipment can, however, make your job as a photographer easier. Treat your equipment as tools in your kit. The appropraite tool can often help save the day when you're attempting to correct those imperfect lighting situations.

Suppose you are photographing in a room with mixed light. It's not the flash that makes a good photograph. It's your understanding of light, gels, flash settings, and how to interact with your subject that helps make a good image.

Throughout the book, we recommend a wide array of equipment. These are the tools that we prefer and have experience working with in our photographic careers. That does not mean that they are the only tools for the job. When it comes to gear, the final decision depends on you, your budget, and your shooting style.

This appendix lists the equipment that worked best for us while photographing the images for *Shooting in Sh*tty Light*. In each category, we will tell you what we used throughout the book, and why. More importantly, to help you choose your own equipment, we'll discuss the basic features that you actually need in each tool.

In the end, it's all about doing your research. Experiment with these different tools, read reviews, talk to friends. You'll find the solution that fits you just right.

Camera

Nikon D800 DSLR www.nikon.com

Why We Used It

In the Canon versus Nikon war, we are on opposite fronts! Lindsay shoots Canon, and Erik shoots Nikon. Truly, both brands are superb and offer great cameras for photographers of every level. For this particular project, we decided to shoot with the Nikon D800. We wanted a camera that was capable of creating large image files, and the D800 shoots at a whopping 36 megapixels! With files this big, we had plenty of pixels allowing us to crop-in when designing the book and for editing purposes. We, of course, wanted a digital camera with interchangeable lenses. Furthermore, we selected a camera with great-quality high ISO (for demonstrations in low light). Finally, we wanted a camera with a full-frame sensor. The D800 has all of these great features.

What You Need

To achieve images like those in this book, you certainly don't need the top-of-the-line Nikon or Canon digital camera. All you need is a camera that allows you full manual control, meaning the ability to fully adjust aperture, shutter speed, and ISO. You also want the option to use interchangeable lenses so that you can select a lens specific to your subject and latest photographic challenge. If you have a recent digital camera, it will have sufficient high-ISO performance and enough megapixels to get the job done—and get it done right!

Lenses

Nikon 24–70mm f/2.8 and Nikon 70–200mm f/2.8 www.nikon.com

Sigma 85mm f/1.4 www.sigmaphoto.com

Why We Used It

When we shoot, we always prefer to use the widest aperture lenses possible. These wide-aperture, or fast glass, lenses allow us narrow depth of field and also the ability to shoot in lower light. We selected the 85mm f/1.4 as a great portrait lens with narrow depth of field, which isolates the subject by blurring the background of the photograph. The 24–70mm and 70–200mm gave us the flexibility of zoom lenses while maintaining a constant wide aperture. Also, we selected an image-stabilized lens (VR, IS, OS) to help ensure a steady image in lower light situations with slow shutter speeds.

What You Need

Any lens will do, although we recommend purchasing lenses with the widest aperture capabilities you can afford. In fact, in this book we shot nearly all of the images at f/5.6, which is an available aperture in even the most affordable lenses. This way, you can duplicate our results no matter how tight your lens budget may be. Zoom lenses with constant apertures (like the ones we used in this book) are versatile, convenient, and have high-quality optics. These lenses can be expensive, though. Instead, you might opt for prime (fixed) lenses with wide apertures. You lose the versatility of a zoom lens, but if you're willing to move your feet a little, you'll gain the benefits of wide-open apertures for a fraction of the cost.

Tripod

Vanguard Carbon Fiber Tripod with Ball Head www.vanguardworld.com

Why We Used It

A tripod gives you hands-off stability. With three legs, you get a sturdy base that you don't have to hang onto or balance between shots. A tripod also guarantees consistency from shot to shot. Once that camera is locked into position, the composition doesn't change until you want it to. Carbon fiber tripods have the added benefits of being light and durable, which is important when you take your tripod to events and on the road.

The lighter a tripod is, the more likely you are to actually take it with you! Finally, the ball head allows for quick and easy adjustments of the camera's position.

What You Need

You really just need to stabilize your camera for low light. This can be achieved with a tripod, monopod, or even a beanbag if you're shooting from a lower vantage point. Keep in mind, though, that you usually get what you pay for. A very inexpensive tripod may not be overly stable, especially in windy situations, which might still produce camera shake. We recommend carbon fiber for good quality and light weight, but it's certainly not necessary.

Flash and Flash Accessories

Nikon SB-800 Flash and Nikon SC-29 TTL Coiled Remote Cord www.nikonusa.com

PocketWizard FlexTT5 and MiniTT1 www.pocketwizard.com

ExpoImaging Rogue Gels www.expoimaging.com

Why We Used It

Because we shot the book with a Nikon camera, we selected a high-quality Nikon flash that allowed us full manual control as well as TTL capabilities. The SB-800 flash (**Figure B.1**) allowed us wireless communication between camera and flash, optical triggering, as well as TTL metering.

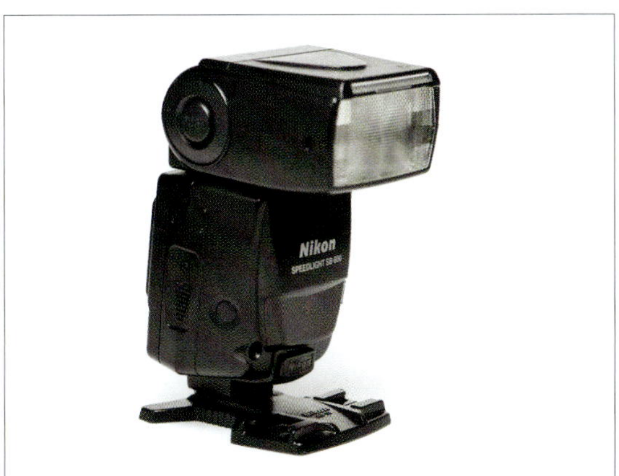

FIGURE B.1
We used the Nikon SB-800 flash unit for the photos in this book.

To trigger the flash wirelessly, we used the MiniTT1 and FlexTT5 units from PocketWizard. These triggers use radio frequencies to tell the flash to fire, without the need for long sync cables or line-of-sight visibility between the camera and the flash. They also allow for the use of TTL functions, wirelessly, which is a kind of auto-metering mode for your flash (**Figure B.2**). These tools offered the most functionality and the consistency that we need when working in the field.

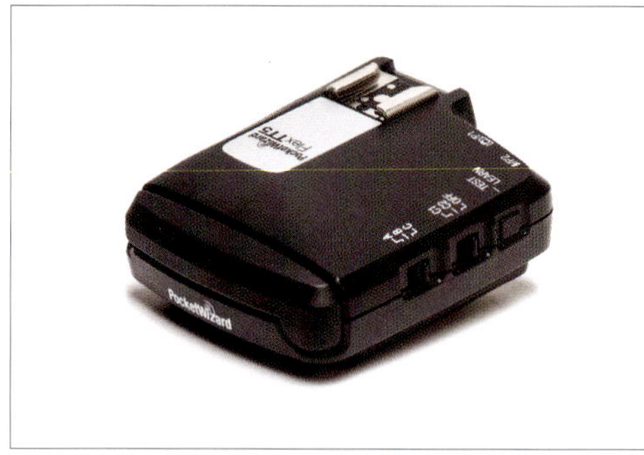

FIGURE B.2
PocketWizard radio triggers were used to wirelessly fire the flash.

When we wanted to get the flash off the camera's hot shoe, but not too far, a TTL cable fit our needs. When we used a TTL cable, we wanted one with an AF-Assist Illuminator to help out with focusing in low light. Conveniently, the Nikon's SC-29 TTL Coiled Remote Cord has one built in (**Figure B.3**).

Rogue Gels (**Figure B.4**) come in a wide range of colors and are designed to easily attach to variety of different size flash heads. They also list specific exposure compensation info and Kelvin temperatures on each gel so that we could precisely gel our flash to match the existing light temperatures in a room. This convenience, selection, and precision gave us the control we needed.

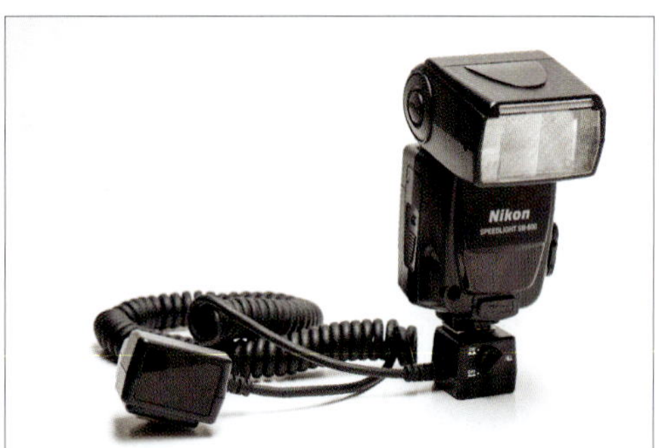

FIGURE B.3
This Nikon SC-29 TTL cable allows you to fire your flash off camera and also has a built-in focus-assist beam.

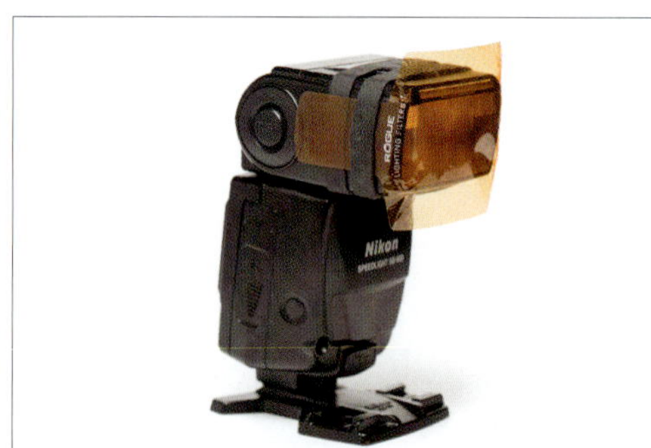

FIGURE B.4
Rogue Gels give you a very precise ability to adjust and match Kelvin color tempertures.

What You Need

You don't necessarily need the newest model, just one that has the option to manually set the flash's output power. This allows more control of the flash as you become more experienced. Also, look for a flash with TTL (Through-The-Lens metering) capabilities so that the flash can help you determine the proper exposure. A few flash accessories are essential for conquering challenging lighting. First, you need to find a way to get your flash off your camera's hot shoe, which will give more direction to your light. This could be a TTL cable, the PocketWizard wireless system, Radio Poppers, or whatever you are comfortable with. Just be sure that the option gives you radio triggering (as opposed to line-of-sight triggering). Next, you need some sort of gels. Many flashes already come with a pack of gels for basic color correction!

Flash Modifiers

Westcott 60-inch Umbrella with Removable Cover and Westcott Large PocketBox www.fjwestcott.com

ExpoImaging Rogue FlashBender Kit www.expoimaging.com

Why We Used It

Larger modifiers result in softer light—the larger, the softer. The Westcott 60-inch umbrella greatly enlarged the light from our flash, producing soft light to illuminate the scene. Also, the removeable back cover gave us the ability to use it as a reflective bounce umbrella or a shoot-through diffusion umbrella. This versatility is key when shooting on location where packing light can really save you.

The Westcott PocketBox gave us the benefits of a softbox (soft directional light) without the usual weight and hassle of internal rods and metal speedrings (**Figure B.5**). Its compact design makes it mobile while still producing flattering light.

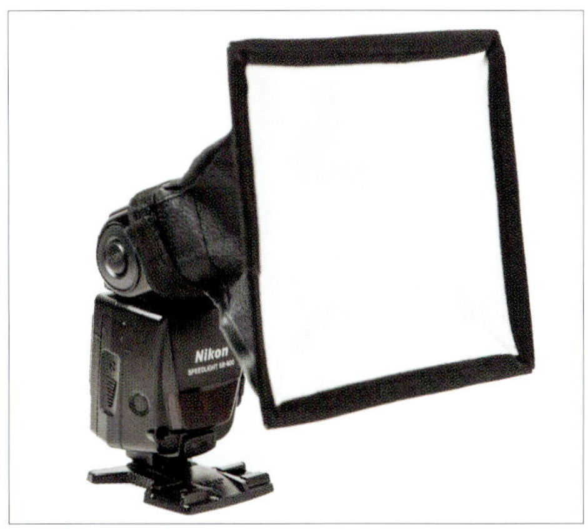

FIGURE B.5
The PocketBox helps to enlarge and soften the light from your flash.

The Rogue FlashBender with optional front diffusion panel was a very useful modifier because of its extreme versatility. Once attached to the flash, it acted like a large bounce card, reflecting more fill light onto the subject, while still allowing light to be bounced off a ceiling or wall for better direction. With the front panel in place, the FlashBender became a small softbox with more control and direction of the light. Finally, the FlashBender can be used to flag off, or block, light from spilling onto the scene where we don't want it.

What You Need

There are dozens (if not hundreds) of different flash modifiers to help you change the quality and direction of the light from your flash. The key things to look for when shopping around are size and control. By enlarging the light, it becomes softer. By controlling the spill of that light, you are better able to direct it. The options are endless. Experiment and find the solution that works for you. But remember: The most expensive or complicated option is not always the best one.

Reflectors

Westcott PhotoBasics 40-inch 5-in-1 Reflector and Westcott 72 x 72-inch Scrim Jim www.fjwestcott.com

California Sunbounce Reflectors www.sunbounce.com

Why We Used It

When using a reflector, we like to have a variety of options without the need to carry four or five separate reflectors around with us. The Westcott PhotoBasics 40-inch 5-in-1 reflector (**Figure B.6**) gave us the ability to use soft bounce (white), hard bounce (silver), diffusion, and subtractive light all in one diffuser—no need to carry extra equipment. For something a little bigger, the California Sunbounce makes a variety of large reflectors that are particularly useful when lighting groups. While not as versatile as a 5-in-1 reflector, their metal frames make them easy to mount and hold for catching light in unusual places.

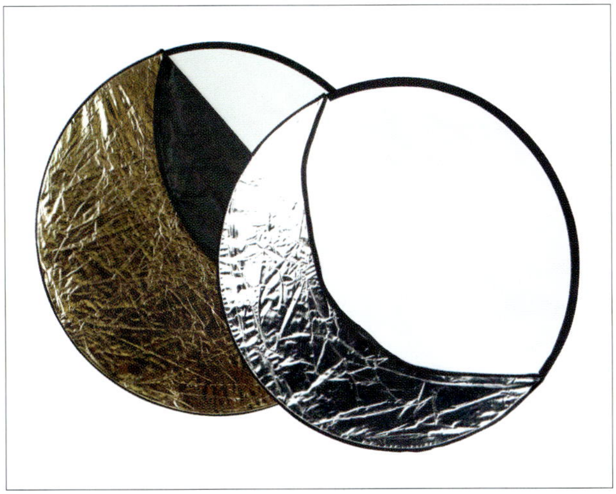

FIGURE B.6
A 5-in-1 reflector gives you a great deal of versatility, including silver, white, gold, and diffusion material options.

What You Need

Reflectors by nature aren't high-tech tools, and they needn't be expensive either. Try using a simple piece of white foam core to start. It's very affordable, and you can recycle it when you are done. We do recommend that you get a reflector as soon as possible, though. A minimum size of 32 inches should be enough to light a single person, and if you go with a 5-in-1 type reflector, you'll have all your bases covered. Look into larger reflectors if you need to photograph small groups or want full-body illumination.

Diffusers

Westcott 72 x 72-inch Scrim Jim and
Westcott 7-foot Parabolic Umbrella www.fjwestcott.com
California Sunbounce Sun-Swatter www.sunbounce.com

Why We Used It

For those days when we have to venture out into the harsh sun and need to bring our own shade with us, we like to pack the Westcott Scrim Jim. It's an extremely versatile piece of equipment because of its modular design. When we need to create shade in the wide open, we simply assemble the frame, attach a scrim or piece of diffusion material, and hold it up between the model and the sun. What's really great is that it breaks down into a small carry case and has optional silver and white panels that turn it into a large reflector if needed.

Another quick and easy solution for diffusion is Westcott's 7-foot shoot-through parabolic umbrella. It's as simple to use as opening a rain umbrella and shading your subject with it. It's also very affordable.

Sometimes you are shooting a wider scene or bigger group and need to get a diffuser way up above your subjects. If you don't have time, space, or budget for large light stands (or multiple really tall assistants), then we suggest you break out the Sun-Swatter. It's similar to the Scrim Jim but designed to be used easily with an extension arm, allowing a single assistant to hold it up in place.

What You Need

You need something to help soften direct sunlight or dappled light. Honestly, this could be achieved with a simple white bed sheet if you are able to stretch it over the scene. When you are looking for more durability and ease of use, you'll have to look into scrims or smaller diffusers. Keep in mind how big of an area you need to diffuse and that will help you make decisions on which solution will work for you.

White Balance Tools

ExpoImaging ExpoDisc www.expoimaging.com

Lastolite Gray Card www.lastolite.com

Why We Used It

An ExpoDisc (**Figure B.7**) is an easy and precise way to achieve custom white balance on the fly, even in mixed lighting scenarios. We find that an ExpoDisc is the best way to get it right in camera. A basic gray card, like the Lastolite gray card, allowed us to quickly and easily create a neutral point of reference in our images that we could then further correct in post-processing when shooting in RAW. By getting it right in camera and getting a reference point to refer to in post-production, we were able to guarantee optimum color accuracy.

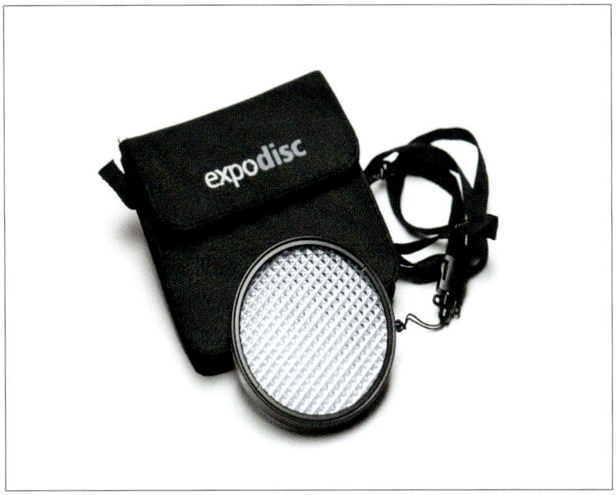

FIGURE B.7
An ExpoDisc helps you to create custom white balances that take into account all of the light sources within a scene.

What You Need

All you truly need is something to help you address the issues of white balance, whether that be in the field or in post-production. Don't cross your fingers and leave white balance to chance! One way is to set your camera to capture RAW files, then photograph a 18% gray card or color checker to use as a neutral reference when you're back in Adobe Lightroom or Photoshop. Or you can set the white balance correctly before you even begin shooting. Something as simple as white printer paper can be used to make a custom white balance profile in your camera. Read your camera's manual for specifics on how to set a custom white balance.

INDEX

E